Studies of revolution generally regard peasant popular support as a prerequisite for success. In this study of political mobilization and organization in Zimbabwe's recent rural-based war of independence, Norma Kriger is interested in the extent to which ZANU guerrillas were able to mobilize peasant support, the reasons why peasants participated, and in the links between the post-war outcomes for peasants and the mobilization process. Hers is an unusual study of revolution in that she interviews peasants and other participants about their experiences, and she is able to produce fresh insights into village politics during a revolution. In particular, Zimbabwean peasant accounts direct our attention to the ZANU guerrillas' ultimate political victory despite the lack of peasant popular support, and to the importance that peasants attached to gender, generational and other struggles with one another. Her findings raise questions about theories of revolution.

ZIMBABWE'S GUERRILLA WAR

AFRICAN STUDIES SERIES 70

GENERAL EDITOR
J.M. Lonsdale, Lecturer in History and Fellow of Trinity College,
Cambridge

ADVISORY EDITORS
J.D.Y. Peel, *Professor of Anthropology and Sociology, with special reference
to Africa, School of Oriental and African Studies, University of London*

John Sender, *Faculty of Economics and Fellow of Wolfson College,
Cambridge*

PUBLISHED IN COLLABORATION WITH THE AFRICAN STUDIES CENTRE,
CAMBRIDGE

A list of books in the series will be found at the end of the volume.

ZIMBABWE'S GUERRILLA WAR

Peasant Voices

NORMA J. KRIGER
Associate Professor, Department of Political Science,
The Johns Hopkins University

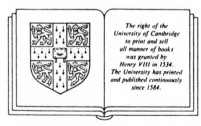

*The right of the
University of Cambridge
to print and sell
all manner of books
was granted by
Henry VIII in 1534.
The University has printed
and published continuously
since 1584.*

CAMBRIDGE UNIVERSITY PRESS

Cambridge

NEW YORK   PORT CHESTER   MELBOURNE   SYDNEY

CAMBRIDGE UNIVERSITY PRESS
Cambridge, New York, Melbourne, Madrid, Cape Town, Singapore, São Paulo

Cambridge University Press
The Edinburgh Building, Cambridge CB2 8RU, UK

Published in the United States of America by Cambridge University Press, New York

www.cambridge.org
Information on this title: www.cambridge.org/9780521392549

First published 1992
This digitally printed version 2008

A catalogue record for this publication is available from the British Library

Library of Congress Cataloguing in Publication data
Kriger, Norma J.
  Zimbabwe's Guerrilla War: Peasant Voices. – (African
  studies series; 0065–406X, 70).
  1. Zimbabwe. Guerrilla warfare, history
  I. Title II. Series
  355.0218

ISBN 978-0-521-39254-9 hardback
ISBN 978-0-521-07067-6 paperback

Contents

Maps

* After independence, many places that had been named after colonial heroes were given African names. Where the settlers had used African names but misspelled them, the new government corrected the errors. For example, Mtoko district became Mutoko district and Mrewa district became Murewa.

Acknowledgements

This book grew out of my Ph.D. dissertation, completed in 1985, in the Department of Political Science at MIT. I am indebted to my supervisor, Lucian Pye, and Suzanne Berger, Sara Berry, and Myron Weiner for their support and encouragement. Michael Bratton, Gwendolen Carter, Michael Schatzberg, Terence Ranger, and anonymous readers also commented on the dissertation.

I have benefited from presenting papers at conferences, of which two stand out. The 'Culture and Consciousness' conference at Manchester University in September 1986 was a consciousness raising experience. I am especially grateful to David Lan, Ken Manungo, Terence Ranger and Richard Werbner for increasing my awareness in different ways. In April 1988, the Humanities Centre at the University of Copenhagen hosted a conference on southern Africa and I appreciate the participants' useful suggestions.

Many people read parts of this book in its early stages. I thank Stephen Bunker, David Cohen, Steven David, Toby Ditz, Michael Doyle, Will Moore, Robert Peabody, Laurie Salitan, Michael Schatzberg, Ron Weitzer, and William Zartman. A number of people read and commented on a draft manuscript completed in November 1988 and I thank them too: David Cohen, Matt Crenson, Phil Curtin, Dick Flathman, Germaine Hoston, Preben Kaarsholm, Dick Katz, Michael Schatzberg, and James Scott. I am grateful to John Lonsdale, editor of the African Studies Series, and Jessica Kuper at Cambridge University Press for expeditiously reading it and sending it to other readers. Terence Ranger, Michael Bourdillon, and an anonymous third reader provided helpful suggestions.

I feel very fortunate to have studied an event that attracted the research interest of others. Two district-level studies of Zimbabwe's war of independence have been extremely valuable. I owe a special debt to David Lan and his *Guns and Rain* and Terence Ranger and his *Peasant Consciousness and Guerrilla War in Zimbabwe*. Their different findings, despite data often remarkably similar to my own, were provocative and helpful. David Caute's *Under The Skin* was the first book written by someone sympathetic to the guerrilla cause to give so much attention to guerrilla coercion. It allowed me to be bolder. My debt to those social scientists who in the 1960s and 1970s asked why peasants participated in revolutions is obvious in the text.

In Zimbabwe, I was affiliated to the Centre for Applied Social Sciences, and I thank its director, Marshall Murphree, and acting director, Joan May, for their help throughout my stay. I thank Marshall Murphree too for suggesting I ask questions in the field about totems which turned out to have a special significance. The people of Mutoko district must remain anonymous because of possible, although not probable, government retribution for the kind of information they gave. There would be no study without their help and support. I am indebted to Bothwell Kowo, my interpreter, and to Bruce Maitland for accommodation in Mutoko.

A grant from the Social Science Research Council supported field work for nearly two years. I also thank the Department of Political Science, The Johns Hopkins University, for a semester of leave in fall, 1988 which enabled me to produce the first draft of this book.

Bill Huggins generously allowed me to use his laser printer and provided free computer consulting. I thank Dean Pendleton for producing the maps and Stefan Cornelis for proofreading.

Evelyn Brodkin and Janet Levine helped in innumerable ways from the outset of this project. Lastly, I pay tribute to Steve Wilson for the special, all-encompassing interest that only an aspirant spouse could show.

Introduction

Guerrilla wars are the primary form of armed conflict today. They are fought mostly in Africa and Asia and often involve regional and international powers. The far-reaching implications of guerrilla war attract the attention of scholars interested in military issues, international relations, and the relationship between wars and national development. Guerrilla wars have also caught the attention of scholars who work on peasant revolutions. Most anti-colonial and anti-imperial revolutionary wars this century have involved rural-based guerrilla armies. Peasants, widely held to be conservative and parochial, have been prominent in revolutionary guerrilla movements, both as the source of guerrillas' logistical support and as war victims – about 80 per cent of those killed in contemporary guerrilla wars have been civilians. The prominence of peasants in revolutions surprised analysts who had anticipated proletarian revolutions and they turned their attention to trying to understand why peasants participated in these wars. This book is about peasant mobilization by a guerrilla army and internal struggles within the peasantry that motivated peasants to participate in Zimbabwe's anti-colonial war.

Zimbabwe takes its name from the most spectacular of its many stone ruins that were built by indigenous people from the thirteenth century to the fifteenth century. Bounded by the Zambezi River in the north and the Limpopo River in the south, the country is some 391,000 square kilometres – slightly smaller than the state of California and 60 per cent greater than the United Kingdom. Zambia borders it in the north and northwest, Botswana in the southwest, Mozambique in the east and South Africa in the south (see map 1). In the early 1970s, on the eve of the guerrilla war, the country had about 275,000 whites, mostly from Britain and South Africa, and five million Africans. Africans are composed of two major ethnolinguistic groups: the Shona and Ndebele. Some 80 per cent of all the Africans are Shona, who are themselves made up of geographically concentrated groups who speak different dialects, including Zezuru, Ndau, Karanga, Manyika, and Korekore. Most whites lived in the urban areas, whereas about 80 per cent of Africans resided in the rural areas. From the

1

time of white conquest and colonization in 1889 until Africans won their political independence in 1980, the white minority monopolized economic and political power to further its own interests.

Map 1: Zimbabwe and its neighbours

Source: Ministry of Internal Affairs, National Service Research Unit, Resource Survey No. 1, Mrewa-Mtoko-Mudzi, 1979.

Zimbabwe has a distinctive constitutional history. From 1889 to 1923 the territory was ruled by the British South Africa Company on the basis of a British royal charter. It then became a British colony – named Southern Rhodesia after its imperialist conqueror, Cecil John Rhodes – and the tiny white minority was given the right to govern itself. Nowhere else in Africa, except South Africa, did Britain (or any other colonial power) give self-government to white settlers in its colonies. Consequently, when African nationalism became a powerful force most colonial overlords could

2

decolonize and override white settler sentiments. But in Rhodesia, Britain had to contend with a strong white nationalistic home government whose fear of African political advancement grew as other colonies won their political independence. Fearing that Britain would eventually grant political independence to Africans, the white minority government declared independence unilaterally in 1965. This brought it international opprobrium, symbolized by the United Nations imposing first selective and then mandatory sanctions against it. In another unprecedented move in the history of decolonization in Africa, the white Rhodesian government introduced a constitution that provided for universal suffrage and an African majority in parliament in 1979, while executive and judicial power remained under white minority control. The hope was that the international community would recognize the legitimacy of a black majority government and lift sanctions. However, Britain and other countries (except South Africa) withheld recognition of the new African government because it excluded two exiled nationalist parties that had been fighting a guerrilla war beginning in 1966. In late 1979, Britain held a conference with the key military and political actors in the conflict and settled the constitutional impasse of the past fifteen years. The talks restored the legality of Rhodesia and it reverted to its former status as a British colony under a British governor. Ironically, in his four months of office, Lord Soames exercised more power than any British governor before him. A ceasefire was arranged, and Britain supervised elections in February 1980 in which the two exiled parties participated. The result was an overwhelming victory for an avowedly Marxist-Leninist nationalist party, ZANU (Zimbabwe African National Union), and its leader Robert Mugabe became Prime Minister of the politically independent state of Zimbabwe.

This study examines ZANU's efforts to mobilize political support in the countryside in the war of independence against the white settler minority. In the 1960s, ZANU's rival, ZAPU (Zimbabwe African People's Union), was in the forefront of the armed struggle against the white minority government. But from 1972 ZANU forces, called ZANLA (Zimbabwe African National Liberation Army), dominated the struggle for independence. At the end of the war, in December 1979, estimates were that 19,300 guerrillas out of a total of 28,000 inside Zimbabwe belonged to ZANU while the rest belonged to ZAPU. There was also an unknown number of guerrillas in training camps, mostly in Mozambique and Zambia. In January 1981 an estimated 37,000 guerrillas had returned; by 1989 this figure had grown to 50,000.[1] ZANU forces passed through Mozambique and operated mostly in Shona-speaking parts of the country, while ZAPU's army, called ZIPRA (Zimbabwe People's Revolutionary Army), operated chiefly in Ndebele-speaking areas in the west and south-west, infiltrating through Zambia and Botswana. At the peak of the war the government could call on about 20,000–25,000 regular and conscripted armed forces, 36,000 police (regular and conscripted), and

27,000 paramilitary forces, many of whom were Africans. When the war ended in 1979, official estimates of the war dead were 30,000 and almost the entire countryside had been affected. Today the estimated number of war dead stands at 40,000.[2]

1

Peasant revolutions: theories and methods

This is a study of political mobilization and organization in a rural-based war of national liberation. The book addresses standard questions raised by those interested in political mobilization in nationalist or Marxist revolutionary guerrilla wars that take place in the countryside. How do guerrillas try to mobilize peasants' support and what accounts for their success or lack thereof? What are the peasants' motives for participating? What linkages, if any, are there between the mobilization process and post-war outcomes for peasants? The distinctiveness of this study derives from its attempt to answer these questions by relying on the direct voices of peasants and other active participants. Ironically, the direct voices of villagers are missing in most accounts of the revolutionary events in which they play so central a role. What peasants themselves have to say about their experiences in a revolutionary guerrilla war highlights what goes on at the village level and raises questions about the language of revolutionary elites, scholars, and others who write about peasants and revolutions.

Direct peasant voices are usually absent in studies of revolution regardless of the theoretical approach they adopt. Studies that are based on the premise that human agency determines revolutions – so-called voluntarist assumptions – might be expected to depend on what actors say and do. In fact, such studies generally infer evidence about peasant ideas from peasant behaviour that is itself inferred from non-peasant sources. An alternative approach assumes that structures rather than human agency determine the causes, processes, and outcomes of revolutions. It is reasonable to expect scholars who accept the theoretical premises of structuralist studies not to seek out the direct voice of active participants. Theda Skocpol's *States and Social Revolutions* contains an unusually explicit rationale for not listening to what individual actors say and do. Most importantly, she believes that revolutions are not made or begun by a revolutionary movement but arise when particular structures no longer relate to each other in a functionally compatible way and produce crises.[1] Skocpol does not give a systematic analysis of her concept of structure, but one can make inferences based on what she says about structure, and how

5

it functions in her account. Structures appear in her work as determinate relations – of states, of the landed upper class and the state, of peasants and landlords – that are objective and impersonal. They 'condition', 'shape', and 'limit' differently situated actors, but structures are not to be identified with people's actions. In their intentional acts, people unintentionally reproduce and sometimes transform the structures governing their activities.[2] Skocpol rejects a voluntarist approach, that emphasizes the values, beliefs, intentions, and goals of actors, chiefly on theoretical grounds: structures can best explain the causes, processes, and outcomes of revolutions. But she also offers empirical reasons for rejecting voluntarism. Actors in a revolution are not always clear about their motives and goals because they are often complex and poorly formulated. And even when revolutionary actors have clear aims, the outcomes of revolutions do not necessarily conform with them. The virtue of her structural approach, she claims, lies precisely in its ability to 'rise above' the viewpoints of the participants and avoid getting embroiled in their intentions and actions.[3]

Skocpol's observation that people's stated aims and revolutionary outcomes frequently diverge constitutes a cogent reason for rejecting the voluntarist assumption that human agency determines outcomes, but it ought not to lead to eliminating people's voices from accounts of revolutions. A revolution is unlikely to fulfil the aspirations of all its participants but this does not diminish the importance of understanding their hopes and how these may affect the revolutionary process. Indeed, Zimbabwean peasants actually help to shed light on how peasant structures affect their dreams of a better world. Skocpol raises valid concerns about the difficulties of establishing values, intentions, beliefs, and goals when the actors themselves might express confusion. Understanding people's motives is inherently difficult and any such project confronts notoriously daunting pitfalls. How can one know that individuals actually believe what they say or say what they believe? What do you do when individuals give conflicting renditions of the same event or when an individual makes contradictory statements? How do you weight the intensity of people's views? How do you understand the gaps between what people say and how they behave? What of the problem of people being unaware of their real interests because of false consciousness? Do you treat all individual viewpoints and actions as equally important? The slippery problems of unravelling the multiple, confused motives and actions of individuals are compounded when one tries to aggregate individual data to make statements about group behaviour and interests, as this analysis attempts to do. Still other difficulties that confront a researcher who attempts to elicit participants' viewpoints are dealt with in the discussion of methodological issues affecting the Zimbabwe case study. But the difficulty of establishing people's motives and interests is not a compelling reason to eliminate them from investigation. The premise of this study is that what people say and do matters.

6

It must be acknowledged that even if one had an interest in obtaining peasants' voices about their experiences in wars and revolutions, it is usually difficult. Even if researchers were willing to accept the risks of trying to interview peasants during such crises, they are generally denied access to peasants. Access is invariably contingent on demonstrable political allegiance to the incumbent regime or the revolutionary organization and these stints in the bush usually serve, as they are intended to, as propaganda for their respective sponsors. Failure to bolster their sponsors' cause might affect future access with serious consequences for careers. In the aftermath of a revolutionary upheaval the newly established victorious government is often involved in external wars and is generally preoccupied with consolidating its power. Again, researchers are unlikely to obtain access to war-torn rural areas unless they have credentials as reliable friends of the ruling party. Consequently, since most peasants are illiterate and leave behind few documents, one is forced to rely on the documents of revolutionary organizations, private memoirs of ruling and revolutionary elites, and other participant observers. Journalists and scholars often supplement these sources with elite interviews. There are also official government records. But peasants appear in these insofar as they present a problem or are perceived as a threat to the state, or as anonymous figures in statistics on conscription, crop production, and taxes. As such, official records are unilluminating about how peasants see each other, elites, rulers, or guerrillas. To obtain the direct voices of peasants in revolutions, whether as civilians or rank-and-file in armies, is inherently difficult.

What difference does it make to theories of revolution to actually take into account peasant ideas and actions? Voluntarist studies that assume that individual actors' attitudes and behaviour can determine revolutions maintain that revolutionary organizations must win popular support if they are to come to power. We learn from peasants in Zimbabwe's war of independence that their participation in organizations set up to provide logistical support for the guerrillas was unpopular, yet this did not prevent the revolutionary movement from coming to power. Peasants reported on how they invented ways to avoid positions in the organizations because they perceived the work to be physically demanding and very risky – at any time, peasants working for the guerrillas could be caught by government forces. Peasants inform us of how much they suffered, not only from the abuses of government forces but also from guerrilla coercion. Even though they worked very hard and sacrificed their meagre resources to meet the guerrillas' logistical needs, they were often beaten and threatened by the guerrillas. Voluntarists are wrong, therefore, to assume that revolutionary success requires popular support, although as I note later, they are correct to emphasize the importance of individual participants' ideas and actions. On the other hand, this study's finding that a revolution's success is independent of whether or not it enjoys popular support is consistent with studies that assume that revolutionary success is determined by impersonal, objective structures (e.g. class

7

relations, state–class relations) and that popular support is an irrelevant issue. Also, Zimbabwean peasants' descriptions of being squeezed by the demands of the government and guerrilla armies support the important role of structures on behaviour. But the findings of this study repudiate the structuralist assumption that individual attitudes and behaviour cannot have a determinative influence on revolutions. Although lack of peasants' popular support for the guerrillas was not an obstacle to the eventual success of the Zimbabwean revolution, their attitudes and actions did influence the revolutionary process and outcomes in ways that are alluded to below.

Peasants can also enlighten us about why they participate in revolutions. Zimbabwean peasants participated in the guerrilla war of independence only partly because they wanted to remove the racially discriminatory policies of the white minority government. More importantly, oppressed peasants saw in the breakdown of law and order during the war an unprecedented opportunity to transform oppressive village structures. While the guerrillas were persuading and coercing peasants to sweat and toil on their behalf, oppressed peasants were forging alliances with the guerrillas to try to restructure village relations. Unmarried peasant children challenged their elders, women battled their husbands, subject clans sometimes tried to usurp power from ruling clans, and the least advantaged attacked the better-off. Theories of revolution, regardless of approach, locate the grievances that motivate peasants to join revolutionary movements outside their villages. Most studies of revolution account for peasant involvement in revolutions by dwelling on peasant resentments against the state, markets, capitalism, imperialism, other classes, or other external agents or forces. But these studies fail to capture the potentially powerful role that peasants' dissatisfaction with internal peasant structures can play in motivating them to participate in revolutions. Voluntarists do not take into account how peasant ideas and actions are affected by peasant structures; structuralists focus on the influence of class, state, or other structures in determining peasant participation, but not on peasant structures.

Finally, listening to what peasants have to say may enhance our understanding of the linkages between revolutionary processes and outcomes. Zimbabwean peasants won some advantages after the war from the new party-state in return for having provided the guerrillas with logistical support. However, peasants continued to fear the party because of their experience of coercion from its guerrilla representatives during the war and because local party representatives often continued to coerce peasants after the war. Peasants were also at least as interested in how any benefits from the party-state were distributed within their communities as they were in their relationship with the party and the state. Many studies of revolution, both voluntarist and structuralist, claim that the success of a revolutionary organization in mobilizing peasants during a revolution results in a continuing close relationship between peasants and the party-state after the revolution and that it benefits not only the party-state but also peasants. But these studies, for different reasons, ignore the potential for coercive mobilization and hence do not consider its post-war influence on peasants. Nor do most works on revolution examine how conflicts internal to the peasantry may persist into the post-revolutionary period.

It should be apparent from the foregoing that this study rejects a determinative role for either human agency or structures. Instead, it seeks to show how an investigation that begins with peasant ideas and actions ends up highlighting how they are important and how structures influence them, thereby contributing to both theoretical approaches. Whereas the following chapters engage the existing literature on Zimbabwe's war of independence, here I seek to show where my case study on Zimbabwe stands in relation to the wider literature on revolutions. The primary concern of this book is peasant mobilization in revolutions with Zimbabwe's war of independence as a source of data. Consequently, much of the rest of this chapter elaborates on how my Zimbabwe case study findings, derived from direct peasant voices, compare and contrast with those in landmark studies of revolution that depend on inferred evidence from non-peasant sources. My review of the literature must be selective because an examination of the voluminous works on revolution is beyond the scope of this book. But I have sought to include studies that are structuralist, studies that are voluntarist and others that, as one would expect, do not fit unambiguously into either category. Skocpol's study of revolution in France, Russia and China is, as I have noted, an exemplar of a structuralist approach. Less self-conscious and less 'pure' structuralist studies are represented by Barrington Moore's work on China and Eric Wolf's comparative study of Algeria, Cuba, Mexico, Vietnam, China and Russia. James Scott on south-east Asia and Chalmers Johnson on China represent studies that do not fit neatly structuralist or voluntarist labels: for example, both examine peasant and organizational behaviour within the context of peasant value structures. I use them sometimes to illustrate an aspect of a structuralist approach and other times to highlight a feature of a voluntarist approach. My exemplary voluntarist studies are Joel Migdal's work on twentieth-century revolutions and Samuel Popkin's study of the Vietnamese revolution against the French.[4] These, as well as other studies, provide an entry point for my comparative analysis of studies of revolution. I try to reveal how studies of revolution, despite diverse theoretical and methodological approaches, converge in important ways. In particular, their failure to consult peasants directly about their participation and mobilization creates the potential to misread evidence and to neglect or omit issues that are important to peasants. Peasant voices can produce new insights. Instead of the centrality of popular support in understanding revolutionary successes, peasant voices direct us to the potential for guerrilla coercion against peasants to coexist with successful revolutions.

Without repudiating a role for markets and states, imperialism and capitalism in their self-understandings of what has gone wrong with their world, peasants give more prominence to structural conflicts internal to the peasantry. Moreover, peasant voices in the Zimbabwe case study underscore how individual actions and ideas interact with structures, thereby challenging both structuralists and voluntarists. The chapter concludes with a fairly detailed examination of methodological issues such as why particular individuals were selected for interviewing and what kinds of questions they were asked. Other issues such as the mediating influences of the researcher, contemporary politics, and interpreters are also raised.

What peasant voices can contribute to theories of revolutions

Two questions arise: can one label Zimbabwe's war of independence a revolution, and, if one can, does this justify a comparative analysis of revolutions that have been very different? Most definitions of revolution depend on the extent of violent political and social change – although the peaceful transformations in Eastern Europe in 1989 and 1990 may change that common understanding of a revolution. Certainly Zimbabwe's war of liberation meets the criterion of violent change. But how much change is needed for a violent event to qualify as revolutionary? Some accept political changes in personnel as sufficient.[5] Zimbabwe's war of independence, which ushered in a new African political leadership to replace the former white rulers, meets this criterion too. Skocpol's concept of revolution requires that a revolution bring about drastic structural changes in society: state–class relations, inter-class relations, and inter-state relations should all be revamped.[6] Even though Skocpol directs us to particular structural relations, she gives us no measure of what constitutes fundamental change. Also race was not a factor in the revolutions that Skocpol studied but it was central in Zimbabwe's war of liberation. The structure of race relations in Zimbabwe has been transformed radically at the political level. Race relations in society have changed too, but the extent of this change is less easy to assess. Whether one labels Zimbabwe's war of independence a revolution depends then on whether one accepts change in personnel or fundamental structural changes as the criterion. If one adopts the latter criterion, one must consider what is 'fundamental' and what are relevant structures. To the extent that Zimbabwe's war resulted in a change in the racial structure, I consider it a revolutionary outcome. But one might separate outcomes from process, as Charles Tilly does.[7] Tilly defines a revolutionary situation as one in which revolutionary movements compete with the government for resources from the population and create a dual sovereignty. Definitions of revolution that focus exclusively on outcomes, he reasons, close off from purview such revolutionary periods and make it impossible to study why some revolutions succeed and others fail. Both movements that fought the war in Zimbabwe competed with the government for resources from the population; in this respect, Zimbabwe's war of liberation constitutes, at a minimum, a revolutionary situation. Most of this study is concerned with revolutionary process.

There is the further question of the legitimacy of comparing Zimbabwe's revolution with other revolutions. Differences among revolutions abound. Labelling revolutions communist or nationalist ascribes to them a unity of ideas and organization that they seldom, if ever, have; but the labels do at least suggest the revolutionary elite's aspirations. The Chinese and Vietnamese revolutions, on which many of the theories of revolution are based, have been labelled communist; Zimbabwe's war of liberation cannot share that label. These revolutions also differ from Zimbabwe's revolution (and other African cases – the ex-lusophone colonies and Algeria – that could be called revolutions by the same reasoning that was applied to Zimbabwe's war of independence) in that they witnessed regular armies developing alongside guerrilla armies. In the African cases, victory was achieved ultimately through political negotiations rather than on the battlefield. China was different in this respect, and some argue that Vietnam was too. These differences should not be minimized. But the purpose of comparing and contrasting my findings with those of other studies of different revolutions is premised on revolutions having certain important commonalities. Indeed, many of the studies of revolution that will be examined here in light of the findings of this study make a similar assumption and themselves include communist and nationalist revolutions, African and Asian cases. The comparison between my findings, based on peasant voices, and other studies, dependent on indirect inferences about peasants, is undertaken for the limited purpose of illustrating how influential studies of peasant revolutions may be enriched and revised by incorporating peasant voices. The critical review of important literature on revolutions is organized around three questions central to this study. What is the relationship between popular support, guerrilla coercion and revolutionary success? What are peasant motives for participating in revolutionary guerrilla wars? What is the relationship, if any, between the experience of peasants during the mobilization process and in the immediate post-revolutionary period?

Popular support and coercion

Peasant responses, based on interviews with Zimbabwean peasants who were active participants in the war of independence, point to the guerrillas' inability to offer utilitarian appeals (e.g. land redistribution, alternative marketing systems) and hence guerrilla reliance on nationalist appeals and coercion. The lack of positive utilitarian guerrilla appeals (and indeed the costly sacrifices that peasants' logistical support for the guerrillas required) must be understood in terms of the guerrillas' inability to win enduring control over territory from the state's military forces. The prominence of guerrilla coercion in peasant accounts – this study uses coercion parsimoniously to include only violence and threats of violence to persons and property and not the withholding of benefits as some do – underscores the difficulties experienced by the guerrillas in winning peasants' active voluntary or popular support by relying on cultural nationalist appeals. Yet despite the lack of popular support among peasants, the revolutionary organization that the guerrillas represented was successful in terms of securing routinized logistical support from peasants and in ultimately coming to power. These findings, based on peasant interviews, about the relationship between popular support and revolutionary success and the role of coercive guerrilla appeals, can enhance structuralist and voluntarist perspectives.

Consistent with its premise that structural relationships as opposed to people's attitudes are the key to understanding revolutions, Skocpol's *States and Social Revolutions* asserts that revolutions succeed or fail regardless of whether they enjoy popular support. However, she identifies a weakening of state power, measured partly by its shrinking military capacity,[8] as a prerequisite of a successful revolution, and this enables her to characterize the relationship between peasants and revolutionary organizations as one based on mutual exchange. Hence the possibility of revolutionary coercion playing a prominent role never arises.

The findings of the Zimbabwe case study support Skocpol's proposition that revolutionary success does not depend on popular support but, unlike Skocpol's structural analysis, also underscore the importance of peasant experiences in the revolutionary process. In particular, peasant experiences of guerrilla coercion and immense material sacrifices occupy a prominent place in an account of revolutionary process in Zimbabwe. Moreover, the coercive nature of mobilization has repercussions for peasant relations with the revolutionary party in the post-war period (see page 30), and for this reason, too, ought not to be neglected.

The Zimbabwe study does not support Skocpol's claim that a revolution will not occur unless there is a weakening of state power. Nor does the Zimbabwe study support her argument, contingent on the weakening of state power, that the relationship between peasants and revolutionary organizations will be based on mutually beneficial exchange. In Zimbabwe, despite the economic damage inflicted by both the guerrilla war and international economic sanctions, the state was able to expand its military capacity, largely by recruiting Africans and purchasing arms directly from, or through, South Africa. This did not prevent the exiled nationalist movements from waging a successful revolution, but it did affect the character of the relationship between guerrillas and peasants. The expanding military power of the state, and the state's virtual monopoly of services such as schools and clinics, made it difficult for the guerrillas to offer any new utilitarian benefits to induce voluntary peasant participation. Zimbabwean peasants dwelled on the lack of utilitarian benefits offered by guerrillas in return for their costly sacrifices to provide logistical support for guerrillas. Consequently, the guerrillas had to rely on cultural nationalist appeals and coercion. Although the Zimbabwe case does not support Skocpol's argument that a prerequisite for a revolution is that state power be weakened, the connection that I establish between a strong state (in terms of military capacity) and the lack of a mutually beneficial exchange relationship between guerrillas and peasants supports Skocpol's argument that a prerequisite for a mutually beneficial relationship between peasants and revolutionaries is a weakening of state power.

Skocpol remarks critically that even avowedly Marxist analysts, whose theoretical assumptions orient them toward the impersonal and objective, often lapse into a misplaced concern with mass grievances against a state as a cause of revolution.[9] They thereby make the occurrence of revolutions contingent on popular support. Barrington Moore's *The Social Origins of Dictatorship and Democracy* is at once an example of how structuralist analysis obviates the need to examine actors' self-understandings of their ideas and actions, and an illustration of how structuralists often stray from their theoretical tenets and allow people's subjectivities to creep into their analyses. Moore identifies peasant revolt as most likely when the landed upper class fails to commercialize. The only way it can remain competitive and maintain its living standards is by extracting a larger surplus from a peasantry whose social institutions remain intact into the modern era. Intensified objective exploitation and the survival of a peasantry with strong horizontal links but weak vertical ties with the landed upper class produce the conditions for peasant revolt. For Moore, peasant revolutionary potential depends on objective forces: growing agrarian class conflicts, objective class exploitation, and the presence of certain institutional conditions. In this analysis, there is no need to elicit peasant views; peasants' revolutionary potential may be inferred from the presence of these objective forces. In this sense, Moore's analysis is structuralist and precludes a role for people's subjectivities. Insofar as the conditions exist for peasants to have revolutionary potential, the issue of revolutionary organizations employing coercion to mobilize peasant support never arises.

But despite Moore's argument that objective historical and institutional conditions account for the revolutionary potential of peasants, subjective conditions enter his text. For the revolutionary potential of peasants to become politically effective, other classes must form alliances with peasants and provide leadership. Moore also asserts the key importance of peasant grievances in revolutions[10] and again introduces a subjective element when he says that peasants may revolt even when their objective situation is improving if they realize that the 'lord's exactions increased and his contribution . . . declined'.[11] Here Moore introduces the notion of upper class violations of peasants' subjective ideas about what constitutes fair reciprocity in their relations with landlords as a vital component

13

contributing to peasants' revolutionary potential. Moreover, when he discusses the Chinese Communist revolution, his case of a peasant revolution, he cannot escape assigning a crucial role to peasant sentiments. He records that the 'decisive ingredient' in the Communist Party victory was the Japanese conquest and occupation policies. The behaviour of the foreign conqueror engendered peasant hatred, thereby forging the peasant solidarity that is a prerequisite for peasant revolt.[12] To the extent that Moore's analysis of the conditions for revolution depends on peasant popular support, he simply infers it from the existence of those objective forces that create the potential for revolutionary peasants, the fact of peasant participation, and the fact of a revolutionary organization's success. Like Moore, Eric Wolf's *Peasant Wars of the Twentieth Century* also emphasizes the objective historical forces that mould peasants into potential revolutionaries, but occasionally lapses into the relevance of peasants' popular support, [13] and infers evidence for popular support from peasant behaviour and the fact of successful revolutions.

Most voluntarists assume that revolutions will only succeed if they enjoy popular support. Whereas popular support is regarded as an inevitable by-product of objective historical conditions for structuralists who stray from their theoretical premises, voluntarists frequently view mobilization of popular support as a central problem confronting revolutionary organizations that seek to make revolutions. Samuel Popkin's *The Rational Peasant* assumes that peasants are rational, cost-calculating individuals who will choose not to engage in costly collective action to bring about a revolution, even though it would be in their common interests, because the benefits of a revolution are like a public good from which no individual can be excluded. Drawing on Mancur Olson's *The Logic of Collective Action*, Popkin cites two alternative approaches to ensure that rational individuals will pursue their common interests. One path is to coerce them by using violence, threats of violence, and withholding benefits; the other is to entice them by offering special incentives independent of any benefits that will ensue from collective action.[14] Popkin goes on to examine how the leadership of organizations succeeded in winning popular participation by offering peasants immediate concrete benefits, invariably material ones, such as literacy, a progressive tax, or land reform. However, he never pursues the possibility of effective coercive appeals. One might expect that Popkin, with his interest in individual peasant behaviour and attitudes, would be interested in what peasants themselves have to say. Indeed, Popkin did extensive fieldwork in Vietnam between 1966 and 1970 and later made two extended research trips, during which he conducted 'masses of interviews' with past and present political activists.[15] Yet we almost never hear directly from peasants and he acknowledges his primary reliance on library research. This mars his evidence for the Viet Cong's popular support among peasants because he must rely on indirect evidence. He shows that the revolutionary forces induced peasant participation by offering utilitarian benefits. From the fact of participation and the Viet Cong's ultimate victory, he infers that peasant support was voluntary. Even though Popkin seems to believe in the importance of peasant self-understandings, we are never presented with what individual peasants say about why they participated. Peasant voices in the Zimbabwe study challenge Popkin's argument that popular support is a prerequisite to revolutionary success and draw attention to the important role of a revolutionary organization's coercive appeals, a possibility that Popkin leaves unexplored.

Joel Migdal's *Peasants, Politics and Revolution* shares much in common with Popkin's *The Rational Peasant*. Like Popkin, he focuses on how an organization employs selective material incentives to obtain popular support and collective action. Migdal notes that revolutionary organizations, like governments, depend on a mix of sanctions and benefits to achieve goals. However, he assumes that sanctions, and especially coercive ones, will not be able to elicit the routinized behaviour without which an organization seeking to build its power base cannot function long.[16] Since he considers that no revolution will succeed unless it has popular support, and since he regards widespread coercive appeals by a revolutionary organization to be self-defeating, he can dismiss further consideration of coercive appeals. Migdal never obtains direct peasant voices to support his argument about the centrality of popular support in a revolution, but draws on an impressive volume of secondary literature to show that organizations that offered utilitarian appeals could induce rational, cost-calculating peasants to participate. From the fact of participation in successful revolutions, he, like Popkin, infers peasant popular support.

Chalmers Johnson's *Peasant Nationalism and Communist Power* also examines the appeals that a revolutionary organization used to win peasants' popular support, which he considers an essential ingredient of the success of the revolution. Johnson recognizes the importance of the Japanese invasion of 1937 in transforming peasant ideas and values: it destroyed the traditional rural social order in the north and east of China, in which pre-political peasants were totally absorbed in local affairs, and 'unified and politicized' them so that they became aware of a Chinese national politics and identity.[17] The success of the Chinese Communist Party was to recognize the new peasant nationalism and appeal to it. The revolutionary leaders' normative appeals accounted for their success in mobilizing peasant popular support although the structural context was provided by the already transformed peasant values. Johnson does not examine coercive appeals and his evidence for popular support depends on a series of inferences from non-peasant sources. He makes ingenious use of Japanese archival holdings of captured documents of the Chinese Communist party and the Kuomintang that had been translated by the Japanese, and of Japanese investigations of Chinese conditions, especially in Japanese-occupied areas. Johnson notes that the Japanese archives tell us that the Chinese Communist Party carried out successful guerrilla operations. Further, we know from Mao and comparative guerrilla war studies that successful guerrilla war requires the closest collaboration between peasants and guerrillas. Since the Communist Party did conduct successful guerrilla operations, he concludes that widespread Communist–peasant collaboration existed.[18] Johnson uses other inferred evidence of peasant support. He shows that the Communist Party used nationalist appeals to win peasant participation and that peasants participated because the invasions had awakened their nationalism. Peasant nationalism is inferred from archival sources that described the breakdown of traditional rural social order. This, Johnson argues, made peasants available for a new kind of politics beyond village politics.

The notion that popular support is a prerequisite for revolutionary success and that popular support is incompatible with coercive appeals by a revolutionary organization appears in the writings of revolutionary strategists too. Structuralists in the sense that they often use Marxian language of class conflict and objective exploitation in understanding revolutions, they also share voluntarist assumptions about the importance of the intentions, actions, and goals of revolutionary organizations and a revolution's popular support. Mao's *On Guerrilla Warfare* cautions against the use of force against the people. 'The people must be inspired to cooperate voluntarily. We must not force them, for if we do, it will be ineffectual.'[19] Elsewhere he rejects the use of terror by the Party against its comrades or the enemy. 'No matter with whom you are dealing, a false show of authority to instil terror is always uncalled for.'[20] Terror is of no use against the enemy and he forbids indiscriminate killing or beating of landlords, and it only does harm when used against the comrades.[21] Mao's reasons for using guerrilla terror (and violence in general) against special targets only are not based on tactical considerations that indiscriminate coercion will antagonize peasants but on a conception of violence as a means of self-transformation and class victory.[22] Che Guevara's *Guerrilla Warfare*, like Regis Debray's *Revolution in the Revolution?*, differs sharply with Mao on a host of issues such as the role of the party in mobilizing peasants, the leadership role of the party over the guerrillas, and the importance of mobilization by political persuasion.[23] Both Guevara and Debray make the case for guerrilla control of all aspects of the armed struggle, and regard the demonstrated military capacity of the guerrillas against the enemy to be a more important tool for mobilizing the popular support of peasants than political mobilization orchestrated by the party. Again unlike Mao, Che Guevara suggests that it may be necessary to use coercion in addition to political persuasion and military success to win popular support. He poses the question: will coercion intimidate or alienate the civilian population? His answer is ambiguous. On the one hand, he favours 'just punishments' for 'treason' by initial sympathizers. On the other hand, he insists terrorism is a negative weapon that fails to produce the desired effects. It can turn a people against a given revolutionary movement and brings with it a loss of lives among those taking part that is much greater than the benefit to the organization. To the extent that Guevara rejects terror, therefore, it is for practical reasons rather than Mao's ideological one.[24] Not surprisingly, James de Nardo's *Power in Numbers*, using revolutionary strategists' texts to develop a theory 'that can demonstrate the common patterns of reasoning and calculation that underlie the various strategic perspectives' from which radical movements may choose,[25] concludes that 'resorting to more violent tactics invariably diminishes the dissidents' support'.[26]

Some scholars share the assumption that popular support is a prerequisite for revolutionary success, but acknowledge that widespread guerrilla coercion may occur in twentieth century anti-colonial nationalist struggles without undermining the revolutionary organization's popular support. They argue that revolutionary organizations, unlike alien governments, can use terror to pressure civilians to comply with their demands without undermining their legitimacy because they can appeal to nationalist sentiments to justify their actions. For example, Paret writes: 'The Algerian was caught in a cross fire, but of the two sources of danger – the French and the Nationalists – France in the long run proved the weaker. Despite its control of the machinery of government and administration, and despite its psychological-warfare armoury, France was unable to match the diffused but continuous moral and physical pressure that a native, nationalistic revolutionary movement can exert on the people.'[27] John Dunn, writing on Vietnam, argues along the same lines in *Modern Revolutions*. 'The reason why the coercion applied by the insurgents has been so much more effective is that pure coercion is necessarily less effective than coercion exercised on behalf of intelligible moral solidarities. No doubt one would not present too roseate a view of the intimate moral solidarity sensed between bemused peasantry and harassed guerrilla organizer. But it hardly seems surprising that in bulk the notion should seem more plausible along lines of ethnic identity than when stretched to the French or the Americans.'[28] Both Paret and Dunn rely on assertions that the instinctive nationalist support enjoyed by anti-colonial movements permits them to use terror against the colonized without undercutting their popular support. Paret, it should be noted, in another study draws attention to the lack of systematic analysis of guerrilla terror and the need to redress this neglect.[29] Peasant voices in the Zimbabwe study support the argument that guerrilla coercion may be important in winning the compliance of the population. But they repudiate the view that guerrilla coercion will not adversely affect peasant popular support for an anti-colonial movement because the latter can rely on the efficacy of its nationalist appeals. Cultural nationalist appeals were found to be inadequate to compensate peasants for their material sacrifices, risks of government coercion, and experience of guerrilla coercion.

Martha Crenshaw goes beyond claiming that a revolutionary organization's compliance terror does not undermine its legitimacy and argues that it actually contributed to the popularity of the Algerian nationalist movement, the FLN. Algerians feared FLN terror but realized that if they failed to comply with FLN demands the FLN would label them traitors to justify violence against them to their fellow Algerians. 'Thus to fear were added feelings of shame and dishonor. Considering the pride and status that could be gained by joining the FLN, it is not surprising that many opted for this solution, and it is difficult to separate actions motivated by fear from those motivated by choice.'[30] But her argument for the efficacy of Algerian terror in winning popular support rests on inferences from non-peasant sources and suppositions. She notes how the FLN justified killing Algerians by labelling them traitors, and asserts without supporting evidence from those who were targets of coercion: 'This policy of polarizing loyalties was also a means of legitimizing both the revolution and FLN violence by equating terrorism with governmental punishment of traitors. The FLN thus encouraged acceptance of its authority while it was simultaneously enforcing compliance with its demands through coercion.'[31] She also speculates on the legitimacy of terror by Algerian nationalists against other Algerians. 'The habit of obedience that was acquired through compulsion might also have served as a basis for accepting the commands of the FLN as normal and right, particularly since French authority, which was weak among Algerians, if not nonexistent, had long ago lost its legitimacy.'[32] Nor does she offer data to support her claim that the fear of FLN terror and the shame of being labelled a traitor was offset by the pride and glory of belonging to the FLN. Peasant experiences of guerrilla coercion in Zimbabwe's anti-colonial war underscore the importance of guerrilla coercion but they inform us of how guerrilla coercion contributed to undermining peasant support for the guerrillas.

Leites and Wolf reject the widely held voluntarist notion that revolutionary success depends on popular support without rejecting the voluntarist idea that what revolutionary organizations do can account for the success or failure of revolutions. Leites and Wolf argue that compliant behaviour from most of the population is more important for the success of the revolutionary organization than the population having positive attitudes towards the guerrillas. They provide the most explicit and extended consideration of revolutionary guerrilla organizations' use of coercive appeals.[33] Explicitly rejecting a focus on positive material and normative reasons for providing popular support, they write: 'the effort to limit damage may prevail over aspirations to better one's condition or act according to one's ideals: the more so, the fiercer and longer the conflict'.[34] Leites and Wolf consider the cases of both government and guerrilla coercion to obtain compliance with their demands. Whereas Paret, Dunn, and Crenshaw argued that individuals would still support the guerrillas because of their shared nationalism, Leites and Wolf claim that individuals will make a choice of whom to support based on what type of coercion will limit damages. 'One may prefer a high probability of death to its certainty, if those are one's alternatives. Or one may choose a side threatening a merciful death against the side promising a painful one.'[35] Leites and Wolf explicitly acknowledge the speculative nature of their claim and lament the absence of empirical studies about how people will behave when confronted with government and guerrilla coercion. 'If both opponents use coercion and indicate to populations their willingness to punish with death every violation of their commands, what will determine the outcome? It is an obviously crucial question on which extant knowledge or even reflection is meager.'[36] Peasant voices in the Zimbabwe study support the compatibility of revolutionary success and lack of popular support. But when faced with government and guerrilla coercion, peasants responded in ways that suggest that their decisions about which side to support were not made entirely on the basis of how to limit damages; peasants had their own ideas and agendas and saw the guerrillas as potential allies or susceptible to manipulation to further their own goals.

The preceding review of influential studies of revolution illustrates that an abiding assumption is that revolutions have legitimacy or popular support. The idea that revolutions enjoy legitimacy has had its critics: structuralists like Skocpol explicitly reject the idea that any actors' attitudes and actions matter in a revolution; others like Leites believe that the revolutionary organizations' conscious actions matter but that popular support is unimportant for their success. Despite these critics, the notion that revolutions do not occur without popular support has been remarkably resilient so that even structuralists whose theoretical assumptions ought to steer them away from people's attitudes often cannot escape its grip. For all the emphasis on the necessity for popular support in a revolution, peasant voices are strikingly mute in the vast corpus of literature that mostly infers their popular support for revolutionary movements from indirect evidence. Zimbabwean peasant voices draw attention to the potential for spurious inferences when individual attitudes and motives are derived from data other than what individuals themselves say and do as well as for missing important aspects of peasants' self-understandings. Peasant voices in the Zimbabwe study support Skocpol's 'pure' structuralist perspective that revolutions may occur and succeed without popular support, but do not confirm her argument that a prerequisite for revolution is a weakening of the state or her claim that peasants and guerrillas establish mutually beneficial exchange relations. Peasants also provide valuable insights into guerrilla–civilian relations by emphasizing how the guerrillas made onerous demands on their resources without providing material benefits. At least one reason for the guerrillas' inability to offer utilitarian appeals, I argue, was the ability of the state to augment its military strength.

Peasant experiences of coercion are of no interest to those structuralists who assume that the subjectivities of individuals are unimportant in understanding social processes. Peasants speaking about their experience of guerrilla coercion and their lack of popular support for ZANU guerrillas challenge voluntarists who assume that popular support and revolutionary success go hand in hand, and, therefore, choose not to examine guerrilla coercion in cases of successful revolutions. Zimbabwean peasant responses also repudiate those voluntarists who recognize the role of guerrilla and government coercion in anti-colonial struggles but assume either that guerrilla coercion will not dent popular support for the guerrillas because, unlike the government they can exploit nationalistic support, or that guerrilla coercion actually contributes to popular support. Zimbabwean peasants spoke of both government and guerrilla coercion and while they deeply resented government coercion it did not mitigate their negative sentiments towards guerrillas who beat and threatened them. Guerrilla coercion, even in a nationalistic revolution, must be recognized to be potentially damaging for a revolutionary movement's popularity. Peasant views support the unusual perspective that asserts that revolutions may succeed without popular support and that gives prominence to the role of guerrilla coercion in effecting compliance from the majority of the population in revolutionary success. But in a situation, such as Zimbabwe's war of independence, where peasants found themselves squeezed between government and guerrilla coercion, peasants often did not behave as if they were motivated primarily by a desire to limit personal damages. Instead, peasants often took further risks to try to promote their own revolutionary agendas even when they clashed with guerrilla goals.

Peasant motives for participating in revolutions

Direct peasant voices in the Zimbabwe study raise questions about theories of revolution, both structuralist and voluntarist, that attribute peasant motives for participating in a revolution to their unsatisfactory relationships with capitalist states, markets, or other classes. Peasants' responses suggest that gender, generational, and other structural inequities within villages may be more powerful motivating factors than peasant grievances arising from their externally oriented relationships. Peasant voices indicate that these motivations may operate even in the context of guerrilla and government coercion and in opposition to guerrilla appeals for unity. Peasant voices may direct structuralists towards structures that influence peasant behaviour which they may otherwise overlook or underestimate. Voluntarists can learn from what peasants say about how structures shape individual responses. Women, youth, subject clans, and the less well-off all had different motives for participating because of their different structural positions in society. Both structuralists and voluntarists assume that markets, states, capitalism, imperialism, and other classes are the primary source of peasant woes. Peasant voices suggest peasants are more likely to blame their neighbours for their woes and act on this understanding of the source of their problems. Arguably, one might consider peasant concern for village inequalities in a revolution to be misplaced because peasant structures prevent them from seeing the larger picture that would inform them of where their interests really lie. Instead of blaming a peasant with more land for one's shortage of land, one might argue that peasants might be better off if they understood that behind the inequalities of land were state policies and the influence of capitalism. Even if one chooses to see peasant anger turned inwards against other peasants as irrational, their ideas and actions are important for understanding revolutionary process and outcomes.

Wolf's *Peasant Wars of the Twentieth Century* examines how objective historical forces create the conditions that give rise to peasants with a revolutionary potential. Wolf argues that the spread of capitalism in the periphery undermined traditional or precapitalist social institutions in which the relationship between landlords and peasants and among peasants was governed by social obligations that effectively protected peasants from the risks that threatened their security. Under capitalism, these relationships become governed by a quest to maximize profits in the market and peasants are likely to rebel. 'Perhaps it is precisely when the peasant can no longer rely on his accustomed institutional context to reduce his risks, but when alternative institutions are either too chaotic or too restrictive to guarantee a viable commitment to new ways, that the psychological, economic, social and political tensions all mount toward peasant rebellion and involvement in revolution.'[37] But peasant motives for rebelling or participating in revolutions are to restore their precapitalist institutions eroded by an exogenously imposed world capitalism. Wolf recognizes that peasants and revolutionaries, whose role is to provide the outside leadership necessary to get peasants involved in a revolution, seek different outcomes from revolutions. Peasants wish to free themselves of state control and subjection to the laws of markets. Wolf describes 'the peasant utopia' as 'the free village, untrammeled by tax collectors, labor recruiters, large landowners, officials'.[38] Peasants see the state only negatively as something to be removed. In contrast, revolutionary organizations seek to extend the interventionist role of the state and centralize power further.

For Wolf (as for Skocpol, Moore, and other structuralists) peasant ideas about their interests are unimportant: they can be inferred chiefly from objective historical forces – the impact of capitalism on peasant–landlord relations and peasant relations with each other – but also from the fact of peasant participation in successful revolutions. But the Zimbabwe study emphasizes the importance of what peasants themselves say about their motives for participating in a revolution. Zimbabwean peasant voices protested against a racially discriminatory and intrusive state and in that respect support Wolf when he attributes peasant hostility to a state that seeks to regulate and control. But Zimbabwean peasants also point to their dissatisfaction with oppressive peasant structures. Even though Wolf emphasizes structures, he fails to identify how peasant structures influence peasant behaviour and ideas. Wolf begins *Peasant Wars of the Twentieth Century* with the promise of exploring internal peasant structure. He notes that peasant differences are important because different kinds of peasants behave differently and have different outlooks. But when Wolf discusses peasants, he is not interested in gender differences and refers to peasants using masculine forms only. Nor is he interested in generational differences in peasant societies. The differences he has in mind relate to property ownership between tenants and proprietors, to poor and rich peasants, part-time and full-time peasants, self-employed and employed peasants, and to peasants more or less linked to the market and communications.[39] Moreover, his interest is not in how this limited set of peasant differences affects peasant interaction with other peasants but in how it relates to the external domain of power. In particular, he argues that different peasant strata have different material and organizational advantages in their relationship to external power domains and that these influence whether their revolutionary potential will materialize. What all peasants share is low risk behaviour with respect to the market and an interest in social status in a narrow set of relationships. But Wolf's focus on peasants' relations with an external power domain steers him away from investigating potential status conflicts among peasants during revolutions. Peasant voices can direct attention to internal peasant structures that shape peasant behaviour during revolutions.

Like Wolf, James Scott attributes peasants' revolutionary potential to the influence of an exogenously imposed capitalism (or other crises such as famine and war) that undermines social institutions that guarantee peasant security. But, unlike structuralists such as Wolf and Moore, Scott maintains that even when objective exploitation by landlords is increasing, peasants might not revolt. What matters is peasants' subjective understanding of exploitation and this is influenced chiefly by peasant values but also by peasant social structure.[40] Scott dwells on the informal kin and market networks that provide opportunities for coordinated peasant action. Often invisible, these informal networks can escape state control and cooptation more easily than proletarian formal organization. Peasant values provide an even more important source of cohesion. They are, and always have been, in opposition to the state and landlords. As long as the peasants' belief that the community has a right to some minimum subsistence is respected, they will subordinate opposition and be accommodationist. When crises lead to their subsistence ethic being violated, they will be ready to revolt.[41] Like Wolf, Scott recognizes that peasant interests in a revolution diverge from those of the revolutionary elite. Peasants are interested in subsistence, land, and autonomy; revolutionary elites are interested in nationalist rule and seek to reconstitute the state. With his deep interest in peasant subjectivities, Scott also emphasizes how revolutionary elites and peasants have different ideas about organization, strategy, and tactics. Elites prefer secular, centralized and disciplined party bureaucracy; peasants opt for banditry, secret societies, and millenial movements. Nationalist revolutionary elites often prefer gradualism and coalition building; peasants opt for immediate justice and resist coalitions. Peasant concerns focus on their villages and their lost local rights rather than on the nation; their notions of justice revolve around a strict equality within villages rather than equality across villages.[42]

Despite Scott's obvious concern for peasant self-understandings, he assumes that the behaviour of subsistence-oriented peasants is governed by a belief in the inviolability of their culturally determined subsistence and then relies on evidence from peasant culture (e.g. songs, myths) and peasant behaviour to support his assumption. Direct interviewing of peasants was not an option available to Scott in his study of historical rebellions; his explicit interest in peasant views suggests that he would otherwise have interviewed peasants. Scott misses the potential importance of how internal conflicts within the peasantry may influence peasant motives to participate not because he is entirely unaware of internal differentiation within the peasantry – although he does neglect gender and generational differences – but because these differences pale in importance when one considers how shared peasant values give peasants similar motives.

In *Peasant Nationalism and Communist Power*, Chalmers Johnson combines structuralist and voluntarist assumptions. He is acutely aware of how peasant goals may differ from those of revolutionary organizations. He argues that after the Japanese invasion of China in the late 1930s, the Chinese Communist Party deliberately downplayed its socialist intentions, which had no appeal to peasants and capitalized on peasants' new spirit of nationalism awakened by the invasion and the horrors of the Japanese occupation. But Johnson infers peasant interests from peasant values, themselves inferred from non-peasant sources. Direct peasant voices, as in the Zimbabwean study, might have highlighted the potential for internal peasant structures to generate grievances that motivate peasants to participate in revolution. Johnson is interested in the internal structure of peasant societies but he perceives it to be one of shared values. Consequently, there is no scope for internal conflicts within the peasantry to motivate peasant participation in revolutions.

Migdal's *Peasants, Politics and Revolution* and Popkin's *The Rational Peasant* make peasant ideas and behaviour central to their studies and recognize that peasants and revolutionary organizations have different agendas. While the latter are concerned with state power and ideologies, peasants participate in revolutions because they seek immediate benefits. In particular, they wish to improve their links to markets and states. Unlike Migdal (and Scott and Wolf), Popkin argues that colonialism was not unequivocally harmful to peasant welfare and he focuses not just on peasant grievances against the state and landlords but also on the injustices in traditional or 'feudal' institutions: the exploitative power of landlords and village notables who use their power to exclude, in different ways, poor peasants, outsiders, and the wives of poor migrants.[43] Popkin's emphasis on peasant grievances against 'feudal' village arrangements that exclude certain groups from equal rights and benefits in villages is unusual but we learn of their role in a revolution only through the apparently effective appeals made by revolutionary organizations to redress them. Despite the importance of these village inequalities in his theoretical exposition about why peasants participate in revolutions, their empirical illustration is not well developed. Moreover, he entirely bypasses potentially conflicting identities in peasant societies, such as gender and generation, especially unmarried youth, and the possible role they may play in spurring peasants to participate in revolutions. Both Migdal and Popkin portray peasants as individuals making decisions without reference to peasant structures; that is, they do not consider how peasant interactions with each other influence their decisions. Both share the voluntarist assumption that peasant ideas and actions matter but both infer peasant motives from peasant behaviour and other non-peasant sources. Voluntarists can learn from peasant voices how structures do influence individual decisions.

There are several striking features about this literature. Particularly glaring is that none of the studies reviewed consider gender or generational differences within the peasantry to influence peasant motives for revolutionary participation. To the extent that scholars concern themselves with peasant differentiation, it is usually in the debate about which socio-economic strata in the peasantry are most likely to participate in revolutions. Scott argues that it is subsistence-oriented peasants who will have the greatest revolutionary potential because they are most vulnerable to landlord violations of the subsistence ethic. For Wolf, it is the middle or landowning peasants, cast by most other scholars as the culturally most conservative stratum of peasants, who are most likely to play the role of 'dynamiting the peasant social order'. Although subordinate to external power, they have the most internal leverage to rebel: they own their land and can use family labour. Moreover, 'it is also the middle peasant who is relatively the most vulnerable to economic changes wrought by commercialism, while his social relations remain encased within the traditional design'. Middle peasants are also most exposed to the influences of a developing proletariat because they send their children to work in town. 'This makes the middle peasant a transmitter also of urban unrest and political ideas.'[44] Migdal suggests that peasants undergoing the most rapid, disruptive exposure to newly penetrating market forces will be the most likely to respond to organized political movements that offer solutions to their market-induced woes. Similarly, Popkin claims that peasants with a small surplus can take risks that those at the margin cannot afford and are more likely to initially respond to organizational incentives. These examples illustrate how these scholars' views about who in the peasantry is most likely to participate in revolutions are linked to their arguments about what motivates peasants to participate. Debates on both these issues failed to allow for the possibility that gender and generation might account for notable differences in peasant motives and behaviour during revolutions. Peasant voices in the Zimbabwe case study draw attention to the important role of unmarried peasant youth in aiding the guerrillas, and to how gender and generational conflicts within the peasantry spurred women and youth to participate.

All the studies reviewed, whether structuralist or voluntarist, share the view that states and markets, and class (peasant–landlord) conflicts are the primary sources of peasant grievances underlying peasant motives for participating in revolutions. Structuralists (Wolf, Moore, and Skocpol) do not concern themselves with peasant ideas about peasant interests and motives for participating in revolutions; they simply infer peasant interests from objective forces. Voluntarists (and I include for the moment Scott and Johnson who share voluntarist and structuralist assumptions) assert an interest in peasant ideas but also do not consult peasants. Structuralists (and I include for the moment Scott and Johnson) are more likely to concern themselves with peasant structures and how they influence peasant behaviour than are voluntarists (such as Popkin and Migdal) but even structuralists do not focus on structural conflicts within the peasantry as a source of peasant motives for participating in revolutions. Beyond the failure to consult peasants themselves and these broad theoretical assumptions, other factors appear to have also steered us away from recognizing how conflicts arising from grievances that are internal to villages may be potential sources of peasant motivation for revolutionary participation.

Our concept of peasant, I believe, is an obstacle to allowing a larger role for grievances about internal village politics in the revolutionary process. To illustrate the point, I will discuss two influential and radically different conceptions of peasants. In *Peasant Society and Culture*, first published in 1956, Redfield offers a loose definition of a peasant class or type to assist the comparative study of such societies. He defines peasants as small producers who live off the land to which they have a special attachment and over which they are in effective control even if they do not own it. Unlike farmers, peasants do not regard agriculture as a business for profit but produce for their own consumption. Whereas primitive societies are 'self-contained' cultures, isolated and remote, peasants are part of a larger society and culture. A literate elite (in the manor or city) gives guidance to peasants in the 'moral sphere', providing them with a justification for their existence and continued survival. Peasants relate to the elite, but in no specified way. Elites have a different 'way of life' from peasants in that it is 'more civilized' but it is also like that of peasants. Peasant societies lie on a continuum between primitive and urban societies, and are understood in terms of their differences from either pole.[45] Notions of 'tradition', 'way of life', and peasant–elite relationships, seen as ideational influences, are central to Redfield's peasant concept.[46]

Eric Wolf also defines peasants with respect to primitives and farmers. Peasants are rural people subject to the dictates of a superordinate state; primitives are rural dwellers who live outside the confines of the state. However, not all rural people who are subject to the dictates of the state are included in his peasant concept. Peasants include only 'populations that are existentially involved in cultivation and make autonomous decisions regarding the processes of cultivation. The category is thus made to cover tenants and sharecroppers as well as owner-operators, as long as they are in a position to make the relevant decisions on how their crops are grown. It does not, however, include fishermen or landless laborers.' Peasants are distinguished from farmers by their different psychological orientations and institutional contexts. Peasants favour smaller risks rather than larger profits, and their major aim is subsistence and social status gained in a narrow range of social relationships. In contrast, farmers seek to maximize profits, participate fully in the market, and seek social status in a wide social network.[47]

Two differences between Wolf's and Redfield's definition of peasants are noteworthy. First, Wolf introduces unequal power relations between peasants and the state that are absent in Redfield's work.[48] Second, Wolf gives importance to economic (and ecological) processes, seen simultaneously as relations of power, whereas Redfield focuses on peasant 'tradition' and 'way of life'. But the point I wish to make here is how both definitions, representing different anthropological approaches to the study of peasants, still have much in common. Peasants are still located on a continuum that places them between 'others': 'primitives' and farmers. Wolf distinguishes peasants from primitives by the former's subjection to the dictates of the state; for Redfield the distinction is that peasants, unlike primitives, are a 'part society' related to the city and elites rather than a separate self-contained culture. The distinction between peasants and farmers that both authors make highlights a particular relationship between peasants and markets. But there are important differences within peasant communities from which the peasant concept is likely to divert attention. As long as we are more interested in pointing to the differences between peasants and 'others', we will minimize or bypass the differences within peasant communities, and, thereby, their potential political importance in peasant revolutions. As Polly Hill observed in her critique of the peasant concept in *Development Economics on Trial*, many who engage in defining peasants are primarily concerned with the peasantry as a political entity, yet peasants do not usually act as an 'organized political force to be reckoned with'.[49] Revolutions, rather than uniting peasants against others, may actually accentuate everyday political struggles among peasants.

Another factor vitiates against examining conflicts internal to the peasantry. Despite an expressed interest in peasants, most studies of rural-based revolutions – and much of social science itself – have ultimately been interested in elites.[50] One manifestation of this elite bias is the way in which scholars privilege revolutionary organizations' intermediate goals: popular support, unity, collective action. Even when peasants are a central topic of investigation, studies of revolution tend to examine them as a means to furthering these prerequisites of revolutionary organizations. As already noted, most voluntarist studies focus on how an organization can find appropriate appeals to induce peasants to engage in collective action and win their popular support. Such studies understand that organizations will manipulate peasant grievances for their own ends, and often acknowledge that peasants will try to manipulate organizations. But peasant manipulation of organizations is regarded ultimately as a threat to organizational goals. The interest in peasant agency therefore is limited to how peasants may further organizational ends. I have already argued that structuralists, despite their theoretical orientation away from individuals' attitudes, frequently drift into a concern with popular support. For them, collective class action, like popular support, is not a major problem: objective forces will create the necessary conditions that will give rise to them. By allowing these concepts of popular support, collective action, and unity to permeate the study of revolutions, scholars often unwittingly adopt the perspective of the revolutionary elite. In doing so, they relegate peasant agendas that might jeopardize the attainment of these intermediate organizational goals to obstacles to be contained and controlled.

Just how much scholars' organizational perspective resonates with revolutionary elites' concerns becomes apparent in Richard Solomon's *Mao's Revolution and the Chinese Political Culture*. Solomon discusses how Mao advocated mobilizing politically passive peasants by promoting their hostility and aggression against their class oppressors. 'The dynamic aspect of Mao's approach to building a unity of revolutionary forces derives from his belief that people are sustained in their political involvement through the tension of conflict with their oppressors . . .'[51] But the Communist Party had to maintain discipline in the class conflict it encouraged and ensure that its goal of party and coalition unity was not compromised. During the land reform programme in the civil war, 'the personalized hatreds which Party cadres stimulated in the village "speak bitterness" struggles were difficult to control. The peasants, lacking the discipline of political "consciousness", tended to be indiscriminate in using the violence of land reform to settle old personal grudges or to embark on an orgy of "eating up" the material possessions of their class enemies. The Party faced the danger of "tailism" – of becoming a mere appendage manipulated by the peasant violence it sought to use.'[52] Mao also regarded peasants' 'narrow loyalties' such as exclusive commitments to family, clan, school class, and region as a threat to party and coalition unity and therefore a problem to be overcome.[53]

27

Gregory Massell's *The Surrogate Proletariat* represents another example of the concerns of a revolutionary elite – in this case the Soviet central elite – with how to control mobilization. Massell describes how the Soviet regime tried to use legal and administrative means to stimulate and exploit women's grievances in Moslem traditional societies to undermine the traditional order. Legal and administrative reforms did spur the mobilization of women as intended but the reforms also provoked the mobilization of others. Inequalities and divisions based on sex could not be made consistently synonymous with those based on class: women valued some connections that they had to men and the new Soviet reforms challenged them, inviting resistance from some women. Also, Moslem male personnel who had to implement the new Soviet laws at the grassroots level were mobilized to oppose the attempted reforms. The Soviet central elite also failed because it was unable to induce (positive) tensions that would undermine the traditional order and at the same time control those (negative) consequences of the induced tensions that threatened to affect the regime's stability and developmental objectives. Both Massell and Solomon illustrate the fine line that revolutionary organizations must tread to ensure that those they mobilize remain under their control and that the process of stimulating mobilization does not trigger the spontaneous mobilization of others with agendas that are at odds with their own.[54]

The organizational bias in the literature on revolutions also asserts itself in privileging revolutionary elites' national objectives over local and parochial peasant goals. Just as revolutionaries may legitimately manipulate peasants to further intermediate organizational goals, so they may manipulate peasants to guarantee that national rather than local goals prevail. Patrick Chabal emphasizes the 'internal contradiction' for revolutionary parties in Africa that must mobilize on the basis of ethnicity in order to create a sense of national identity and remarks that successful political mobilization requires that the revolutionary party control and submerge ethnic identities that it arouses. 'The paradox is that successful mobilisation demands, not the abolition of ethnic sentiments (if that were possible), but rather the politicisation of ethnicity for nationalist purposes. Here the role of the party is crucial: it is both the agency through which ethnic mobilisation is channelled and the organisation through which ethnic particularisms are transcended into a new state. The party must reconcile its conflicting interests between the need to achieve national unity and the use of local and parochial issues for purposes of mobilisation.'[55] Even James Scott, who is aware of the elite bias in studies of revolution, ultimately sanctions their national objectives. Scott criticizes the elite bias: 'When we call a complex and momentous historical movement a nationalist or communist revolution we thereby acquiesce in a form of instant analysis and historiography, the implications of which are rarely appreciated. We describe, in shorthand fashion, the motivating ideology of the movement and implicitly ascribe to it both a certain unity at the level of ideas and a certain coherence at the level of organization. Inasmuch as traditional scholarship has been, above all, interested in the elites of such movements and in the ideas which they carry, there may be something to be said for such convenient labels.'[56] The thrust of much of Scott's work has been to uncover how peasant ideas and interests differ from those of revolutionary elites. He takes issue with those who regard peasant goals as inferior to the national goals of a revolutionary party and observes that a revolutionary leadership with its emphasis on organization, bureaucracy, coalition building and the like may dampen the spontaneity of peasants' revolutionary zeal. Ultimately, though, he too submits that party goals must prevail if the revolution is to achieve national objectives.[57]

It is difficult to escape the conclusion that the study of peasant involvement in revolutions has often been motivated by an interest in how peasants contribute to the revolutionary elite's success rather than an intrinsic interest in peasant agency. Many scholars accept that if what motivates peasants also challenges the agenda of national interests defined by a revolutionary organization, the latter should prevail. Joel Kahn's review of studies of peasant ideologies in the contemporary third world led him to a similar conclusion. He found the studies curiously removed from how peasants understood their interests and revealed more about academic perspectives on modernization. He claimed that even academics who engage in dialogue with peasants to discover peasant consciousness and ideologies tend to treat the peasantry as an object of study: 'no matter to what extent the process of discovering peasant ideology and culture is a matter of self-consciousness [sic] dialogue between peasant and investigator, the longer-term evaluation of the academic text tends to have very little to do with peasants or, perhaps more accurately, the participants in the concrete struggles in which peasants are involved'.[58] Peasant voices in the Zimbabwe case study valorize peasant ideas and interests in a revolution, even when they are at odds with those of the revolutionary elite, and show how peasants sought to manipulate a revolutionary organization to promote their own local objectives. Indeed, peasant struggles that conflicted with the revolutionary elite's nationalist objectives serve as a critique of nationalism and its intolerance for other identities.

The widespread legitimacy of revolutionary organizations' national objectives at the expense of local peasant goals, I believe, stems partly from an uncritical acceptance of nationalist revolutions in the twentieth century. Nationalism is a slippery concept, the meaning of which is disputed. However, whether analysts see it as a reaction to colonialism,[59] imperialism or capitalism,[60] or a cultural reaction,[61] all share the idea of nationalism as a reaction to an alien intrusion. The force of nationalism overwhelms differences internal to society. Hodgkin writes: 'The fact that the economic claims and interests of different sections of African society – traders and entrepreneurs, farmers and fishermen, labourers and clerks – may be divergent is of subordinate importance, so long as for all sections that

29

colonial regime is regarded as the main obstacle in the way of economic advance.'[62] Renan expresses nationalism as an essential condition for a 'nation': a sense of common history, especially a memory of common sufferings that seem more important than the conflicts and divisions also to be found within that history.[63] A similar notion appears in Deutsch's discussion of one of two processes that result in nation-building and the formation of nationalities. Cultural assimilation is described as the process by which information fed to members of different groups exceeds the different stores of information that feed their different groups' memories.[64] In short, like the peasant concept, the concept of nationalism with its focus on united action against an external enemy fosters an orientation away from conflicts internal to the peasantry.

Mobilization and revolutionary outcomes

Peasants' voices in the Zimbabwe study alert us to how they perceived the party as a symbol of fear and coercion despite its revolutionary success. Peasants associated a victorious revolutionary party with coercive mobilization and continued acts of party coercion in the post-war period. These peasant views underscore the importance of the subjective realm if theories are to understand party-state relations. Zimbabwean peasants also remind us that in the post-war phase, as in the mobilization process, they were at least as concerned about their social relations with other villagers as they were with their relationship to the party and the state. That is, peasants draw attention to the influence on their ideas and actions of internal peasant structures and of new divisions introduced by their experience of the war itself, such as who had really provided material support for the guerrillas.

Skocpol contrasts the outcomes of two patterns of revolutions based on whether organized revolutionaries mobilized peasants. She groups together the French, Russian, and Mexican revolutions where political mobilization of the peasantry was not a factor in the revolutionary process and contrasts it with the direct mobilization of peasants in the Chinese, Vietnamese, and perhaps Cuban revolutions, and the revolutionary anti-colonial movements of Portuguese Africa. She argues that the latter pattern produced favourable outcomes for peasants. 'Because of this direct mobilization, peasant resources and manpower have ended up participating in the building of new-regime social institutions and state organizations. Peasant participation in this revolutionary pattern is less 'spontaneous' and autonomous than in the first pattern, but the results can be much more favourable to local peasant interests, because during the revolutionary process itself direct links are established between peasants and revolutionary political and military organizations.'[65] In *States and Social Revolutions* Skocpol is more specific about the benefits of revolutionary mobilization in China. The unique relationship between the party and peasants forged while completing and consolidating the Chinese social revolution 'created special possibilities afterwards for the Party-state to mobilize peasants for active involvement in socialist transformation'.[66] Also, at the same time that the revolution strengthened the Chinese state, it also strengthened 'local-level collective democracy'.[67]

Skocpol's optimistic prognoses for peasants in the post-revolutionary period are predicated on revolution only occurring once the power of the state has been weakened, making possible revolutionary mobilization based on a mutually beneficial exchange between peasants and revolutionary organization. Peasant experiences in Zimbabwe's war, as already discussed, direct attention to the possibility that a successful revolution may occur even without a weakening of the state's military capacity. Consequently, mobilization may occur but without a mutually beneficial exchange between peasants and revolutionaries. Skocpol's attempt at strict structural analysis precludes an interest in revolutionary participants' subjective experience during mobilization and after the revolution. Such an analysis cannot uncover, as the Zimbabwe study that relied on peasant voices did, the potential for coercive mobilization and how it might continue to influence peasant perspectives of the party and even the behaviour of grassroots party officials in the post-war period. Also, Zimbabwean peasant voices about their post-war experiences again remind us that structuralists may not always know which structures are important influences on peasant behaviour and interests. Just as structuralists neglected how internal peasant structures shaped peasant behaviour and interests in the mobilization period, so too does Skocpol neglect these structures in the post-war period in favour of peasant relationships to the party and state.

Writing about revolutionary parties in the ex-lusophone African colonies, Ali Mazrui and others, who share many voluntarist assumptions, have argued, like Skocpol, that the revolutionary mobilization process should offer benefits to both peasants and the party. According to Mazrui, 'organizationally, the movement should have acquired considerable advantages over the usual political parties in Africa. The apparently sustained attempt to mobilize the peasantry as part of the war against the Portuguese, and then institutionalize the ethos of purposeful transformation in the liberated rural areas, helped to deepen the experience of genuine collective organization and commitment . . . The party's experience in mass mobilization against the Portuguese should be an asset in this new struggle for reconstruction and rejuvenation.'[68] Mazrui adopts the vantage point of the revolutionary party but his emphasis on its 'experience of genuine collective organization' suggests some lasting mutual benefit for party and peasant based on their war-time relationship. Chabal finds the idea that the beneficial exchanges established between peasants and party during the mobilization process in the people's wars in the ex-lusophone colonies will continue into the post-independence period to be widespread. However, while agreeing with this characterization of mobilization, he rejects the so-called 'optimists'' predictions that the legacy of armed struggle would inevitably produce revolutionary post-colonial states that would continue to align themselves with peasants. His central objection is that one cannot infer post-war outcomes from the mobilization process and that one must take into account the absence of structural conditions for post-colonial socialist states.[69] Chabal is right to alert us to the pitfalls of inferring post-war outcomes from processes and to advocate direct investigation of the post-colonial state and its relations to peasants. However, he accepts the characterization of a popular mobilization process that was mutually beneficial to both peasants and party when this view is itself based on indirect inferences. Peasants in the Zimbabwe study inform us of the coercive aspects of mobilization, and of how their war-time and continued experience of party coercion influenced their interaction with the party. Zimbabwean peasants also alert us to the external bias in these studies that focus on the relationship between peasants and the state and neglect the influence of internal peasant structures and divisiveness about who in the peasantry had contributed to the material support of the guerrillas in shaping conflicts after the war.

The foregoing discussion has attempted to highlight how incorporating peasant understandings of their experiences in a revolution can contribute to existing theories of revolutions on three issues: the relationship between popular support, coercion, and revolutionary success; peasant motives for participating in revolutions; and the linkage between mobilization and revolutionary outcomes for peasants. Structuralists cannot ignore individual ideas and actions even if they wish to understand structures only; voluntarists cannot ignore how structures influence individual choices and behaviour. Beginning with peasant voices, this study seeks to emphasize the importance of both individual ideas and actions and how they are influenced by structures.

To obtain direct peasant voices requires fieldwork. The research on which this study is based was possible largely because it took place before the new Zimbabwean government had established a bureaucracy to deal with outside researchers. The first two years of independence were remarkably open to foreign researchers. Government research permits did not yet exist. Stories circulated at the University of Zimbabwe about how university students had to obtain government and party approval before undertaking rural research, and I was advised to submit a proposal to the Minister of Local Government and Housing. Perhaps approval was easier than it might have been because we had met previously in the United States. During the nearly two years of fieldwork for this study, the bureaucracy to cope with researchers was slowly being installed. Today there is an elaborate procedure, taking up to eighteen months, to obtain a research permit. This applies even to obtaining access to the national archives. How one selects a physical area and respondents, the questions one asks, whose answers and what fragment of these answers one chooses to record all reflect crucial choices that influence research. Other factors, such as the timing of the research and the identity of the researcher may also profoundly affect one's findings. For this reason, these and other methodological issues call for explicit attention.

Selecting a district to study

Fieldwork for this study was done in Mutoko district in the north-eastern part of Zimbabwe (see map 1). Mutoko district comprised a so-called European farming sector dependent on African labour, a Tribal Trust Land where the majority of Africans in the district lived, cultivating individual plots and grazing cattle in communal areas, and a Purchase Area where Africans leased land from the government or owned private farms. The chief reason for selecting Mutoko district was that the war had been intense and more protracted there than in much of the country, and there was a presumption, based on the writings of the proponents of the radicalization thesis, that therefore mobilization would have been extensive. The much earlier start of the war in Mutoko district had to do with its location on the ZANLA guerrillas' infiltration route from Mozambique. The centre of the district lies only 94 kilometres from the Mozambican border post at Nyamapanda, itself close to the Mozambican town of Tete (see map 2). Government countermeasures also affected Mutoko earlier. At the end of 1972 when the government first became aware of guerrilla activity in the northeast, it tightened administrative control in Mutoko. The area north of Mutoko Tribal Trust Land had always had an extremely thin administrative presence, and in mid 1973 this was changed by establishing a second district for this sparsely inhabited area[70] (see map 2). In 1976, well before the war had spread to most of the country, the first 'protected villages' were established in Mutoko Tribal Trust Land. Beginning with an understaffed paramilitary force of about 70 guards at the 'protected villages', the armed guard force grew to 600 by March 1977.[71] To economize on the costs of the guard forces, 'protected villages' in Mutoko and the rest of Mashonaland East Province were built to accommodate 1,000 to 3,000 people – many more than elsewhere in the country. Mutoko became the base for the Security Forces' Joint Operations Command for the Operation Hurricane area covering the north-east in 1976. It was also made the forward deployment base for the Selous Scouts – government forces that masqueraded as guerrillas.[72] Until at least January 1977, when the war began to spread outside the Operation Hurricane area, almost all available forces of the army, air force, and British South Africa Police were concentrated in this region. The higher casualty figures in Operation Hurricane zone compared with other government operational zones indicate its importance in the war. Operation Hurricane had nearly three times the number of casualties as the next most important operational area (see table 1.1). As the war spread, Mutoko had to compete for security forces with eastern districts that had become important infiltration routes, and with European areas of higher national economic value. However, it remained a most savagely contested zone throughout

Map 2: Land divisions in Mutoko and Mudzi districts

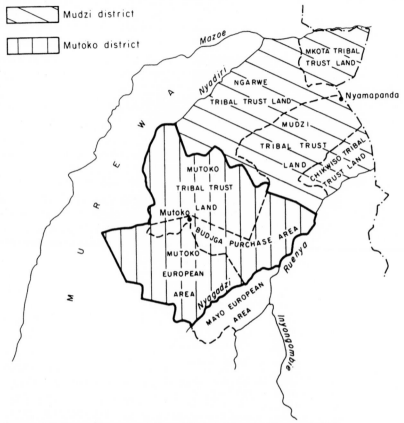

Source: Ministry of Internal Affairs, National Service Research Unit,
Resource Survey No. 1, Mrewa-Mtoko-Mudzi, 1979.

the war.[73] Given the prevailing view in the Zimbabwe war literature about
the beneficial aspects of a protracted mobilization, Mutoko district ought to
have constituted a most desirable case for examining the relationship
between revolutionary mobilization and post-war rural politics.

Two other reasons made Mutoko a compelling case study. Throughout
the war, ZANLA was the only guerrilla army to operate here, so the district
would be free of the complications that affected mobilization in areas such as
the Midlands Province where ZANLA and ZIPRA forces clashed with each
other. Post-war electoral data suggested broad support for ZANU. The
February 1980 parliamentary elections were on a provincial rather than
constituency basis, and Mashonaland East province, in which Mutoko
district is located, was solidly behind ZANU. In the local government
elections in August 1981 in Mutoko Tribal Trust Land, ZANU won all the

Table 1.1 *Casualty figures per operational area up to 30 January 1977*

Operation	Persons	Killed	Missing	Wounded	Captured	Total
Hurricane	Insurgents	1,033			372	1,405
	Security forces	106		769		875
	Civilians	525	4	740		1,269
	Total	1,664	4	1,509	372	3,549
Thrasher	Insurgents	359			46	405
	Security forces	41	1	324		366
	Civilians	269		263		532
	Total	669	1	587	46	1,303
Repulse	Insurgents	262			53	315
	Security forces	29		138		167
	Civilians	96	7	104		207
	Total	387	7	242	53	689
Tangent	Insurgents	18			13	31
	Security forces	14		30		44
	Civilians	36	3	37		76
	Total	68	3	67	13	151

These are official figures, the only ones that are available, and they are known to exaggerate the numbers of guerrillas killed by including African civilians. [74]
Source: Cilliers, *Counter-Insurgency in Rhodesia*, p. 36.

seats. Lastly, some European farmers had already been bought out under Muzorewa, and so land was available for resettling Africans. Many other farms belonging to whites in the so-called European area had been abandoned during the war and Mutoko district was going to be a major resettlement area. ZANU and scholars presented land resettlement as a crucial development issue and Mutoko provided an opportunity to observe its progress. These, then, were the reasons for choosing to work in Mutoko. It was to be the first of three case studies on the relationship of mobilization to post-war rural politics. I fully expected to move on and work in a district in which ZIPRA alone had operated during the war and where ZAPU had control over the local government after the war. Afterwards, I hoped to study a district in which ZIPRA and ZANLA had contested against each other as well as the government forces for control during the war. As things turned out, all I managed was the Mutoko study, and then only selected parts of the district.

Trying to cover the entire district raised its own problems. The distances I was travelling daily consumed too much time, given that the road network, albeit surprisingly extensive, was largely unpaved. People's accounts of what had happened seemed too contingent on local specifics, and required much deeper probing if information was to be cross-checked or some understanding acquired of why such differences surfaced. I focused the rest of my interviews on four administrative divisions or wards in Mutoko Tribal Trust Land – Charewa (fifty-eight villages), Nyakuna (six villages), Nyamatsahuni (twenty-seven villages), and Nyamanza (twenty-seven villages)[75] (see map 3). Work in Manyange ward had to be aban-

Map 3: Wards in Mutoko Tribal Trust Land

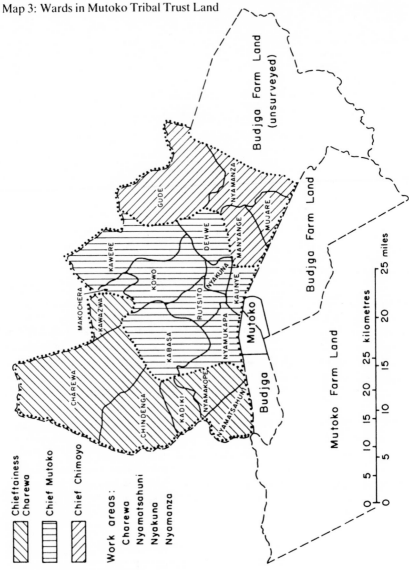

Source: Ministry of Internal Affairs, National Service Reseach Unit, Resource Survey No. 1, Mrewa-Mtoko-Mudzi, 1979.

doned for reasons I will go into later. My choice of wards was guided by two criteria: their distance from the district centre, and whether the headman had survived during the war. The district headquarters were in the general area of the Joint Operations Command, the Selous Scouts' and paramalitary camps, and I thought that areas closer to the centre would have been under greater Security Force pressures and less exposed to the guerrillas. It had also seemed reasonable to assume that the survival of the headman, unlikely to be sympathetic to competitive political actors, might have made it more difficult to establish party organizations. Consequently, Nyamanza and Charewa wards were chosen because both were some distance from the district centre, and in Nyamanza the ward headman had died, while the ward headman in Charewa had survived the war. Nyamatsahuni and Nyakuna wards were chosen because they were both close to the district centre and only headman Nyakuna had survived the war. Factors other than distance from the district centre turned out to be crucially important in giving government forces access to villages. These were the existence of roads, which varied enormously within wards, the location of army camps and airfields that had been established in some remote areas, and the presence of paramilitary troops that were occupying school buildings in many parts of the district. These considerations made mileage from the district centre less important than I had anticipated. Moreover, the whole concept of distance from the district centre for an entire ward was difficult to apply as a part of the ward might be close to the district headquarters while the rest of it might be a considerable distance away. In practice, what mattered was accessibility to parts of a district and that turned out to depend on the road network. Whether the headman had survived the war also turned out to much less important than I had expected.

Selecting respondents

My interest in political leadership during and after the war led to me to seek interviews with past and present court officers, chiefs, local government representatives, and party leaders. It was easy to learn who local leaders were when they were paid government officials, and all but the party leaders were on government payrolls. Government records contained the information and villagers could usually name officeholders. The main difficulty was identifying party leaders during the war. Many villagers served as committee members during the war and people often could not remember who committee members had been. Also, there were many reasons, as I will discuss, why cooperation was not always forthcoming. Present day party members were sometimes difficult to identify because there had been so many elections since the war and people were often confused about who had been elected most recently. Declining interest in party affairs also made tracking down committee members a little more arduous than it might otherwise have been. Most of my time was taken up interviewing war-time and post-war party committee members. Some war-time leaders slipped through the net, but in the four wards I worked in, a majority were interviewed. Also important in this study are the children of villagers, the so-called *youth*, who also had active roles in the war. Unfortunately, many had left the district after the war, either to work in the towns or to go to school in other districts. Although the study focuses chiefly on peasants and *youth* and their relationships with the guerrillas and one another, I also examine their relationships with the African rural elite. Members of the African elite – teachers, ministers of religion, storekeepers, local government officials, agricultural extension staff – are few and conspicuous. They were easy to identify and find at schools, clinics, missions, businesses, and government offices. Actively involved in the war too, albeit in different ways from peasants and *youth*, they contribute significantly to this study. They were generally eager to talk, and because they were usually proficient in English, I interviewed most of them without a translator.

Limitations on presenting peasant voices

To refer to a direct peasant voice only has meaning as a contrast to data on peasants that are inferred from other sources. Although peasant and other voices appear in quotation marks in the rest of the study, these responses were preceded and followed up by my questions. Influenced by the scholarly portrait of a relationship of guerrillas and peasants based on popular support and mutual interests, I initially asked questions that reflected these presuppositions. The cracks in this picture of mobilization first began to appear when I tried to find out who the village party leaders had been during the war so that I could map out continuities with contemporary leadership positions. When I realized that almost every adult villager had been thrust onto party committees to organize logistical support for the guerrillas, my questions shifted to probing the sources of conflict between guerrillas on the one hand and peasants and other rural Africans on the other (see chapter 4). My interest in social conflicts among African civilians grew out of an increasing awareness of how resentments among villagers had become intertwined with their participation in the organizations set up to supply guerrillas' logistical needs (see chapter 5). Not all my questions were directed at understanding conflicts between guerrillas and peasants and among peasants during the war. I tried to find out if leaders in the post-war period thought their positions were influential or prestigious, and how they felt about government policies and the changes since independence (see chapter 6). I also tried to get personal information from interviewees about the number of wives they had, how much schooling they and their children had, their job histories, family income and wealth (their landholdings, cattle, and so on). For some time I began interviews with such questions, thinking that they were less contentious than the issues of more immediate interest to me. I hoped that the kind of data I collected would make it possible to develop a socio-economic profile of my sample population. Some of the responses were helpful in this respect. Visiting people at their homes was also a useful way of getting some idea of their socio-economic status. Brick homes suggested some degree of affluence, as did furniture, bicycles, ploughs, scotch carts and the availability of purchased food. But I abandoned any attempt to collect systematically socio-economic data through interviews. It was time-consuming: interviewees often had many children and it took much thought and perhaps family consultations before they could give their ages and educational levels. Questions about how much land they had were answered by detailed descriptions of the boundaries of their fields. But it was not just that quantitative data were produced slowly, if at all, that made me abandon such questioning. Many of these questions provoked suspicion, when I had hoped that they would help to put people at ease before I moved onto the more overtly sensitive questions about the war. Shortly before I left the district, the interaction between a local government representative and his constituents instructed me on what would have been the most effective opening questions. Encouraging a reluctant assembly to speak to me, he suggested that they tell me of how they suffered during the war, of the cattle they had lost and of the government soldiers' brutality. Everyone wanted to speak at once.

The peasant voice is also mediated by the choice I have made of who to cite and what excerpts of responses to include. My study is open to the allegation that it focuses so exclusively on conflict that it is blind or deaf to instances of voluntary cooperation between guerrillas and peasants. I did encounter respondents who described their relationship to guerrillas in slogan-like phrases like 'we were all one' or 'we were united'. However, in the light of what I regard as strong and consistent counter-evidence, such claims, never buttressed with specific evidence, seemed unworthy of inclusion. They sounded more like the guerrilla voices appealing to the civilian population.

Another mediating issue was my identity as a foreign white woman. Had I been a local African asking similar questions, I doubt that people would have been as willing to discuss their conflicts with each other and the guerrillas. A black Zimbabwean who came to Mutoko would be more likely to inhibit peasants: that person would return to Harare and could not escape being seen as partisan. Being a foreigner and a white made the distance between us greater than it might have been for an African researcher but ironically the effect was to allow people to offer more intimate revelations about their internal conflicts than they might have shared with an African whom they perceived as a comparative insider.

But there were definite disadvantages being a foreign white researcher. Lacking any prior connections, I found myself being introduced to the African community via whites: a white farmer, an American at a publishing house, an American-born missionary. It would have been preferable to make contacts in the district through Africans so that I did not seem so aligned with whites, especially after a war that was racial in origin and objective. Being white and trying to interview Africans in such a society was often a burden. The skills required to survive a war had made people more alert to potential threats to their security, and a member of the formerly dominant racial group, asking war-related questions triggered a variety of fears so that people were extremely suspicious and afraid to talk to me. But many of these fears were related as much to the timing of the research so soon after a brutal war as to my white identity, as I discuss below. The Minister of Local Government and Housing, who was also the Acting Publicity Secretary of the ruling party ZANU-PF (as ZANU was renamed at the time of the election in 1980), gave me letters that indicated that I had permission from both the government and the party to conduct the research. While these letters were indispensable, they rarely allayed people's different fears. Nor did my efforts to bury my South African identity and present my less provocative face as a student from an American university studying the history of the district ameliorate the suspicion and fear. Sometimes people's fears were expressed explicitly in my presence at village meetings as a village tried to decide whether to talk to me. At other times their concerns leaked out. Throughout my stay at Mutoko, their suspicions were never entirely laid to rest. I had only to leave the district for a single day, and fresh rumours about who I was and what I was doing confronted me on my return.

Despite all the difficulties I experienced in finding people to talk to, some of the meanings that people constructed about who I was suggest that African images of a white are not entirely negative. Some thought I was helping to administer an existing government scheme to compensate people who lost family members or had war injuries. They eagerly reported these and other losses such as cattle that had been fed to the guerrillas or homes that had been burnt by soldiers, for which they still hoped to be compensated. Some volunteered to speak to me in the hope that if I advertised their sufferings to the world, they would receive material aid. Believing this, they insisted on being identified by name. A memorable example of such expectations occurred in one village, where people had met with me at a gathering arranged by their ward representative. Before he had arrived, considerable discussion had taken place about whether they should talk to me, and they had decided in the end against it. When he arrived, many people were still milling about. Admonishing villagers for refusing to talk to me, he warned them not to complain when the adjacent area, where people had cooperated, received aid from the United States and they did not. Over time, people saw they could use me as an intermediary to the government. They correctly recognized that I had easier access to top government officials than they or most of their representatives had. For many, though, it was a matter of preserving the historical record of their district so that their children and future generations could be educated. Several teachers, when consulted by villagers uncertain whether to be interviewed, helped of their own accord by advancing this argument to encourage people to talk. Amidst all the resistance that I generated, the hospitality and generosity of so many villagers was all the more remarkable. I have devoted so little space to the cooperative relationships I formed because the data on which this study is based are their testimony.

The timing of the research must also be recorded as a mediating influence. What difference did it make that people were being questioned about their war experiences with ZANU guerrillas, and their attitudes to ZANU's current policies and practices when ZANU was the ruling party? Had early signs that many of ZANU's war promises would not materialize caught peasants in a bitter and resentful mood towards it, thereby leading them to focus on negative features of their relationship with ZANU guerrillas? People were undeniably disappointed that many of ZANU's war-time promises had not been fulfilled, but certain promises had been honoured. Despite disappointments, people were often reluctant, even fearful, to discuss questions about ZANU. Some refused to talk at all, others answered questions with safe slogan-like answers handed down by the party, and still others spoke circumspectly about ZANU. But perhaps the mediating influence of a ZANU government being in power at the time of fieldwork was less important than that research was undertaken so soon after the war had ended. The experience of a costly and brutal war had made people extremely cautious and suspicious.

For some, governments were indistinguishable. During the war, it was pointed out, Muzorewa's government had given them free food, and then they had got into trouble from the guerrillas for accepting it. Why should they accept my government permission to do the research as an assurance that nothing would happen to them if they spoke to me? Some questioned whether the government had given me research permission. How could they know that I had not forged the official letterhead stationery and the signatures, or bribed government officials? Only white officials ever visited African homes, and then usually on punitive missions. It was common for adults walking past a home I was visiting to call out to the interviewee: 'Are you under arrest?' Children too had learned to be afraid of whites, and at my approach many ran in terror to warn their parents that the war had started again. Treating me as a white government official, people sometimes refused to give the names of war-time committee members because to tell would be 'selling-out'. Others chose to see me as representing Mugabe's government and saw in the letters a government trap to ensnare those who had 'not worked hard' during the war. Many of villagers' fears about talking to me concerned the repercussions it would have on their relations with neighbours. Some informants gave interviews only once because of co-villagers' threats to punish them for betraying their village. Thinking that I was alleviating people's fears, at first I promised them anonymity. To my surprise, on occasions this provoked villagers' suspicions as it reminded them of the Security Forces' promises of protection to 'sell-outs'. If they were going to speak, they preferred to do so publicly in a group and be identified. Others, it should be noted, preferred private interviews. Everywhere there was concern that talking about the war would lead to discussion of the 'selling-out' that had occurred, reviving war-related tensions that were barely under control. Yet only rarely would people talk about 'sell-outs' in their villages that they were anxious to present as exemplary models of unity during the war.

All over the district there was either disbelief that the war had really ended, or fear that some seemingly insignificant event might revive it. Having spoken freely, some people expressed immediate regrets that if another war were to start, 'everyone will know where they hid and how we ran the war. We will have no secrets left.' A school committee in a remote part of the district held its meetings at night, despite the inconvenience, believing that it was still not safe to meet during the day. Repeatedly I ran into concern that my presence in the district might start another war. The first guerrillas, I was told, had arrived unexpectedly. Initially everything had seemed fine but then a long war had ensued. They saw parallels in my ostensibly innocent arrival, and could not be sure that it too would not entrap them. Presumably the parallels ran deeper. Had not the missionaries also arrived decades earlier promising no harm? And had not Rhodes struck what appeared an unthreatening bargain with Lobengula, that then led to the expropriation of their land and their subjugation by whites? Innocent appearances could not be trusted.

In Manyange ward in Chimoyo chiefdom, I was forced to abandon research when people repeatedly made and broke arrangements. Some people avoided having to make excuses, others left messages. An extraordinary number of funerals occurred in the six-week period I spent trying to work here, a strategy of polite avoidance with which I had become familiar. It was rumoured that an ex-guerrilla had warned people not to talk to me. Even after the war, a single guerrilla could still command obedience. Not even an introduction by the local Member of Parliament and the district party chairman at an election meeting could remove suspicion. Indeed, after the chair's opening remarks and assurances that people could speak to me, one woman in the audience observed that I had not joined in the party slogans. 'Why did I not know party slogans?' she asked accusingly. Helpful as some of these officials were on occasions, they sometimes compounded my difficulties. For example, at one meeting at which these same officials were seeking to give me some legitimacy, it was explained that the government knew about my research and would read my notes carefully before I left the country. This seemingly wild statement was certainly not reassuring to those who did not share these officials' benign view of Prime Minister Mugabe's government.

When I returned to Mutoko for a week in January 1989 the mood was dramatically different. The changed climate was conveyed to me most vividly by the young man who had been the primary interpreter in 1981–2. 'Sometimes I meet people who were too afraid to speak to you,' he said, 'and today they are embarrassed.' Those were extraordinary times, and difficult as the research might be today, life in Mutoko has returned to normal. I had hoped to return to Mutoko in 1988 to investigate if people spoke differently about the war. What did they remember as important in 1988 that may not have seemed memorable in 1982? How significant were conflicts that had erupted during the war, and had any of these continued to simmer in its immediate aftermath? But the research environment in Zimbabwe had changed and all research, according to university guidelines, required government authorization that took up to eighteen months (and even longer in practice) to obtain. It remains an intriguing question to examine how people would speak about their participation in the war today.

This research was conducted in a period when local leadership was in a state of flux, and this too must be taken into account. Since the political fluidity at the time was a subject of my inquiry, it also complicated fieldwork. In every ward I wanted to interview political actors to establish links betwen local leadership during and after the war and to come to grips with the competition for local power in a new regime that had not yet established its authority in the rural areas. The government had removed the prewar rights of 'traditional' leaders and the war-time authority of party committees to hear court cases. New legislation provided for elected village court officers to settle disputes, and democratized local government so that 'traditional' leaders were not ex officio voting members. On the ground, though, the competition for power was intense. For example, 'traditional' leaders, party committees, and spirit mediums (who by customary law were entitled to hear certain cases) all still heard cases in different areas. To interview party committees first might offend chiefs, and vice versa. The power of spirit mediums also had to be reckoned with. In Nyamanza ward, people who spoke to me without the medium's permission had to pay a fine to her. The intertwining of a research problem with an intense ongoing battle for power that differed from area to area in its configuration made it impossible to learn from experience.

This study is removed from the direct peasant voice in still other respects because I worked through translators. The problems of language equivalency have received considerable attention in the literature on comparative inquiry and methodology. A study based on peasant views is obviously preferably done by a scholar with the appropriate linguistic skills. I went to Zimbabwe prepared to interview white Zimbabweans about sanctions and although I made an effort to learn some Shona when my topic changed, I was not proficient in it (see appendix). Nor am I persuaded that a few months of language training would have reduced the problem significantly. I would still have been using a language that I was not familiar enough with to appreciate its nuances. Using a translator is not optimal, but under the circumstances it was the best option.

Translators become a mediating influence too. I worked with different translators in different phases of the research (see appendix). But all the peasant interviews, as well as interviews with many others, were conducted by a young man in his twenties who had grown up in the Kowo area of Mutoko (see map 3), had attended an American Methodist missionary secondary school at Nyamuzuwe, and was completing high school by correspondence. From about 1976 he had been living in Chitungwiza, a huge sprawling township with municipality status, some miles from Harare. I was introduced to him through a former school-teacher, an American-born missionary at the United Methodist Mission centre at Nyamuzuwe in Kabasa ward (see map 3). Questions are bound to arise about the way in which he may have filtered information to me, and some have suggested my data show he was anti-ZANU. There is no evidence to support this. Many people were willing to be interviewed because they knew and had regard for his mother and late father who had lived all their lives in Kowo. To my knowledge, there were no allegations about his political past. Given my earlier experiences with a trainee teacher, who turned out to have been against ZANU, I am confident that had there been any suspicion about his politics, it would quickly have come to light (see appendix). The only hostility he ever informed me about came from a few younger teachers and high school students who urged him to stop working for me. Rather than help a white woman write African history, they told him that he or other educated Africans should write their own history. It is worth noting how interdependent we were. My Shona was too rudimentary to use in interviews, and whenever he tried to do any work on his own – even if it were only scheduling interviews – he reported back with stories of how uncooperative people had been.

It is not possible to produce, on behalf of peasants, an uncontaminated narrative of their perspectives on their participation in the guerrilla war. The interlocutor's identity and the themes chosen for inclusion and exclusion constitute, as Todorov says, a 'massive' and 'diffuse' intervention.[76] Todorov, who examines the texts of Columbus and Spaniards of the sixteenth century to learn about how they perceived Indians in America, states that his goal was to engage in dialogue with his texts.[77]

> I have tried to avoid two extremes. The first is the temptation to reproduce the voices of these figures 'as they really are'; to try to do away with my own presence 'for the other's sake'. The second is to subjugate the other to myself, to make him into a marionette of which I pull the strings. Between the two, I have sought not a terrain of compromise but the path of dialogue. I question, I transpose, I interpret these texts; but also I let them speak (whence so many quotations) and defend themselves. From Columbus to Sahagun, these figures did not speak the same language as the one I speak; but one does not let the other live merely by leaving him intact, any more

than by obliterating his voice entirely. I have tried to see them, both close and distant, as forming one of the interlocutors of our dialogue.

Todorov is dialoguing with existing texts; the problems for a researcher who seeks to obtain peasants' voices is that dialogue is the vehicle for creating the text that must then be interpreted.

The limits of generalizing the district study

To what extent can the findings of a case study based on four wards in a single district be generalized? A priori, there is no reason to expect that the conclusions of this study about guerrilla–civilian relations, and the inter-twining of the war with African rural social relations would not apply to other predominantly Shona-speaking districts that were exposed to ZANLA guerrillas. For reasons already offered, Mutoko was a priori an ideal case for the presumed mutually supportive relationship between guerrillas and civilians. There is no reason to expect guerrilla or govern-ment strategy and tactics or the character of Shona society to have been notably different in other Shona districts. Hence my conclusions ought to apply to other Shona districts.

This study makes no claim for the validity of its findings for ZIPRA areas in Matabeleland, northern Midlands and northern Mashonaland West. Although ZIPRA officially adopted a strategy giving more attention to mass politicization (see chapter 3), it allegedly placed less emphasis on politicizing the population or preparing it for protracted struggle. It is said to have fought a war that was military rather than political in character. That is, it relied on scoring spectacular military successes against the Security Forces or symbolic targets – such as the shooting of the two Viscount civilian planes – for mobilizing political support. Its guerrillas did not devote much time and effort to winning over civilian support for its political programme through political education and meetings. They left this task to ZAPU's network of supporters built up throughout Zimbabwe in the early 1960s when ZAPU was legal and further developed during the period when the party went underground.[78] The conventional wisdom is that ZANU won the independence elections in 1980 because of its successful strategy of politicizing the rural population (see chapter 4). Consequently, ZIPRA's apparent lack of interest in political mobilization is contrasted unfavourably with ZANU's focus on it. But such contrasts should be treated with caution. Possibly Nkomo's ZAPU with its long-established roots in Matabeleland also had less need for mobilization than ZANU that had no grassroots presence in the country when the war intensified from 1972. Perhaps, too, the findings of this study will deroman-ticise or demythologize the existing portrait of ZANU's successful politici-zation.

Apart from differences that may be related to the strategy and tactics of the nationalist parties or allegiance to their leaders, the structure and

45

history of Ndebele society are markedly different from that of Shona society. A few examples follow. First, after the conquest in 1896–7, Ndebele chiefs often sent their children to school, sometimes in South Africa, while Shona chiefs displayed little interest in education. A second difference between Shona and Ndebele history and social structure stems from their varied responses to impending defeat in the 1896–7 rebellion. The Ndebele agreed to negotiate with Rhodes. Consequently, their senior *indunas* (chiefs) were offered salaries and officially recognized as chiefs in the reformed system of native administration. They continued to exercise widespread influence over their people. In contrast, the Shona continued to rebel until defeated. Many Shona chiefs were hanged or prosecuted and removed from office, while those who had fought with the white adminis- tration were rewarded with chieftainships.[79] Yet another difference is that the Ndebele had a concept of themselves as a nation, and had evidence of a previous kingship. The Shona had no such concept of being a united people with a shared history: their histories were of tribal competition and allegiances.[80] These are among the reasons why the experiences of peasants in Matabeleland are unlikely to have corresponded with that of their counterparts in Mashonaland. However, like ZANLA, ZIPRA would have had to operate in the context of a powerful colonial state and a differentiated African society.

ZANU guerrillas and workers in the camps

The guerrillas are omnipresent in this study but their direct voice is missing. The purpose of this book is to explore peasant perspectives on their war-time participation but something must be said about ZANU's guerrillas whose presence had such an important impact on peasants and *youth*. Several people have interviewed former guerrillas to find out who they were, why they joined the struggle, what their war experiences were, and what has become of them today. These provide useful information, but there is as yet no comprehensive analytical study of the guerrilla armies and guerrilla experiences during and after the war.

The first guerrillas had work experience in the major cities and mines of southern Africa and were often living in exile in Tanzania or Zambia.[81] During the 1970s, the overwhelming majority of the guerrillas came from the rural areas. They were the sons and daughters of the villagers and the siblings of the *youth* whose voices appear in this study. Many were teenagers with, at most, a primary education. In June 1980 the Mugabe government announced that 50 per cent of the guerrillas in the Assembly Points were between nineteen and twenty-four years old and only 15 per cent were eighteen years or less.[82] This means that the percentage who joined the struggle at eighteen years or less must have been much higher. Of the women fighters and workers in ZANU camps in Mozambique in 1978, 75 per cent were between fifteen and twenty-four years old, and 25 per cent were twenty-five to twenty-nine years old.[83] Members of the Commonwealth team that was sent to observe the transition to independence estimated that there were 228,000 refugees, 160,000 of whom were in ZANU camps in Mozambique, and a high percentage of whom were under twenty years.[84] ZANU guerrillas were drawn chiefly from the Shona, and more especially from the Karanga who also provided most of the African troops in the Rhodesian army.[85] From 1970 when tensions led many Shona guerrillas to leave the party, most ZAPU guerrillas were Ndebele. However, the party executives of both armies were more representative of the population and ZAPU's national executive committee had a Shona majority. ZAPU reportedly also had many Shona officers in its army.[86]

Why did people leave the country to join the struggle, whether to fight as guerrillas or work in the camps? In the 1960s, guerrillas were often recruited in Rhodesia or from Zimbabweans living in Tanzania and Zambia. Kidnapping and pressganging were used by both nationalist parties to build up guerrilla armies in the 1960s and the early 1970s. Neither party paid the guerrillas it pressganged unless they won battles – a policy of the FNLA, one of the three Angolan liberation movements fighting the Portuguese.[87] Party representatives also tried to recruit Zimbabwean students in Britain for training as officers and medical aides. Students were offered free airline tickets for training in communist countries. Those who resisted recruitment were threatened with withdrawal of party scholarships and, on occasion, blackmail and violence.[88] Those who went to the camps after 1974 often did so because of the political influence of their teachers in rural schools, the encouragement and promises of opportunities from the guerrillas, the brutality of the government forces, and sometimes apparently on guerrilla orders. Some young women chose to leave the country to join husbands and lovers. These and other motives are expressed by women who were in ZANU camps. The accounts of women who joined guerrilla forces, either as fighters or to work in the camps, reveal that motives often changed with changing circumstances.

Caroline, who came from Mutoko, joined the struggle when she was a fifteen-year-old student at Nyamuzuwe, a Methodist boarding school.[89]

> I had been there for about one and a half years when the first freedom fighters came to the school. We knew there was a war. The Smith forces came and told us there were 'terrorists' in the area. At first, the freedom fighters came only once or twice a month. Some of our relatives were in hot soup at that time because the Smith forces had told them to report the presence of 'terrorists'. Some people were killed because the comrades thought that they were traitors and had informed on them.
>
> Then the teachers, almost all of them, were taken away to gaol. We did no schoolwork in those days. At night, the freedom fighters came to teach us about the war and our oppression, and we stayed up until the dawn, singing and talking with them. This meant that we slept during the day. Then one day

47

in 1977, the comrades came and closed the school. They took the fittest, about 15 of us. We were not trained, of course, and when we heard firing during the night, some people ran and were shot. I think that about five or six children died that night. We had to leave them, since we could not take or bury them.

Altogether, we walked for three days. When we finally crossed the border into Mozambique, FRELIMO comrades looked after us and gave us food and clothes. Then we walked about 120 km to a camp called Mororo, in Tete. That is where I stayed until December 1979 . . .

Life was hard for the women. Most women comrades, like myself, were political commissars. I could have done nursing, but I did not like that, so I became a political commissar.

Another fifteen-year-old joined soon after attending her first meeting with the guerrillas who 'were dancing and singing slogans' and who told them 'about the war, about why they were fighting and how we were oppressed'. The guerrillas visited one more time, before the government forces came and punished the villagers for aiding the guerrillas. 'They took away the Headman and I never saw him again. My aunt was beaten and left as dead. All these terrible things made me want to join the struggle. The next night, I took some food and I and two other girls left' (for Mozambique).[90]

Comrades 'rounded-up' about 200 children and teachers at a mission boarding school, according to a fourteen-year-old. Weiss recounts her story.[91]

Comrades had come often and so they were doing little work at school. It was a mission with a hospital, and the missionaries were giving treatment at night to the wounded comrades. For this reason, they were rounded up one night and told to leave. It was no longer safe for them to remain, because the Smith forces would find out sooner or later about the missionaries and would beat and kill everyone . . . Muriel was one of a group of 30 who made it into Mozambique. There, everything was quite different from what she had expected – she had thought they were marching to freedom and riches, not to a refugee camp with no blankets and little food.

A sixteen-year-old was inspired by a talk given by her teacher after Herbert Chitepo, the Acting President of ZANU, was assassinated in Zambia in 1975. Twelve boys left that night to go to Mozambique, and the police visited the dormitories to interrogate other students. 'Then we talked about only one thing: how we could get to Mozambique ourselves.' She eventually left the country a few weeks later. 'I think I was simply adventurous, and I'd heard so much about the war.'[92] A young girl of thirteen met guerrillas one day while getting water from a river and was swayed by their promise that life in the camps offered freedom from drudgery.[93] Many were reportedly lured into the camps with promises of education. Only 12 per cent of primary school graduates were admitted into secondary schools, creating deep resentments.[94] In fact, life in the camps was extremely difficult, and there were always shortages of food.[95] Only a select minority were sent abroad for further education.

Organizational outline

The next chapter examines peasant grievances in the colonial period. Most studies of anti-colonial peasant-based revolutions dwell on the grievances against colonial policies and neglect resentments emanating from within peasant communities. The purpose of this chapter is to redress the literature's inattention to internal peasant grievances without neglecting the grievances of peasants and other rural Africans against the white minority regime.

Chapter 3 argues that the existing literature on Zimbabwe fails to give due weight to the repressive capacity of the state and its influence on the type of appeals that the guerrillas were able to use. The periodization of nationalist strategies, that differentiates the commencement of ZANU's guerrilla war with its emphasis on revolutionary political mobilization from the earlier period of African nationalism, contributes to a focus on change and thereby conceals from analysts the extent to which the appeals before and during the guerrilla war were similar. And the reasons for their similarity lie in continuities in structural conditions, and in particular, the enduring repressive capacity of the state. An analysis of guerrilla appeals shows the prominence of cultural nationalism and coercion and the dearth of utilitarian appeals and links this particular mix of appeals to the ability of the state to continue to expand its military and paramilitary forces, chiefly by recruiting Africans. By representing historical data on nationalist party appeals, the chapter seeks to underline the resemblance between the appeals throughout the mass nationalist period even after the onset of the guerrilla war. The continuity in the weakness of nationalist appeals underscores the problems of organizing under a repressive state. More militant nationalist strategies and appeals provoked an expansion of the state's repressive capacity. This chapter paves the way for seeking peasant evaluations of the impact of ZANU's guerrilla war strategy, emphasizing revolutionary mobilization through political education.

Chapter 4 reviews critically the literature on Zimbabwe's war of independence that makes the case for ZANLA guerrillas having the popular support of the peasants. The arguments for popular support are rejected because the case for popular support almost never rests on peasant voices, it overstates the efficacy of guerrilla normative appeals, and understates the effects of utilitarian and coercive appeals. When the full impact of coercive and utilitarian appeals are incorporated in an analysis of popular support, the costs for peasants of the exchange relationship with the guerrillas outweigh the benefits. Using interviews with peasants, the rural elite and *youth*, I conclude that the peasants were at best reluctant supporters of the guerrillas but among the *youth* were enthusiastic guerrilla supporters. These divergent findings for peasants and *youth* underline the need for some generational distinction in evaluating rural civilians' responses to the guerrillas.

49

Chapter 5 analyzes the literature on Zimbabwe's war of independence to try to understand why conflicts internal to the peasantry and between peasants and the African rural elite receive so little prominence. Clues are sought in the peasant concept, the privileging of organizational goals of unity, the concept of nationalism, and the reliance on non-peasant sources. The chapter describes how oppressed groups in the peasantry – women, *youth*, non-ruling clans, the very poor – used the party committees and the guerrillas themselves as resources in their own battles. Peasant struggles complicated the guerrillas' efforts to forge unity and collective action but they also motivated peasant participation. Oppressed groups sought a restructuring of African social relations and, in this regard, their agenda was more radical than the primarily nationalist goals of the guerrillas that aimed merely to remove racial inequalities.

The concluding chapter challenges variants of the radicalization thesis that link popular revolutionary mobilization to particular post-revolutionary outcomes in Zimbabwe. Whereas proponents of the thesis found democratic grassroots party structures to be a legacy of the war, this study stresses villagers' fear of party committees and the committees' use of coercion. The chapter also examines internal peasant struggles after the war that the radicalization thesis neglects because it is oriented to peasant relations with the state and party. Finally, the chapter reinterprets peasant relations with the state in the first years after the war.

2

Inequalities and peasant grievances

The grievances of rural Africans against the white minority regime are a necessary backdrop to this study as they form the basis for the appeals used by the guerrillas to mobilize and unite rural Africans (see chapter 3). However, a central argument of this book is that peasant resentments against inequalities with other Africans provided even more powerful drives to participate in the nationalist guerrilla war than did peasant hostility to colonial policies and whites. These inter-African inequalities within the peasantry are also potential grievances available to a revolutionary movement that seeks to mobilize peasants. Chapter 1 discussed how the concepts of nationalism and peasants, reliance on non-peasant sources, and an elite bias in the literature on peasant revolutions contribute to bypassing grievances emanating from internal peasant organization. The purpose of this chapter is to rectify that neglect without excluding racially discriminatory colonial policies that produced anti-white and anti-colonial grievances. Elite–mass or incipient class tensions among rural Africans are given more weight than they ordinarily receive in accounts of grievances underlying Zimbabwe's anti-colonial nationalist movements. Where possible, the study of racial inequalities and African rural inequalities will draw on Mutoko district data.

A definition of who to include in the peasant category in the Zimbabwean context is necessary. Commonly, Tribal Trust Land cultivators and Purchase Area farmers are lumped together as peasants.[1] Even teachers, businessmen, and storekeepers are sometimes included in the peasant category.[2] Such broad peasant categories are especially problematic when the peasant concept assumes that peasants' shared political interest *vis-à-vis* others supersede their political differences with each other. Since this chapter seeks to highlight the importance of rural African inequalities, it employs a narrow peasant category that includes only Tribal Trust Land cultivators who earn more income from agriculture than other activities.

Racial inequalities

Racial policies and practices tended to shift in small but significant ways under different constitutional orders. From 1899 until 1923, when the British South Africa Company (BSAC) ruled the territory based on a royal charter, the belief guiding race relations was that eventually Africans would assimilate into white society.[3] After 1923, Rhodesia became a self-governing colony ruled directly by white settlers. For the next thirty years, a policy of separate development governed race relations. In their own areas, Africans could occupy top positions; in land set aside for whites, they should accept white domination. From 1953 to 1963 Southern Rhodesia formed a federation with the British Protectorates of Northern Rhodesia and Nyasaland. Especially from the late 1950s the white minority government in Rhodesia was under British pressure to make progress towards racial partnership as a condition of renewing federal status. In 1961 provision was made for African parliamentary representatives. In exchange for this minimal concession to African political advancement, Britain gave up almost all its constitutional powers to protect Africans from discriminatory legislation. Right-wing pressures were growing as whites became concerned that Britain might insist on further constitutional concessions to Africans. In 1962, there was the first major shift in party government since 1923. Whites now wanted to be rid of any vestige of Crown control, even though Britain had never once used its constitutional powers to veto discriminatory legislation. In 1965 when the Rhodesia Front party government declared unilateral independence (UDI), it simultaneously introduced a new constitution that freed it completely from the Crown. The 1969 constitution declared Rhodesia to be a republic and was frankly white supremacist. Under Rhodesia Front party government (1962–79), race relations came to resemble even more closely those in neighbouring South Africa.[4] Racially discriminatory legislation and administrative practices had evolved to give colonial authorities such tight control over Africans that some have drawn analogies between African life under settler rule and 'total institutions' such as prisons, slavery, and concentration camps.[5] This section addresses racially discriminatory policies and the inequities they produced in land, agricultural policies, wages and labour conditions, the national franchise, local government, and education and health. These inequities were sources of African grievances.

Land

A hallmark of Company rule was its policy of selling land cheaply and quickly to attract white settlers and revenue. White encroachment on African land bred resentment and rebellions by the Ndebele in 1893 and the Shona and Ndebele in 1896–7. Both uprisings drew the attention of the British government to the need to set aside areas where Africans could be guaranteed that their land would not be alienated by whites. The first Reserves (called Tribal Trust Lands from 1961) were set up in Matabeleland in 1894 and were extended to Mashonaland in 1898. Only Africans could live in the Reserves, and they were intended to be occupied by tribes or parts of tribes according to existing African communal tenure practices. After it was found that the earliest Reserves in Matabeleland were in extremely arid areas, the British government required that future Reserves contain adequate water. In practice, the only requirement that was observed was that Africans be allowed to practise communal tenure in the Reserves. When Reserves were created, the only common guiding principle followed by Company officials was to leave undisturbed the healthy and fertile highlands where land was already occupied or alienated by whites. In 1920, when the British government reduced the total amount of Reserves land, the assumption had been that eventually Africans would assimilate. Of the total land area in 1925, Reserves covered 22 per cent and land alienated by whites another 32 per cent. Most Africans preferred not to live in the Reserves, but to continue living where they were even though this meant paying rent to white landowners or the Company, that regarded itself as the owner of unalienated land.

When Company rule ended and Rhodesia became a self-governing British colony in 1923, the new constitution protected the land already set aside for Reserves and the right of Africans to purchase land outside the Reserves on an equal basis with whites. Any constitutional change affecting these provisions required an extraordinary majority in the legislature and British parliamentary approval. In 1925, a bill was introduced to distribute 45 per cent of land in the colony that had not been alienated. The version of the bill that was passed as the Land Apportionment Act of 1930 set aside 17 per cent of the unalienated land for the creation of Purchase Areas where only Africans could purchase or lease land on an individual tenure basis. Another 40 per cent was allocated for exclusive European purchase, and the rest was left as Unassigned Land. The Act, approved by the British parliament, repudiated the liberal assimilationist premises of the Reserves system and introduced racial land segregation. European areas constituted 50 per cent of the land, African areas 30 per cent and Unassigned Land 20 per cent. Contrasted with the 1925 allocation of land, the 1930 Act allotted another 8 per cent of land to Africans and an additional 18 per cent to whites.[6]

The republican constitution of 1969 replaced the Land Apportionment Act by the Land Tenure Act according to which the land was divided roughly equally between Europeans and Africans. The main difference between the 1930 and 1969 land divisions was the increase in the African share of the land, from 30 per cent to 53 per cent and a small decrease in European land from 50 per cent to 47 per cent. The inequity concealed by almost equal racial shares of land is highlighted by racial population densities. The European population in European rural areas was 1 person per square mile; the African population density in African rural areas was an estimated 45.8 persons per square mile. The latter figure combines the much lower population density in the Purchase Areas with the higher population density in the Tribal Trust Lands where most Africans live. The figures therefore conceal the extent of racial inequity in population density that contributed to making landlessness and land shortage in the Tribal Trust Lands a major African grievance.[7] Land grievances were exacerbated by the generally inferior quality of African land compared to European land, and by Africans witnessing large areas of unused European land that amounted to almost one-tenth of the total land area in 1961.[8] Moreover, African Purchase Areas, originally envisaged to cover 7 million acres were only 3.7 million acres, or 9 per cent of the total African land area, in the Land Tenure Act of 1969. When the land allocated for Reserves in 1930 proved inadequate, land was taken from the land allotted for Purchase Areas rather than from the European allocation.[9] In 1976, 35 per cent of even the whittled down Purchase Area allocation was still unplanned or vacant, breeding resentment among aspirant African landowners and Reserves cultivators who were often moved to clear areas for African purchase.[10]

Much of the land within the pre-1973 boundaries of Mutoko district was undesirable, so Europeans alienated a much smaller percentage of it than in more fertile districts.[11] The area north and east of Mutoko Tribal Trust Land is intensely hot and dry, infested with tsetse fly and virtually devoid of natural water.[12] The government did not even settle Africans here until population pressures in Mutoko Tribal Trust Land became acute. Ngarwe was settled in 1957 and Mudzi in 1962.[13] Even the land that Europeans did alienate is ecologically unsuitable for intensive crop production and lies within natural regions 3 and 4.[14] The almost equal sizes of Mutoko Tribal Trust Land and the European area conceal the racial inequities in land per capita. In 1969 the Tribal Trust Land had 74,410 Africans (and 110,000 people in 1981)[15] while the European area had only about 500 Europeans (100 farms and an estimated family size of 5) and 14,500 African farm-workers, chiefly Malawians and Mozambicans.[16] Mutoko Tribal Trust Land was identified as one of the two most densely populated districts in the country in the 1950s.[17] About twenty years later, its population density was estimated to be 44 persons per square mile, compared with an average of 28 persons per square mile for other Tribal Trust Lands in the Mazoe River catchment area.[18] Despite the shortage of land for Africans, in the 1970s the government sold at low prices Unassigned Land on the Nyagadzi River to European tobacco farmers who were having financial difficulties[19] (see map 2).

Wages and labour conditions

The importance of migrant labour to rural Africans warrants including African grievances about wages and labour conditions. Africans were concentrated in the lowest-paid economic sectors as unskilled workers – first the white-owned mines and farms, and later domestic service and the farms. In the 1970s, agriculture and domestic service still accounted for over 50 per cent of African wage earners. Most African women who were in the formal sector worked in these lowest-paid jobs where they were paid even less than their African male counterparts. Africans who worked on white farms and in domestic service were denied the right to form unions; instead, they were subject to the Masters and Servants Act of 1901, designed to protect employers from the high rates of desertion among African workers.[20] Low mine and farm wages discouraged Africans from seeking work so that until recently these sectors depended chiefly on foreign Africans from Nyasaland (Malawi), Portuguese East Africa (Mozambique), and Northern Rhodesia (Zambia). Gradually more indigenous Africans, propelled by the negative effect of colonial land and agrarian policies on the viability of their agricultural endeavours as well as by a desire to satisfy their new wants created by the colonial economy, became migrant labourers.

The manufacturing sector, despite its increasingly important contribution to economic growth from the 1940s, employed only a small proportion of African wage earners. The Europeans had a monopoly of the higher-paid, skilled jobs – initially as artisans on the mines, and later in the manufacturing sector too. In the early days of Company rule, European artisans received high wages because their skills were in demand. However, statutory means were introduced in 1934 to guarantee Europeans skilled jobs at high wages and block the entry of Africans into skilled and semi-skilled work. One such measure allowed Europeans to form registered trade unions but denied the same right to Africans.[21] The statute was amended in 1959 during the more liberal federal period to provide for Africans in secondary industry to form registered trade unions. But only about 7 per cent of the small proportion of Africans in secondary industry joined unions.[22] The high rate of turnover of African labour and the cost of membership subscriptions kept union membership low. Table 2.1 shows the disparity in average wages per annum for Africans and Europeans in industry in the 1950s and 1960s. It also highlights the preponderance of African workers who provided almost 90 per cent of total wage labour. Low pay, wide pay differentials, systemic obstacles to more skilled employment, and unequal pay when Africans and Europeans did the same jobs and had the same qualifications, embittered Africans against the colonial regime and white employers.

Agricultural policies

Early in the twentieth century, the state promoted European agriculture while it deliberately undermined African agriculture to induce Africans to work on the mines and farms. State concern for African agriculture, first

Table 2.1 *Employment opportunities and average earnings of Africans and Europeans in the industrial sector*[23]

	Africans		Europeans	
Year	Number in employment	Average earnings (pounds per month)	Number in employment	Average earnings (pounds per month)
1954	555,000	65	64,400	884
1958	628,000	88	84,600	1,091
1962	616,000	110	88,500	1,186
1967	605,000	138	90,900	1,361

Europeans includes a small number of Asians and Coloureds. Separate figures for Europeans are not available.

expressed in the 1920s, remained of limited scope until independence. European agricultural development policies were comprehensive, and encompassed agricultural research, credit, marketing, extension as well as soil conservation and physical infrastructure such as roads and dams. By contrast, African agricultural development policies and expenditures were narrowly focused on soil conservation and physical infrastructure. A considerable portion of the costs of African development was borne by Africans themselves through taxes, such as a levy on their marketed production. Public expenditure on European agriculture came from general revenues that included Africans' indirect tax payments.[24] These discriminatory policies disadvantaged rural Africans *vis-à-vis* European farmers, engendering resentment against the colonial regime.

Soil conservation

Early soil conservation measures tried to persuade Africans to either sell or kill cattle, but after 1941 statutory measures made cattle destocking compulsory. The cattle population in the Reserves had increased sixfold between 1911 and World War II, and its pressure on limited grazing was a major source of soil erosion. The 1951 African Land Husbandry Act stands as the most ambitious conservation effort in the Reserves. Its main purpose was to end migrant labour that produced inefficient part-time farmers, and create a stable and contented farm population that would not seek political advancement. Only cultivators resident in the Reserves qualified for farming and stock rights that had been calculated to ensure each holder subsistence with a small surplus. A form of limited individual tenure was introduced but communal grazing was continued. Grazing and arable land were strictly demarcated, and violations were subject to criminal prosecution. If farm holders were convicted three times for failure to protect their land or use it properly, they could be forced to sell their land. Rural people resented the scheme as they identified their central agricultural problem to be lack of land, and they feared that there would not be enough land for everyone to get a farming right – a fear confirmed by an official report in 1962 that estimated that the Act would make 30 per cent of the African rural population landless. To conform with stock rights, Africans often had to sell cattle. Urban Africans were resentful because they were ineligible for farm rights yet were not offered security of tenure in the urban area. Widespread protests forced the government to abandon the Act in 1962.[25] The Land Husbandry Act was proclaimed in Mutoko Tribal Trust Land in 1956. By the time it was abandoned, all stock rights had been allocated in Mutoko Tribal Trust Land but only 25 per cent of arable allocations had been made. Those left landless by the Act had the option of resettling in Ngarwe and Mudzi (see map 2). These areas had been classified as unalienated European land in the Land Apportionment Act of 1930 but were later considered unsuitable for European habitation. No Europeans ever settled in these areas, and the government declared Ngarwe and Mudzi African areas in 1957 and 1962 respectively.

In Mutoko Tribal Trust Land soil erosion was more severe than elsewhere in the country. Huge granite hills made the ratio of arable to non-arable land smaller in nearly half of Mutoko than was normal in the rest of the country. The serious shortage of arable land drove people to cultivate their chief crops – maize and some groundnuts – on theoretically non-arable land, contributing to soil erosion. An official survey noted the hopelessness of government soil conservation measures given Mutoko's ecology and population expansion.[26] Even after repeated destocking campaigns, the Tribal Trust Land was still estimated to be 145 per cent overstocked in 1974.[27]

Credit

European farmers had access to low-cost government credit from the Land Bank from 1913 and later from other parastatals. In contrast, rural Africans first obtained access to government credit in 1945. The main government lending agency for Africans was set up in 1958 and became known as the Agricultural Loan Fund in 1964. The major source of commercial finance was the African Loan and Development Company that began lending money to Africans in 1962. In 1977 these pivotal private and government lenders had less than R$900,000 outstanding; the corresponding figure for a single parastatal, the Land Bank, with its almost exclusively white clients, was R$110 million.[28]

Prices and markets

The government's marketing and pricing policy discriminated against Africans in the depression and post-depression years. The government Maize Marketing Board, one of the first statutory marketing boards established in the 1920s, set higher prices for domestic than export maize sales and allocated maize to either pool using a method that restricted African participation in the small but higher priced internal market. This system, eventually scrapped, was intended to protect small-scale European producers from African competition.[29]

Statutory marketing boards became more prominent and powerful in agricultural marketing, especially after 1965 when Rhodesia unilaterally declared its independence from Britain. The boards had a monopoly over the sale of the commodities under their jurisdiction and prescribed producer prices. Whereas 35 per cent of agricultural sales were by statutory boards in 1965, this figure was over 70 per cent in 1973. Statutory marketing boards ceased to discriminate by law against Africans. However, the boards' practices and the institutional context in which they functioned favoured the larger European producers and help to account for the disparity in the value of European and African marketed agricultural production. In the early 1960s, 6,000 European production units were responsible for 90 per cent of marketed output; 300,000 African producers contributed only 10 per cent.[30]

Certain boards dealt exclusively with Europeans by virtue of Africans not producing the commodities for which they were responsible. For example, Europeans produced almost all dairy cows and the bulk of beef and cereals. But even when Africans produced the regulated commodities, they were disadvantaged. The system of payment in two instalments, with the second received only at the end of the season, eliminated most Africans who could not afford the delay in receiving the full price. Transport costs were much higher for African farmers since the marketing depots were usually in European areas, and they generally lived off the line of rail and away from the major road networks. The Rhodesia Motor Services that offered road transport between railheads – especially for livestock – did operate in African areas but its minimum load requirements were burdensome for smaller African producers. The payment system and transport problems left African producers reliant on selling through officially approved buyers in African areas, either traders or general dealers, who then sold to statutory boards. This avenue overcame the difficulties Africans had of selling direct to the marketing boards, but they received less than the official price offered by the statutory boards because the traders charged handling and transport fees. The Cooperatives Society Act of 1956 introduced another option for African producers. Cooperatives, by combining many small-scale producers into one organization, can purchase services that would otherwise be too costly for individual producers and thereby reduce handling and transport costs charged by traders. In the 1970s African cooperatives marketed only about 15 per cent of the small amount of African marketed agricultural produce, mainly because the costs of registering were almost the equivalent of registering with a statutory board.[31]

African market participation was discouraged further by an agricultural levy on a wide range of commodities and livestock sold to the marketing boards. A levy, at times as high as 15 per cent of the retail price, was introduced in 1948. The proceeds were paid into the African Development Fund, renamed the African Production and Marketing Development Fund in 1969, and were used exclusively for African agriculture and related services – building roads, bridges, dams, cattle dips for inoculating cattle against disease, grazing and conservation schemes, and servicing a World Bank loan to implement the hated African Land Husbandry Act. The levy, imposed only on African products, was inequitable and discouraged legal marketing. From 1967 African Purchase farmers were able to exempt themselves from the agricultural levy.[32] But Tribal Trust Land producers continued to have to pay it and resented it.

National franchise and parliamentary representation

Most Africans were denied the franchise and this was a source of resentment especially among more educated Africans. Europeans controlled elected national political bodies even though Africans outnumbered them by 45:1 in the early days of Company rule and thereafter usually by about 20:1. Until the Rhodesia Front's republican constitution of 1969 the franchise regulations were colour-blind in principle. In practice, though, they ensured that the numbers of registered African voters never reached even one per cent of the total African voting population. Rhodesian Africans first obtained limited parliamentary representation in the federal parliament established in 1953 and then in Rhodesia's lower house of parliament under its 1961 constitution. The proportion of elected African seats in the lower house declined under the republican constitution of 1969 but senate seats were reserved for chiefs.[33]

African local government

The system of local government for rural Africans, like all other aspects of life, was separate and unequal from that for Europeans and a source of African resentment. African local government bodies were first introduced in the 1930s under the pressure of proto-nationalist demands for an extension of the national franchise. The earliest councils were composed of chiefs and elected representatives, and were purely advisory. In 1944 they acquired the authority to tax, pass by-laws, and take some responsibility for local development. Few councils were formed, though. Chiefs feared the younger, better educated elected representatives; the latter resented their illiterate elders and the native commissioner's authority as chairman; and most Africans resented paying taxes that produced few visible benefits.[34]

In the more liberal federal period, a new initiative was planned for local

government in the Reserves that envisaged wholly elected local government bodies. When ready, African councillors could cast aside the native
commissioner as chair and elect an African chairman. Councils would be
formed voluntarily by communities that could select whatever development projects they desired. Like their predecessors they would have taxing
authority, but significant central government grants were projected. These
were the intentions of the architects of the African Councils Act of 1957.[35]
But by the time their ideas had won legislative approval, there had been an
upsurge of African nationalist activity. Nationalists attacked councils,
rejecting them as substitutes for the right to vote in national politics. Under
the apartheid-oriented Rhodesia Front party (1962–79), brought to power
by white reaction to African nationalist militancy, the major suppositions
and legal provisions behind the African Councils Act were violated.

The central government did not generously subsidize councils' development activities, councils and development projects were imposed from
above, and chiefs were not removed from councils. Instead, the government interpreted community development to mean that councils would
take increasing financial and administrative responsibility. An official,
disapproving of the government's community development policy, summed up government's intent to be: 'Let's get the African off our back.'[36]
Facing strong opposition to African councils and the policy of community
development, the central government threatened to withdraw grants for
self-help projects in 1969.[37] The government also announced that if
councils did not take over the running of primary schools from missions,
whose generally liberal political influence it wished to eliminate, it would
withdraw its financial support for paying the teachers at mission schools.[38]
This measure was also consistent with government policy of devolving
financial and supervisory responsibility onto Africans. Missions were the
primary providers of education and without government support would not
be able to function. Communities had little choice but to form councils
given these indirect government pressures. They grew most rapidly
between 1969 and 1972, increasing from 87 to 241 out of a possible total of
260 councils.[39] The Smith government's policy of bolstering the power of
chiefs to offset the influence of African nationalists included returning
chiefs onto councils from 1972 and creating African provincial governments for each of the eight provinces on which chiefs would be prominent.
African provincial councils had the same functions as African councils and
exercised jurisdiction over them. It was anticipated that the provincial
authorities would gradually relieve the central government of its functions
related to African local administration, and would constitute a step in the
evolution of a separate African civil service, the nucleus of which would be
Africans transferred from the European civil service.[40]

Africans in Mutoko Tribal Trust Land were first introduced to councils
in 1971–2 as part of the Smith government's community development
policy.[41] Electoral participation in the new councils and rates payments

underscore the low enthusiasm for councils. Only about 18 per cent of the eligible voters participated in the first election for the council in Mutoko chiefdom and less than 15 per cent for the council in Charewa chiefdom. Adult males resented paying council rates of R$2 per annum, in addition to dipping fees, licence fees and other taxes, and government records dwell on the difficulties of rates collection. Chimoyo council collected 78 per cent of its rates in the first year, but only 30 per cent in 1973/4 when the population saw no immediate benefits.[42] Councils spent their revenue on council offices, staff housing, and administration. Following colonial practice of using African beerhall profits to finance African administration and services, each council built a beerhall. Councils provided few new services. By 1977, the three councils controlled three beerhalls, three clinics (one of which was council-built) and forty-one schools, almost all at the primary level and inherited from missions.[43] The Purchase Area council differed from the African councils in each of the three chiefdoms of Mutoko Tribal Trust Land. It was formed voluntarily by the people in 1965/6 and all twelve of its councillors were elected. Because there are no chiefs in the Purchase Area, the council could not be used as a government vehicle for strengthening the chiefs as it was in the Tribal Trust Land. Male farmers paid R$10 per annum in 1975/6; male non-farmers R$5. District records described the council as unenthusiastic and lacking in ideas, but it did build a clinic and seven schools, council offices and housing for council staff, roads and bridges.[44] Residents of Mutoko township, today the commercial hub of the district and a major bus terminus, were administered by the European rural council.[45] Township revenue came from ratepayers (who still had neither running water nor inside toilets in 1982), a government-owned beerhall, and licence fees paid by the small businesses that form a semicircle around a large sandy square that serves as a major bus terminus and market place.

Education and health

Inadequate and inferior government provision of health and education for Africans compared with Europeans aroused African indignation towards the colonial regime. A pattern of mission responsibility for African health and education and government concern with European needs was established during Company rule and persisted until independence. Government grants to mission schools remained small when compared with state expenditure on European education, and missions continued to rely chiefly on overseas funds. Africans continued to pay school fees at mission schools and at the first government schools for Africans that appeared in the 1920s, while Europeans attending government day schools paid no fees until 1964. African education remained available only in the rural areas (except for a few privately run night schools in the urban areas) and at the primary level until after World War II.[46] In the post World War II period, education became compulsory for European children between seven and fifteen years of age, but not for Africans. Although the government paid more attention to African education after World War II, the basic pattern of inequalities persisted, as did the grievances that they spawned.[47]

On the eve of the guerrilla war, racial inequalities in education were still pervasive. Even though aggregate government expenditure on African education per enrolled African student increased, the absolute racial gap widened between 1972/3 and 1976/7. At the beginning of this period, government expenditure per enrolled African pupil was R$29 compared with R$338 per enrolled European pupil; at the end of the period the respective figures were R$46 and R$531.[48] In 1967, nearly 80 per cent of Africans never finished more than five years of schooling. In the same year, more than half of European children attended school for between ten and eleven years compared with not even one half of one per cent of African children. Over a third of all whites completed a full secondary education whereas the comparable figure for Africans was 0.04 per cent. Those Africans who did go to school and remained in school for a few years were more likely to be males than females. The net effect of these educational levels was that European school leavers were much more competitive than Africans in a colour-conscious labour market.[49]

Missions have also been the primary providers of health care for Africans. Government provision and financing of health services were biased in favour of urban health services for Europeans throughout the colonial period. In 1976 the government provided one hospital bed for every 1,261 Africans compared with a corresponding 1:255 ratio for whites. Missions provided two-thirds of all rural hospital beds. The Rhodesia Front's community development policy encouraged African councils to provide primary health care in the rural areas. By 1977 they had established 363 clinics, generally built with volunteer local African labour and supported in part by fees. In 1977, the central government provided only 9 per cent of its total health budget in grants to local authorities, missions, and voluntary organizations.[50]

Mutoko district seems to have suffered greater government neglect in the provision of social services (and infrastructure) than better endowed districts. Even native commissioners' reports over a twenty-year period from 1936 to 1956 repeatedly lament that though Africans loyally paid their taxes, they received little in return.[51] This was especially true for the part of the district north of Mutoko Tribal Trust Land. In Mutoko Tribal Trust Land, the Methodist Episcopal Church was the first to get a foothold in 1911, followed by the Catholics in 1929.[52] For years, the Methodist village schools only offered three to five years of education, after which children had to go to the Methodist school at Nyadiri Mission in adjacent Murewa district. This changed when the Catholic primary school at All Souls' in the eastern part of Mutoko Tribal Trust Land introduced a sixth year of schooling. Only in 1956, though, when the new Methodist mission centre at

Nyamuzuwe in Mutoko Tribal Trust Land developed a secondary school did it become possible to go to secondary school in the district.[53] In 1964, when the missions were still the primary providers of education and health, the Methodists had twenty-nine schools with just under 7,000 students, and two clinics, mostly located in the western area of Mutoko Tribal Trust Land. The Catholics, never able to overcome their late start, had eleven schools with almost 3,000 students and a clinic, all concentrated in the eastern part of Mutoko Tribal Trust Land.[54] The missions were not active in Budjga Purchase Area, but the local authorities had established a clinic and seven schools by the 1970s.

To sum up, racially discriminatory colonial policies were the source of numerous African grievances. Africans resented the way in which Europeans had appropriated their land, consigning them to infertile and overcrowded Reserves or Tribal Trust Lands. African agriculture was further undermined by pricing, marketing, and credit policies and Africans resented policies that focused on soil conservation when they identified the problem to be lack of land. Migrant labour – entrenched in the economy by the refusal to recognize the right of Africans to reside as permanent residents in urban areas – was poorly paid, drew men away from the fields, and divided families. Most Africans were not allowed to join registered trade unions even when they were legally recognized. The provision of education and health was woefully inadequate and inferior to what was available for Europeans. Africans were unable to use the vote in national politics to bring about change, and instead were encouraged to participate in local government councils that were dominated by chiefs. These were among the many grievances provoked by discriminatory colonial policies.

African rural inequalities

Peasant grievances also emanated from resentment about inequalities within their villages and with the African rural elite. Colonial policies and the spread of a money economy deepened inequalities existing in Shona society on the eve of European conquest, in particular gender and generational inequalities and those between rulers (chiefs, headmen, and village heads) and their subjects. The colonial era also produced new forms of differentiation, creating rural elites and significant differences among peasants.

Rulers versus ruled

The structure of Shona chiefdoms has changed little since the late nineteenth century. The chiefdom stands at the apex of the hierarchically organized Shona polity and beneath it are wards made up of villages. Both chiefdoms and wards have distinct boundaries, and since the colonial period, villages do too. Chiefdoms are composed of patrilineal clans, which are groups who claim a common origin through the agnatic line. Even though members of a patrilineal clan may not be able to trace kinship, they share a common totemic clan name (*mutupo*) and sub-clan name (*chidao*).[55] Members of the chief's clan (*macinda* – plural; *mucinda* – singular) usually form the largest single clan in any chiefdom, but most subjects of a chief usually belong to other clans and are called *strangers* (*vatorwa* – plural; *mutorwa* – singular).[56] Patrilineal clans and sub-clans rarely, if ever, acted as corporate groups and had no political significance. The classification of people into *macinda* and *vatorwa* 'does not imply a position of political or social subordination or inferiority of *vatorwa* generally to *macinda* generally. It mainly serves to distinguish between members belonging to the same lineage as the chief and people of different origin. No *mucinda* (*jinda*) unless he actually occupies a position of authority in the tribal organization, ranks socially higher than a *mutorwa*.'[57] Chiefs are almost always drawn from the chiefly clan, but ward and village heads sometimes belong to *stranger* clans because a chief might have awarded these positions to friends in return for allegiance or for other reasons.

Chiefs, ward, and village heads are positions that are inherited according to the patrilineal and collateral rules of Shona succession. The former means that the position of chief is inherited by his male descendants (and seniority is respected) and the latter that the position of chief circulates in one generation before passing on to the next. A man cannot be chief while he has a 'father' (a father's brother or father's agnatic cousin) alive. This collateral aspect results in the chiefship (or other positions) alternating in some houses of the chiefly family, while excluding other houses. Hence not all ward heads are necessarily eligible for the chiefship. The collateral rule also guarantees that power will reside in a male gerontocracy.[58]

Colonial rule altered the relationship between rulers and subjects. Instead of having to be responsive to their subjects if they wished to retain their positions, rulers had to satisfy the colonial authorities. From the time of European conquest, the chiefship and other positions depended not only on the application of inheritance laws but also on government approval. Chiefs who had rebelled against Company rule in 1896–7 were removed, and loyalists rewarded – a process that continued throughout the period of white rule. Governments sometimes intervened in succession disputes to veto eligible candidates of whom they disapproved or to support rivals who were not strictly eligible but whom they trusted to be subservient. Chiefships might be demoted to ward head or even village head positions, and ward head positions upgraded to chiefships.[59] In Mutoko Tribal Trust Land, the government created a headman in Charewa chiefdom. Those who occupied the position of chieftainess Charewa had refused for decades to meet with Europeans. Frustrated in their efforts to impose administrative control over the area, the government instructed the chieftainess to appoint a headman to attend meetings with government officials. Although this person's status was high from the government's perspective, it was low in the indigenous polity.[60] In Chimoyo chiefdom in Mutoko Tribal Trust Land, the Nyamanza ward headmanship was created by the government in 1951.[61] In that year the government embarked on a major reorganization of chieftanships, eliminating old and ineffective chiefs, pensioning them off, re-ranking office-holders, and occasionally creating new offices.[62]

White governments interfered with the powers formerly held by chiefs and other rulers and undermined their authority by making them implement unpopular government policies. Precolonial rulers' main secular powers related to land and settling disputes. A hierarchy of power prevailed with village heads at the bottom and chiefs at the apex. The Shona believe that chiefs inherit from the founding father the 'ownership' of the land: the chief protects the land that is the common property of inhabitants in the chiefdom. For most of the colonial period village heads allocated arable plots, as they had done in the past, to married male household heads. Village heads also settled village disputes. If they failed, the matter was referred to the ward head's court, and if he too failed, it would go to the chief's court. Usually rulers tried, as they had in the precolonial past, to reconcile the parties and to make judgements that would meet with public approval. Punishments took the form of paying compensation, except in cases such as witchcraft or adultery.

Chiefs were also associated, as they still are, with religious and magical powers. The legendary spiritual power of the founding chief and his close relatives is expressed in the belief that their spirits remain the powerful guardians of the chiefdom. They are believed to continue their rule through the living chiefs, their successors, whom they protect and support, and who in principle must have their approval. They assert themselves by possessing individuals who then become spirit mediums. The spirit of the founding ancestor is called the *mhondoro* or lion spirit. Founder chiefs may have had to engage in battle to obtain the land, and often traditions of their conquest impute magical powers to them to explain their victories. Chiefs also mediate between the founding ancestor and their subjects. If there is a drought, the chief must consult the medium of the senior spirit guardian and organize appropriate rituals to pray for rain and appease the spirits. Chiefs' spiritual powers are also expressed in their unusually elaborate burials in which senior spirit mediums are usually prominent. Also, deceased chiefs are usually buried at a sacred site, believed dangerous to anyone approaching it without the approval of the senior spirits.[63]

Colonial rulers first decreased and then increased indigenous rulers' powers but their authority was undermined because their powers were decided on by an alien government. Even though the Company Charter provided for respect of African civil law and custom, rulers were reduced to police constables whose duty was to uphold European-imposed law and collect European-imposed taxes. Village heads came to be called 'keeper of the book' (*sabuku*), referring to the tax register, instead of head of the village (*samusha*). Native commissioners assumed many of the rulers' former powers. European law imposed on Africans a distinction between civil and criminal law, and, in theory, rulers lost their jurisdiction over Africans in criminal cases until it was partially restored in the 1930s and again in 1969. Witchcraft, homicide, and other offences, formerly tried by chiefs, were classified as criminal and had to be tried in commissioners' courts.[64]

In the 1930s, chiefs were given administrative powers through ex officio representation on experimental African local government bodies that were intended as substitutes for the demands of educated Africans for an extension of the national franchise. In 1957 legislation was passed that envisaged the introduction of wholly elected councils. After 1972 when the guerrilla war spread and security deteriorated, Smith's apartheid-oriented government returned to the policy of bolstering the administrative powers of chiefs to counter nationalists' quest for power. The Ministry of Internal Affairs changed the administrative boundaries of councils from districts to chiefdoms in 1973 to give every chief some status and power.[65] By February 1977, 130 out of 220 established councils had their warrants altered to provide for appointed members, subject to the approval of chiefs.[66] The notion of developing a local leadership alternative to chiefs was so entirely abandoned that the Minister of Internal Affairs admitted in the House of Assembly in August 1973 that the chief embodied local government and was the development authority for the whole tribal area.[67] Legislation introduced in 1972 provided for African provincial councils that would be a tier of African government above chiefs' councils. Just as African councils became the development arm of chiefs, so provincial councils were related to a body of chiefs, the provincial assembly of chiefs.[68] Chiefs were given prominence on provincial councils too.[69] These councils came to be presided over by two regional bodies, the Matabeleland and Mashonaland Cabinet Councils, also composed of chiefs.[70]

Governments had always held that chiefs were the true representatives of Africans, rural and urban. In 1951, the government created chiefs' provincial assemblies as vehicles for expressing African views on legislation affecting Africans. Threatened by young, educated nationalists, chiefs used the provincial assemblies to their advantage in 1959 to petition the government to ban nationalist meetings. In 1962 the government authorized chiefs' provincial assemblies to elect delegates to represent Africans at the national level in the National Council of Chiefs – a reward for chiefs' loyalty in approving the 1961 constitution rejected by African nationalists.[71] Chiefs unanimously approved the government's proposed unilateral declaration of independence from Britain in 1964 and requested then that they be given parliamentary representation. The 1969 republican constitution, drawn up after Rhodesia had declared its independence from Britain, reserved seats for chiefs in the Senate and House of

Assembly. From 1976 the Smith regime also tried to involve chiefs in national government by appointing some to the national cabinet.[72]

Chiefs' powers were boosted in other ways. In 1966 the African Affairs Act was amended to delete the reference to chiefs as having merely the powers and duties of police in their areas. The 1967 Tribal Land Authority Act restored to chiefs their right to allocate land and control its use within their chiefdoms – a right that the Land Husbandry Act of 1951 had removed and given to agricultural demonstrators. Loss of the right to allocate land had so enraged chiefs that in the early 1950s it looked as if they and nationalists would forge a lasting alliance. The African Law and Tribal Courts Act of 1969 broadened further the right that certain chiefs had won to hear criminal cases in the 1930s. It also established an appeal court comprising chiefs appointed by a government minister.[73]

Government efforts to boost chiefs' powers only exacerbated their dilemma. According to the rules of the indigenous polity, they were supposed to be responsive to their people. But as government servants they had to implement often unpopular policies or either be deposed or suffer salary deductions. Freed of popular pressures, chiefs could violate with impunity precolonial mores that protected the right of all married men to a fair and equitable use of land. Floyd, a doctoral dissertation student, found that it had become common for village heads to favour close relatives, kin, and special friends with more land than they could cultivate or an unfair share of the land.[74] A Zimbabwean sociologist, Gordon Chavunduka, obtained village data that provide further support for the corruption of Shona precolonial mores of land allocation and the vulnerability of *strangers*. Between 1948 and 1968 the percentage of lineage members in a Shona village who were linked matrilaterally to the dominant lineage declined significantly. Chavunduka suggests that children linked matrilaterally to the village may have found it easier to claim land rights in the village where the fathers' lineage lived.[75] Weinrich, a social anthropologist, describes how inhabitants in a chiefdom responded differently to headmen who regained their power to allocate land when the district commissioner abandoned land allocation under the Native Land Husbandry Act because of opposition. 'This decision pleased the relatives of traditional leaders but distressed the *strangers*, for wherever land was allocated by civil servants, all families received an equal share in the village land; where allocation was left to village headmen and chiefs, great inequalities resulted. For example, in one village in the south of Shiri chiefdom, married men had land holdings ranging between 23 acres and one acre before the Land Husbandry Act was implemented; after the implementation all married men had between seven and nine acres. Members of the chief's clan therefore, who had a stake in the tribal system, were more opposed to the government's control over the land than *strangers*.'[76] Tensions between chiefly families and *strangers* also appear in a novel on the guerrilla war. The novelist describes how the chiefly families, and particularly its elders, enjoyed privileges. Only the senior elders of the local tribe could go and see old gold workings in caves, and those who had not lived there as long were regarded as 'immigrant upstarts'.[77]

In the colonial period, land alienation by whites and growing African population pressures produced land shortages and it became difficult for *strangers* to emigrate and join other chiefdoms when they were dissatisfied or establish new ones, as they could in precolonial times. Hence an important safety valve for resolving the conflicts that build up in small communities was eliminated. Once the government presided over the allocation of fixed arable plots to household heads under the Land Husbandry Act in 1951, mobility became even more difficult.[78] One way in which *strangers* tried to overcome their dwindling influence in chiefly politics was to seek status in other arenas: school committees, separatist churches, missions, nationalist parties, and business ventures.[79] But *strangers* and even those from the chiefly clan who were only remotely related to the ruling families had no vehicles through which they could express discontent in the colonial period.

A 1966 survey conducted by a doctoral dissertation student was an unusual opportunity for subjects to express sentiments about the chiefship. The survey revealed widespread dissatisfaction with the practice of appointing chiefs and having mediums approve them. Most respondents preferred chiefs to be elected.[80] In a survey of African township residents near Salisbury published in 1972, many agreed that chiefs should be represented in parliament but preferred chiefs to be younger and educated.[81] These surveys indicate that neither rural nor urban Africans wished to abolish the institution of the chiefship, but many wished to see a change in how it functioned. The institutions of the indigenous Shona polity might have evolved towards elected chiefships or alternative forms in the absence of such strong support from the authorities. Although the chiefdom was no longer the main focus of Shona loyalties as it had been in the late nineteenth century[82] and even in the Shona and Ndebele rebellions against the Company in 1896–7,[83] it still competed for Shona loyalties. The perpetuation of dynastic politics worked well to discourage rural Africans from forging broader political loyalties and suited colonial governments that feared a broad-based African political organization. Also, the arbitrating role of Europeans in dynastic disputes encouraged Africans to look to the administration for support rather than build alliances against it. Colonial policies also intensified dynastic disputes. In the precolonial past, an unsuccessful candidate for office could emigrate and establish a chiefdom elsewhere, but racial land legislation that demarcated African areas in the colonial period placed a ceiling on the number of chiefly offices, intensifying succession disputes. The pay associated with political office added to its appeal and heightened competition.[84]

Rural socio-economic differentiation

Precolonial Shona society was less differentiated than it is today. Wealth of a patrilineage was measured by the numbers of wives, children, and cattle because they helped to reproduce the kin group as an organic unit. The concept of individual property was unimportant and largely limited to goods that had a personal value such as clothing, tools, ornaments, and weapons.[85] Wealth differentials among the Shona, primarily subsistence cultivators, were small. Some obtained wealth from small-scale internal trading and long-distance trade.[86] The Shona egalitarian ideal was, as it remains for some, that wealth should be evenly distributed in the community. Many still believe that when an individual or family is successful it is because of witchcraft against others or because of praying too hard to senior spirit elders. The rich bring unpopularity and suspicion on themselves and allegations of prospering at the expense of the good of the group. To escape these suspicions, they must use their wealth for the benefit of the group, and restore the equality that is the norm.[87] So chiefs were obligated to use the tribute they received to satisfy their subjects.

The uneven spread of education, limited wage-labour opportunities, and the creation of individual land ownership in the Purchase Areas all contributed to the emergence of a more differentiated African society and individual property came to be the most valued form of wealth. Although the socio-economic gap between whites and Africans was much larger than socio-economic differences among Africans, the latter became important potential sources of African grievances. In particular, differences between Purchase Area and Tribal Trust Land cultivators, between educated government-paid personnel and other rural Africans, and among Tribal Trust Land producers must be considered as potentially explosive.

Purchase Area versus Tribal Trust Land cultivators

The differences between Purchase Area and Tribal Trust Land producers created mutual resentments. Purchase Area farmers, a creation of colonial policy, represent less than 2 per cent of all African producers. They live outside the authority of chiefs, own or lease their land, and usually live some distance from neighbours with whom they are unlikely to be related. Many Purchase Areas have not been settled for long. Budjga Purchase Area in Mutoko had only nine occupied farms in 1952. The numbers grew to 124 in 1959, 244 in 1962, and 318 in 1976, with some areas settled earlier than others.[88] All Budjga farmers are Shona-speaking but Shona and Ndebele reside side by side in some Purchase Areas. In contrast, most African producers live in the Tribal Trust Lands under the authority of chiefs. Land is vested in the chiefdom and household heads are granted arable plots for their use while grazing is communal. People live in villages close to kin and friends.

Purchase Area and Tribal Trust Land cultivators generally grow the same basic crops, chiefly maize with some groundnuts, but their farm sizes, incomes, labour requirements, marketing arrangements, access to credit and extension services differ. The average Purchase Area farmer has a much larger farm. The average farm sizes in Budjga Purchase Area were 123 acres (including grazing) and in Mutoko Tribal Trust Land about 15 acres (excluding grazing because it is communal).[89] There were corresponding differences in average incomes in each division. Pre-independence data on African agriculture in the rural areas are based on rough estimates by government field workers or sample studies. Based on a sample size of only fifteen Budjga Purchase Area farmers, the average farm income from farm and non-farm related activities was R$1,117, but the range was between R$316 and R$2,750. Those at the bottom range are close to the living standards of many in the Tribal Trust Lands.[90] Larger farm sizes imposed more demanding labour requirements on Purchase Area farmers, and account for their higher rates of polygyny and the large numbers of relatives living with them.[91] A condition of freehold was that farmers live on the land, and consequently, the average Purchase Area farmer obtains 70–80 per cent of income from the land. Their sons are likely to migrate to towns or settle in the Tribal Trust Lands, but they keep their earnings for themselves. In contrast, most Tribal Trust Land producers rely on migrant labour of family members for a significant proportion of their income.[92] Purchase Area farmers produced most of African marketed production and were more likely to use cooperatives than Tribal Trust Land cultivators. The most widely used marketing agents in the Tribal Trust Lands were traders whom Purchase Area farmers never used. Because they often owned land, Purchase Area farmers were also more likely to obtain credit. Finally, Tribal Trust Lands were less well-served with extension advice than Purchase Areas.

How do these institutional and other differences affect the relationship between Purchase Areas and Tribal Trust Land farmers? Daughters from the Purchase Area may marry in the Tribal Trust Lands, and farm owners in the Purchase Area seek additional wives from the Tribal Trust Lands. Purchase Area farmers also market surpluses unofficially (and illegally) to Tribal Trust Land residents. But Tribal Trust Land cultivators envy the wealth of their neighbours.[93] People residing in chiefdoms, as in Chimoyo chiefdom in Mutoko, were often evicted from their land when it was earmarked as Purchase Land, only to observe it unoccupied and unsurveyed. Purchase Area farmers reciprocated Tribal Trust Land producers' negative sentiments. They preferred to identify with European commercial farmers and the African urban petty bourgeoisie, whose origins still come disproportionately from freehold farmers. And they excluded Tribal Trust Land producers from membership in the African Farmers' Union that promoted almost exclusively the interests of Purchase Area farmers.[94] There was little mobility between Tribal Trust Land and Purchase Area producers.[95]

Educated government-paid personnel

The authorities' antipathy towards educated Africans influenced the slow pace of development of an indigenous educated African elite. Initially, the most that educated Africans could aspire to was employment by churches as clergy – there were a mere twenty-four African clergy by 1930 – or government-paid teachers. Later they could become civil servants, usually in the rural areas in the segregated African departments.[96] Education was prestigious: one-third to a half of African university graduates between 1968 and 1974 joined the Ministry of African Education.[97] The elite remained small. As already noted, in 1967 nearly 80 per cent of Africans never finished more than five years of schooling and only 0.04 per cent of Africans completed a full secondary education.

In the period before African mass nationalism in the late 1950s, African organizations failed to pull together varied interests: rural and urban, Shona and Ndebele, educated and uneducated, workers on the farms and mines and in the towns.[98] The relationship between the African educated elite and other Africans in this period has been characterized in divergent ways. One view is that African elites were conscious of their links to the masses because racial discrimination ensured their marginality to European society.[99] Others have commented on the political gap between the African elite and other Africans because of the former's identification with Europeans. Van Velsen asserted:

> Just because it is realised or at any rate assumed by the rank-and-file that some of his [the elite's] non-political interests lie much closer to those of counterparts in the white community with whom he shares similar professional, economic, intellectual and other interests and aspirations, therefore he tends to be suspected of being liable to fall for the blandishments of the white minority.[100]

This view has much in common with Fanon's observation that those Africans who acquired the skills or values associated with the colonizers were frequently stigmatized as 'having acquired the habits of a master'.[101]

The data with which to evaluate either proposition are minimal. There is some evidence that the tiny group of African professionals were slow to join the so-called mass nationalist movement that is dated from the founding of the Southern Rhodesian African National Congress in 1957. Only in 1961 and 1962 did university graduates and others join.[102] Weinrich studied the attitudes of rural African elites, defined by their western education and incomes, to other Africans and Europeans in the 1960s but gave little attention to how rural Africans perceived the elite. The study divided rural African elites into an upper and middle stratum. The upper stratum comprised Catholic priests, doctors, hospital administrators, school inspectors, and extension officers. They were found to seek acceptance from Europeans, who rejected them. No longer tied to the land, they were reported to have consciously separated themselves from peasant life and to feel a great distance from members of their own race.[103] Politically, they were often neutral or at least inactive, 'because either their religious commitment does not allow them to engage in active politics or their economic rewards bind them to submit passively to a social order which discriminates as much against them as against the less educated of their race'.[104] Primary school teachers, successful businessmen (who are included as elites because of their high incomes rather than their education), extension supervisors and assistants, nurses and Protestant ministers were included in the numerically largest middle stratum. 'Because they have less to lose than the wealthier members of the elite, many of them criticize European dominance in Rhodesia . . . A significant number are willing to participate actively in political movements to bring about a changed social order. Being less alienated, their commitment to African society is much more intense than is that of members of the top elite.'[105]

The third stratum, according to Weinrich, must be considered a sub-elite, because of its members' lower education and income. It comprises successful farmers, petty traders, some church pastors, and craftsmen, most of whom are cultivators and obtain additional and erratic income from their crafts. The study found storekeepers to be envied by African peasants, and successful traders were often the butt of witchcraft allegations. Peasants are reported to believe that if a man becomes successful in business, he must have killed a close relative and buried his heart under the counter in order to attract customers. Besides envy, storekeepers in the Tribal Trust Lands also generated peasant resentment. Storekeepers, as agents of the government marketing board, bought peasant grain and sold it to the government. Peasants resented that storekeepers profited from these transactions and often cheated them by systematically underweighing their produce. Some storekeepers also insisted that producers purchase goods at high prices in return for handling grain. They charged higher prices than white businessmen and were also allegedly less polite. Somewhat at odds with the case for peasant resentment and envy of storekeepers, Weinrich notes that storekeepers were also a source of credit, and, as long as they did not demand debt repayment when peasants found themselves in a financial squeeze, they were popular.[106]

Socio-economic differentiation within the Tribal Trust Lands

Farming incomes. Income differences arose from the varied responses of cultivators to government extension advice and the failure of government extension to reach more cultivators. Master farmers, plotholders, cooperators, and ordinary cultivators are government categories signifying the degree to which producers have been exposed to government advisory services and the use they have made of these services. Master farmers have most completely accepted government extension advice: they rotate crops, are attentive to the timing of farm operations, and use fertilizer.

Plotholders follow prescribed farming methods, and if they perform satisfactorily, will be certified as master farmers. Cooperators are less influenced by extension advice but at least exposed to it whereas ordinary producers are outside such influences.[107] Extension advice contributes to significant differences in yields, and hence potential market production and incomes. Five-year averages of grain yields in bags per acre were 7.3 for master farmers, 6.3 for plotholders, and only 2.1 for ordinary cultivators. Purchase Area farmers only obtained 3.8 bags per acre and were therefore not as efficient in their land use as the better farmers in the Tribal Trust Lands, but their larger land allotments and other advantages enabled them to earn higher average incomes.[108] Master farmers constituted only about 3.2 per cent of all Tribal Trust Land cultivators, and all those who cooperated to some extent with government agricultural advisors amounted to some 30 per cent.[109] Estimates of market-oriented producers, all cooperators with government advisors, ranged from 3 per cent to 30 per cent, and even higher, in the 1970s.[110]

To my knowledge Weinrich's effort to determine how these differences in farming success affect the attitudes of Tribal Trust Land producers towards each other is unique. Based on data gathered in the 1960s, Weinrich argued that successful producers in the Tribal Trust Lands – unlike in the Purchase Areas – were not held in high esteem by their less successful neighbours.[111] Although providing leadership in farming, successful farmers were found to be otherwise marginal to their communities and often aspired to move to the Purchase Areas.[112] But she gives different reasons for the different levels of farming success. On the one hand, she asserts that most ordinary cultivators refused to adopt extension advice from an alien government because they were nationalists.[113] On the other hand, she argues that ordinary cultivators were not interested in farming and proposes that the government allow them to live permanently in the urban areas.[114] At other times, she attributes ordinary farmers' failure to embrace modern farming methods to their 'traditional' values that accord priority to social relationships rather than investment in land and individual advancement. For them, chiefs, 'the most tradition-bound group of tribesmen', represent an alternative role model.[115] Regardless of what one attributes the farming skill differentials to, they evidently produced tensions among cultivators.

There were significant differences in landholdings and cattle herds in the Tribal Trust Lands. A 1978 study claims that 16.5 per cent of Tribal Trust Land cultivators had less than 8 hectares (20 acres) and 70 per cent less than 15 hectares (37.5 acres).[116] Another study in the 1970s concluded that most producers lacked the minimum amount of land for subsistence, and that in many areas 20 per cent of cultivators were landless while others had plot sizes twenty times that required for subsistence.[117] A study of Karangaland in the 1960s found that 30 per cent of families had no cattle, 22 per cent owned 1–3 head, and 23 per cent over 6 head.[118] A 1984

Table 2.2 *Chiefs' and headmen's basic allowances per annum*[121] (R$)

	July 1976–Feb. 1980	Feb. 1980
Chiefs with more than 500 followers	1,620	2,136
Chiefs with less than 500 followers	960	1,272
Headmen with more than 500 followers	420	552
Headmen with less than 500 followers	120	

No. of posts, 21 July 1976: 480
New posts, 21 July 1976: 156

household survey found size of existing and past remittances of members of the household in paid employment to be a more important indicator than cattle and land in distinguishing rich and poor in rural areas. Over one-third of all households reported receiving remittances.[119]

Chiefs' government income. Precolonial chiefs (and other leaders) had larger fields and more wives and children than their subjects. They also got various sources of income from their people – such as tribute from hunters or from *strangers* requesting land and protection – but they were supposed to use them for the benefit of their subjects. Hence the wealth differential between chiefs and their subjects never became significant. In the colonial period, the chiefs used their government salaries for their personal benefit, thus fuelling already strained relations with their subjects. Chiefs' and headmen's pay was substantial (see table 2.2), and the average chief's salary, though small, exceeded the average earnings of black workers.[120] This comparison of pay ignores other salaries and allowances that the colonial government paid to chiefs and sometimes headmen. Chiefs and headmen were eligible for personal allowances of up to R$1,860 and R$480 per annum respectively for exceeding 'normal standards' in carrying out their duties, and travel and subsistence allowances to cover the costs of attending meetings for serving on local and provincial government bodies as well as provincial and national assemblies of chiefs, indigenous rulers could earn still more.

Councillors' pay and allowances (African councils). Headmen and chiefs were ex officio members of African councils and received R$3 for attending meetings. Sometimes they were also elected as African councillors, whose pay just before independence was R$360 per annum. If elected chairmen of an African council, headmen and chiefs received R$600 per annum. In the seven years preceding independence, chiefs who became members of the Council of Chiefs were paid R$240 per annum, while the President of this body received R$480 per annum. Through their participation in provincial authorities, as elected, ex officio, or coopted members, chiefs were entitled to a monthly allowance of up to R$85 and a R$6 per day allowance for attending meetings. These payments were raised to R$100 and R$10 respectively, just before independence.

Gender

Precolonial laws regarding marriage, divorce, custody of children, and property favoured patrilineages, and more specifically, married men. These so-called traditional or customary laws, which discriminated against women, remained largely unchanged during the colonial period and were a potential source of grievance.[122] The British South Africa Company's Charter determined that traditional law should prevail in domestic life unless it was considered repugnant to 'natural justice and morality', which were deemed to be 'universal standards'. White courts rarely found traditional law repugnant.

In traditional marriages the groom's family had to pay bridewealth (*lobola*) to compensate the bride's extended family and lineage for the loss of her labour and reproductive capacities. Any children from the marriage belonged to the groom's extended family, which also had rights to their labour and the bridewealth of future daughters. Marriage was polygynous and virilocal. The former meant that men could marry more than one wife, which they did if they could afford the bridewealth payments because more wives meant broader lineage affiliations for a patrilineage and family, more labour for agricultural production, and more children. Virilocal marriage required the wife to go and live in the village of her husband's family. Yet the woman continued to belong to her father's clan, and did not become a member of her husband's clan. She was expected to respect and serve her husband's family, and the women in her husband's family made her perform the unpleasant chores around the house. She and other women in her lineage call the women in her husband's lineage *vamwene* (owner) underlining her subordinate position not just to her husband but also the women in her husband's family. On the other hand, marriage raised a woman's status in her father's family. In contrast to the subordination of females in the wife-giving lineage, males in the wife-giving lineage are paid deference by males in the wife-receiving lineage, who, regardless of their generation, call them 'father'. Males in the wife-giving lineage call all males in the receiving lineage 'children'.

Colonial law required Africans to register their marriages with a state authority. Of those who adhered to the law, most registered polygynous marriages under the African Marriages Act. From 1917 the Marriages Act provided for Africans to register monogamous marriages – also called 'civil' or 'Christian' marriages – but the men could not then marry additional wives without committing a criminal offence. As it happened, polygyny declined everywhere, except in the Purchase Areas, for various reasons that had little to do with legal efforts to limit it.[123] The Marriages Act did not interfere with other aspects of traditional law such as bridewealth payments, virilocal residence, and the treatment of women as legal minors. In contrast to African women, white women under the Marriages Act became legal majors entitling them to enter contracts, open bank accounts, and represent themselves in court. Interestingly, chiefs' courts came to interpret traditional law that prohibited women from representing themselves in court more flexibly than European courts, and often allowed women to speak for themselves. The treatment of women as minors is also evident in their funeral rituals. A man who is married and has a child has full adult status and when he dies a ritual is performed to bring home his spirit and install it among the spirit guardians of the family. There is no such ceremony for a deceased adult woman, suggesting that women do not acquire full adult status.[124]

Divorce in the precolonial period was rare, in part because it required settling the amount of bridewealth to be returned to the husband's family. Because a bride's family would use bridewealth to pay for a son's marriage, returning any part of bridewealth entailed complex lineage transactions and the bride's family was likely to prevail on her to remain with her husband. Also, since children remained with the husband's family when their mothers divorced, a woman was reluctant to divorce. If the husband were at fault according to traditional divorce laws, he would have no interest in bringing about a divorce since he would have to return some of the brideprice.

The grounds for divorce in traditional law discriminated against women. Shona women could be divorced on the grounds of barrenness or the production of daughters only, adultery, failure to cook and perform other domestic duties to their husbands' satisfaction, disobedience, and insubordination. Wives' adultery was often considered less compelling grounds for divorce than neglect of domestic duties. Rather than seek a divorce for his wife's adultery, a Shona man was more likely to obtain compensation from her lover and punish his wife by beating her severely. It was more difficult for women to find grounds for divorcing their husbands. Shona husbands could not be divorced for adultery, impotence, or sterility. If a husband beat his wife continually and cruelly, or so severely that she could show the results of his physical assaults, then her family could seek a divorce. Either party could seek divorce on the grounds of insanity, refusal of conjugal rights, or the practice of witchcraft. Most divorces were settled by the families and only if they were unable to reach agreement did they take the case to court.

In the colonial period, divorce had to be settled by courts. Divorce also became more common. Once young men obtained wage employment, they gained some independence from their extended family for bridewealth payments and hence more freedom to seek dissolution of their marriages. Also, an economy built on cheap migrant labour separated men from their wives and children for extended periods and contributed to the erosion of family. Even when marriages did not dissolve, married women were worse off in some respects. For women, the lower profile of the families in the marriage meant a loss of outside protection against abusive husbands. Fear of losing access to the children if they divorced led many women to tolerate such behaviour and avoid the courts. African women in 'civil' or 'Christian' marriages could seek dissolution of their marriages on the grounds of their husbands' adultery, and claim maintenance. However, most African marriages fall outside this legislation.

Precolonial Shona inheritance laws also discriminated against women. When the family head died, traditional law required that livestock (the most important form of property) and other family property be inherited by collateral succession – that is, by male relatives in the same generation as the family head.[125] The new family head also inherited the deceased's children and usually marital rights to the widow, subject to her consent. If she chose instead to return to her father's home and if she were still of childbearing age, then her family would have to return some *lobola*. Concern for her children, who would remain with her husband's family, usually dictated that she would remain in the village if she got along tolerably well with her affines. If the widow was past childbearing age and elected to continue living among her deceased husband's family, the new head of the family was supposed to ensure that she had land to cultivate and a place to live.

Few changes in traditional inheritance laws occurred in the colonial period. Instead of inheritance being based on collateral rules, it was more likely to follow primogeniture according to which the eldest son inherits his father's property.[126] The Marriages Act provided for white women to control all their own property unless they elected to marry in community of property but there was no similar protection for African women. After 1933 an African man married under this Act could stipulate in his will that his wife should be guardian of his children and inherit his property. Again, few Africans were married under this Act and still fewer were aware of this provision or chose to take advantage of it.

Opinions differ on whether women's status and autonomy in Zimbabwe (and other African contexts) increased or declined under colonial rule.[127] An estimated one-third of household heads in the 1970s were women – the spouses of migrant men, divorcees, or widows.[128] Some argue that the migration of younger men, especially between twenty and forty-five years, enabled women in the Tribal Trust Lands to win considerable autonomy in their daily lives. While their husbands were away, they had more influence over their children and more opportunity to build matri-segments. They won more control of household income, more economic prominence as *de facto* household heads, and more political significance in local affairs.[129] Yet women's increased responsibilities in the Tribal Trust Land were not matched by an improvement in their legal rights.[130] Others maintain that migrant husbands still made major decisions affecting the household on their home visits, despite women being the primary agricultural producers.

77

They add that agricultural work became low status once men became engaged in wage labour. Other women's roles, such as mediumship and midwifery, lost status to European-trained nurses and western medicine, both promoted by missions that simultaneously denigrated these traditional roles. The availability of cheap European-produced goods and colonial prohibitions on trade of certain items deprived women of some sources of income that they were able to control in traditional law and that gave them some economic independence.[131] Precolonial African demand for baskets and pottery was eliminated early in the colonial period by the availability of cheap, mass-produced goods, and the British South Africa Company prohibited African men and women from participating in the alluvial gold trade with the Portuguese. Home-made beer-brewing from sorghum had to compete for sales with council beer-halls. New sources of revenue that women were able to take advantage of in the early colonial period were later prohibited. Beer sales on the mines and in the towns to single men were outlawed, and by the mid 1930s the right to sell vegetables and food in the European areas was also prohibited. Also, European courts generally interpreted traditional law as requiring women to give their wages to their husbands even though traditional law allowed women rights to income from their own skills.[132]

Distinctions must be made between most African women who live in the Tribal Trust Lands and women in Purchase Areas. It is generally acknowledged that Purchase Area women were unambiguously worse off than their Tribal Trust Land counterparts. Under the constant attention of their husbands whose continued ownership or leasing of land depended on abiding by the requirement that they not migrate, women's time was strictly controlled to maximize the benefits of their labour.[133] Therefore mothers in the Purchase Areas often assisted their daughters to find husbands in the Tribal Trust Lands.[134] Also, Purchase Area women were much more likely to be in polygynous marriages. Purchase Area farmers use wives and children as a means of accumulating capital, and almost half the men still practice polygyny – many have four to five wives.[135] Although women in polygynous marriages may find support from co-wives, senior wives often resent junior wives who get more attention from their husbands, creating the potential for domestic conflicts.

Traditional laws of marriage, inheritance, and divorce clearly discriminate against women, and have been sources of gender tensions. Men resent what influence women are able to exercise in spite of the male-oriented structure of society. Women are most likely to be accused of practising witchcraft and it has been suggested that this reflects men's recognition of their subtle influence. It also reflects women's vulnerability: as outsiders to their husband's lineages, they are most likely to be blamed for any quarrels that destroy the ideal of patrilineal unity.[136]

Generational inequalities

Rank according to age was a fundamental characteristic of precolonial Shona society. Older people had more status than younger people, and the spirits of the dead enjoyed more stature than even the oldest living people. Status was enhanced by marriage, and still further by children and grandchildren. Children had low status: they were fed after their parents, and when they died, did not join the spirit world. The relationship between children and parents, and especially that of father–child, was based on strict obedience and respect. The ideal of father–child relationships was one of distance and authority.[137] Males had to marry in order to be eligible for land, so marriage was essential for young men to obtain economic independence. Fathers decided when and whom their children should marry. Daughters' marriages enriched families with bridewealth from the husbands' families, but fathers had to pay bridewealth for their sons to marry and once married, they lost the value of their labour. On the other hand, lineages needed to expand if they were to grow in power and status, so fathers had an interest in marrying sons.[138]

The colonial period opened opportunities for youth to become more independent of their families. Migrant labour for cash wages or food rations reduced dependence on families. This affected primarily young males. Colonial labour statistics often regarded African males as adults from the age of sixteen years,[139] although there is plenty of evidence of even younger Africans working in the towns during and after World War II, and on white farms.[140] Missions targeted the young as potential converts and concentrated educational efforts on them. Missionary success required alienating young Africans from their traditional roots and missions were always ready to assist and abet those seeking to escape family controls by offering training and asylum. Education and training increased the prospects of the young obtaining better wages, and hence the possibility of even more autonomy from family control. The independence of young men from their elders has been most pronounced among males who reside permanently in the European centres of employment, in particular the towns, mines, and farms, less so for those who live in the Purchase Areas, and least for those in the Tribal Trust Lands. To a large exent, their degree of independence coincides with their level of education, and hence earning power.[141] The new towns, mines, and later the white farms which all had large concentrations of single male migrant workers, offered opportunities for female prostitution which was often a means of escape from parental control or husbands' authority. A study in the 1960s found that a surprisingly high number of wives, sisters, and daughters of Purchase Area farmers engaged in prostitution not to flee male control but to earn money to feed and educate their children because their husbands and fathers neglected them.[142] Another alternative for women escaping male control was to go and live at missions.

The sources of tensions between elders and the younger generation in the Purchase Area differ from those in the Tribal Trust Lands. Land shortages in the Tribal Trust Lands drive many young men to seek work away from home. A study of two Tribal Trust Lands in the 1960s found over 80 per cent of males between fifteen and thirty years old to be landless compared with only 5.5 per cent of men over forty-five years.[143] In the Purchase Areas only the eldest son can hope to inherit his father's farm. Because Purchase Area farmers cling to controlling their farms until death, tension arises between the farmer and his eldest son if the latter is eager to become a farmer. Other sons must seek employment in European centres or try to find land in generally overcrowded Tribal Trust Lands. Also, fathers often want to use their wealth to acquire another wife rather than help their sons to pay bridewealth. The problem is more pronounced in the Purchase Areas because of its higher rate of polygyny than in the Tribal Trust Lands. A study of two Purchase Areas in the 1960s found that 58 per cent of males over fifteen years of age were unmarried compared with only 37 per cent in the Tribal Trust Lands surveyed. Fathers and daughters come into conflict too. Fathers would prefer their daughters to marry neighbours to help them form alliances but daughters often choose to escape and marry in the Tribal Trust Lands where they have more autonomy from husbands who are frequently away as migrant workers. Also Tribal Trust Land marriages are less likely to be polygynous and so lower the risks for married women of having to put up with potentially thorny domestic conflicts among co-wives.[144] For these and other reasons, sons and daughters constantly emigrate from their fathers' farms.

Male elders sought to retain their dwindling authority. For example, the Vapostori or Apostolic Church which grew rapidly in the 1930s and is today the largest independent African church in Zimbabwe, rejects church teaching on polygyny and church education as a basis for prestige and power. Its members resent the way in which the church has undermined the power of male elders and an ill-educated male gerontocracy monopolizes all secular leadership positions in the movement. But they do not endorse all aspects of precolonial society. They reject ancestor worship and belief in witchcraft, and they are willing to eliminate bridewealth.[145] Male elders may try to prolong the dependence of young men and capture some of their wealth by demanding more bridewealth (and in cash rather than cattle), especially for well-educated children. Political movements, both protonationalist and nationalist, opposed the political power of less educated and often elderly chiefs and attracted the better educated, who were also younger.[146]

Conclusion

Colonial policies, the spread of a money economy, and education created peasant grievances against the colonial regime. But these same factors also generated inequalities, and associated grievances, among peasants and between them and a rural African elite. Most studies of anti-colonial and peasant-based nationalist revolutions can show that colonial regimes, whether chiefly as alien rulers or as capitalists, were the root cause of the colonized's grievances. But they cannot document that peasants understood that the colonial state was responsible for their misery. At least for the colonial period in Zimbabwe, scholars have shown little interest in how inequalities among Africans were experienced. Like the colonial authorities, they have been preoccupied with the relationship between the colonized and colonizers. Hence this chapter has had to infer grievances from African inequalities. The next chapter discusses nationalist parties' appeals, the core of which were based on racially based grievances.

3

Strategies, goals and appeals: continuity and change

Mass African nationalist activity in Southern Rhodesia is conventionally dated from the founding of the Southern Rhodesian African National Congress (SRANC) in September 1957. Nationalist strategies changed between 1957 and the attainment of African majority rule in 1980. Periodizing the shifts in strategy is complicated because legal party activity inside the country overlapped with armed struggle from exiled bases, and armed struggle with constitutional negotiations. None the less, there is a consensus that between 1969 and 1972 ZANU adopted a Maoist strategy stressing guerrilla mobilization of peasants through revolutionary political education. Scholars have scrutinized leaders' utterances, often aimed at external audiences, to understand the movement's strategy and goals. This has led to a neglect of structural constraints affecting the guerrilla movement. An analysis of ZANU guerrilla appeals highlights the realities that confronted the fighters on the battlefield. Guerrilla appeals shared similar weaknesses with those of the legal nationalist parties. Coercive appeals against other Africans were prominent throughout the period of mass nationalism and utilitarian appeals were almost non-existent. These shared weaknesses in organizational appeals are linked to a growing state capacity, and especially repressive military capacity.[1] Before illustrating the similarity between guerrilla and earlier nationalist parties' appeals, and the increasing state capacity, the nationalist parties' changing strategies and goals are discussed.

Nationalist strategies and goals

Organized political party activity inside Zimbabwe, 1957–79

The SRANC came into existence during the Federal period (1953–63) and was influenced by the trend towards greater African political participation in Northern Rhodesia and Nyasaland. The new body was the product of the amalgamation of two protonationalist organizations, the Salisbury-based City Youth League (whose members were adults) and the

82

Bulawayo-based African National Congress of Southern Rhodesia. The City Youth League, formed in 1955, was critical of the African elite who sought advancement through participation in anti-democratic institutions such as white political parties and the federal parliament. The African National Congress of Southern Rhodesia, founded in 1945, was an elitist organization that perpetuated the tradition of its predecessors. It selectively opposed discriminatory laws, particularly those that prevented the African elite from participating fully in the white-dominated political system. After World War II it tried to appeal to an expanding working population but it lost the initiative to workers' organizations. When it merged with the City Youth League, it was almost defunct. It was the politics of the City Youth League that shaped the new mass nationalist organization's agenda, although the top leadership position went to Joshua Nkomo who had not been a member of the organization.[2]

The goals of the SRANC were modest insofar as it declared its loyalty to the Crown and rejected the idea of independence from the United Kingdom before progress towards an integrated society was well advanced. However, it demanded universal suffrage and parliamentary democracy, the repeal of all racial legislation, and a society based on individual freedom and equal opportunity for all. Like African nationalist organizations to the north, it objected to a federal constitution being imposed without consulting Africans and without regard to vocal African opposition. In the socio-economic sphere, the organization favoured a mixed economy open to foreign capital, techniques, and skills, a closing of the gap between the lowest and highest income groups, and free and compulsory universal primary education. The SRANC identified racially discriminatory legislation as the major problem in the country, and singled out for attack the franchise laws, the Department of Native Affairs, and the Native Land Husbandry Act. Africans who worked with anti-democratic white political parties, labelled 'so-called African moderates', were impugned. Effective appeals to rural and urban socio-economic grievances boosted its organizational drive.[3]

The National Democratic Party (NDP) succeeded the SRANC in January 1960 soon after the latter was banned. In contrast to the SRANC, the NDP opposed organized efforts to break socio-economic segregation and pursued more doggedly the political battle for universal African franchise. Nationalists now called for African self-rule and not merely the right to participate in government. Interestingly, the NDP called for chiefs to be ex officio members of the judiciary and saw no conflict between this constitutional proposal and its belief in a meritocratic society.[4] The life of the NDP coincided with intense constitutional politics that absorbed the energies of the nationalist leadership. The London conference to review the federal constitution at the end of 1960 had been suspended until each of the constituent territories had produced constitutions that showed satisfactory progress towards granting Africans greater political participation. The

Southern Rhodesian government was eager to obtain more independence from Britain for itself. It wanted to remove Britain's right to review and veto legislation affecting Africans, even though Britain had never used these reserve powers, in return for making concessions towards African political advancement. The NDP called on Britain to retain its reserve powers until Southern Rhodesia had a democratic parliament and universal suffrage, and warned that if Britain were to accede to the white government's desire for greater independence, it would be tantamount to accepting the ruling minority's racial discrimination. However, the NDP, like its predecessor, believed Britain would uphold democratic values: 'We believe that it is Her Majesty's Government's intention, as evidenced by recent constitutional developments in Kenya and Tanganyika, to steer clear of policies based on race discrimination and minority rule.'[5] The NDP failed to understand that Britain's decolonization policies did not apply to colonies with sizeable white settler populations. The NDP also initiated links with international and regional organizations that exerted diplomatic pressure on Britain to pursue democratic goals in Southern Rhodesia.[6]

Tensions about the nationalist movement's strategy and leadership date from this period. Joshua Nkomo's vacillating leadership and prolonged absences from the country while he campaigned abroad fuelled discontent within the party. Many felt that the leadership gave too much attention to international diplomacy and constitutional change and neglected building a mass organization. An episode that allegedly contributed to the eventual split in the nationalist movement was the behaviour of Nkomo and NDP representatives at constitutional talks with the British and Southern Rhodesian governments in Salisbury early in 1961 – the first time that African nationalists were formally included in constitutional negotiations. The NDP was committed to immediate parliamentary majority rule and universal suffrage or to retaining Britain's reserve powers. Yet its representatives allegedly agreed to a constitution that removed virtually all Britain's reserve powers, did not allow for parliamentary majority rule for another fifteen years, and was based on a qualified franchise. Facing protests from the rest of the executive and the rank and file, the representatives denied that they had ever approved the proposed constitution – a view accepted by one analyst of these events.[7] But those who accept that the NDP did not adhere to the party's principles at the constitutional conference claim that the initial disregard for the party platform by Nkomo and others embittered NDP executive members. The NDP then held its own referendum on the constitution that was rejected, and organized eligible African voters against registering on the new electoral rolls that the 1961 constitution had introduced or voting in the 1962 general election.[8]

Days after the banning of the NDP the Zimbabwe African People's Union (ZAPU) was formed to replace it. Britain held that the African nationalists had initially agreed to the 1961 constitution and refused to respond to their call for it to convene a fresh conference to devise a constitution based on universal suffrage and parliamentary democracy. ZAPU broadened the nationalists' international campaign and appealed to the United Nations to intervene in the constitutional dispute with Britain and the white government. Still refusing to distinguish between Southern Rhodesia and British colonies to the north, it insisted that Britain had the power and responsibility to legislate for Southern Rhodesia without the settler government's prior consent.[9] Apart from intensifying its international diplomatic efforts, ZAPU also engaged in widespread sabotage of churches and government property – school buildings, dip tanks, communications installations, beer gardens. All were seen as the symbols of an alien administration and the segregated and inferior public services that it provided for Africans. The hope was that sabotage would quickly bring about a collapse in law and order and induce Britain to intervene and seek a constitutional settlement. However, ZAPU was banned in September 1962 and its leaders detained. When most of them were released, they issued an order to cease sabotage because they perceived that it was hardening white attitudes and the anticipated British intervention had not materialized.[10]

The nationalist movement split into two organizations in August 1963. Those disaffected with Nkomo's leadership and strategy formed a new party, the Zimbabwe African National Union (ZANU), under Ndabiningi Sithole's leadership. Its first policy statement committed it to a non-racial, democratic socialist, Pan-Africanist state within the British Commonwealth. The major goal of its Pan-African policy was to liquidate colonialism, settler rule, neo-colonialism, and imperialism in Africa. Although it proposed to nationalize all major industries, it encouraged private enterprise, foreign investment, and foreign technicians. It declared an open immigration policy to all Africans but specifically prohibited South African and Portuguese whites. Universal free health and free compulsory education for children were in its programme.[11] ZANU's anti-colonial, anti-imperial and socialist language departed from that used by earlier nationalist organizations. In his inaugural address, ZANU's President Sithole criticized ZAPU for relying on the United Nations and the Afro-Asian bloc to liberate Zimbabweans. He declared ZANU's commitment to continue the strategy of boycotting elections because change would not come through the ballot box.[12] 'Time for fine speeches has gone', he said. 'This is now time for action in order to solve the problem facing us.' Quoting the Algerian nationalist leader Ben Bella, he pleaded: 'we must be prepared "to die a little" if need be'.[13] The major difference between the two rival nationalist organizations at this stage was ZANU's more radical rhetoric rather than its strategy. After ZANU had announced its creation, ZAPU formed the People's Caretaker Council (PCC) so that it would have an organizational presence to rival ZANU. In keeping with its commitment not to form another party, the PCC had neither dues-paying members nor offices. It resumed ZAPU's strategy of international diplomacy and sabotage of government property to try to induce British intervention.

The African National Congress (ANC), led by Bishop Muzorewa, came into existence in the context of efforts to settle the constitutional problems arising from the Rhodesian government's unilateral declaration of independence in 1965. Both ZANU and ZAPU had been banned in August 1964 and were operating from exile in Zambia. The British and Rhodesian governments tried to negotiate a constitutional settlement on three occasions between 1966 and 1970. Talks in December 1966 and October 1968 failed, even though the British government retreated from the negotiating principles it had enunciated in 1964 when the threat of the white government declaring unilateral independence seemed imminent. After the failure of the first talks, Britain called on the United Nations to intervene, and the Security Council imposed first selective, and later, comprehensive mandatory sanctions. In November 1970 the two governments reached agreement on constitutional proposals. Although the proposed constitution legalized Rhodesia's independence and accepted the 1969 white supremacist constitution as the basis for independence, the British government claimed that it conformed to its original negotiating principles. These had provided for progress to majority rule and ending racial discrimination, an immediate improvement in the political status of Africans, guarantees against retrogressive constitutional amendments, and that the basis for independence be acceptable to the Rhodesian people as a whole. Despite Britain's claims, the proposed constitution marked a further retreat from its negotiating principles of 1964.[14] However, Britain adhered to its original commitment that the basis of independence meet with African approval. The Rhodesian government consented to allow Africans to engage in normal politics so that they could prepare to meet a British commission under Lord Pearce that would test African opinion in January 1971, and the ANC was founded.

Bishop Muzorewa became the ANC president mainly because he had been untainted by the internecine rivalries between ZANU and PCC/ZAPU in 1963/4. The ANC's executive balanced ex-ZANU and ex-ZAPU officials, many of whom had been released recently from detention. In May 1972 the Pearce Commission reported that it was satisfied that most Africans rejected the proposals. The ANC favoured legal and non-violent means to bring about majority rule and universal suffrage in a non-racial democratic society. It guaranteed protection for minority rights. It appealed to whites to influence the government to participate in a national convention, and called on the United Nations and the Organization of African Unity to help to effect political change. It called for the United Nations to help enforce sanctions and for punitive measures against member states who broke sanctions. The Commonwealth nations or the United Nations were asked to set up a scheme to assist whites who did not wish to live under African rule to emigrate to the place of their choice. The hope was that white emigration would reduce support for the Rhodesian armed forces and discourage aspirant immigrants. Two aspects of ANC policy led many ZANU members, who had joined it to fight the proposed constitution, to leave the ANC and the country. In early 1973 ANC leaders had dissociated themselves from over 200 members who were arrested for supporting the guerrillas who had begun an offensive in the northeast. Also, the ANC shifted its original opposition to holding constitutional talks with Smith.[15]

Muzorewa became the compromise choice to lead a different ANC, formed under pressure from the front line states – Botswana, Mozambique, Angola, Zambia, Tanzania. The ANC was supposed to unite ZAPU, ZANU, Muzorewa's ANC, and FROLIZI.[16] For a period between late 1975 and 1977 when Muzorewa sought in vain to match his formal position as head of an umbrella ANC with control of the exiled movements and their armies, he condemned negotiations, accepted the inevitability of armed struggle, and declared the ANC to be in favour of socialism.[17] Once he had clearly lost the struggle for control of the exiled movements, Muzorewa (and Sithole, who had lost the battle for the political leadership of ZANU) returned to Rhodesia and accepted Prime Minister Smith's offer in late 1977 to negotiate a constitutional settlement. Muzorewa re-established his leadership of the ANC inside Rhodesia, and renamed the party the United African National Council (UANC) while Sithole established his own political party. Under growing pressures from the war, sanctions, and South Africa, Smith was willing to grant majority rule based on a universal adult suffrage to 'moderate' leaders. In March 1978 Muzorewa, Sithole, and two African chiefs signed an 'internal settlement' with Smith. It provided for a transitional government headed by an executive council composed of the four signatories, a new constitution allowing for universal suffrage, an African parliamentary majority, and the first African Prime Minister. Elections were held in April 1979, four months later than planned. Electoral turnout was officially estimated to be 64 per cent and Bishop Muzorewa's UANC won 52 out of 72 African seats, making him the first African Prime Minister of the country, renamed Zimbabwe Rhodesia. The remaining 28 seats were reserved for whites. Muzorewa had returned to his pre-August 1975 goals: minority guarantees, protection of private property, and constitutional change through negotiations and the ballot box. But, having shunned violence to overthrow the white minority most of his life, he built up a paramilitary force to help the Security Forces defeat the guerrillas. With 16,000 Security Force Auxiliaries, Muzorewa's army had only 5,000 fewer people than ZANU's guerrilla army had inside Zimbabwe at the end of 1979.

The nationalist movements in exile

Conventional phase, 1966–1970

During 1964, ZANU and ZAPU established themselves in exile in Zambia. The Zambian government refused to allow them to train the armies they were building on its territory, but it permitted them to pass through and turned a blind eye to transit camps north of the Zambezi River.[18] The NDP had commenced training an army in 1960, and ZANU and ZAPU stepped up efforts from 1963/4. Both nationalist parties still hoped to create such chaos inside Rhodesia that Britain would intervene and negotiate African majority rule. When the Rhodesian government declared unilateral independence from Britain in November 1965, the exiled nationalist parties were unprepared for any organized activity, having expected a mass insurrection and encouraged it in broadcasts from Zambia. No uprising occurred, although for some months groups of guerrillas, many sent into Rhodesia in 1964–5, engaged in incidents of stonings, crop-slashing, livestock mutilations, industrial action, and arson, using explosives and ammunitions provided by the exiled parties.[19]

From 1966 to 1970, the exiled nationalist parties continued to try to disrupt law and order and compel Britain to intervene.[20] However, acts of sabotage gave way to engaging the Security Forces in conventional battles. Armed groups often brought in arms and explosives and hid them, but they gave little attention to recruiting or mobilizing local people. ZANU remained the more radical of the two movements in its official rhetoric. While ZANU was calling for socialism, a ZAPU statement proclaimed in 1969 that Africans as a whole were neither communist nor capitalist: although their history was one of communalism, they admired the good in both systems. Especially after the inter-party rivalries of 1963–4, ZANU had attempted to redirect its attacks on Africans to whites, and condemned white liberals to be as much part of the problem as Smith supporters. ZAPU was still willing to differentiate between those white settlers who were enemies of the people and those who were friends.[21]

The first clash with Security Forces that the regime acknowledged involved ZANU armed groups who hoped to seize the town of Sinoia and precipitate an insurrection on 28 April 1966. ZANU dates this battle as the start of the guerrilla war of liberation, and since independence has celebrated it as *Chimurenga* Day (Liberation Day). However, the initiative in this period lay with ZAPU groups. Most of the armed men sent into Rhodesia in this period belonged to ZAPU – it had the larger armed force and fought most of the major battles. After a series of defeats in 1966, ZAPU invited the South African African National Congress (SAANC), itself headquartered in Zambia, to assist it. From July 1967 together they sent into Rhodesia groups of between 80 and 150 men, who then split up into smaller groups of about 20. Most of their battles took place within 100 miles of the Zambezi River.[22] Although the Security Forces conceded that some of the insurgents' morale and training had reached a high level, these battles resulted in serious defeats for both movements. By the end of 1968, more than 160 guerrillas had been killed compared with only 12 Security Force members.[23] Some claim the nationalists lost many of the best trained fighters they would produce.[24]

Guerrilla warfare and negotiations, 1972–9

During 1969 ZANU and ZAPU re-evaluated the merits of engaging in conventional battles with a numerically superior Security Force, aided by air power. Also, the British government's negotiating position in the constitutional talks with the Smith government in 1968 marked a retreat from the terms it was willing to accept in the 1966 talks, and disillusionment set in among African nationalists about depending on Britain to represent African interests.[25] Both parties decided to infiltrate smaller armed groups that could move about less conspicuously, and to give greater emphasis in practice to establishing links with the population inside Rhodesia.

Announcing a change in policy in October 1969 the acting president of ZAPU said: 'We will go to our own areas and infiltrate ourselves in the population and organize our masses.' The guerrillas were instructed to avoid battles with the Security Forces, but to recruit, train, and arm ZAPU underground in preparation for a rebellion.[26] In September 1972 a ZAPU document stated that the guarantee of a successful revolution depended on the 'revolutionary masses . . . without which our army would be like a fish out of water'. This Maoist tone from a party that received most of its military support from the Soviet Union was surprising.[27] As it happened, intense leadership conflicts paralysed ZAPU's war effort till 1976.[28] The party was compelled to reject FRELIMO's offer of a base in Tete in Mozambique in 1971 because of internal leadership conflicts and concern that its largely Ndebele army would have to operate in Shona-speaking areas. FRELIMO (Front for the Liberation of Mozambique) then made its offer of a base in Mozambique to ZANU, which was able to accept the offer since its party organization was in better shape than ZAPU's and, unlike ZAPU, had a predominantly Shona army. Access to base areas in Mozambique marked the beginning of a new phase in ZANU's strategy.[29]

ZANU spelled out its new emphasis on political education and political mobilization in the armed struggle also in 1972. It proclaimed the armed struggle to be primarily political, and asserted that the entire guerrilla zone of operations was a school to discuss, analyse, and find solutions to the felt needs of peasants and workers. The war of liberation was perceived as an educational project and part of a long-term goal of mental decolonization. ZANU reiterated the greater importance of the armed struggle inside Rhodesia over international diplomacy. Its military objective was to liquidate the South African and Rhodesian military units. It aimed to create national unity that would be based on a common struggle against white rule and a common purpose to build an independent, democratic, non-racial, Marxist–Leninist socialist state. Africans who resisted national unity and served the interests of white settlers directly or indirectly had to be converted. Provision was made for the private sector, which was expected to persist for a while. However, all land and natural resources would be state-owned. In its foreign policy goals, ZANU repeated its fight against imperialism and capitalism and its desire to unite with world progressive forces.[30] This study is concerned with peasant mobilization by ZANU guerrillas; hence its focus on ZANU's guerrilla war strategy and involvement in negotiations from about 1970 to the end of the war.

The military initiative shifted to ZANU between 1969 and 1972 as it took advantage of FRELIMO's offer of a base area in Mozambique and infiltrated guerrillas into north-eastern Rhodesia where they began to lay the political foundations for Maoist guerrilla warfare. That is, ZANU guerrillas made revolutionary political education of peasants central to their military strategy according to which they hoped to gradually take political control of the rural areas, surround the cities, and eventually take control of them too. In December 1972 ZANU mounted an offensive in the north-east with about 60 guerrillas inside the country and 250 in holding and training camps in Zambia and Tanzania. By the end of 1974, before the front line states interrupted ZANU's guerrilla war effort for over two years, Rhodesian intelligence sources estimated that there were 70–100 guerrillas in the north-east.[31]

From 1974 the nationalist parties had several opportunities to negotiate a constitutional settlement. Since ZANU had declared its support for a military victory and already had an army with some vested interest in fighting, the question of whether it should participate in negotiations was bound to be potentially divisive. The front line states had leverage over both ZANU's and ZAPU's leadership struggles over strategy because they provided both parties with sanctuaries, holding camps, and refugee facilities.[32] In December 1974, just when many ZANU political and military leaders believed their guerrilla strategy was beginning to pay dividends, the front line states pressured them to unite with other nationalist parties and negotiate with the Rhodesian government. Many in ZANU opposed negotiations as disruptive of the guerrilla strategy. They included military leaders and Acting President Herbert Chitepo, who had been appointed to lead the exiled movement after the detention of President Sithole and other central committee members in 1964. Robert Mugabe, who had just been released from detention along with other key nationalists as a result of South African pressure on Smith to seek a negotiated settlement, also opposed negotiations. While in detention, central committee members had removed Sithole from the presidency and replaced him with Mugabe in 1970. Their chief complaint against Sithole was that he had violated ZANU policy when he publicly denounced his commitment to violent change. Sithole favoured negotiations in 1974, and the front line states, eager to pursue the opportunity to negotiate a settlement, insisted that Sithole represent ZANU at unity talks. These talks led to the formation of the new umbrella group, the ANC, with Muzorewa the head of its constituent elements: FROLIZI, ZANU, ZAPU, and Muzorewa's ANC inside Rhodesia.

In March 1975 the front line states helped to take the steam out of ZANU's guerrilla war again. They chose to believe that Acting President Chitepo had been assassinated because of ethnic conflicts – a position promoted by Sithole (and later his brother Masipula Sithole) and endorsed by an International Commission of Inquiry appointed by Zambia. Eager to proceed with constitutional talks, the front line states ignored ZANU leaders who attributed tensions in ZANU leading to Chitepo's death to ideological differences and held the Rhodesian secret service responsible for assassinating Chitepo.[33] Zambia detained almost all the top political and military leaders of ZANU, Zambia and Tanzania closed their training camps, and Mozambique handed over ZANLA commanders to Zambia. These actions effectively halted the guerrilla war and constitutional talks between the nationalists represented by the new umbrella group, the ANC, and the Rhodesian government took place at Victoria Falls in 1975.

The front line states were ready to allow the nationalists to resume the guerrilla war after these talks failed. They expected ZANU forces and the smaller ZAPU army to combine to become the military wing of Muzorewa's ANC. But there was too much opposition from ZANU party and army leaders and rank and file, and when Muzorewa appointed Sithole in charge of the military hoping to placate ZANU, he further alienated it. When a more promising alternative, the Zimbabwe People's Army (ZIPA), planned to revive the war in November 1975, the front line states abandoned the ANC and denied Sithole and Muzorewa access to training camps. ZIPA united ZANU and ZAPU guerrilla forces under a military leadership (because of disappointment with the political leaders), and a Marxist–Leninist banner. It opposed negotiations and revived the guerrilla war in January 1976 after more than a two-year break. Its hopes of a united army were short-lived after ZANU and ZAPU guerrillas clashed inside Rhodesia and in camps in Mozambique. Within months, ZAPU guerrillas returned to Zambia and ZIPA was composed exclusively of ZANU guerrillas. Just as the front line states had abandoned the ANC and allowed the rise of ZIPA, in 1976–7 they abetted the re-emergence of ZANU's political leaders and the demise of ZIPA. Again, the front line states pressed ZANU to participate in constitutional talks that had reopened following a visit by Kissinger to southern Africa in September 1976. They insisted that ZANU and ZAPU present a united front at talks; hence the birth of the uneasy alliance, the Patriotic Front. As a quid pro quo, ZANU leaders detained in Zambia since March 1975 were released.

Guerrilla strategy and Patriotic Front diplomacy, aided by the front line states, aimed at discrediting the African signatories to the 'internal

91

settlement' and the 1979 elections. They pointed out that African control of parliament was meaningless because parliament had lost its former powers to the security sector during the war, and the new constitution guaranteed white control of the army, police, courts, and civil service.[34] The guerrillas had to ensure a low electoral turnout to demonstrate that the new constitution was unacceptable and therefore should be denied international recognition. For its part, the government needed free and fair elections and a high electoral turnout to obtain international recognition and the lifting of economic sanctions. The government hoped that the new constitution, calls for a ceasefire, and an amnesty for guerrillas who surrendered would undercut the exiled movements.[35] As already noted, Bishop Muzorewa became the first African Prime Minister to be elected by universal African suffrage. Even though an estimated 64 per cent of the electorate voted, and a Conservative Party observer had reported the elections to be free and fair, and the constitution conformed with the negotiating principles Britain had itself laid out in 1964, Britain did not recognize his government and nor did other countries except South Africa. Ultimately, Muzorewa's UANC, Smith's Rhodesia Front, and the Patriotic Front negotiated a constitutional settlement at Lancaster House in December 1979, and the war ended. Ironically, the exiled movements accepted reserved parliamentary seats for whites and protection of private property although these were among the reasons they had so bitterly opposed the 1979 constitution that grew out of the 'internal settlement'.

The 'internal settlement' marked a massive intensification of the war by the government and the guerrillas. In mid 1977, before the talks, ZANU had 3,000 guerrillas in the country, and ZAPU only 100–200. Once talks for the 'internal settlement' began, the number of guerrillas inside the country grew rapidly. In the 1977/8 rainy season, almost the entire country was affected and the guerrillas inside the country reached about 9,000, 85 per cent of whom belonged to ZANU. At the ceasefire in December 1979, there were an estimated 20,000 ZANU guerrillas and 8,000 ZAPU guerrillas.[36] ZANU guerrilla recruits grew so rapidly that in 1977 the party appealed on Radio Mozambique to aspirant guerrillas to remain inside Rhodesia because it was unable to supply those in camps with adequate food or training.[37] Another indicator of the intensification of the war after 'internal settlement' talks began is the rise in the official death rates of civilians, guerrillas, and Security Forces. Between December 1972 and the beginning of 1979, 310 white civilians, 3,845 black civilians, 760 Security Force personnel and over 6,000 guerrilla personnel were killed. Of these deaths, 60 per cent of white civilians, 45 per cent of black civilians, 37 per cent of Security Forces, and just under 50 per cent of guerrillas were killed in 1978 alone.[38] Of the total deaths in the war, 33 per cent – apparently excluding those killed outside Rhodesia – occurred in 1979 alone.[39]

ZANU always insisted on the primacy of guerrilla war over negotiations to achieve its goal of a socialist country under African rule. Some scholars and ZIPA leaders have questioned the commitment of ZANU's political leaders – named the 'old guard' for their longstanding involvement in the nationalist movement – to socialist change and military victory. They allege that these 'petty bourgeois' politicians, raised in an era of constitutional politics, saw the guerrilla war as facilitating constitutional negotiations for national independence. Their lust for power made them susceptible to divisive factional disputes and ethnic politics. This 'old guard' triumphed over younger men in ZIPA who became involved in nationalist politics later in the nationalist struggle. The latter group had experience of armed struggle and single-mindedly pursued it as the only route to a socialist Zimbabwe. They strove to unite the military forces of ZANU and ZAPU under military Marxist–Leninist leadership to prevent the bickering politicians, bent on a negotiated independence settlement, from disrupting the war effort (see chapter 6).

Political appeals and their limitations

David Lan's *Guns and Rain* notes that people were caught between two armed forces.[40] But he never analyzes its implications for guerrilla appeals. Lan focuses on guerrilla violence against 'sell-outs', which he regards as 'perhaps the most controversial of the techniques used by the guerrillas to gain support'.[41] He considers government collaborators and witches as 'sell-outs' whose deaths enhanced guerrilla legitimacy. But he neglects guerrilla coercion against people who simply failed to comply with guerrilla instructions. They are too important a group to be omitted. Lan's neglect of guerrilla coercion against this group is related to his failure to take into account in his analysis the effects of having to mobilize when state power was largely intact. This circumstance made coercive appeals to comply with guerrilla commands frequent (see chapter 4).

Ranger's *Peasant Consciousness and Guerrilla War in Zimbabwe* remarks that no area was completely under guerrilla control and that therefore there was no opportunity to reorganize production or marketing, or set up a regular school system.[42] Ranger does not explicitly link this to the guerrillas' inability to offer utilitarian appeals, and in particular material benefits. Elsewhere Ranger refers to the 'fearsome military power' of the Rhodesian Security Forces, but again does not discuss how this might have affected guerrilla appeals.[43] Nowhere in this volume does he explicitly discuss guerrillas' coercive appeals although he mentions that especially in the late 1970s peasants sometimes perceived the guerrillas 'to be acting arbitrarily and without respect for the moral economy of the war'.[44] However, in an article 'Bandits and Guerrillas: The Case of Zimbabwe', Ranger confronts directly the issue of guerrilla violence towards peasants during the war. It only became a problem in 1978 and 1979, when the guerrillas came under 'intense pressures' and at the same time were receiving less training than before.[45] Guerrilla violence is never linked to the problems of mobilizing support in the context of a state whose repressive power has increased. Instead, it is treated as merely a problem of inadequate training.

David Caute's *Under the Skin* gives unusual prominence to coercive appeals by guerrillas and links them to guerrilla indiscipline that he maintains was especially low in 1978 and 1979.[46] Caute's study is also distinctive for its sensitivity to the absence of utilitarian appeals by guerrillas. He dwells on the material costs of the war to rural Africans – the food, money, and clothing that they had to provide for the guerrillas – and the costs to African students and teachers of the closing of schools by guerrillas.[47] But Caute does not link the prominence of coercive appeals, the absence of utilitarian appeals, and the costly normative appeals to close schools to state power in a settler colony.

Others also discuss guerrilla abuses and attribute it to the lack of guerrilla training, even though they disagree on when it was a problem. One study emphasizes the decline in ZANU's capacity to train and equip its rapidly growing guerrilla recruits between 1972 and 1976.[48] Another comments on the lack of basic training given to the guerrillas infiltrated around the time of a constitutional conference in 1976 because the guerrilla leaders desired to put maximum pressure on the Smith government and thereby increase their negotiating power at the conference.[49] As noted, Ranger points to the lack of training of guerrillas infiltrated in 1978 and 1979 and Caute also identifies 1978 and 1979 as years in which guerrilla indiscipline increased. Linden's study of church relations with the state during the war, published in 1979 before its most intense year, identifies a serious decline in the discipline of the liberation armies in the 1977/8 rainy season, when 'acts of gratuitous and random terror became more common.'[50] Bandits owing allegiance to no-one terrorised the rural population.'[50] Linden attributes some of this guerrilla violence to widespread 'social disruption that created a breakdown of normal moral codes' and brief training periods.[51] In short, there never was a time in the 1970s when guerrilla abuses could not be attributed to inadequate guerrilla training. Presumably guerrilla training can produce a more disciplined army, but the emphasis on training in exile detracts from the structural problem facing the guerrillas: how could they mobilize civilians in the context of a state with an increasing repressive capacity? The terminology of guerrilla abuse is appropriate from the peasants' perspective, but coercive appeals to win compliance might better convey the guerrilla perspective.

An article that seeks to explain ZANU's electoral success in the independence elections in 1980 does discuss the strength of state apparatuses and its effect on guerrilla efforts to organize and mobilize rural civilians. 'In some areas, such as the liberated zones of certain TTLs [Tribal Trust Lands], there was no police presence whatsoever and meetings could be held openly, whilst in the other area [sic] far greater caution was required.'[52] The kinds of activities that civilian committees established by the guerrillas engaged in 'probably varied depending on how effectively the Rhodesian state apparatuses had been excluded'.[53] Yet when the article discusses why the guerrilla armies, despite their claims to the contrary, largely failed to establish liberated zones, it omits to highlight colonial state power. FRELIMO, an African guerrilla movement that won independence in Mozambique, established liberated zones or 'whole regions capable of generating and maintaining their own infrastructure and of isolating areas from any contact with a colonial regime, which to all intents and purposes was some hundreds of miles away'.[54] In contrast, ZANU was faced with a heritage of racial land patterns that made it possible to create only 'semi-liberated' areas in most Tribal Trust Lands. 'Ingenuity and a somewhat different approach was required on the part of ZANU, faced as it was with this fragmented pattern of African reserves, interspaced with white areas through which passed the major arteries.' These difficulties make sense as obstructions to mobilization if one links them to the continued power of the state. If the state were unable to protect European areas, racial land divisions would lose their significance. If the settler communications infrastructure were not maintained, sometimes improved, and used by expanding government forces, its existence would be of little consequence for mobilization. If the settlers did not receive adequate state protection, they would leave their land (as some did) and not hinder mobilization. Moreover, the article never explicitly discusses guerrilla coercion, even when informants suggest its importance.[55] So the need to explain guerrilla coercion never arises. Ibbo Mandaza also recognizes that the guerrilla movements confronted a still powerful state and reminds his readers that the war was not won on the battlefield but ended as a result of the Lancaster House constitutional settlement. But he does not spell out the implications of a strong state for guerrilla appeals to mobilize support.[56]

The literature on ZANU's war of independence seldom, if ever, links the type of appeals the guerrillas used to the power of the state. Nor does it address the continuity of appeals in the guerrilla war and the earlier nationalist period, and its links to the repressive capacity of the state. The rest of the chapter highlights similarities between earlier nationalist party appeals and those of ZANU guerrillas and attributes their shared weaknesses to the increasing repressive capacity of the state.

Normative appeals

The primary normative appeal used by the earlier nationalist parties and ZANLA guerrillas was African cultural nationalism. Socialist appeals were prominent in official ZANU pronouncements, but, with a few notable exceptions, scholars and journalists downplay their importance in the guerrilla repertoire.[57] Cliffe and Stoneman write: 'There was virtually no Marxist influence in the formation of the Zimbabwe national movement.

Like the movements in English-speaking Africa it was set in the African nationalist mould.' From the early 1970s:

> Political-education documents and practices . . . were clearly influenced by Marxian approaches, including ideas about 'a just war', 'national liberation', 'the role of cadres', culled in part from Chinese formulations. But rather abstract discussions of this sort were supplemented, though not thoroughly integrated, with some Zimbabwean historiography that pointed to racial oppression and social injustice, but not in terms that were analytically different from nationalist perspectives based on essentially liberal and ethical critiques of settler colonialism. Thus there was only a partial working out of the implications of a Marxist approach for the strategy of struggle in the specific context of Zimbabwe, in terms of which class forces could be mobilized for which demands and for what kind of post-independence transformation – even in the thinking of those (by no means a majority) influenced by such thinking. The process did go a little further, at least in the sense of an organized group which debated and articulated such notions if not their further elaboration, with the creation of ZIPA.[58]

Ibbo Mandaza argues that the armed struggle did not contain within it even the idea of a socialist revolution. 'National independence was the central goal.'[59] With Marxism such a tenuous strand among the movement's leaders, it is not surprising that peasants and many guerrillas reported the absence or insignificance of socialist appeals.[60]

The NDP tried to build a spiritual and cultural base for African nationalism and to denounce European culture. This became an important goal for the NDP's successors in the 1960s, and nationalist youth played an especially prominent role in its promotion.

> The party encouraged its supporters to value those things which were African – customs, names, music, dress, religion and food and much else. Many nationalists changed their English-style names to African ones . . . In religion young Africans increasingly rejected the view encouraged among their elders by missionaries that worshipping ancestral spirits or gods of idols was heathen superstition . . . At meetings, prayers are said to Chaminuka [a spirit medium who played a heroic role in the 1896–7 rebellion], but all in the name of God who is accepted as the Almighty Father over the Mashona prophet.[61]

Side by side with the promotion of ancestor worship and prayers to spirit mediums, rank and file nationalist youth denounced Christianity as the white man's religion and encouraged Africans to stop going to church. Shamuyarira, a leading African nationalist, overheard the following conversation between young people in the rural areas. 'God is for us all, but this Jesus is for the Europeans', said a girl to her mother. 'In actual fact', elaborated a young man, 'Jesus is like a big Colonial Secretary for the Missionaries. They use his preachings to blind us, while Europeans take our land and our heritage.'[62] According to a dissertation by a Methodist missionary based on data collected in Makoni district, political party members were more likely to approve of ancestral worship and consulting *ngangas* ('traditional' doctors) than non-party members.[63] Other aspects of European culture were rejected too. Youth groups directed their anger at Africans who used perfume, wore short skirts, straightened their hair and in other ways participated in the symbols of European cultural domination. At political meetings in the towns, 'Youth Leaguers ordered attendants to remove their shoes, ties and jackets, as one of the first signs in rejecting European civilization. Water served in traditional water-pots replaced Coca-Cola kiosks.'[64]

The City Youth League and the SRANC introduced appeals to Africans to withdraw from white political institutions and dared slander top white politicians and district commissioners. In the context of the times, debasing district or native commissioners (NCs) was especially important. 'Nobody could have made any headway in organizing rural Africans or even bringing a sense of human dignity until the NC's artificial position of Lord-and-Master had been destroyed. The NC was necessarily the first target in a wider programme to show that Europeans were not superior beings.'[65]

The SRANC appealed to Africans to engage in civil disobedience and defy racially discriminatory legislation, and these were continued and intensified by its successors. The police statement by Headman Nyamatsa-huni in Charewa chiefdom in Mutoko Tribal Trust Land suggests the popularity of appeals to disobey the Native Land Husbandry Act that made it a criminal offence to use arable land for grazing.[66]

> We want to plough in the grazing area, but our kraalheads are chasing us and they stop us. They are bad people. They are worrying us. We must plough the grazing area . . . There are other people who go to demonstrators and ask them to teach them. They are bad people. They should be assaulted or killed.
>
> At our places, kraalheads stop us from ploughing the grazing area or cutting poles. They are stopping us from doing what we want. Such kraalheads must go; they must be changed and new ones appointed.
>
> You people, you have said you want to plough in the grazing area. You have been told you are not allowed to. You can be arrested for it. People have already been arrested for this. You must be strong. Do not give up and do not fear. You may be arrested. If you are arrested, don't give up; you must still keep ploughing.

People were also called on to defy compulsory livestock dipping and dip fees because they did not apply to Europeans. These appeals were particularly strident and successful in June 1964 when some 7,500 cattle owners in Mutoko Tribal Trust Land refused to dip.[67]

The guerrillas' cultural nationalist appeals were more militant but remarkably similar to those of earlier nationalist parties. At political meetings with villagers, called *moraris* in Mutoko, ZANLA guerrillas promised that African grievances would be rectified in a liberated Zimbabwe. There would be employment for all, equal pay for equal work, more and improved free public services – schools, clinics, piped water, modern toilets – and dignity for Africans. Africans would inherit whites' farms, houses, cars, and jobs. The following recollections of guerrilla promises are drawn chiefly from the African rural elite.

> Whites would not be in offices – all jobs would be Africanized.

> Comrades told us: 'parents, you can't live like this in the mountains. You must go and live in the valleys on the white farms'.

> European houses would be taken by blacks.

> Down with these whites. Down with Smith. Whites have everything: cars, enough to eat, nice houses. You have nothing. After independence, you can have all they have too.

> Comrades said they wanted a true independence with no segregation in bars, hotels, buses. All such injustices were to be removed. The chief enemy was the white man. If he were driven off the land, there'd be enough land for everyone and people could plough and live where they liked. They would give examples of people with sandy soil, and identify a white farm where some people had been working with lots of good land.

> They'd discuss salary scales and tell of how African teachers and European teachers, equally qualified, were paid differently. They'd give specific examples of African teachers who'd left teaching because of this injustice. This aroused unity in the people. They were aware of these injustices before, but they had not dared say anything . . . Comrades would say: 'We want people to be judged fairly and live in peace. We don't want people to be called "kaffir" or "boy" when an old African man is being addressed.'

Guerrillas continued to assert, as nationalist parties from the time of the NDP had, that Africans were competent to rule.

Ordinary rural people, supporting the view of a leading nationalist that even the most dynamic speeches are quickly forgotten by the uneducated,[68] often claimed that all that they remembered of political education at the *moraris* were the *chimurenga* (liberation) songs and the guerrilla slogans. Slogans such as these were commonly remembered.

Forward with Unity	*Pamberi ne Kubatana*
Forward with Bravery	*Pamberi ne Kushinga*
Forward with the War	*Pamberi ne Hondo*
Forward with ZANU	*Pamberi ne Zanu*

Many of the *chimurenga* songs appealed to the spiritual and cultural base of African nationalism. The following song, for example, enjoins village heads to reform their corrupt ways and to remember Nehanda, an ancestor who played a leading role in the 1896–7 rebellion.

> Kraalheads, the way you live with the society, as if you have got hatred and as if you are handicapped and you are a fool. See kraalhead, see kraalhead, it is now a new era. If I think of *Mbuya* [grandmother] Nehanda, I end up joining the struggle. It is now a new era.

Chimurenga songs were brought into the rural areas by the guerrillas, and therefore cannot be regarded as a source for understanding peasant culture.[69]

To persuade people of the power of the ancestors and their commitment to liberation, guerrillas told people that they were 'the bones of the dead ancestors that have now risen and are fighting'. They encouraged locals to pray to the spirits for protection against the hazards of living through the war. This is described by a former United Methodist churchgoer who played an active role in providing logistical support to the guerrillas.

> They taught me to use bush roads and pray to the spirits. I'd always been a churchgoer. They taught me how to use snuff. They told me to go to a *munondo* tree, take off my shoes, pick the leaves and place them next to the tree trunk and place snuff on leaves as an offering to the spirits to protect me. They gave me the snuff. If after praying, the *chipungu* [bateleur eagle] came and flew above me, it would indicate that I should not carry on.[70] If the bird came and flew on, I should follow that direction and it'd be safe. If the bird didn't come, it would mean there was nothing bad. We knew of *chipungu* from childhood. Even if the *chipungu* came and flew above us at a base, we'd all flee. And then soldiers always came.

By example, too, the guerrillas promoted ancestor worship. They commenced *moraris* with an invitation to village heads or elders to offer prayers to their ancestral spirits. The guerrillas themselves were instructed by spirit mediums how to interpret the signs displayed by animals, such as the *chipungu*. For these protective techniques to work, the guerrillas were not allowed sex on duty, physical contact with menstruating women, or food cooked by them. Nor could the guerrillas kill wild animals in the bush. They had dietary restrictions too: no okra, beans, groundnuts (only a certain type of groundnut, *nyimo*, according to my informants), and only certain parts of animals. Heads, limbs, intestines, lungs, hearts, and anything in the abdominal cavity were prohibited.[71] If the guerrillas broke any of these rules, many of them adhered to by mediums themselves, the spirits could punish them. When relating awful events during the war, rural people often blamed them on guerrillas disobeying the mediums' commands.

Sometimes the spirits were invoked to arbitrate in cases where the guerrillas were not sure if alleged informers were guilty. By calling on the spirits, the guerrillas underlined their own power and also absolved themselves of responsibility for killing innocent people. A member of the Vapostori Church, also known as the Apostolic Church, described how

> a very mysterious thing happened after a contact at Shena [during which helicopters bombed a guerrilla base]. The comrades had the four alleged sell-outs. They checked the information. They prayed to the spirits and said that if there were an innocent one among them, that person would not be killed by the gunshot. When they fired, the one girl survived. She was innocent. Thereafter, the comrades would always pray to the spirits and say that if a person were innocent, they'd survive the gunshot.

The guerrillas also tried to promote indigenous beliefs by persuading African clergy and lay people to abandon Christianity, the religion of their alien conquerors.[72] The following comments by an African Catholic father, an African United Methodist minister, and a white Catholic missionary respectively attest to the anti-Christian propaganda in Mutoko.

> Missionaries hold a bible and sweets in front, but a gun behind their backs. This deception has been going on all our history. People were deprived of their own religion, and government made use of missionaries. Missionaries told people that consulting *ngangas* [traditional healers] and mediums was sinful, and they replaced ancestral worship with prayer, incense, and mass. The religion of the whites, missionaries told them, was better than their own. Comrades would sometimes say: 'Who's that bloke on the crucifixion?' I'd say: 'An historical figure'. They'd say: 'Oh, these whites again. Do you pray to him?'

> The church is a white man's rule. It made us to be quiet. The white man came with the gun and then the bible.

> Guerrillas didn't want people to go to church. They were anti-white and they said Christ was a European. They aimed to alienate the people from anything white. They encouraged people to worship their ancestral spirits.

ZANLA guerrillas sometimes appealed to their shared linguistic, ethnic, or national background with rural people. To arouse people's sympathy they told of how they were suffering to fight for freedom for 'the sons and daughters of Zimbabwe'. Appealing to parental responsibility, they reminded them: 'we are your children'. This was especially moving to parents whose children had joined the guerrillas and who knew that their children's survival depended on the support of their counterparts in a foreign district. ZANLA guerrillas who operated in Ndebele-speaking areas tried to promote the Shona language and culture. A local teacher reported that he would have voted for ZANU, renamed ZANU-PF in the independence elections, but its guerrillas 'did not treat us in a good way. They tried to compel us to speak Shona. They were ruthless on those who asked why. All the slogans and songs were in Shona and they were not be translated [sic] into Sindebele. Every thing tended to 'change' us to Shona.'[73]

In the spirit of promoting unity among peasants, the guerrillas tried to eliminate the sources of marital disharmony: men's violence towards their wives, their excessive drinking, and extra-marital affairs.[74] The implication of these guerrilla appeals was that people were to behave in a moral and socially responsible way.[75] 'There were no divorces during the war', according to a female teacher. 'It was not allowed . . . What would happen to the children?' A man who had been a party chairman during the war remembered a 'comrade' saying: 'You must live in peace and unity. We want no quarrelling. Husbands should not beat their wives. They must live well with their wives.' A primary school headmaster joked about how the 'comrades' would ask women: 'How are you living with your husbands?' and they would answer, 'they drink too much, take other women, waste money'. He proceeded to relate how the guerrillas 'encouraged recently divorced couples to unite and told men not to take other women. Comrades could call men responsible for illegitimate children and beat them and try to persuade them to take responsibility for the child.'

Even though the guerrillas called on people to unite, like ZAPU/PCC and ZANU in the 1960s, they actively promoted inter-party conflict. Their slogans identified not only Smith but also the other nationalist parties as the enemy.

Down with Smith	*Pasi ne Smith*
Down with Muzorewa	*Pasi ne Muzorewa*
Down with Nkomo (or euphemistically)	*Pasi ne Nkomo*
Down with fat stomachs	*Pasi ne vanematumbu*
Down with sell-outs	*Pasi ne vatengesa*
Down with witches	*Pasi ne varoyi*
Down with troublesome people	*Pasi ne nhunzvatunza*
Down with disobedient people	*Pasi ne nharadada*

Coercive and violent appeals

Some use a concept of coercion that includes the withholding of benefits and rewards.[76] Others, such as Michael Bayles, define coercion more parsimoniously. He defines 'dispositional coercion' as a threat by one person to another (victim) with a sanction if the latter fails to act as requested. Bayles draws attention to the voluntary component in this type of coercion – a person always has a choice to do as told, or do something else and receive a sanction. But, in the absence of a threat, the person would have chosen differently. Sanctions imposed for non-compliance must entail harm and deprivation. The interpersonal relations that are central to coercion distinguish it from force, compulsion, constraint, and restraint that are the result of impersonal circumstances. What distinguishes coercion from bribery, warnings, advice, and some other forms of exercising power over another is that the agent of coercion desires to bring about certain behaviour from the victim, and will impose sanctions if it is not forthcoming.[77] It should be added that coercion directed at an individual can affect indirectly, as often intended, the behaviour of a wider audience. The concept of coercion used in this study is even narrower than Bayles' concept and includes only physical threats and attacks on persons and property.

My sources on coercion call for comment. For the early period, I often rely on the government record, including police statements that are notoriously unreliable sources as they may have been coerced. By doing so, I lay myself open to a charge of accepting government propaganda of party nationalists and guerrillas intimidating otherwise contented Africans. However, one does not have to subscribe to government propaganda to accept that there was coercion in the era of nationalist party politics. ZANU itself called for an end to intimidation of other Africans in 1964. For coercion in the guerrilla war period, I have used government records and interviews with white farmers, African farm-workers, and the African elite in the white government. Again, it may be alleged that two of these sources – white farmers and the African rural elite in government – have a pro-government bias. However, farm-workers and their employers told similar stories, and many incidents of guerrilla coercion could be cross-checked. Local people's accounts confirmed government records that chiefs and headmen had been killed by guerrillas. The rural African elite employed by the government kept careful tabs on the fate of their colleagues, and their accounts also converge. Moreover, guerrillas would probably agree that the categories of people identified below were 'enemies' who deserved their fate.

From the time of the NDP until the banning of ZANU and ZAPU in 1964, petrol bombing residential, business, and government property was a common tactic of seeking compliance with nationalist demands. Other Africans rather than Europeans were identified as targets. They included informers and 'moderate' Africans who did not show the requisite nationalist enthusiasm or who belonged to the multiracial United Federal Party or the liberal Centre Action Party. Africans who helped to maintain settler domination by working for European churches or the government were also targeted: chiefs, teachers, agricultural demonstrators, police, and church staff.[78] How much of this was party policy is a thorny question. Much of the coercion against other Africans in 1961–2 and 1963–4 was by youths, and Van Velsen believes it was 'an expression of the large number of unemployed and landless . . .' rather than the result of an intensified policy of confrontation.[79] While it is debated whether coercion against other Africans was party policy, there is no doubt that ZANU, the NDP, and ZAPU/PCC pursued policies of sabotaging government property.

In October 1961 Headman Charewa's hut was burned while he was in it, and he subsequently died of severe burns. From his hospital bed where he lay dying, he blamed nationalists for the attempt on his life. He complained of their challenge to 'tribal elders' and related how they had bypassed his authority by sending a delegation that included a village head and the main NDP organizer in Charewa to Chieftainess Charewa to complain about the Land Husbandry Act.[80] Hut burning, according to Murphree, 'has been a technique of political coercion in common use in Budjga, since it has disastrous consequences for the victim, requires no special equipment and can be carried out with little fear of detection'.[81] Many members of the Vapostori Church had their huts burned for refusing on religious grounds to participate in politics, even though they were known not to support the government, itself suspicious of them.[82]

The police report on political activities in Mutoko between March and June 1964 cited forty-six cases of intimidation.[83] A person on trial for throwing stones into a dip tank claimed intimidation. 'The kraalhead told us to go to the dip tank. We were told we'd be assaulted if we didn't throw stones and sticks into it.'[84] Chief Chimoyo, in his police statement, also spoke of intimidation.

> Five youths arrived at my house; then some girls came also. Then many other people came. They said to me: 'Let's go to the dip tank.' We went there and they told me to throw a stone into the dip. I threw a stone in and other people also did; then they told me to leave. The dip was then full. I had been the first to throw in a stone. Then they took me back to my kraal. There they gave me a fur hat and made me shout 'ZAPU' three times and they told me I was now a member of ZAPU.[85]

The same report listed sixty-eight cases of arson and seventy-one incidents of malicious intent to government property. About 200 to 300 people participated in each of thirteen attacks on dip tanks in Mutoko Tribal Trust Land.

Also, church members were frequently intimidated not to attend services. According to Murphree,

> Political rallies have been scheduled on Sundays at service times, earning the disapproval of the ministers and priests. The church leaders have advised their members to 'attend the political rallies, but only after you have rendered your first allegiance to God by attending church', a compromise unacceptable to many of the politicians. Irresponsible members of the youth wing of the nationalist parties have on occasion appeared outside the homes of church members at night demanding that the daughters of the house be sent out 'to attend a youth rally', when what in fact is intended is a dance which the Christians consider inappropriate for their youth.[86]

Violence between nationalist parties that competed for dominance first manifested itself when some NDP members, disillusioned with their leaders for allegedly abandoning party principles at the constitutional conference in 1961, broke away and formed two rival parties. But they were 'castigated, beaten up and called traitors' by NDP loyalists and the parties did not survive.[87] When the united nationalist movement split after 1963 into ZANU and ZAPU/PCC and party rivalries began, those suspected of loyalties to the other party were subjected to attacks on their homes and persons. ZAPU rank and file members remained committed to their organization, and in Mutoko, as in the rest of the country, ZANU found it difficult to build up a mass base.[88] Teachers in Mutoko who had joined ZANU in 1964, when interviewed in 1981–2, recalled how ZAPU members would visit the homes of suspected ZANU members and beat them. They could not remember ZANU holding a single mass meeting. During the Pearce Commission's visit to Rhodesia, although the ANC rejected violence, there were incidents of intimidation against Africans who were thought to be willing to support the proposed constitution on which the Rhodesian and British governments had agreed.[89]

During the guerrilla war, coercion was more widely used, threats were more likely to be enforced, and the categories of people who were potential targets expanded. All Africans directly or indirectly involved in European institutions might become victims of guerrilla coercion if they failed to respond to non-violent appeals to cooperate with the guerrillas. To the old list of targets – church leaders, chiefs and headmen, government agricultural advisors, Africans who belonged to other parties, informers – were added: farm-workers on white commercial farms, better-off farmers who engaged in marketing surpluses, elected or nominated councillors and appointed council staff, teachers, and all African government employees. White farmers, white missionaries, and district government officials, African and white, became listed too. In chapter 4, I argue that anyone was liable to become a victim of guerrilla coercion if they dared disobey guerrilla commands.

The guerrillas killed one of three chiefs and six of fifteen headmen in Mutoko district, and were responsible for the suicide of another headman and the escape to Harare of still another.[90] One night in May 1978 guerrillas murdered Acting Chief Chimoyo and carried off all his regalia and burnt them.[91] The district commissioner remarked that the acting chief had done 'a good job under difficult conditions at that time [when he was appointed in July 1966], when African nationalists were active in this area'. He added that he had 'motivated his people to build a number of small dams and was responsible for the establishment of an African council'. The district commissioner's satisfaction with the chief's performance may be enough to explain why the guerrillas killed him.[92] Also in Chimoyo chiefdom, two of the three headmen and a spirit medium were killed. Headman Mujare, the successor to the Chimoyo chieftainship, was murdered by guerrillas at his home on the night of 5 September 1976. According to the district commissioner, 'a group of terrorists called him out of his hut and accused him of co-operating with Government in the protected village programme. They then beat him on the legs with poles and shot him three times. The kraal dwellers also were made to watch the incident, were then ordered to disperse and were given the usual orders about reporting, etc.' The district commissioner goes on to acknowledge that what may have contributed to Headman Mujare's murder was that he was 'most co-operative and was the possible successor to the Chimoyo chieftainship'.[93]

Headman Kadiki of Charewa chiefdom was travelling on a bus on 30 July 1976 when it was stopped and robbed by guerrillas. He insisted 'that the matter be reported to the Police post at Charewa despite terrorist instruction to the contrary'. When the guerrillas learned this, they went to his house the next day and abducted him.[94] Until April 1980 rumours circulated about the headman's fate, but then his body was identified on a hill near his home.[95]

Government files contain warning signals of Acting Headman Makochera's pending death. The district commissioner invited village heads and elders to attend a meeting at his office in August 1977 to discuss the appointment of a substantive headman for Makochera ward in Mutoko chiefdom. In the words of a government researcher, Acting Headman Makochera was 'the only one brave enough to come to the office'.[96] Three months later *youth* murdered him when he was outside the area of his jurisdiction. Not until early 1980 was his body discovered.[97] Two other headmen from Mutoko chiefdom were murdered. Headman Kawere supported the government's villagization programme in his area. *Youth* abducted him from his home and took him to Makochera area, where they murdered him the following day. In Dehwe, the guerrillas became embroiled in a longstanding feud over the legitimacy of the incumbent headman. Supporters of his rival claimed that years ago the district administration had favoured the incumbent in defiance of customary rules of succession. Labelled a traitor by the opposing faction, the headman was murdered by the guerrillas.[98]

Those chiefs, headmen, and village heads who survived severed their links to the district administration: they stopped working for district administration and no longer went to the district commissioner's office to collect their monthly allowances. None of the families eligible for succession made any claim to the positions of the deceased rulers. Customary rules of succession require that deceased rulers be buried and appropriate rituals be carried out before new appointments can be made. Since the guerrillas refused to allow their victims the customary burial rituals, no appointment could be sanctioned. Consequently, murdered traditional leaders were not replaced during the war. The one exception was Acting Chief Chimoyo who was succeeded by the government's preferred candidate, Headman Mujare, who obtained permission from the tribal spirit to accept even though the customary burial rites had not been performed.[99]

Guerrilla coercion helped to bring about the swift collapse of the council system. As early as July 1977, a memo from the Ministry of Internal Affairs acknowledged that 'councils in the affected areas are in a difficult situation, with many being on the point of collapse'. It added: 'beerhalls and offices have been robbed, vehicles and buildings burned, staff intimidated, councillors threatened and in some cases murdered'.[100] The three councils in each of the chiefdoms in Mutoko Tribal Trust Land stopped functioning. Councillors and staff resigned or failed to attend meetings so that the legal quorum could not be met. On 1 March 1977 Charewa council was hit by the resignations of its secretary, who claimed to have found better employment, and its driver and clerk. The coincidence and suddenness of these three staff resignations led the district commissioner to infer guerrilla intimidation.[101] District records also note the resignations of the Chimoyo council secretary during the war.[102]

Guerrilla activity forced the African Development Fund staff to operate from 'protected villages' or 'protected sub-offices' – the base from which some 'protected villages' were commanded. Although district staff increased by nearly three times between 1972 and 1977, most of the expansion was in paramilitary personnel. District administrative staff declined during the war as trained staff resigned or became war casualties, and 'generally speaking, . . . district stations were better off fifteen to twenty years ago'. In November 1977 the Ministry of Internal Affairs was short of some twenty-three assistant district commissioners and thirty-two district officers. Many district stations were virtually in a state of siege, and administrators were unable to move outside a restricted radius of the station.[103] About 1,031 ministry personnel were wounded and 395 killed by guerrilla activities, most of them Africans.[104]

Specific information on government staff in Mutoko is scanty, but some information on the experience of agricultural extension officers was obtained through interviews. The guerrillas were suspicious of these Africans because they were government employees, and Tribal Trust Land villagers had a long combative history with them because they had implemented some of the most hated government policies: destocking, land allocation under the Land Husbandry Act, and conservation measures. Guerrillas murdered two extension assistants in about August 1976 for participating in the establishment of a 'protected village', whereupon the district commissioner ordered the remaining seventeen officials to withdraw to Mutoko centre and confine themselves to working within a six kilometre radius of it. Still feeling exposed, eleven of the seventeen who lived outside the district returned to their homes.[105] In sharp contrast, the extension assistants working in the Purchase Area and employed by the Department of Agriculture that was responsible for white commercial farming had good relationships with the farmers. When they left the Purchase Area, they did so usually because of harassment from government forces.

Better-off farmers were subjected to careful guerrilla scrutiny for two reasons: they often marketed produce through official channels, and they also cooperated with extension agents. Indeed a master farmer's certificate was issued to confirm that farmers had cooperated with government agricultural staff and met government farming standards. An agricultural extension assistant who worked in Mutoko Tribal Trust Land noted that 'those master farmers who survived had to drop their standards if they didn't want to be killed. Master farmers were taken as associates of the government. They were adhering to government orders.'

Guerrilla coercion was used to compel Africans to desist from using government services. A villager who owned cattle and valued the dip facilities encountered problems when he preferred not to participate in destroying the dip tank.

> I resisted. I didn't want to destroy the dip. The comrades demonstrated how we should destroy the dip. They threw huge stones into the dip. Then we had to do this. Most of us didn't want to . . . This was our dip and we knew we should dip our cattle to keep them healthy. When I resisted, the comrades beat me very badly.

White farmers and their property were victims of guerrilla violence.[106] In Mutoko Intensive Conservation Area, guerrillas' coercive appeals directed at white farmers may be inferred from their dwindling numbers. In September 1975 there were 73 white farm owners/occupiers, 77 in 1976, 75 in 1977, 66 in 1978, and 47 in 1979.[107] As part of their strategy to pressure white farmers to leave their land, the guerrillas tried to persuade their farm-workers to leave. To get farm-workers off the land, they set alight their huts in the labour compounds and sometimes shot resisters. Typical of the experience of farm-workers is the account given by a 'boss-boy' – an African with some authority over other workers.

> The boys came and burned the compound one night. I think it happened in 1979. I couldn't tell how many boys were there because it was night. But they were fierce. Nobody was hurt. We were all told that we shouldn't work for Europeans, that we weren't paid enough. We should leave the farm and go to the Purchase Area. Comrades were pushing people from their huts and burning them at the same time. Some of our luggage was burned. After the burnings that night, we all left our compounds.

Several white farmers in Mutoko told of how guerrillas had shot their workers in their compounds. In one case, thirty workers had been killed; in another the guerrillas lined up and shot five of forty workers. Such massacres had a demonstration effect, according to a white farmer, and 'farm-workers would just disappear off other farms out of fear. Workers got the message that they weren't wanted to be working on European farms.'

Although self-employed, storekeepers were common guerrilla targets because they were a vital source of food and money. Many reported guerrilla coercion and several were killed. Headman Kabasa, himself a storekeeper at Nyamuzuwe small business centre, described a threatening letter he and other storekeepers in Nyamuzuwe received from guerrillas in 1976. 'The letter said if we didn't meet their requests [for groceries, soft drinks, money] we'd be asked to contribute more money for a bazooka and then comrades could kill us.'

Those who refused to switch party loyalties after the guerrillas came to the district risked guerrilla coercion. Others have passed over the extent of guerrilla coercion against supporters of other parties. Ranger claims that Makoni peasants had supported ZAPU earlier but by 1977 ZANU guerrillas 'demanded exclusive allegiance to ZANU/Mugabe. Those pioneer nationalists who could not stomach having to change parties at the behest of younger strangers found it wise to leave the district and take refuge in Salisbury.' Ranger appears to ignore the demonstration effect of guerrilla coercion against supporters of other parties when he writes: 'The great majority of Makoni peasants, as the war developed and they confronted whites together with the guerrillas, came naturally enough to transfer their allegiance to ZANU/Mugabe.'[108] Cliffe and Stoneman also describe how ZANU guerrillas had to build up local support without the benefit, as ZAPU had, of a significant earlier period of legal existence. Perhaps referring to Ranger's study, they write: 'there are accounts of how communities initially stated "they had only known ZAPU", but that they were open-minded enough to give this new group a hearing'.[109] They, too, neglect the possible role of compliance coercion (see chapter 4).

Supporters of Muzorewa's UANC posed the greatest problem for the guerrillas. Many people believed that Muzorewa and ZANU were working together, and that Muzorewa's party was merely the internal wing of exiled ZANU and ZAPU. Some guerrilla groups, reflecting their varied loyalties, adopted a hardline attitude towards Muzorewa from 1976, others seem to have only stiffened their opposition to Muzorewa supporters after the signing of the 3 March 1978 agreement. The absence of a clear policy regarding Muzorewa and his supporters was the source of costly confusion for civilians. The following comment by a villager is a strong, blunt statement about coercion towards UANC supporters.

> Those who had positions in UANC in our branches are dead. They either hung themselves or they died. Wherever you move, you don't find people saying that they had positions in UANC. You can waste your time trying to find that out. You'll never find it out. Muzorewa bombed people when he was in power, so even those who had positions in UANC when it was good, today will say nothing.

An eighteen-year-old secondary school student describes how the guerrillas coerced him to become a *youth*. More pertinent for the moment, the boy's story highlights how the guerrillas used coercion to ensure that people abandoned other party affiliations.

> I was at primary school in Makosa where I lived with Mr S. [a teacher]. The headmaster was known to be UANC supporter. One night as S., a friend, and I were leaving a *morari*, about four comrades called us back. They accused S. of being a UANC supporter and recited his history from the time he left Salisbury and came to Makosa to teach. They said he was working for the headmaster delivering messages to the UANC office in Mutoko. Even though S. denied the allegations, he was beaten. Because the comrades didn't want to kill a teacher in front of us, we were told to return to the *morari*. We heard S. screaming as they beat him: 'I don't know nothing. You can ask X. and Y.' By the time we were called, S. was dead. We both told comrades that S. was not UANC. The comrades said: 'You're lying' and then beat us and told us we were to be *mujibas*. We were told to patrol the area and alert people if soldiers were seen. We also had to learn the names of the central committee in Mozambique . . .

The guerrillas attacked 'protected villages' to release villagers from constant government surveillance. The basic technique involved the guerrillas cutting the security fencing and standing guard in case paramilitary administrators were alerted to the attack. Meanwhile *youth* would go inside, give villagers a warning to flee, and then burn their homes, forcing them to run away. During 1977 the guerrillas burned nearly 10 per cent of the 'protected villages' and 'consolidated villages', mostly in the Mutoko/ Murewa areas.[110] The benefit to villagers of being freed of tight government control must be offset against the coercive means used by the guerrillas and villagers' material losses from the guerrillas' tactic of burning their huts.

Utilitarian appeals

Both the political parties and the guerrillas could offer only a few concrete utilitarian benefits to attract members because neither could substantially diminish the power of the state. The SRANC successfully defended African cultivators' rights against loss of cattle and land as a result of the Land Husbandry Act.[111] The nationalist movement's help, however, merely restored property to owners. Otherwise, the early nationalist parties, themselves lacking in resources, offered few, if any, concrete material benefits. Nor were they able to protect Africans who participated in nationalist politics from government sanctions.

The guerrillas disrupted rural administration, and hence the payments that Africans made to various government agencies, and encouraged Africans to stop paying their council rates and fees. They told Africans that their money was being used to support the government's war effort, that Europeans did not have to pay for many of these services, and that Africans did not get benefits commensurate with what they were paying. An African religious minister and a cattle-owning villager respectively recounted what guerrillas had told them.

> Our ancestors had beasts and they never needed dips. You're being cheated. Fees are being used by the government to buy ammunition. Next time we come we don't want to see tanks open.

> *Youth* came to call us. They knocked on the door some time late at night and said: 'Wake up. Let's go.' At the dip tank, the comrades were there. They said we must destroy the dip because it didn't belong to us, but to the oppressors. We had to pay thirty cents per head to use the dip and we were forced to dip on a certain day every week. The whites could dip whenever they liked.

More as a compensation than a benefit, guerrillas encouraged farmworkers, many of them Malawian and Mozambican, to leave their European bosses and resettle on the Purchase Area farms, where guerrillas had appealed to farmers to accept farm-workers who found themselves without jobs and homes.

Utilitarian appeals were limited because the guerrillas were forced to contend with the military capacity of the state as they tried to mobilize civilian support. Skocpol's observation that a weakening of state repression is a prerequisite for a mutually beneficial exchange between peasants and revolutionaries is pertinent.

> It is hard to imagine the successful institutionalization of such social exchange between peasants and revolutionaries except in places and time unusually free from counterrevolutionary state repression. Marginal, inaccessible geographical areas are the most suitable places for the process to begin, but for it to spread and succeed, no doubt 'exogenous' events must intervene to drastically weaken the existing state power . . . In both patterns of revolution [autonomous and mobilized], defeats in wars and international military interventions are the most likely ways for existing state power to be disrupted.[112]

To sum up, political appeals to mobilize support were similar in the early nationalist party period and during the guerrilla war, although the latter period was marked by greater militancy. Utilitarian appeals both before and during the war were overshadowed by cultural nationalist and coercive appeals. A link between coercive and negative utilitarian appeals ought to be highlighted. The colonial state was the main provider of African rural services and infrastructure, always inferior and unequal to those for whites. These existing benefits were also symbols of state oppression and therefore targets of coercive appeals. The reliance on coercive and normative appeals to mobilize support reflect the continued repressive capacity of the colonial state and are also a measure of state capacity. Other, sometimes more direct measures of state capacity are discussed below.

Increasing state capacity

Although the first mass African nationalist organization, the SRANC, posed no threat to the status quo, whites were alarmed at what they perceived to be a militant African organization. The ruling party anticipated a loss of white voters to the political parties to its right in the pending election unless it appeared tough on law and order issues. From February to April 1959, the government declared a state of emergency. Immediately after the emergency was lifted, parliament passed several statutes to make possible a *de facto* emergency.[113] Over the next few years, security legislation proliferated.[114] The effect of all these laws was to increase the relative power of the executive, in particular the arbitrary powers of the security sector, over other branches of government.[115] The security legislation introduced since the emergency in 1959 was matched by greater capacity to enforce law and order. Personnel in the Ministries of Internal Affairs and Justice and the British South Africa Police nearly doubled between 1958 and 1962. The numbers of police stations increased from 102 in 1958 to 134 in 1962. Britain's decision to transfer the equipment of the federal air force to Southern Rhodesia when the federation broke up in 1963 added to state military capacity.[116]

Repression increased after the apartheid-oriented Rhodesia Front party came to power in December 1962. Radio and television became state controlled. The death penalty became mandatory for petrol-bombing residential property,[117] people who had been officers in unlawful organizations were forced to resign from other organizations, and gatherings on Sundays and public holidays – ideal times for political meetings – were prohibited. New laws tightened control of urban townships, where both parties had established cells. The Rhodesia Front government introduced a state of emergency in selected areas in March 1964. After the banning of ZAPU and ZANU in August 1964, no organized party activity took place till the end of 1970. Heeding the African nationalists' threat of a mass uprising if it declared its independence from Britain, which it did, the government extended the state of emergency to the entire country in 1965, and it was renewed annually until 1990. Draconian security legislation had the desired effect on African political activity and political crimes dwindled to an insignificant number between 1964 and 1969.[118]

After ZANU's attack on Sinoia in 1966, the Rhodesian Security Forces were put on a counter-insurgency basis. The primacy of the police in internal security ended. A period of cooperation followed among the police, the Ministry of Internal Affairs (INTAF), and the army. For the first time, the air force was used to give air support to ground troops, making for effective counter-insurgency against large groups of guerrillas in sparsely populated areas where they had insufficient local support.[119] The involvement of the South African African National Congress (SAANC) provoked acrimonious charges between ZANU and ZAPU and between the SAANC and its rival organization, the Pan African Congress (PAC). ZANU and the PAC alleged that the joint venture gave the pretext for the Rhodesian government to receive South African paramilitary police units, but ZAPU sources maintain that they worked with the SAANC in response to a pact among the armed forces of Rhodesia, Portugal, and South Africa to support each other.[120] South African police units operating in Rhodesia probably matched the size of the Rhodesian regular army and were only withdrawn in 1975. At the same time that the state expanded its capacity, it continued to multiply its security laws.[121]

By 1976 as much as a third of the regular army of about 3,500 was made up of foreign white mercenaries.[122] The regular army had grown to 5,000 by 1978.[123] African regulars, mainly from the Fort Victoria area, were in the white-officered Rhodesia African Rifles while most whites were in the Rhodesia Light Infantry or the smaller, specialized units. Most of the increase in the army came from more rigorous conscription of all white males over eighteen years for national service (2,400 conscripts in 1977; 3,250 in 1978)[124] and the introduction of compulsory duty for ex-servicemen between twenty-five and fifty years old who formed the all-white reserve or territorial force. Those on active duty at any one time in the latter force grew from 10,000 in 1973 to 15,000 in 1977–8.[125] In 1978 the government introduced compulsory conscription for blacks with at least three years' secondary schooling. A small but important force that was associated with the army was the Selous Scouts. They were used as pseudo guerrilla gangs and by the end of the war numbered 1,800; they were chiefly Africans among whom were some ex-guerrillas. In the words of their creator, their objective was 'to infiltrate the tribal population and the terrorist networks, pinpoint the terrorist camps and bases and then direct conventional forces in to carry out the actual attacks. Then, depending on the skill of the particular Selous Scouts' pseudo group concerned, their cover should remain intact which would enable them to continue operating in a particular area . . . perhaps indefinitely.'[126]

Critical to the success of the Selous Scouts was air support. The air force comprised about 1,200 whites and grew little during the war.[127] The regular forces of the British South Africa Police also expanded, relying more heavily on African recruitment for its growth than the army. Between 1966 and 1970 the regular police force was about 6,400 men, of whom two-thirds were Africans. In 1974 the regular force was some 8,000, and in 1979 about 11,000 with roughly the same ratio of African to white police. Most of the police reservists were whites over fifty years old. Their numbers grew from 28,500 in 1970 to nearly 35,000 in 1973 and remained this size until the end of the war.[128]

Throughout the war, the state expanded its paramilitary forces chiefly by recruiting Africans. The Guard Force was first introduced to guard the 'protected villages'. From early 1978 when the guerrillas threatened economically important farming areas, key economic installations, and lines of communication, the Guard Force was sent there and replaced by Security Force Auxiliaries at the 'protected villages'. By the end of the war, there were 7,000 Guard Force and 20,000 Security Force Auxiliaries, 80 per cent of whom were under Muzorewa's control.[129] With generous government subsidies, European farmers contributed to a farm militia that was supposed to protect the African farm-workers' compounds. Its recruits were chiefly black farm-workers but like the other paramilitary units included foreign white mercenaries too.[130] These paramilitary forces, it should be underlined, were entirely new.

Another indicator of growing state capacity was the ability to finance increases in the military and paramilitary forces. Total defence or 'security' costs, which include not only the armed forces but also all ministries involved in the war effort such as the police, law and order, and internal affairs soared between 1967 and 1979. As a percentage of total government expenditure, war costs rose 6.5 per cent in 1967, 9 per cent in 1973, 12 per cent in 1974, 25 per cent in 1976, and 47 per cent in 1979.[131] Moreover, the central provincial administration survived and expanded chiefly through the recruitment of Africans into the civil service. This middle administrative tier assumed much of the responsibility for African rural administration when district administration crumbled under guerrilla pressures.

The enduring capacity of the state even in the face of a mounting guerrilla war is also evident in less direct measures. Comparative aggregate data have well-known limitations but may provide insights. For a government to be successful in an anti-colonial guerrilla war, where the guerrillas have the advantage of intimate knowledge of terrain, defensive organization, and the sympathy of the population, Bernard Fall asserts that combined government forces must outnumber guerrilla forces by at least fifteen to one. In Malaya, 250,000 British, Commonwealth, and native troops and militia defeated a maximum of 8,000 guerrillas. Able to bring in large numbers of foreign troops, the alien British-run government raised troops that exceeded the guerrilla force by thirty-one to one.[132] In contrast, the Rhodesian government, alienated from its metropolitan colonial power, had to rely chiefly on internal recruits. Although it recruited a surprising number of Africans, the ratio of its troops, military and paramilitary, to the combined guerrilla forces at the end of the war was less than four to one. Yet its military losses were low compared to those of the guerrillas. According to official figures, the guerrillas killed 350 white and some 700 black Security Force members,[133] while the regime forces killed over 10,000 guerrillas between 1977 and 1979 alone.[134] Even though the official figures exaggerate guerrilla deaths by including civilians, they do underline the glaring differences in military losses by both sides and the relative power of the state. The strength of the state relative to the guerrillas is also evident in the guerrillas' inability to prevent the Rhodesian government from obtaining an estimated 64 per cent turnout in the elections in April 1979. The guerrillas attacked only 18 of 932 polling booths and were unable to force any of them to close.[135]

How an expansion of military capacity was possible requires an appreciation of the social structure in a settler society and the regional and international forces. Rhodesia's relationship with international powers and the regional power, South Africa, mitigated the effects of sanctions on essential military equipment, the financial burden of the war, and the need for military personnel. After the unilateral declaration of independence in 1965, the international powers often turned a blind eye to violations of mandatory international economic sanctions and themselves skirted them. The United States supplied aircraft to the minority regime from 1975, thereby increasing its combat capacity by five times, made no effort to stop the illegal recruitment of mercenaries to the Rhodesian army, and imported chrome from 1971 to 1977. Neither Britain nor the United States interrupted the flow of investment funds from parent companies to subsidiaries or the movement of skilled personnel. Private British and American corporations clandestinely sold oil to Rhodesia. Even though Harold Wilson's government was informed of these violations from 1967, it never acted against corporate transgressors. In these ways, the international environment was not as hostile to Rhodesia as its rhetoric implied.[136] The South African government refused to impose economic sanctions and supported the regime in various ways. Much South African capital was invested in Rhodesia, especially after the unilateral declaration of independence in 1965, and trade between the two countries expanded rapidly. The

South African government assisted the war effort with loans (US$300 million), arms, and military personnel. It served as a major conduit for equipment from sanctions-busters in Europe after Portugal lost control of Mozambique and a new route became necessary.[137] Also, the Rhodesian government was able to raise taxes although the tax base declined as large numbers of whites chose to emigrate rather than fight the war. In 1971 the country registered + 9,403 net immigration, in 1976, – 7,072, and in 1978, – 13,709.[138]

Domestic factors are also important. White minority regimes maintain themselves by making white unity a security issue, and by dividing and controlling Africans. The subordinate role of Africans in every aspect of such regimes is essential to their survival. The state could still exploit the colonial social structure. By the end of the war the state had recruited almost as many Africans into its paramilitary forces alone as ZANU had guerrillas operating inside the country. Government recruitment of Africans in the guerrilla war presents a striking contrast with the 1896–7 rebellion in which the rebels were able to win over Africans from the Company's forces. African willingness to participate on the side of the European colonial power in the 1970s may be attributed largely to the effect of colonial rule on the power structure and inter-group relationships in colonial societies. Michael Adas' study of five anti-colonial rebellions, which were all suppressed, highlights this distinctive feature of colonial societies. 'The co-option of indigenous elite groups, the skilful manipulation of cultural differences and longstanding rivalries, and the extensive recruitment of colonized peoples into colonial armies and police forces provided the most immediate and most frequently employed props supporting the European colonial order.'[139]

Power realities, rather than socialist ideology, influenced ZANU's choice of a Maoist strategy. The rural areas in the north-east became accessible once FRELIMO established control in parts of Mozambique, and the entire eastern border was opened as an infiltration route after Mozambique became independent. The cities and mine compounds remained under tight administrative control, and urban guerrilla war was never a possibility.[140] More than failures of leadership or ideology, the military power of the state helps to explain gaps between ZANU's strategy and Mao's strategy, such as why ZANU never built up a conventional army, a culminating phase in Mao's strategy of guerrilla war, or why it skipped the important Maoist phase of organizing guerrilla bands composed of locals, and moved immediately to a mobile guerrilla army.[141] At the heart of Mao's strategy of guerrilla warfare is the idea that the political support of peasants is a stepping stone to military victory. But without a lessening of state military control, how can a movement begin to mobilize support through political means? Cognisant of this conundrum for revolutionary movements, many regard the weakening of the repressive capacity of the state to be a prerequisite for successful political mobilization.[142] This condition was not met in Zimbabwe, where state capacity, and in particular military capacity, expanded.

Conclusion

A periodization of African mass nationalism (1957–79) that demarcates the beginning of ZANU's guerrilla offensive at the end of December 1972 and differentiates it from earlier nationalist strategies is valid. But it has had the effect of obscuring from analysts how the growth of the state's military capacity during the nationalist period affected the mixture of appeals available to the guerrillas. Those who have written about ZANU's war have also overlooked the striking similarities between the appeals used by the guerrillas and the earlier nationalist parties. ZANU guerrillas shared the problem of earlier nationalist parties, and ZANU's own prior weakness, of being able to offer only limited utilitarian appeals, and of having to rely on a combination of cultural nationalist appeals and coercion to mobilize civilian support. The power of the state must be at the centre of an analysis of civilian mobilization in the guerrilla war. It illuminates why the guerrillas used normative and coercive appeals and rarely utilitarian ones. This repertoire of guerrilla appeals becomes critical to an understanding of peasant evaluations of the success of ZANU appeals to effect a revolutionary political mobilization, the subject of the next chapter.

4

Guerrilla–civilian relations: the issue of popular support

The notion of popular support permeates the literature on peasant revolutions although evidence for it is seldom based on peasant voices (see chapter 1). Peasants' popular support for ZANU guerrillas and the effectiveness of guerrilla appeals is a central issue in the literature on Zimbabwe's guerrilla war. Existing studies concur that ZANU's guerrilla movement won the popular support of peasants. This chapter evaluates critically the case for popular support in the most significant studies of ZANU's war, paying careful attention to their evidence and data. Like most other studies of revolution, those on Zimbabwe's revolutionary war do not specify how much support is needed to make it popular. Here support is defined to be popular provided it is voluntary and shared by a significant majority of the population. By not requiring the voluntary support of a minority, the chapter employs a more relaxed notion of popular support than others might but one that is perhaps more relevant from the viewpoint of a revolutionary organization's needs. The chapter offers an alternative interpretation of the effect of guerrilla appeals on peasants, using interviews with peasants, *youth*, and the African rural elite who actively supported ZANU guerrillas. The most important vehicles for peasant participation were civilian organizations or committees and these are described first.

The organization of logistical support

The guerrillas organized peasants, *youth*, and the African elite to meet their logistical needs for resources – food, money, clothing, and intelligence about the regime forces and informers. Coordinating many contributions in kind and deed during war conditions was a remarkable achievement for both guerrillas and civilians. A much more extensive system developed in the Tribal Trust Land than in the Purchase Area. The densely populated Tribal Trust Land offered more protection for the guerrillas than the comparatively sparsely populated Purchase Area. Organizing group activity was much easier in the Tribal Trust Land where

116

villagers lived close to one another than in the Purchase Areas where farmers lived farther from each other. Also, villagers had no choice but to combine their resources to try to cope with the demands of large guerrilla groups whereas the better-off Budjga Purchase farmers could often feed a group without help from neighbours. Security on white farms and around Mutoko township was so tight that guerrillas could not organize the agricultural workers or the township residents. The origins and structure of the organizational network of civilian support in Mutoko Tribal Trust Land reveal peasants and guerrillas' preoccupation with physical security and highlight the problems of organizing support when the state's military power is still intact (see chapter 3). The description that follows is based on a mass of confusing data, collected from *parents* and *youth* active in the civilian network of organizations. The confusion about organizational structure and functions itself reflects the problems of organizing in unstable political and military conditions.

Initially the few small groups of guerrillas contacted selected individuals – those with nationalist histories or chiefs and headmen – for food and information. According to a Member of Parliament who worked with guerrillas in Mutoko during the war, only about two unarmed guerrilla groups tried to work with civilians for a brief spell in 1973 and 1974. They operated only in the north-east of Mutoko Tribal Trust Land. District records point to guerrilla influence in 1972 in Charewa chiefdom in the north-west of Mutoko Tribal Trust Land where Headman Chindenga was suspected of contacts with guerrillas in the neighbouring Murewa district.[1] In their first encounters, the guerrillas were reportedly anxious to assure people that they were not *gandangas* (terrorists), as they were called in government propaganda, but freedom fighters. Civilians were warned not to report their meetings with guerrillas to others unless directed to.[2] As the guerrilla army expanded, its growing food requirements impelled it to broaden its bases of logistical support. It also became increasingly difficult for guerrillas to keep their presence in the villages a secret. They began to meet entire villages in 1975 and 1976. Usually the guerrillas would send brief advance warning of their pending arrival, the objective being to give any traitors the minimum possible time in which to betray them to the government. Civilians would quickly collect food for the guerrillas. Women from each household would bring uncooked food to a villager's home or a clearing in the bush that the guerrillas had selected because they were close to where they would be spending the night. Here at the 'kitchen', the women did the cooking.

Gradually a more efficient system evolved that was better suited to the military realities. Elderly women took too long to carry food from the villages to the 'kitchen' and to prepare huge barrels of food such as *sadza* – a stiff porridge made from mealie meal. The guerrillas wanted to eat quickly. Often they were walking up to fifty kilometres a night and were hungry; also they might have to move on if soldiers suddenly arrived.[3]

Efficiency considerations resulted in young boys and girls being drawn in to help transport and cook the food. Still wanting to improve the efficiency of logistical support, the guerrillas suggested married adults form village committees and unmarried youths over the age of fifteen form youth wings. These two groups came to be referred to as *parents* and *youth*. Once the committees were formed, villagers found ways to ensure the smooth functioning of the committees. Instead of waiting for *youth* to tell them that guerrillas were en route and then frantically going house-to-house to collect food and money for them, *parents* developed a system of storing food that did not spoil, such as maize, and having a money supply. In late 1977 and early 1978 branch committees composed of a cluster of villages were introduced to improve the efficiency of the system and to ensure that the same villagers were not being asked to meet demands from many guerrilla groups.

A committee comprised a chairman, secretary, treasurer, security officer, organizer, 'logistics' representative and a political commissar. Each position was filled with an alternate for when the incumbent was sick or away from home. The chairman coordinated the various tasks and ensured that the guerrillas got the resources they asked for; the secretary kept records of who contributed what. The security officer detected potential spies by tracking movements of strangers into the village and of village residents to Mutoko centre and other areas where security forces were based. The organizer went from house to house collecting rice, maize, vegetables, and other food supplies, and collected money to buy meat, cooking oil, salt, bread, sugar, and other cash items. The 'logistics' staff supervised cooking for the guerrillas and ensured that there was adequate food for them. The political commissar gave political instruction to the people and conveyed what happened at *moraris* (political education sessions conducted by the guerrillas) to those who did not attend. The most intense interaction between guerrillas and civilians occurred at *moraris*, usually held after dusk at a spot close to the guerrilla base and protected from easy Security Force access. The direct contact with civilians was an opportunity for the guerrillas to offer political education. One at a time, guerrillas would step into the centre of a circle formed by the villagers, introduce themselves, repeat slogans and lead in songs glorifying the past. Perhaps they would make a speech before withdrawing from public view to their *poshto* – a Mozambican word to describe the hiding-places where guerrillas in twos and threes would sleep while the *morari* was in progress. The guerrillas also adjudicated cases involving alleged 'sell-outs' at *moraris*.[4]

In addition to elected committee members, the guerrillas appointed adults to do especially dangerous and demanding tasks, often involving long-distance travel. One such 'special appointee' described his job as follows:

> Comrades at Shinga would give me letters to give to chairmen. If there were three hundred comrades at Shinga you'd say there were none. They'd be there in the thousands. Even soldiers feared to go there. They would give me

a date by which the money had to be returned to them. I'd go to each chairman and tell them to bring the money to my house before that date. Then I'd return to Shinga . . . Later as the war intensified, I had to walk. It got too dangerous to cycle along the main road where I'd meet soldiers. I'd leave here at five in the morning and get to Shinga at eleven at night. I might put up for the night on the way – sometimes in the bush, sometimes at the house of my wife's family who lived near Shinga.

The most strenuous work was usually reserved for *youth*. They were responsible for gathering much of the information, reporting alleged traitors to the guerrillas, and patrolling villages to warn of approaching regime forces. They also provided a courier service connecting dispersed guerrilla groups to each other and guerrillas to villagers. Usually carrying letters from the guerrillas, *youth* conveyed guerrilla requests for money, food, clothing, and other items. The following letters, translated from Shona, were exhumed by a war chairman from a hole in his yard where he used to hide them. Both letters were written after the ceasefire by guerrillas in the Assembly Points.

> Forward with ZANU (PF). Forward with Unity. Forward with Comrade Mugabe. Down with Rebels, Down with Muzorewa, A Luta Continua. How are you parents? Thank you very much for the things you sent us. Thank you. Forward with unity. See you don't forget to vote for JONGWE [The ZANU-PF symbol]. Received 10 packets of cigarettes worth $2.00, 4 Romance soap, Blue surf, Colgate, batteries – supersonic. Can you help us with clothes please. We are really suffering.

> Forward with ZANU(PF). Forward with President Mugabe. Down with UANC. So how are you parents. We are fine. We seek help from you in the form of money. Any amount you can afford. We do want to use it somehow, please.

Probably because these letters came from guerrillas in the Assembly Points where they were provided with basic shelter and food, their requests were modest compared with those made during the war. 'Sometimes you could receive three letters from different groups of comrades for say $50, $70 and $100', said a war chairman. 'You could not afford to collect for all groups. You would just collect small amounts for each group.'

Youth also had other duties. They washed the guerrillas' clothing and cooked for them. They might help *parents* to transport food from their villages to the guerrillas' overnight bases. After a *morari*, they were required to spend the night with the guerrillas. They had their own leaders and base commanders, the latter being responsible for *youth* maintaining base areas and leaving no trace of guerrilla visits after they left. Sometimes *youth* were assisted by 'junior youth' – children under fifteen who carried messages within the village precincts. Sometime in 1977 the guerrillas selected *youth* for military training in their home areas rather than in Mozambique. The former guerrilla practice of walking recruits to Mozambique had become increasingly dangerous as guerrilla groups escorting the

119

recruits frequently became embroiled in contacts with Security Forces or were bombed by helicopters. Also, the camps in Mozambique were already overflowing with recruits who needed training, food, and other amenities. Lastly, *youth* had proved their value to the guerrillas. Familiar with the terrain and the local population, they were able to advise the guerrillas, who were ignorant of local conditions.

Between 1976 and 1978 many villagers in the Tribal Trust Land were in 'protected villages' where any systematic organization of supplies to the guerrillas was impossible because of tight government surveillance. Individuals collected food and money for the guerrillas, but many villages were unaware of these efforts. Even those personally involved in supplying the guerrillas were unable to agree on who else participated or how their help was organized. This confusion underscores the problems of organizing under the gaze of regime forces. Even when people were released from the 'protected villages', some villages could be more easily penetrated by government forces than others. Concerns about security continued to influence the shape of the organizations.

In areas that were not easily accessible to government forces, each village was likely to have its own committee, and neighbouring villages were usually represented on a branch committee. Tasks were divided among many people, with women frequently having their own committees. Women tended to collect maize meal and money to buy cooking oil, salt, sugar, and bread. Men collected money for meat, vegetables, and clothing. Villages located close to the road network and therefore most accessible to government forces had more centralized organizations. Instead of village committees and branch committees, there were usually only branches comprised of representatives of each village. Most of the party work was concentrated in these few representatives. Women were unlikely to have separate committees. Because men and *youth* were the targets of regime force scrutiny, women were often sent to purchase salt or cooking oil from Mutoko centre where stores remained open throughout the war.

Besides the unstable military environment, *parents'* committees and *youth* wings were also influenced by the social structure. Teachers, clergymen, nurses, and storekeepers who often lived among peasants in the Tribal Trust Land but had more resources than them, preferred to organize as occupational collectivities rather than become integrated in a system with the peasants. There is some evidence that peasants also preferred this arrangement. The committee system and the *youth* wing also were influenced by status hierarchies of the patrilineal system. Where possible women organized themselves separately, and *youth* and *parents* had their own organizations. That is, the support organizations entrenched existing generational cleavages, and sometimes gender differences too. The separate organization of the African elite and peasants also laid the foundation for the expression of emergent class conflicts.

These organizational features became important in intra-peasant and peasant–elite conflicts (see chapter 6).

The case for popular support: a critique

Cliffe and his co-authors, and Gregory and Rich all discuss in articles why, to the surprise of many, ZANU (renamed ZANU-PF after the ceasefire) won fifty-seven of eighty African parliamentary seats and 63 per cent of the votes cast in the election of 1980.[5] ZAPU (renamed Patriotic Front or PF) won twenty seats and just over 24 per cent of votes cast, while Muzorewa's UANC won only three seats compared with the fifty-one out of seventy-two seats it had won in the 1979 election, when the exiled parties were excluded from participating. All three articles emphasize how the political education that ZANU guerrillas gave to peasants and their effective normative appeals won them popular support during the war and contributed to ZANU's electoral victory in 1980. Only the article by Cliffe et al. is analyzed here because its evidence for popular support during the war is more detailed than Rich's and it is drawn on in Gregory's work.

Cliffe et al. argue that people voted for the exiled parties because they promised to remove African grievances (land shortage in the Tribal Trust Lands, appallingly low wages in white farms, problems of access to loans for Purchase Area and master farmers) and to end the war.[6] But it was their 'ability to organize which proved decisive. The people had to be "educated" and there was scant time or freedom allowed to do this during the election campaign . . . The grass roots organisational frameworks that were so crucial were in fact a product of the period of the liberation struggle.'[7] ZANU guerrillas had established a level of party organization in the rural areas 'that began to be revealed during the elections' and that surprised even observers sympathetic to their cause. 'It was both a measure of the support that ZANU had received and a reason for that support.'[8] These organizations could not have been set up without 'a considerable input of political education', of which the chief vehicle was *pungwes* (meetings) between civilians and guerrillas. Here guerrillas gave political instruction, taught slogans, and used *chimurenga* (liberation) songs and other cultural symbols such as mediums to make links between the war of national liberation that they were waging and the wars of resistance of the 1890s.[9] These organizations not only provided for the guerrillas' logistical needs but also catered for some of the local population's needs.[10]

The authors infer popular support for the guerrillas from the existence of political organizations, from which in turn they deduce considerable political education. But the existence of organizations and the extensiveness of political instruction say little about how peasants themselves felt about the guerrillas. The tumultuous election period was no doubt unpropitious for interviewing peasants about their experience of the guerrillas. But it is interesting that the authors did not interview peasants about why they voted the way they did in 1980 given that they saw the elections as the first opportunity in over sixteen years to find out something about the 'popular dimension' of politics or 'the mood of the African people'.[11] Instead, they relied mainly on the voices of two teachers, a headmaster, a businessman, a colleague who interviewed guerrillas in a few Assembly Points, ranking ZANU-PF officials, and a ZIPRA commander. They refer to speaking to peasants exposed to ZIPRA,[12] and cite a peasant, an unidentified man, and 'local people' from Matabeleland.[13] Even before he was able to obtain empirical data, Lionel Cliffe had argued that the logic of protracted guerrilla war would be an important radicalizing experience for both guerrillas and peasants, and would necessitate political mobilization and political education of the peasantry.[14]

In a book entitled *Zimbabwe: A Revolution That Lost Its Way?* Andre Astrow, a political scientist, answers unequivocally the question posed in its title. He holds the petit bourgeois nationalist leadership responsible for the revolution's failure. Astrow argues that historically the masses (peasants and workers) were more militant than the petit bourgeois nationalist leaders who frequently sought to moderate their militancy in the early period of the nationalist movement.[15] After the Rhodesia Front (RF) party's unilateral declaration of independence in 1965, the African masses became increasingly radicalized.

> The repression that the settlers sustained against the African people, combined with their declining living standards and increased landlessness helped to ensure mass support for the armed struggle. Africans increasingly came to understand that the RF would never be prepared to relinquish the power they had amassed, unless the African people waged a war of national liberation to overthrow them. The radicalization of the African masses and their support for the war enabled the nationalist movement to become a decisive force in undermining settler society.[16]

The intensification of the war of liberation and counter-insurgency measures further intensified mass radicalism.[17]

> As a result, the leadership of the nationalist movement had to react accordingly in order to maintain its support among African workers and peasants . . . ZANU, the political party most susceptible to the radicalization of the African people, became transformed, particularly through ZANLA, into a 'party of the people'. Its political programme was modified over the years to encompass the democratic aspirations of the African people. During the war the 'struggle for socialism' and the 'fight against imperialism' came to be increasingly emphasized by the petit bourgeois leadership. Such rhetoric about fundamental transformations and socialism was essential for retaining credibility among the more and more radicalized African population.[18]

But the petit bourgeois nationalist leaders saw the war as a way of achieving majority rule rather than of transforming society.[19] In contrast, 'the struggle of the African people in Zimbabwe was for more than the replacement of the settler state by an African one. It required the overthrow of the social relations defended by the settler regime, and which restrict production to the narrow limits set by the criterion of profitability.'[20] Although its radical rhetoric won ZANU popular support in the war, its political programme had little to offer the African masses other than 'a continued period of capitalist development'. In this respect, it 'was not offering the African masses anything radically different from other sections of the nationalist movement'.[21]

Astrow's critical study of nationalist leadership politics is insightful, but his assertions of militant radical peasants and their popular support for the guerrillas rest on indirect inferences. For Astrow, peasant radicalism before the war grows from state and settler oppression and discriminatory policies and manifests itself in violent protest against the state in the era of mass nationalism. This interesting interpretation must contend with existing accounts, some of which suggest that the nationalist leadership decided to adopt a policy of sabotage in 1960 – well before incidents of sabotage by the masses – if attempts to effect change through constitutional politics failed.[22] Others maintain that the mass violence of the 1960s was more an expression of frustration because of unemployment and other grievances than of politically conscious protest.[23] After the unilateral declaration of independence, Astrow asserts that government repression and state policies shifted the economic costs of a declining economy onto the African masses, increasing their radicalization. Once the war begins, it too increases their radicalization. But Astrow presents no direct evidence for his claims that peasant radicalization increased. Instead, they are deduced from the existence of peasant grievances, and from the fact that ZANU 'maintained close links with Africans in rural areas and did the bulk of the fighting'.[24] There is no reason why peasant grievances by themselves should lead to growing radicalism, which Astrow defines to be socialist and anti-imperialist.

In her book, *None But Ourselves*, Julie Frederikse, a radio and newspaper journalist, draws effectively on items from the Rhodesian mass media to support her argument that the whites built a mythology about themselves and Africans. She also conducted interviews between early 1980 and 1981 with civilians and guerrillas to show how the guerrillas combatted the technologically superior mass media.[25] She highlights the role of political education in the guerrillas' success at winning popular support and ridicules the Rhodesian media for attributing guerrilla success to guerrilla intimidation.[26] Political education consisted of teaching civilians how the system of racial oppression worked, and, according to some, the evils of capitalism, as well as appeals to spirit mediums and ancestral spirits.[27] The crudity of government propaganda and counter-insurgency operations such as 'protected villages' merely played into guerrilla hands. For example, the government policy of confiscating property belonging to villagers who supported the guerrillas 'not only backfired but served to further radicalize an already resentful population'.[28]

Frederikse does not discuss how she selected her respondents, but her thanks to ranking party officials for facilitating interviews suggest it was not a random process.[29] More serious for her argument about the guerrillas' popular support is the fact that her informants are rarely drawn from peasant ranks. Prominent Africans in her text are seven government media officials (quoted on twenty-two occasions), five ZANLA and five ZIPRA guerrillas (cited respectively thirty-one times and twelve times), three teachers (cited twelve times), three rural store-owners (cited eighteen times), one ZANLA secretary of publicity (cited on twenty occasions), four political detainees (cited seventeen times), and a nurse (cited ten times). In addition, she interviewed whites in the media, the military, and at missions, especially at Berenjena mission. Her reliance on non-peasant sources weakens her case for the guerrillas' popular support among peasants. Guerrilla informants cannot be counted on to give peasant views of guerrillas; nor are committed missionary informants and detainees a substitute for peasant voices. Also, she refers to civilians feeding the guerrillas but omits to evaluate how this cost to peasants affected their relationship. She is clearly aware of problems arising from guerrilla coercion, to which several of her informants allude, but her main purpose appears to be to highlight Security Force brutality. Consequently, she fails to explicitly take into account what impact guerrilla coercion might have had on popular support. Even though informants refer to being coerced by guerrillas to attend political meetings or *pungwes*,[30] she states: 'ZANLA's greater reliance on *pungwes* [compared with ZIPRA's] might also be seen as evidence of its greater rapport with and support from the local population.'[31] Presumably, the reason she downplays guerrilla coercion is that she accepts missionaries' views that the army was more brutal.[32]

Ranger's *Peasant Consciousness and Guerrilla War in Zimbabwe* is a comparative historical study of peasant agency in Zimbabwe, Mozambique, and Kenya. Using Makoni district as a case study for Zimbabwean peasant history, his purpose is to highlight the uniqueness of Zimbabwean peasant history and enhance understanding of the peasant role in the guerrilla war.[33] Ranger's book demands extended critical analysis because it has deservedly been, and undoubtedly will remain, influential. Ranger argues that by the time of ZANU's guerrilla war in the 1970s, the peasants had a revolutionary consciousness. For peasants to develop a radical nationalist consciousness required that the 'peasant option had to be not only restricted and impeded but really threatened with "destruction"; government intervention in peasant cultivation had to reach a peak of coercive intensity which was still only foreshadowed by the developments of the 1930s; peasants had to encounter political movements which spoke directly to rural grievance and held out some sort of hope of alleviating it.'[34] This occurred in the 1950s. 'At its highest stage of development this fusion of Shona cultural nationalism and peasant radicalism proved potent enough to allow the spread of ZANLA's guerrilla action . . .'[35] Compared with Mozambique, peasant revolutionary consciousness allowed for a 'more direct input by the peasantry into the ideology and programme of the war'[36] and there was less 'necessity for political education' by the guerrillas.[37]

The composite peasant/guerrilla ideology focused on the recovery of lost lands and a transformed state 'that would back black farming against white, rather than the other way around' and 'would no longer interfere in peasant production but would content itself wth ensuring high prices, good marketing facilities, supplies of cheap fertilizer and so on'.[38] Mediums were also an important part of the guerrilla/peasant ideology. They had become important as articulators of radical peasant consciousness before guerrillas entered the rural areas precisely because that consciousness was so focused on land and government interference with production and 'above any other possible religious form the mediums symbolized peasant right to the land and their right to work it as they chose'.[39] Moreover, they helped radical peasants to come to terms with the young guerrillas coming from outside the district and 'to come together as one community of resistance'.[40] Because of the high level of peasant consciousness, the guerrillas had merely to intensify peasant resentments through political education, one of their primary functions, and join peasants in disrupting civilian administration.[41] Hence for Ranger, peasant popular support for the guerrillas was primarily based on their shared ideology of African cultural nationalism.

Ranger conceives of peasant consciousness so narrowly that exploitation (or discrimination or oppression) in agricultural production by whites and the state are its primary ingredients. African nationalism incorporated a desire to remove whites from government and to take control of the state. So Ranger has only to show that peasants were opposed to the state and whites who had taken their lands and denied them reasonable access to markets in order for them to qualify as nationalists. To the extent that peasants are always in an antagonistic relationship with the state, it is difficult to separate peasant anti-state sentiments from alleged peasant nationalism. Moreover, because peasant grievances arising from relationships with other Africans are almost entirely absent from his concept of consciousness, if not from his text, there is no way of evaluating how important peasant grievances against whites and the state were. Peasant radical nationalism is overdetermined because of the limited way in which Ranger has constructed the concept of consciousness.

Ranger seldom speaks to peasants to find out about peasant consciousness. Instead, he relies almost exclusively on data about peasant behaviour, reported through others. For the more distant past, he had little choice but to rely on mission and state archives. For the more recent war period, only about one-third of his interviewees (14/52) were peasants and just over half of these enter his text. He relies instead on autobiographical accounts of leading participants, private correspondence with leading nationalists in Makoni, and interviews with nationalist politicians, five teachers, four storekeepers/businessmen, and church-related people. In a review of Ranger's book, I noted that 'The Africans in this group include some unusually dedicated and irrepressible nationalists who chose to confront the coercive power of the state when many others were unwilling to do so. These men were fortunate to be linked to the inspiring Clutton-Brock, based at St Faith's Mission.'[42] Ranger himself paid tribute to the influence that Clutton-Brock, a Welsh missionary (eventually deported by the government), and others at St Faith's had on the spread of African nationalism in Makoni district.[43]

Ranger's evidence of peasant radical nationalism is often weak. In the period of mass nationalism, Ranger notes that mediums are an indicator of peasant radical nationalism because they contribute to a common cultural identity.[44] Mediums become increasingly relevant to 'peasant resentment over land alienation and the enforcement of agricultural rules' in the 1970s.[45] Evidence for the rise of medium worship is contradictory. We are told that mediums played an increasing role in Weya in Makoni district in the 1960s.[46] But in 1981 an informant remarked that in Weya, until the war, 'mediums felt that they had been forgotten'.[47] Also, Ranger's posited relationship between growing peasant radicalism and medium influence does not always prevail in Makoni district. At the Catholic mission at Triashill, medium influence increases in the 1960s. Even though agricultural prosperity improves here, peasants resent increased state intervention in agricultural production.[48] Contrary to what Ranger's posited relationship between growing peasant radicalism and medium influence lead one to expect, medium influence did not continue to grow at Triashill as peasant radical nationalism deepened during the war. Instead, during the war, Catholic priests rather than mediums gave the guerrillas legitimacy.[49] Moreover, other data, sometimes from other districts, challenge his argument about rising medium influence and its association with radical nationalism in the 1960s. As Ranger acknowledged, Murphree and Thomas found mediums in Mutoko and Manicaland province (which includes Makoni district) respectively to be antagonistic to nationalist politics in the 1960s.[50] Thomas also found that most Africans, rural and urban – and especially political party members and urban residents – rejected a continuation of the pre-colonial practice according to which mediums approve the appointment of chiefs.[51] The strongest advocates of a return to African culture were also the most committed to secularizing political life. People in Manicaland apparently wanted a sharper division between secular and religious activities and this suggests a decline in the influence of mediums. Perhaps it is unfair to bring in data from other areas to challenge Ranger's case for the rising influence of mediums and its links to peasant radical nationalism. But Ranger himself sometimes presents his Makoni district findings as if they are applicable to other Shona areas.[52]

Ranger's evidence of peasant nationalism does not take into account differences in peasant attitudes to national politics. Ranger states explicitly that his study is 'an account of consciousness at the grass-roots so that national events and national associations enter the book as they entered the rural areas – intermittently and from the outside'.[53] The focus on informal politics in the nationalist era uncovers an important aspect of peasant activity but should not lead to a neglect of the potential differences between peasants who participate in organizational politics and those who do not. Thomas's survey of African attitudes (rural and urban) in Manicaland in the 1960s, by which time peasants were already radical nationalists according to Ranger, found that 'most respondents had the habit of law-abidingness. Only one in ten displayed that strong rejection of civil authority which leads them into political groups which advocate civil disobedience.' Yet the majority of respondents accepted the principle that they should disobey laws which they consider unjust.[54] Party members also voiced different views from non-party members on the other issues, such as who should vote: 73 per cent of political party members favoured universal suffrage compared with just over 59 per cent of non-party members.[55] This type of survey is difficult to interpret. People may well have been reluctant to reveal their political feelings under a repressive state. Yet it does seem plausible that party members and non-party members would respond differently to political questions. Similarly, peasant attitudes to political questions might reasonably be expected to vary according to level of education. Thomas' study found that education affected people's attitudes to civil liberties: most who answered did not support civil liberties and only those with more than ten years' education showed evidence of having received instruction on the principles of democracy.[56] Thomas warns his readers to treat his data on political opinions about democratic principles with caution because attitudes were unformed. But the majority's lack of ideas or only random ones about civil liberties, an important component of the nationalist agenda, reflects that such concerns were removed from their immediate day-to-day concerns.[57]

Also, Ranger's argument for continued cultural nationalist activity after the banning of the nationalist parties in 1964 may be right for Makoni, although his evidence of peasant resistance, by his own admission, is scattered.[58] Yet this is an important part of his argument to document because it runs against the prevailing interpretation of nationalist history, as Ranger is fully aware. Others have emphasized how nationalist activity in the rural areas declined dramatically after the parties were banned.[59]

Ranger's argument for peasants' popular support for the guerrillas rests on their shared cultural nationalist ideology. But the argument is flawed by his narrowly constructed concept of peasant consciousness that leads to overstating peasant resentments against the state and whites in the sphere of agricultural production. Moreover, from this limited arena of peasant interest, Ranger infers peasant consciousness from peasant behaviour, as described by others. The evidence on peasant mentality is thus indirectly inferred and the potential for erroneous interpretation is wider than were it based on what peasants themselves revealed about their consciousness. Lastly, Ranger's evidence for peasant cultural nationalism intensifying is often weak and contradictory. As noted in chapter 3, utilitarian appeals and guerrilla coercion do not enter his argument about peasant popular support.

It is interesting to juxtapose Ranger's argument about the important role of peasant and guerrilla ideology in peasant popular support of the guerrillas with his bold confrontation of guerrilla coercion in an important article. Ranger begins by diminishing the importance of coercion and asserting that the process by which the guerrillas established legitimacy with the peasants 'remains by far the most important thing to discuss'.[60] Ranger reports isolated incidents of guerrilla misbehaviour before 1978 but found they made no dent on peasant support because peasants had their own reasons for supporting the war.[61] This raises the question of whether the guerrillas' effort to deepen peasant resentments through political education was as important as Ranger maintains in his book. It also raises questions about the alleged influence of the mediums in laying down a code of conduct for the guerrillas that contributed to guerrilla legitimacy and eased initial concerns among the peasants about the guerrillas being young and outsiders. In 1978 and 1979, when guerrilla behaviour deteriorated, 'observers both within and outside the guerrilla movements began to fear a wholesale collapse of rural support'.[62] But Ranger dismisses such concerns expressed in the report of the Catholic Commission for Peace and Justice – an organization that documented widespread government atrocities during the war. When the report cites a local elite's letter about disillusionment among rural people and their desire 'to return to their old way of life even if they were deprived of land and they had to get rid of their cattle', Ranger discounts the comment because it underestimated peasant determination. Moreover, the entire report, he said, depended too much on the evidence of local elites.[63] Ranger is right to require direct evidence from peasants themselves, although it seems unfair to apply the rules of evidence so severely when local elites speak of the negative effects of guerrilla coercion on peasant support for the guerrillas but to allow them to speak for peasants, as he does in his book, when they report peasant popular support. Ranger seems reluctant to consider seriously even peasant voices on the effect of guerrilla coercion on popular support. When a peasant informant reports feeling fear and terror after watching the guerrillas kill alleged 'sell-outs' and witches, he again explains it away. 'In assessing experiences like this, one has to bear in mind two considerations. One is that the "Security Forces" were constantly exposing peasants to much more arbitrary and terrible sufferings . . . The other was that peasants often excused guerrillas of responsibility for unjust punishments or extortionate demands, blaming these on the young boys and girls (the *mujibas*) who acted as go-betweens.'[64] Hence Ranger's attention to guerrilla coercion in this article does not lead him to revise his thesis on peasant popular support in *Peasant Consciousness and Guerrilla War in Zimbabwe*. To discount guerrilla coercion because government atrocities were more severe is merely an assertion that sidesteps inquiring about the effect of guerrilla coercion. My own evidence supports Ranger's data that peasants often absolved guerrillas of responsibility for atrocities and abuses and blamed *youth* instead. But again, such data do not say anything about the effect of guerrilla coercion; they only concede that others were also often coercive.

Lan's *Guns and Rain* is an important anthropological study based on fieldwork in Dande district in the north-east. It is an innovative analysis of how pre-colonial symbols and rituals were incorporated in the resistance ideology of the war, facilitating peasant support for the guerrillas. In Dande the senior mediums, representatives of the spirits of the deceased chiefs or *mhondoro*, had assumed the political authority exercised by living chiefs because the latter had become too bound up with the state.[65] So when the guerrillas came to the district, the people led them to consult with the mediums rather than the chiefs. The mediums and the guerrillas made a pact. The mediums would deliver peasant support and the guerrillas promised that if they were successful in war they would reverse discriminatory legislation 'that limited the development and freedom of the peasantry' and, most importantly, they would return the land to the peasants.[66] Thus began a process that culminated in the symbolic establishment of the guerrillas as the successors of the chiefs. 'Indeed they may be called the chiefs' legitimate successors because, like all legitimate rulers, they were installed by the *mhondoro*. Apart from their recruiting of the peasantry to the resistance, the legitimisation of this succession was the most important contribution the *mhondoro* mediums made to the war.'[67] The mediums, by allowing 'this new feature in the experience of the peasantry', the guerrillas, to be assimilated to established symbolic categories, facilitated the guerrillas' acceptance by the population. For the protective techniques of the ancestors to work and for the peasants to accept the guerrillas, the guerrillas had to abide by restrictions imposed on them by the mediums – for example, they were forbidden to eat certain foods or to have sex on duty – and participate in the possession rituals of the *mhondoro*. In this way the mediums used their moral authority to support the guerrillas and expedite their acceptance by the people. Through a symbolic analysis, Lan draws a parallel between witches in opposition to the moral order of 'the altruistic and benevolent *mhondoro*' on the one hand, and 'sell-outs' in opposition to the moral order for which the guerrillas were fighting, on the other hand. The killing of 'sell-outs', symbolically identified with witches, becomes a further illustration of how closely linked to the *mhondoro* and their moral authority the guerrillas had become. 'The guerrillas' explicit and aggressive policy against witches was the final turn of the key in the lock. The doorway to legitimate political authority was opened wide. With the spirit mediums mounting a guard of honour, the guerrillas marched in and took hold of the symbols of their new power.'[68] Lan is careful to point out that participation in ritual prohibitions did not prevent the guerrillas from taking part in the party programme of peasant mobilization and political education.[69] Also, the guerrillas realized that 'ancestral protection and rigorous military discipline were both essential'.[70]

Lan's evidence that the pact between guerrillas and mediums established guerrilla legitimacy suffers from problems associated with voice: is the reader hearing Lan, mediums, guerrillas, or peasants? Bourdillon's review of Lan's work raises this problem, but not to question Lan's evidence of guerrilla legitimacy.[71] In the text, the direct voices of informants on the relationship between guerrillas and peasants belong to thirty residents of Dande who were asked by Lan to record 'some of their experience of the war as well as a range of other materials they wished to preserve'.[72] They rarely directly address the issue of guerrilla legitimacy. Sidestepping how these residents were selected, these residents' notebooks bias Lan's study towards the thoughts and experiences of the tiny minority of literate people. Also, only eleven of the thirty notebooks appear in the text, and he relies heavily on only four, all of whom were *youth* (*mujibas*). Apart from using these respondents, Lan supports his case that the guerrillas' pact with the mediums facilitated guerrilla legitimacy by reproducing a quote from Tungamirai, the Chief Political Commissar for ZANLA. In short, peasant voices on guerrilla legitimacy are virtually absent in Lan's text.[73]

Lan's argument about guerrilla legitimacy is weakened because he often fails to reproduce what his informants told him, so that one does not know whose voice one is hearing. For instance Lan asserts: 'By these means the authority of the ancestors was tapped to provide legitimacy to armed resistance and violent insurrection and the pact between guerrillas and peasants was struck at such great depth that the peasants began invariably and unthinkingly to refer to the guerrillas as *vasikana* and *vakomana*, our daughters and our sons.'[74] Similarly, he notes, without reproducing any voices, that people transferred their political loyalty from the chiefs to guerrillas 'with a minimum of anxiety'.[75] And again, when Lan maintains that the guerrillas were seen as autochthons or super-autochthons, the reader does not know whose voice is being reproduced.[76] On the legitimacy of guerrillas killing 'sell-outs', an ex-*mujiba* (*youth*) is cited as saying: 'It's very very good to kill those witches.'[77] Otherwise the reader is presented with an occasional guerrilla voice, or Lan's summary of what people said. 'When I arrived in Dande, faith in the ability of the ZANLA guerrillas to deal with witches was still strong. Some people maintained that there were fewer witches than ever before because of the good work the guerrillas had done. Others feared that now the guerrillas had left them the witches would return.'[78]

An additional problem of voice, that complicates evaluating Lan's evidence for guerrilla legitimacy, arises from what he chooses to highlight or ignore from the quotations of those informants that he does reproduce. Lan argues that the most frequent type of guerrilla coercion was directed against government informers and witches and was a boon to guerrilla legitimacy. Consequently, he ignores guerrilla coercion against people who did not 'sell out', even when his respondents comment on it. Lan presents the following portion of a sixteen-year-old female *youth*'s account of how she was recruited by guerrillas.[79]

> I was fast asleep when the guerrillas came. They passed through our village. I asked the boys what they were looking for. They said that they were looking for girls. All the girls are wanted at the headman's village. When I arrived there they said: How are you, sister? I said: I am fine and how are you? They said: Do you want to go where the others are going? I said: Truly, I am not going anywhere. They said: We are not playing games with you today. If you are so lucky that you haven't died before, today you are surely going to visit the cemetery. I started crying. They said: Come. You are going to cook for us. So I went.

Lan's only comment is that 'not all recruitment took place at the *morari*'; he makes no reference to the respondent's point about guerrilla coercion. Lan cites the same young girl later, this time to highlight that 'for those who fled their villages and lived with their children in the forest, life was unbearably hard'. But contained in the respondent's account, there is again a pointed reference to guerrilla coercion to which Lan does not explicitly draw attention.[80]

> The parents began to cry and we said: You must be brave like we are. The parents asked for food. We said: Do you think we grow anything while we are in the bush? They took bamboo shoots and gave them to the children. One woman complained: Do you call that food? And the comrade said: Woman, do you want to stay alive? And she kept quiet. Then she began to speak softly. She said: We people, we are now wild animals. Our children are now wild animals. Do you think we shall ever go back home and grow crops? And she began to cry again.

Lan himself gives an instance of guerrilla coercion against people who were not 'selling out' to the government but were ignoring guerrilla instructions. 'When I arrived in Dande, some nine months after the guerrillas had departed, it was still widely believed that if you defied the *mhondoro* and worked in your fields on the *chisi* rest days you would be fined, beaten or perhaps even killed by the guerrillas.'[81] But the point Lan goes on to make is about the mediums' great (moral) authority during the war rather than the guerrillas' coercive authority. Despite Lan's claim that guerrilla coercion was most frequently against 'sell-outs', the evidence of his respondents suggests that coercion against anyone who disobeyed the guerrillas was common. An evaluation of guerrilla legitimacy must take into account the effects of this type of guerrilla coercion.

Lan's argument that guerrilla coercion against 'sell-outs' enhanced their legitimacy rests on a symbolic analysis that has been rejected. Lan argues that witches, the source of evil, were symbolically opposed to the *mhondoro* mediums, the source of moral authority and goodness. The guerrillas, fighting for a new moral order, came to be seen in the same symbolic category as the *mhondoro* mediums, while 'sell-outs', who opposed the guerrillas and allied themselves to the white government, came to be identified in symbolic terms as witches.[82] Hence the killing of 'sell-outs' fostered guerrilla legitimacy. Bourdillon's review suggests that Lan makes too much of witches being the cognitive antithesis of *mhondoro* and of the symbolic association of the guerrillas with the *mhondoro*. Bourdillon points out that Lan's depiction of the mediums as anti-government symbols is also problematic. Just because mediums observed taboos on Western clothing, cars and other things introduced by whites does not necessarily mean that they were anti-government; it may merely reflect the extent to which they had been untouched by development.[83] He also argues that some mediums did not subscribe to Lan's symbolic system, therefore 'we may reasonably assume that the system was not the cognitive base of many of the people less concerned with religious symbols'. He says: 'I would make more of the guerrillas' recognition of the need for unity in the communities supporting them. Any kind of deviance or conflict would increase the danger of individuals leaking information to government forces.'[84] In short, people did not have to be pro-government to be called 'sell-outs' by the guerrillas. By assuming that 'sell-outs' were pro-government, Lan overstates the legitimacy of guerrilla coercion and hence their popular support.

Another illustration of the problems of evidence associated with Lan's selective downplaying or discounting of what informants actually say is his neglect of the costs of the war imposed on civilians by guerrilla demands for food and other supplies. This omission creates the potential for his analysis to overstate guerrilla legitimacy and popular support. What Lan interprets as a *youth's* 'good times' might seem to others to portray immense hardships. His young respondent wrote: 'We would go on patrol from 5 pm to 7 am and then return and tell the comrades what we saw. We would carry things on our backs, heavy things like guns. We would dig trenches on the road so that if a car comes passed it falls in. We were cooking sadza (porridge) for the comrades at their base. When we were in the bush we were singing and saying slogans: Forward with war! Forward with being brave! These are some of the slogans that I know.'[85] Presumably it is in the reference to singing that Lan finds 'good times', but singing need not express joy or happiness. Again it is Lan's interpretation, and not his respondent's. Moreover, others might be struck by the physical demands on *youth*, on which Lan does not comment.

Citing his respondents, Lan points out how soldiers burnt granaries, depriving people of food.[86] Lan is also aware that people were also having to feed the guerrillas.[87] An ex-guerrilla whom he cites even refers to the tensions between guerrillas and civilians over the issue of having to feed the guerrillas. 'At the end of the meeting we would say to the older people: "Mothers and Fathers, go home now and sleep in peace. But children you must stay here [sic]. The younger people would stay, and we would then say: "What is our support here? Are people in favour of us, are people speaking against us and who is doing so?" Then they would tell us, for example, that some people were saying that they didn't have enough food to eat themselves without giving some to us. And many other complaints came out as well.'[88] Yet Lan does not comment on the effect of the large guerrilla army on civilians' food supplies. Instead, he finds that feeding the population drew it into the resistance and contributed to the guerrillas achieving the status of chiefs.[89] Ignoring the costs of feeding the guerrillas, he blames the regime alone for problems of malnourishment arising from lack of food, and asserts that 'this of course hugely increased the support the guerrillas received'.[90] The case for deprivation increasing guerrilla support rests on the following quote of a respondent. 'Many places were now short of salt, meat, sugar. People suffered from various types of disease. The comrades went and explained this to their leaders and they were given medicines to cure the people. This showed how friendly the comrades were towards us.'[91] The problem with Lan's interpretation of this statement to mean that food shortages led to increased guerrilla support is that we are led to believe that the informant holds the government responsible for the shortages of salt, meat, and sugar because of the context. But, according to what we are told, the informant, a *youth*, never explicitly says that. Nor does he say that food shortages enhanced guerrilla support. He only says that the comrades gave medicines to the people, and that this was seen as a gesture of friendliness. It is Lan's voice saying that regime-related food shortages led to further support for the guerrillas and not the voice of his informants.

In summary, Lan's evidence for guerrilla legitimacy comes from a selective group, chiefly literate *youth* and mediums. His tendency to report to the reader his conclusions about what informants told him rather than to produce their direct quotations raises other problems of evidence. His selective use of evidence leads him to downplay both guerrilla coercion, other than killing 'sell-outs', and the costs of the war to the peasants of having to feed the guerrillas. The effect of these omissions leads him to overstate the extent of guerrilla legitimacy. Lan's argument, based on symbolic analysis, that killing 'sell-outs' heightened guerrilla legitimacy has also been found to be flawed. Whereas Lan emphasizes the frequency of guerrilla coercion against government collaborators, Bourdillon stresses coercion against anyone who fails to comply with guerrilla commands.

In his book *Under the Skin*, David Caute argues that Rhodesian ideology and government propaganda contributed to whites' false consciousness so that they were dazed by the African vote for the exiled nationalist parties in 1980. The book is also a powerful account of government and guerrilla atrocities. Caute finds rural support for the guerrillas despite repeated accounts of guerrilla coercion, the costs of meeting their demands for provisions, and their closing of schools. For Caute, this is the central paradox of rural Zimbabwe, but he never attempts to resolve it.[92] It is, after all, not his subject of study.

Caute courageously travelled through the countryside during 1979 when the war was probably at its fiercest. His account is based on interviews with African teachers and clerics in the rural areas, white farmers, missionaries, and union leaders. He effectively juxtaposes his findings with official war communiqués and statements from the party and army leaders of the exiled movements, which lead him to be cynical about the posturing of all the political and military leaders involved in the conflict. Peasant voices do not appear presumably because it was too dangerous to enter the Tribal Trust Lands. Guerrilla coercion and the costs of the war, though based on data obtained from African elites and missionaries in Caute's study, are important ingredients of my argument against peasants' popular support for the guerrillas. He himself accepts that there was popular support but is content to leave its existence an unresolved paradox.

The most important literature on the relations between ZANU guerrillas and peasants during the war finds that the guerrillas had the popular support of the peasantry. For many, the key factors were the guerrilla campaigns of political mobilization and education. Even Lan, who concentrates on the way in which ancient religious and ritual symbols were used, argues that these merely facilitated the process of guerrilla legitimacy; political mobilization and education were its backbone. Ranger and Astrow place less emphasis on the guerrillas educating the peasants because they characterize peasants as having a radical nationalist (Ranger) or socialist revolutionary (Astrow) consciousness. It is striking how all the studies reviewed emphasize the efficacy of normative guerrilla appeals, and, except for Astrow's, of their cultural nationalist appeals. Caute's study differs from these studies of the war because he does not seek to explain why the guerrillas won popular support. Taking each study, I have argued that the evidence for popular support is flawed and unsatisfactory and almost never relies on peasant voices.

Terence Ranger has described how after 1962 when the Rhodesia Front party came to power, foreign researchers experienced often insurmountable difficulties of research access.[93] He himself had been deported earlier because of his support for the nationalists. During the 1970s, censorship increased and only journalists sympathetic to the government were allowed to travel with an official party to the rural war zones. The only information during the war from the rural areas that was not based on official military communiqués, liberation movement reports, or journalists partial to either side, came from deported missionaries and rural church workers who were sympathetic to the guerrilla cause.[94] Immediately after the war, the new ZANU-PF government was astonishingly open to rural research, and many foreign academics took advantage of this new, and regrettably short-lived, openness. Yet this more open research policy did not produce studies that depended on peasant interviews, despite widespread interest in the war-time relationship between guerrillas and peasants and in rural research.

Re-evaluating the effects of guerrilla appeals and government coercion on civilians

Using interviews with peasants, *youth*, and the rural elite, this chapter proceeds to re-evaluate the effect of guerrilla appeals on peasants. Particular attention is devoted to guerrilla coercion, whose negative effects have often been discounted, and to the lack of utilitarian appeals, that has often been overlooked. The weakness of peasant nationalism and the overemphasis on cultural nationalist appeals in the case for popular support have already been discussed. First, though, the relationship between government coercion, often alleged to abet revolutionary mobilization, and collective action is discussed.

Government coercion and repression

In the literature on the Zimbabwean war, it is often alleged that government coercion abetted mobilization by arousing or intensifying peasant hatred of the government.[95] Fanon's *Wretched of the Earth* asserts that at a certain stage in the history of anti-colonial struggles, settler government repressions encourage the colonized to engage in violent struggle against the colonizers and intensify their national consciousness.[96] Revolutionary strategists also often believe that government repression can help their cause. The Brazilian guerrilla leader Marighella presumed that guerrilla attacks on government installations would provoke the government to retaliate with repressive measures. These would so incense the population that it would throw its support behind the guerrillas.[97] Many other revolutionaries have advocated strategies that would intensify government repression because they believed it would hasten mass mobilization. They reason that peaceful mass agitation fails only because government repression inhibits people from voicing their anti-government feelings. Therefore if they can undermine the regime's repressive strategy through terror, revolutionaries expect to unleash the political energies of the masses and spur mass mobilization. By lashing out at innocent people rather than the terrorists, who are difficult to capture, the government will alienate people and their moral outrage will serve as an incentive to join the movement.[98] De Nardo accepts that 'terrorism can sometimes stimulate mobilization by provoking untoward repression against innocent people' and concedes that the idea has a strong common-sense appeal. But he notes that 'campaigns of repression tend to be short-lived and quickly

135

forgotten. They provide a far less stable source of support than persistent ideological grievances.' Government repression in the guerrilla war was enduring rather than short-lived, but de Nardo's point is pertinent: 'The danger from the radical's point of view is misinterpreting sympathetic moral reactions against a regime's repressiveness as ideological commitment to the movement's demands.'[99]

In contrast to the emphasis that some have placed on how government repression may rebound to the advantage of revolutionary movements, others have described how government repression complicates revolutionary organization and mobilization. Rational choice theories of political participation argue that people are more willing to engage in political action when the risks of government retaliation are low. Hence the degree of protection from government repression that a revolutionary movement is able to offer becomes an important factor in determining whether people will join.[100] Andrei Amalrik's essay, *Will the Soviet Union Survive until 1984?* pointed out how waves of government repression reduced the membership of the Democratic Movement in the Soviet Union.

> The number of supporters of the movement is almost as indeterminable as its aim. They amount to several dozen active participants and several hundred who sympathize with the movement and give it their support. It would be impossible to give an exact number, not only because it is unknown but also because it is constantly changing. Now, when the regime is 'escalating repression', the movement will probably go into decline – some of its members will go to prison and others will sever their connections with it. However, as soon as the pressure subsides, the number of members will probably rise again.[101]

The Democratic Movement was not an armed opposition movement but Amalrik makes an important point about how sensitive people are to government repression when they make decisions about political commitments to organizations. Murphy Morobe, Acting Publicity Secretary of the United Democratic Front in South Africa, speaks about government repression from an organizer's perspective. Addressing the first conference of the Institute for a Democratic Alternative for South Africa, he spoke of the difficulties of 'organizing democratically at gunpoint' and of how 'the need for tight security and secrecy obviously puts a strain on the development of a mass-based democratic practice'.[102]

It is difficult to evaluate either the case for government repression abetting revolutionary mobilization or for it complicating mobilization and organization because of the dearth of empirical data – at least in the literature on revolutions – on how different individuals and groups respond to government repression. Bettelheim's research on how prisoners in concentration camps responded to the brutality of the camps serves as a caveat against assumptions that state brutality inspires hatred of the state and collective resistance to it. He found that the longer prisoners were subjected to the camp regimen, the more likely they were to integrate the values of their oppressors. New prisoners were unlikely to resist as long as they perceived they had a chance of surviving the experience. Prisoners responded to 'normal' slapping and kicking by the SS guards by directing their anger at individual SS guards and not, as one might expect, at the entire institution. Again, counter-intuitively, new prisoners were most likely to experience group unity, freedom from fear and a willingness to resist when they shared a common life-threatening plight, not in more 'routine' instances of brutality.[103] I was struck on several occasions at how villagers directed anger at individual paramilitary members of the Guard Force and Auxiliaries, whom they perceived to be more brutal than government Security Forces. This attitude is reminiscent of the particularly virulent hostility felt by Ndebele after the 1893 war to Shona police rather than, as one might have expected, against white police.[104] We need to know more about individual perceptions towards the different units, and what connections they made between their brutality and the political system before making inferences about the relationship between state brutality, hatred of the system, and collective resistance.

There are other examples where government repression does not lead to resistance but to submission. Barrington Moore's *Injustice: The Social Bases of Obedience and Revolt* tries to understand the socio-cultural factors that lead some people – ascetics, untouchable Hindus, some concentration camp prisoners – to submit to degradation and oppression and to accept the moral authority of their oppressors. He identifies four types of social processes that help to inhibit collective efforts to identify, reduce, or resist collectively the human causes of pain and suffering. Not all derive from government action or the behaviour of dominant groups. First, solidarity within an oppressed group forms readily against an individual protester because any single act of defiance runs the risk of retaliation that threatens the whole group. Hence a group's own efforts at self-defence can easily serve to perpetuate and even intensify its submission. Second, social processes may destroy prior social ties and habits among the oppressed to the point where individuals are left without social support. Third, groups can be co-opted through social learning at an early age to accept their oppression as inevitable and justified. Aggressive impulses produced by oppression will be turned inward against the self rather than against the oppressor. Finally, oppressed groups may fragment according to class, ethnicity, religion, or other categories and intensify existing social bonds that are themselves destructive. Too much social support, or support unsuited to the circumstances, can render a person as ineffective as no support at all.[105] Perhaps most relevant to efforts of the colonized to collectively resist a repressive colonial regime is the process of co-option through social learning. In *Wretched of the Earth* Fanon characterizes the effects of colonial repression on the colonized in this way. Instead of turning the anger and resentment of the oppressed against their oppressors, the colonization process has succeeded in turning their anger inwards on themselves or against each other. According to Fanon, armed struggle liberates the oppressed from these impediments to collective resistance – a subject explored in chapter 5.

Government repression may produce informers who undermine efforts at collective action against the government. The question is who in the population is likely to become an informer. Bettelheim's work on how prisoners in concentration camps responded to the brutality of the camps hints at what groups of people best survive such conditions. He found that those most equipped to survive the first year with personal integrity were the politically educated who could make sense for themselves of their plight. After only one year, all behavioural differences between old and newer prisoners began to disappear, and personality disintegration took its toll indiscriminately.[106] Invidious as comparisons of brutality are, the concentration camps represent a more draconian case than government atrocities and repression in the war in Zimbabwe. Robert Coles' attempt to understand why some civil rights activists in the United States in the 1960s collapsed and others withstood the strain of government repression provides a case of much less severe repression than either the camps or the war in Zimbabwe. Coles could not answer the question but he found, contrary to Bettelheim's evidence, that the most ideological were the least successful in coping with government repression. But in both the concentration camps and the civil rights movement, he maintained that the more ideological tended to keep out of trouble themselves and to persuade others to make the necessary sacrifices.[107] If ideology is important in surviving repression, I would speculate that the educated elite in Zimbabwe would have been better equipped to withstand or avoid coercion than the villagers who, I argue, had a poor understanding of, and low commitment to, nationalist politics.

Certainly, contrary examples exist in which there was collective resistance to state brutality. Da Cunha's *Rebellion in the Backlands* describes how, in the late nineteenth century, a small group of people in the hinterland town of Canudos in Brazil, and with allegiance to a leader-prophet, came to be perceived as a threat to the recently proclaimed Brazilian republican government and became the target of an official military campaign. The community's most fervent and faithful members were women, children, the infirm, and aged. Criminals, cowboys of the north, and backwoodsmen constituted the backbone of the leader-prophet's 1,000 armed men supporters, who also included both religious fanatics and adventurers. Da Cunha, who accompanied the army as a reporter, relates sympathetically the success of the 'rebels' at rebuffing the various official military expeditions sent to crush them. He ridicules the bungling of the well-equipped army against 'rebels' who depended on gunpowder they manufactured themselves, stones, clubs, and, most humiliatingly for the soldiers, yelling ironic calls and names at the soldiers. He expresses contempt and moral outrage at the army's goal of wiping out the backland settlement rather than taking education to the area. 'Rebel' victories against the well-armed soldiers intensified their religious fervour and their brutality toward the soldiers but the army's expeditions exacted extremely high losses on the settlement at Canudos. The final expedition finds the chief inhabitants of the town to be women and children who choose to let the men have the scarce food because collective survival depends on them. Da Cunha notes that the leader's death after he refused to eat because of government attacks on the settlement's church could have marked the end of the rebellion, but instead led to a resurgence. News went out that he was in heaven arranging re-supplies, and, although unbelievers left, fanatics remained. When entirely under siege, and faced with certain death, the 'rebels' did not quit but showed an incredible resistance, which reverses only further stiffened.[108] What made this group respond with collective action and fight to a person, despite all odds, against the state's military might and barbarity? The key seems to lie in its religious fervour and commitment to its messianic leader. This case does not appear to be applicable to peasants facing government repression in Zimbabwe. A central task for the guerrillas was to try to create peasant unity and solidarity.

The case for government coercion against peasants intensifying their nationalist sentiments and fostering mobilization in Zimbabwe has a strong common-sense appeal, but so too does the counter-argument that repressive conditions make democratic mobilization, organization, and political participation more difficult. More empirical work on the relationship between state brutality, peasant resentments against the state, and collective resistance are necessary. What factors might explain individual variation in responses? Who are most likely to become 'sell-outs' in repressive environments? Are some environments especially likely to produce 'sell-outs'?

Utilitarian appeals

The case for ZANLA's popular support in Zimbabwe rests almost exclusively on the guerrillas' normative appeals, and, at least for Ranger and Astrow, on peasants already having a revolutionary consciousness. Utilitarian appeals, positive and negative, receive little attention. Except for Caute's study, none of the existing studies consider the implications of the guerrillas' demands for food and their destruction of government rural services (such as schools and clinics) for peasants' popular support. Nor do they take into account the guerrillas' inability to protect rural civilians from regime brutality. Positive appeals to status and power that individuals might derive from participating in organizations are also neglected. To determine whether there was popular support for guerrillas, the costs and benefits of utilitarian appeals must be assessed. Mancur Olson has argued that 'unless the number of individuals in a group is quite small, or unless

139

there is coercion or some other special device to make individuals act in their common interest, rational, self-interested individuals will not act to achieve their common or group interests'.[109] Special devices include individual material, social, and psychological incentives and coercion covers both violence and threats as well as the denial of benefits. This book's concept of coercion is narrower and excludes the withdrawal of benefits, but it shares the assumption of rational choice theories that individuals are often enough rational and self-interested and will not contribute to their common interests voluntarily unless they are offered special incentives.

Material benefits: resources and services

In cost-benefit calculations of the net flow of material benefits, the distinction between *youth* and *parents* is fundamental. *Parents* enjoyed a reprieve from local government rates (tables 4.1 and 4.2) and fees for government services, such as education (tables 4.3 and 4.4), dipping (tables 4.3 and 4.5), health (table 4.6), and marketing (table 4.7) because of guerrilla appeals that they stop supporting an unjust government. Later the government itself introduced concessions on some taxes and fees. In March 1979 tuition grants were introduced in rural government schools, in effect providing free education, and from July 1979 African Development Fund levies on cattle and produce were abolished. Two further concessions were made after the ceasefire, but they affect the data on rates and fees in the financial year 1979/80. Free dipping came into effect in the Tribal Trust Lands on 1 January 1980 and the newly independent government abolished the prescribed area tax from June 1980 thus freeing councils from having to impose any rate.[110] The tables on the collection of rates (table 4.1) and fees (table 4.3) for Mutoko show an unbroken decline from 1974/5 and 1975/6 respectively, except for the collection of council rates in Charewa (table 4.1), which increased from R$1,712 in 1976/7 to R$2,811 in 1977/8. However, the other tables on council rates and fees by province do not show a continuous decline. For example, table 4.5 shows that the collection of council dip fees in Mashonaland East province, in which Mutoko is located, almost doubled from R$74,094 in 1974/5 to R$138,472 in 1977/8. Government tax collections ordinarily varied from year to year but this huge increase largely reflects government strong-arm tactics. Even before martial law, district commissioners proudly proclaimed their success collecting taxes with the help of police or Security Forces. A district commissioner was cited in the *Rhodesia Herald*, the daily newspaper in Salisbury, in 1977 as saying: 'The people are not paying because they are not being allowed to pay. We have effectively solved this problem in a number of areas by arranging for security forces to accompany the district commissioner of an area when he goes to collect the rates. The effect is quite incredible. The people pay up.'[111] Similarly, the district

Table 4.1 *The collection of council rates in Mutoko district (R$)*

Year ended 30 June	Mutoko	Charewa	Chimoyo	Budjga
1974/5	17,767	10,207	7,980	3,021
1975/6	13,237	8,564	7,260	3,449
1976/7	8,517	1,712	3,390	2,682
1977/8	7,346	2,811	4,327	2,265
1978/9	489	328	238	1,197
1979/80	—	—	—	50

Table 4.2 *Collection of council rates in each province and countrywide (R$)*

Province	1974/5	1975/6	1976/7	1977/8	1978/9	1979/80
Mashonaland East	220,367	236,226	187,636	163,821	48,852	4,532
Mashonaland Ctrl	103,741	106,336	125,081	127,436	89,204	8,540
Mashonaland West	100,468	102,937	130,024	125,417	80,591	3,523
Matabeleland North	93,651	110,608	110,352	95,676	36,971	9,266
Matabeleland South	69,655	77,161	81,542	73,793	43,239	17,448
Midlands	264,689	279,026	288,061	254,147	152,417	27,080
Victoria	231,471	248,113	172,472	175,119	164,800	26,881
Manicaland	96,127	130,402	69,461	25,919	30,616	5,416

commissioner, Murewa district, reported to the provincial commissioner of Mashonaland East in January 1977 that 'an exercise was carried out last year in Uzumba to collect Council rates, Dog tax and School fees. This was done mainly by Internal Affairs but there was also a Police presence. The object of the Police presence was to add more power to the exercise . . . There was no Army present and armed Police and Internal Affairs were responsible for the protection of all concerned.'[112] After 'protected villages' had been introduced, Zimbabwean sociologist Coenrad Brand described how 'when wanting to leave on a trip, receipts for their local taxes may be demanded and if they fail to produce them, they would be stopped from proceeding until these have been paid'.[113] When martial law was introduced, the Ministry of Internal Affairs issued a circular saying: 'As far as this Ministry is concerned, the primary reason for Martial Law is the *restoration of the administration.*' From its vantage point, martial law could 'be used for the collection of rates and taxes', 'to restore a measure of tribal authority', and provide 'the means by which tribesmen will recover the services they have lost through terrorist action'.[114] In November 1979, the Ministry of Internal Affairs, renamed Home Affairs, instructed district commissioners to stop using government forces to enforce collection of current or outstanding rates 'in view of the delicate

Table 4.3 *School and dip fees collected by councils in Mutoko district (R$)*

Year ended 30 June	School fees				Dip fees
	Budjga	Charewa	Chimoyo	Mutoko	Budjga
1975/6	3,904	12,533	12,351	10,485	3,906
1976/7	2,743	3,825	549	1,576	n.a.
1977/8	605	22	4	19	2,286
1978/9	—	—	—	—	497
1979/80	—	—	—	—	30

Table 4.4 *School fees collected by councils in each province and countrywide (R$)*

Province	1974/5	1975/6	1976/7	1977/8	1978/9	1979/80
Mashonaland East	198,090	293,610	254,406	236,779	63,925	48,031
Mashonaland Ctrl	95,810	122,298	98,409	151,480	72,593	6,295
Mashonaland West	160,160	182,805	255,945	201,823	41,728	192
Matabeleland North	81,431	142,190	149,339	54,238	7,508	250
Matabeleland South	61,447	110,667	89,836	31,276	2,035	10
Midlands	245,765	391,988	352,961	140,007	48,706	584
Victoria	236,124	365,929	307,676	128,406	9,429	337
Manicaland	119,506	230,458	89,132	4,220	836	—

Table 4.5 *Dip fees collected by councils by province and countrywide (R$)*

Province	1974/5	1975/6	1976/7	1977/8	1978/9	1979/80
Mashonaland East	74,094	77,060	93,052	138,472	52,540	21,884
Mashonaland Ctrl	41,378	48,146	66,553	68,307	67,119	10,085
Mashonaland West	47,878	52,767	67,556	76,082	32,170	1,256
Matabeleland North	30,635	31,775	39,946	n.a.	11,350	7,254
Matabeleland South	27,573	29,686	27,243	n.a.	9,272	419
Midlands	80,802	81,782	108,174	n.a.	33,377	113
Victoria	132,295	111,596	221,665	n.a.	50,104	114
Manicaland	116,235	123,968	66,318	9,662	86	—

political development at present' – a reference to the Lancaster House constitutional talks.[115] The break from paying government rates and fees was not always as uninterrupted as in Mutoko but was a clearcut gain, *ceteris paribus*. Some *parents* were also able to buy meat from cattle obtained in raids on white farms, and, despite guerrilla policies, from Purchase Area farms. Again, all things being equal, this represents a benefit. But the guerrillas did not merely try to end government tax and fee payments and introduce cheaper meat for peasants. They also demanded that peasants contribute 'war taxes' payable in food, money, and labour.

Table 4.6 *Health fees collected by councils by province and countrywide (R$)*

Province	1974/5	1975/6	1976/7	1977/8	1978/9	1979/80
Mashonaland East	40,743	51,222	60,333	52,464	32,590	27,882
Mashonaland Ctrl	14,919	23,343	30,477	33,400	21,505	16,641
Mashonaland West	13,702	18,333	20,460	21,681	13,694	7,095
Matabeleland North	9,395	16,421	19,246	11,051	6,508	9,524
Matabeleland South	11,012	18,830	21,592	11,167	3,953	4,265
Midlands	47,978	60,346	73,323	60,443	15,781	23,963
Victoria	25,073	27,663	30,122	22,227	20,972	23,187
Manicaland	26,268	34,170	24,294	8,508	5,372	6,408

Source of tables 4.1–4.6: compiled from data obtained from council balance sheets, Chief Internal Auditor, June 1981. Ministry of Local Government and Housing, Division of District Administration.

Table 4.7 *African Development Fund's revenue from fees/taxes (R$)*

	Fees/Charges				
Year	Dip	Levies	Marketing/production	Prescribed area tax	Total
1972/3	954,092	1,627,162	310,440	451,182	4,743,350
1973/4	1,007,476	1,352,046	401,422	379,583	5,270,464
1974/5	942,792	2,241,314	511,237	220,004	6,562,226
1975/6	1,035,383	1,595,830	327,570	138,176	
1976/7	1,518,567	1,990,800	337,298	139,141	7,005,578
1977/8	463,065	575,323	155,162	275,419	5,559,448
1978/9	400,000	1,125,300	90,000	407,260	3,786,407
1979/80	400,000	—	320,000	—	4,831,000

1979/80 figures are unrevised.

Source: compiled from annual estimates of the African Development Fund.

Youth had no financial responsibilities to the government; nor did they have to provide food and money to the guerrillas. While *parents* struggled to pay their 'war taxes', *youth* and guerrillas consumed them. Since they ate together, the more lavishly *parents* contributed to the guerrillas, the better the *youth* ate. With meat regularly included in the guerrillas' diet, *youth* probably ate more of it than usual during the war. What *youth* perceived as benefits for *parents* – medicines the guerrillas sometimes distributed to *parents* and the help they themselves gave to *parents* in their fields when en route to Mozambique with guerrillas – *parents* never even mentioned. Instead, *parents* dwelled on the costs of supporting the guerrillas. Chapter 5 discusses further the different interests and behaviour of *youth* and *parents*. The following comment of a war chairman whose children were enthusiastic and prominent guerrilla supporters underscores

Table 4.8 *Livestock on white farms in Mutoko Intensive Conservation Area*

Year	Farms	Beef cattle	Farms	Dairy cattle	Total cattle
1975	66	35,185	16	192	36,205
1976	67	36,680	16	160	37,729
1977	64	34,901	14	200	35,221
1978	60	26,638	12	88	27,520
1979	47	16,635	10	81	16,716
1980	30	7,109	9	118	7,306

Source: Mutoko Intensive Conservation Area, Department of Statistics, unpublished data.

the different costs and benefits to *youth* and *parents* of the guerrillas' demands for food. His view that *youth* had encouraged the guerrillas' extravagant demands for food was novel.

> *Parents* lost a lot of cattle because of *youth*. *Youth* told comrades: 'Our *parents* are rich; they have lots of cattle.' *Youth* would eat with comrades, so they wanted meat too. If comrades weren't in the area for a while and *youth* wanted meat, they'd go looking for them. They'd bring comrades from Katsukunya and then we'd have to kill cattle. At first, comrades weren't interested in meat but when *youth* started to tell them 'our parents are rich', they'd start demanding a goat from each house and if you didn't have a goat, then four chickens.

To the *parents*, the guerrillas' demands for meat, a luxury in their personal diets, were extravagant. It rankled that they had to watch their meagre assets consumed. At best, they received below market price compensation. Their resentment spilled out in understated comments, such as 'comrades were not satisfied with vegetables, they wanted meat'; 'comrades always ate meat – even at midnight *youth* could wake us to try to find a goat'; 'twenty comrades could eat ten chickens'; 'we could cook five times in a night if the food was not enough for the comrades, and then still be asked to get a goat from each village'. Before his colleagues, a teacher sardonically mimicked how villagers had to cater to the tastes of different guerrilla groups. One group might ask for liver, saying 'it's good. We like it. Give it to us.' Another group might say: 'We don't like entrails. Throw it out. Our *mudzimu* (spirits) don't like this.'[116]

Meat supplies for feeding a large guerrilla army were partly met by cattle raids on white farms. Table 4.8 shows the decline in livestock from 36,205 in 1975 to 7,306 in 1980 on white farms in Mutoko Intensive Conservation Area during the war years. Not all the drop in cattle on white farms can be attributed to cattle raids. As the table suggests, white-occupied farms declined and many farmers took their cattle with them. Others sometimes sold their cattle herds to pre-empt guerrilla raids because although the government offered compensation, it was too meagre to finance rebuilding herds. Although cattle raids reduced guerrilla demands for meat, there were still tremendous pressures on villagers' livestock and poultry holdings. The rapid erosion of what were often villagers' most valuable assets is evident in comments such as 'Every *parent* would rotate giving goats. When they were all gone, they would give cattle.' A war chairman, responsible for seeing that his organizer found a goat for the guerrillas, remembered being anxious because 'the comrades had eaten all our goats' and trying to buy goats 'from villages far away' became difficult because 'they were all used up and scarce by now'. Two other statements by villagers make the point compellingly.

> At first, we'd buy a goat from locals. Then the comrades began demanding that each family take turns in providing a goat without pay.

> At first, when comrades came, we'd give chickens free. When all the chickens were finished, we started with goats which we got paid for.

Villagers were under pressure to sell their livestock cheaply. 'Goats were costing about $6 then – normally even a small one costs $15. If people charged more you could threaten to report to comrades', said a villager. Another villager, speaking before a group, also spoke of social pressures on people to lower their selling prices. 'Goats and cows were cheaper than usual because we couldn't afford more. It was just helping one another. We'd buy three cows in a month for $60; everyday we'd have to get goats for $10–$16.' He went on to say: 'Mostly we paid for the cows and goats, but sometimes we didn't have enough money to buy cattle for the comrades. So we'd borrow a cow or goats. We haven't repaid these people yet.'

To help repay these debts, and to ensure that war taxes were equitably shared, villagers charged those who had fled during the war a resettlement fee based on what they would have had to contribute if they had been in the village. When the Mugabe government prohibited these fees as part of its reconciliation programme, people who were owed money felt cheated. Not only would the government not compensate them for their property losses, but it prevented them from being compensated by other villagers. Their sense of injustice was heightened by their perception that the government had rewarded guerrillas by giving them the choice of a paid position in the army or a generous financial incentive to leave the oversized army and train to join the civilian sector. 'If we went to JOC [Joint Operations Command] Mutoko and asked comrades to pay us now, they wouldn't', was a bitter refrain of *parents* across the district.

Demands for resources coincided with other war-related pressures on *parents'* resources. The 'protected village' programme had disrupted routine farming. Located far from their fields, and having to obey curfews, people often had little time for farming. Those who could afford it bought more food, for which prices had risen. Everywhere rural malnutrition was a problem.[117] Unable to guard their fields at night, many had personal property stolen. Also, government policies to try to cut the guerrillas off from their civilian food supply led to the introduction of legal limits on how much food could be stocked in stores and sold per person, and grain mills were closed.[118] Punitive counter-insurgency measures against entire villages for alleged complicity in cattle raids on European farms often involved seizing and killing villagers' cattle. Guerrilla strategies also contributed to food shortages. The guerrilla prohibition on cattle dipping had resulted in cattle losses through disease and death. As a result of not dipping, tsetse fly killed over one million cattle in the Tribal Trust Lands.[119] In Mutoko Tribal Trust Land, many farmers stopped producing the major cash crops, groundnuts and cotton, because of guerrilla strictures on producing for the market. Ironically, the beneficiaries of these policies were the Purchase Area farmers. When guerrilla orders began to affect them in late 1978, they stopped selling to the Grain Marketing Board, a government marketing organization, but found a ready market for their maize in the Tribal Trust Land because of food shortages there.[120]

Cognisant of *parents'* resentment, the guerrillas – many of whom died of malnutrition – sometimes made wild promises of compensating them for their cattle. A grade seven boy, a child during the war, recalled the guerrillas saying: 'Parents, don't worry about killing your cattle for us. You'll get plenty more when you are independent.' A headmaster also referred to guerrilla promises to *parents* that 'they'd get free animals and money'. Some *parents* and *youth* claim that the guerrillas promised them paid party or government positions after independence.

Some evidence appears to contradict my claims about food pressures on *parents*. Occasionally, *parents* reported an unprecedented abundance of cheap meat obtained from cattle raids. According to *parents*, *youth* instructed them to buy the meat to make them accomplices to the crime of stealing cattle and to reduce the chances of them reporting the thefts to the police. People used the word *macabbages – ma* is a Shona prefix – because meat was as plentiful and commonplace as cabbage. A current branch party chairlady described what cattle raids, referred to by the otherwise meaningless codeword, *kwanguras*, meant for people in her area.

> We were eating good food in the war. But it was difficult. You'd just buy the meat and come back quickly and hope soldiers didn't meet you and find you with the meat . . . If you hear the sound of any truck, you quickly throw the meat away, even if it is already on the fire. We could hide the meat in the mango trees here. Later soldiers found our hiding places and you could watch them climbing up the trees. So we hid meat underground. We'd leave it in the field to dry before burying it. While the meat was drying, the dogs could eat so much meat they'd get tired of it.

Occasional claims of excess meat amidst the preponderant descriptions of shortages can be easily reconciled. Some villages were located on the route back from cattle raids on the Purchase Farms or white farms and often had an abundance of meat.

How can one reconcile the enormous numbers of guerrillas who died of malnutrition with peasant accounts of extravagant guerrilla meals. Many of the guerrillas were malnourished before they reached the camps outside the country. Here food supplies were sometimes problematic. Inside the country, the guerrillas, unlike the rebels who could rely on wild game in the 1896–7 uprising against the whites, were almost entirely dependent on peasant supplies. 'Except in the game reserves, Rhodesia's wild animals had been decimated; cattle-rustlers risked detection by air.'[121] Unlike Malaysia and Kenya, Zimbabwe had no jungles that could provide the guerrillas with some food (and protection) and reduce their dependence on civilians.[122] Moreover, most Zimbabwean peasants themselves struggled to subsist. Comparative aggregate data often conceal more than they illuminate but perhaps the combined guerrilla forces as a percentage of the African population it was depending on for food is a useful indicator of the pressures on peasants. The combined guerrilla forces inside Zimbabwe at the peak of the war were about 27,000 in an African population of about six million. In contrast, there were 15,000 Algerian guerrillas in 1956–8 in an African population over eight million. The Malaysian guerrilla forces peaked at 8,000 in 1951 and the indigenous population was over five million.[123]

Over and above resource pressures on peasants, a combination of guerrilla and counter-insurgency strategies also deprived *parents* of government services to which they had become accustomed. These services included public transport, marketing, cattle dipping, clinics, and schooling for their children. As early as 1976, council-run schools were reported to be experiencing difficulties recruiting and retaining trained teachers because of the deteriorating security situation. All four councils in Mutoko district had been placed under the district commissioner's management: Chimoyo council in July 1977, Charewa and Mutoko in mid 1978, and Budjga council in the Purchase Area in February 1979. In mid 1979 a government report noted that in Mutoko, Charewa council schools were worst hit, with all eleven closed. One of sixteen Mutoko council schools was closed, but six others were 'nearly closing down'. Chimoyo council schools never officially closed and only one of seven Budjga council schools stopped operating. However, all schooling was seriously disrupted, with children commonly described as going 'part-time' to school.[124] In Mutoko and Mudzi, eighty-four United Methodist churches catering to 3,500 members had closed by the end of the war, and twenty-two Catholic centres had stopped functioning by November 1978.[125] Everywhere stores closed. By the end of the war, 1,500 primary schools and 89 secondary schools had closed countrywide, and over 1,000 of 1,500 dip tanks no longer functioned.[126]

The focus of this study is on peasants but the effect of utilitarian appeals on farm-workers on white farms deserves mention. The guerrillas encouraged Purchase Area farmers to allow farm-workers, forced by the guer-

Table 4.9 *Black farm-workers in Mutoko Intensive Conservation Area*

Year ended 30 Sept	Permanent employees			Temporary employees			Total		
	Male	Female	Total	Male	Female	Total	Male	Female	Total
1975	2,586	498	3,084	260	482	742	2,846	980	3,826
1976	2,783	510	3,295	174	680	854	2,957	1,190	4,147
1977	2,773	568	3,341	111	499	610	2,884	1,067	3,951
1978	2,662	359	3,021	131	458	589	2,793	817	3,610
1979	2,207	326	2,533	60	346	406	2,267	672	2,939
1980	1,600	336	1,936	89	254	343	1,689	590	2,279

Source: Mutoko Intensive Conservation Area. Department of Statistics, unpublished data.

rillas to leave their white employers, to live with them or work for them. Table 4.9 shows how farm-workers on white farms declined from over 4,000 in 1976 to 2,279 in 1980. Again, not all the fall-off in farm-workers can be attributed to guerrilla appeals. Many white farmers left their land, some laid off workers as their operations were curtailed during the war, and some deliberately ceased using temporary workers whom they did not know for fear that they might be hiring guerrillas disguised as farm-workers. Also, when the Muzorewa government introduced minimum wages in 1979, and the Mugabe government raised them again in 1980, many farmers laid off workers rather than pay higher wages. But many farm-workers did leave their jobs in response to guerrilla appeals. Table 4.10 indicates that non-family members increased from 261 in 1977 to 426 in 1978, and thereafter data are unavailable. Unless non-family members on Purchase Area farms increased dramatically after 1978, even if one assumes that all the increase in non-family members on their farms came from farm-workers, the scale of Purchase farmers' intake is unlikely to have matched the numbers of farm-workers seeking alternative jobs and homes. Most farm-workers who abided by guerrilla appeals probably suffered net losses as most Purchase Area farmers did not provide jobs and homes to farm-workers.

To assess the material costs and benefits for the rural population, it is necessary to distinguish between the much greater material losses sustained by adults, whether *parents*, farm-workers, or the rural elite, and those experienced by *youth*. In short, *parents* lost resources (food and money) and access to valued government services in return for a reprieve from government taxes and fees. On balance, by any objective measures, it is unlikely that *parents* were better off. Subjectively, they clearly resented the disruptive effects of the war, and the lopsided exchange with the guerrillas. The rural elite's contributions to the guerrillas, mainly in cash, also constituted uncompensated material losses for them. School, store, and clinic closings ordered by guerrillas meant that teachers, storekeepers, and nurses lost

Table 4.10 *Non-family members on Budjga farms*

Year	Farms	Family members	Non-family members
1970	290	3,193	222
1971	289	3,111	247
1972	287	3,203	218
1973	285	3,300	214
1974	286	3,248	192
1975	286	3,265	167
1976	286	3,412	91
1977	288	3,357	261
1978	287	3,385	426
1979	not possible to collect		
1980	not possible to collect		

Source: Budjga Purchase Area. Department of Statistics, unpublished data.

their salaries. The guerrilla strategy of driving farm-workers off white farms entailed a loss of salary for farm-workers that was usually uncompensated.

Youth owned no resources, and therefore were unaffected by the guerrilla demands for food and money. When the guerrillas were based at their villages at night, *youth* ate with them and may have eaten better than usual. A cost-benefit calculation of *youths'* net material contribution to the guerrillas would require offsetting the opportunity cost of the time they spent working for the guerrillas. Neither paid employment nor schooling were options for the majority. A priori, one would expect *youth* in schools to be more resentful of the disruption of schooling than those not in school. However, many schoolchildren voluntarily joined the guerrillas. In the absence of systematic data on *youths'* attitudes to school closings based on level of education, no definitive conclusions can be drawn about their response to the disruption of schooling.

Protection from government forces

The guerrillas were unable to offer civilians protection from the government forces. *Parents, youth,* and the rural elite all walked a tightrope between meeting the demands of the guerrillas and avoiding government sanctions. A villager and a longstanding nationalist headman respectively offer their sense of being squeezed between two forces.

> If you went [to *moraris*] soldiers might find your village deserted and then you'd be in trouble with them. If you didn't go, comrades got angry. You'd go and try to be back by 3:00 in the morning before soldiers came to patrol at about 5:00 [in the morning].

> There was then that war: the mass were afraid of the soldiers; the mass were afraid of the comrades. There was nowhere for the people to go.

Elites suffered the same entrapment between two forces. A report by the African Farmers' Union (AFU) describes how the plight of its constituents, freehold African Purchase Area farmers, worsened after the internal settlement.[127]

> The A.F.U. has 9,000 members who have been suffering intimidation from both sides. The situation changed on 3rd March. The *vakomana* (boys) were not sure of the local attitude to the Agreement and so have hardened towards African farmers. By their ruthless application of Martial Law, the Security Forces are proving that they are in control. The A.F.U. advised the 3 black signatories to consult with Mugabe and Nkomo before signing. The A.F.U. saw the local leaders last week and told them that their situation was much worse as A.F.U. members were victimized by all sides. Sithole and Muzorewa said the auxiliaries were for the protection of the people, but when confronted by evidence of auxiliaries killing farmers, they could not reply. The *vakomana* (boys) are competing with Smith in killing people.

Nurses, storekeepers, and teachers were also faced with an everyday dilemma. They were expected to cooperate with the government; at the same time they were required to cooperate with the guerrillas.[128] A headmaster's experience during the Murozewa election – a time of heightened military pressure by both armies – highlights the dilemma of teachers and describes one man's strategy to survive.

> Like all headmasters, I was supposed to be an election supervisor for the Murozewa election. I knew I'd be killed by the comrades if I did this. If I didn't do it, I'd get six months in prison or a $5,000 fine. For some headmasters it was okay. They could do the job because there weren't any comrades in their areas. But comrades were always in my area. So I left for Salisbury and went to a white doctor. I said I was ill and didn't know what was wrong. She could find nothing wrong. I said to myself: 'Lord help me', and prayed she'd find something wrong. Luckily she discovered I had stomach pains and gave me pills that cost $20. I never took the pills. I didn't need them. I called the D.C. [district commissioner] and said I was ill and couldn't come back for the election. I came back after the election. The D.C. was very cruel and said I should have come back anway. I was taken to JOC [Joint Operational Command] and finger-printed. The next day I was taken to martial court. After three different people phoned my doctor to check my story, I was released.

The security of *youth* was no better than it was for adults. Regime forces knew they were actively aiding the guerrillas, and their movements were constantly observed. Private auxiliaries, introduced in 1978, tried to impress *youth* into their armies. However, *youth* could more easily leave their parents' homes to live with the guerrillas or with other *youth* in mountainous areas than their parents could, tied down as they were by homes, land, and possessions. That *youth* and guerrillas also belonged to the same age cohort also helped to create a spirit of camaraderie between them. The following story by a *youth* shows how the guerrillas tried to help and protect him once he was in trouble. It also illustrates the complex combination of guerrilla persuasion and coercion, and the way relationships between the guerrillas and civilians could change over time.

> I was a fifteen year old at school in Murewa when I met comrades in 1976. Father had sent me to get a spanner from an uncle. It was early morning when I saw the comrades. I ran. They stopped me and said I was hiding something. I denied and explained my mission. They beat me. My village had got the reputation of having a lot of D.A.s [district assistants] and soldiers and Smith government people. They were sure I was running an errand for soldiers. My uncle tried to help me and to explain. But they were so harsh. They wouldn't understand. Comrades were now preparing to leave as it was getting light. I asked to be able to return to my father who would otherwise worry. They instructed two *youth* to accompany me and watch me all day and then take me back to them by 4 [p.m.] that day. They warned me not to tell my father about meeting them and being beaten by them. Comrades feared people to know of them then. They feared that they would be sold out. I was taken back to the comrades at 4:00. They tortured me and asked about the presence and activities of soldiers at my school. They told me to go to them nightly for three weeks, or else they'd kill me. They were about 5 kilometres from the school. Nightly they'd frighten me. After one week they got tired of threatening me. They would show me knives and beat and kill people in front of me. When satisfied with me they told me to find out what connections my headmaster had with the police, and to come with my headmaster to them . . . They wanted me to go to Mozambique with them. I refused and they left me . . . Then it was school holidays. I was now friendly to comrades. I'd spend nights with them, even weeks. Then school opened again. I got a letter from the first comrades I'd met telling me they wanted to take me to Mozambique. I said: 'I must write my J.C. [Junior Certificate] first.' They said: 'You'll go to school in Mozambique. There you can teach Grade 3s and learn yourself. We need people to teach younger children.' The group came to fetch me. We had not even got beyond Nyagui River when we were bombed. From 6:00 in the morning until 6:00 at night the bombing continued. Several comrades died. I lay unconscious . . . Meanwhile comrades who'd escaped from the bombed base told villagers of me and said they should let them know if they found me . . . When comrades found me they said they couldn't help me. What did I suggest? I said: 'Take me to my father.' They left me at my father's and gave me money to have me transported to hospital . . . When I returned to school, soldiers were still asking for me. So early in 1978 comrades took me to live with them in the forest.

Status and power

Rural elites had no opportunity to enhance their status by participating in the civilian support organizations. Indeed, taking orders from uneducated guerrillas and *youth* humiliated them, as it did *parents*. Real gains in status were won by *youth* who enjoyed the authority their war roles gave them over their elders. Children's assertion of authority is apparent in their oft-repeated refrain to *parents*: 'We are the sons of Zimbabwe. We are not your sons.' There is a strong hint of pride in being sons of Zimbabwe that being members of a family did not provide. Many of them aspired to become guerrillas and dreamed of being carried off to training camps in Mozambique. While most respondents when they described their initial meetings with guerrillas reminisced about their fear of being in the presence of armed men, a war chairman's desire to meet guerrillas suggests sometimes peasant fears of guerrillas may initially have mingled with pride. 'I was eager to meet the comrades', he said. 'The people who'd met them were always so proud of having met them.' Both *parents* and *youth* were empowered by their positions in the support organization. How *parents* and *youth* used their newly won power is the subject of chapter 5.

Coercive appeals

The treatment of guerrilla coercion and its implications for popular support were criticized in the review of the literature. To recapitulate, David Caute's *Under the Skin* presents grim accounts of indiscriminate guerrilla coercion but he does not interview peasants to assess its effects. He asserts there was popular support for the guerrillas but leaves it as an unexplained paradox. David Lan's arguments in *Guns and Rain* that guerrilla coercion against 'sell-outs' enhanced their legitimacy was found to be flawed and his 'sell-out' category constructed too narrowly to include only government informers. Ranger's article on guerrilla coercion concluded that although there was much indiscriminate brutality in 1978 and 1979, peasant radical nationalism helped to sustain their support for the guerrilla cause. But the evidence for peasant radical nationalism was unconvincing, and he ignored the concerns of peasant and elite informants on the negative effects of guerrilla coercion. The previous chapter documents how others have also described indiscriminate and random guerrilla coercion, and, like Ranger, link it to lack of guerrilla training, although they differ from him on when ill-trained guerrillas were sent into the country. In that chapter, I argue that a more important factor accounting for guerrilla coercion was the power of the state and the guerrillas' inability to secure military control of areas. The chapter documents the colonial state's expansion of its military forces by recruiting Africans. For this reason, the notion that more guerrilla training might have produced guerrillas inclined to persuade more and punish less should not be pushed too far.

Also, there is no reason to be so sanguine about the leadership's commitment to democratic process. David Moore's dissertation on leadership struggles within ZANU and ZAPU suggests that the leadership itself was inclined to resolve conflicts coercively. Moore cites ZANU-PF's official political history, written for its party congress in 1984, on how the ZANU leaders handled conflicts with the ZIPA leadership when they were released from detention in Zambia. The report first states how the ZIPA troublemakers were detained with Mozambique's permission in January 1977, and proceeds to say: 'This exercise was followed by a politicisation programme in the camps. We warned any person with a tendency to revolt that the Zanu axe would fall on their necks. *Tino tema nedemo* was the clear message!' That coercion was mistaken for politicization in a party officially committed to political education of the masses is an irony that does not escape Moore.[129] Moore also cites a passage, believed to be written in 1976 by Jason Moyo of ZAPU, in which he records his concern with the lack of democratic process among the leadership.

> We should beware that reactionary forces have memorised pat revolutionary phrases which enable them to parade as progressive. Often, we have heard the imperialist press speaking of militant leaders and moderate leaders. Some of our brothers actually cherish being referred to by the imperialist press as militant. For our part, comrades, let us never forget that militancy is not always synonymous with being revolutionary. Hitler was militant but he was a militant fascist.[130]

The conventional distinction in the literature between discriminate and indiscriminate revolutionary violence is of limited use in understanding guerrilla coercion in Zimbabwe's war of national liberation. In a colonial society where the state is so important as an employer of Africans and as a provider of services and infrastructure, few Africans' lives, even in the most remote areas, are untouched by the state. When the state is the enemy, even these few benefits to Africans become symbols of state collaboration. Hence the structure of the colonial economy and state created a seemingly unlimited potential for 'sell-outs'. The bickering among the nationalist parties produced more potential 'sell-outs': those who did not support ZANU, especially after Muzorewa and others signed the internal settlement in 1978, were labelled 'sell-outs'. Moreover, the omnipresence of government forces in the rural areas during the day, often torturing civilians for information about the guerrillas, made the guerrillas always wary of potential 'sell-outs'. If this were not enough, the guerrillas were strangers to the districts in which they operated and did not know whom they could trust.[131] The deliberate posting of people outside their home areas was intended to protect them from conflicting loyalties, and is a common practice.[132] In this insecure environment for the guerrillas, everyone was a potential informer. Anyone who refused to conform with guerrilla demands invited being branded a 'sell-out'. Consequently, for the guerrillas, the distinction between innocently punished 'sell-outs' and deserving 'sell-outs' becomes most difficult to sustain. Taking the perspective of guerrillas, guerrilla coercion is better understood as arising from the extremely difficult environment that they had to mobilize support in rather than as a function of their undoubtedly poor training.

Guerrillas' concern with their personal security was witnessed by all who came into contact with them. Some spoke of guerrilla fears of being bombed. A *youth* observed how guerrilla behaviour was affected after military contacts. 'If there'd been no contacts for a while, comrades and *parents* and *youth* would be happy. If people had heard of a recent contact in the area, no *parents* would be there. Comrades would be harsh. They would beat you for minor mistakes. You would think: "Last time I did this and you didn't beat me. Why beat me now?"' Another *youth* commented on guerrilla fear after a contact. 'Comrades would flee a contact leaving the elderly to be bombed. When they'd return a week later, they'd say they'd run away to prevent the elders being killed in cross-fire. But it was propaganda. They were scared. That's why they ran away. They also had no guns to reply to helicopters and jets bombing.' An International Red Cross official who worked in southern Zimbabwe and on occasion had to meet guerrilla leaders made a similar observation: 'some were bloodthirsty, some weren't. And the same people's behaviour changed. One day they could be free and friendly; the next day they could be monsters. It was just fear. They really feared being bombed by planes. It made them very insecure. They were all terribly young and inexperienced.'

Particularly *parents* and the elite felt that the guerrillas never trusted them. A *youth* leader told of 'how *parents* would ask comrades how they crossed the borders. But comrades would not tell the truth. They'd say that when they crossed the borders, they'd turn into animals. They feared that a *parent* might tell the security forces how they'd really crossed the border.' *Parents* described how civilians would have to eat the food they had cooked because the guerrillas wanted to make sure they were not being poisoned. A headman said: 'Even though I supported them, they were always fearing I'd sell-out. That's how they made me feel. I always felt comrades were watching me to see if I did anything wrong.' A headmaster expressed the same feeling. 'Even though we supported them enormously they never trusted us. We contributed a lot, and even when arrested and tortured, we never sold-out.' And a black clergyman summed up relations with guerrillas as follows: 'Comrades didn't trust anyone, including me. This exercise of weeding out sell-outs would go on all the time, as you could be good today and bad tomorrow.'

Parents, *youth*, and the rural elite had little choice but to identify with ZANU and provide logistical support for the guerrillas. The guerrilla slogan, 'ZANU. *Iwe neni tine basa*' meaning 'ZANU. You and I have got a job to do together' was an appeal to every person to contribute to ZANU's struggle for national liberation. One dared refuse only at the risk of personal physical harm. Indeed, my suggestion that one might have refused to work for the guerrillas was preposterous. A war chairman succinctly expressed the sentiments of others when he explained that 'comrades would know if you refused the job and then you could get beaten. I never knew of anyone who did refuse. There was just that fear that if one did, one could get beaten.' If people did not attend *moraris*, failed to provide resources to the guerrillas, or were alleged to be 'sell-outs' they might be threatened or beaten with huge poles, sticks, or any available implement. Failure to conform with guerrilla demands might also result in death, usually with the same instruments with which the guerrillas beat people. The guerrillas seldom used bullets, preferring to save them for military contacts.

From the vantage point of civilians who risked their lives and sacrificed resources to meet the guerrillas' demands, guerrilla coercion often appeared arbitrary and unreasonable. *Parents* were often afraid to go to *moraris* as they disliked watching 'sell-outs' killed or beaten and they feared that the singing might attract soldiers. Especially after military contacts, neither *youth* nor *parents* were interested in attending *moraris*. To get *parents* to attend often required guerrilla coercion. According to a female war committee member, '*parents* might not respond to the call of the *youth* to go to *moraris*. Comrades would get angry with *youth* and beat them and tell them to go back and get *parents*. Then *youth* would get angry with *parents*, and sometimes beat them. If *parents* still didn't listen, comrades could come and get them.' A *youth* member made the same point. 'Our *parents* often did not want to go to *moraris*. When people near the road were afraid to go, we'd have to force them. Some could say they were cold, others that it was too far to go and come back before it got light in the morning without the auxiliaries seeing them. Sometimes the comrades themselves would have to come to force them to come to *moraris*. Only those who were sick could stay behind. The *parents* were always saying they were sick, and then the next day you could see them moving in the village.' Laconically, a current member of a women's branch committee said: 'Whether you liked it or not, you had to go.' My questions about *moraris* and what they learned at them were often brushed aside, but never so bluntly as by this group of village heads. 'We can't remember. We don't write. Tomorrow we'll have forgotten what you're asking. There was nothing interesting. We went because if we didn't the comrades would say we are not supporting the war.' The sense that guerrillas were unreasonable was expressed by a current member of the women's branch committee, who in her anxiety forgot guerrilla slogans at a *morari*: 'Then they could call you *zakudzaku* [a word used derogatorily by ZANU to refer to Muzorewa supporters] and beat you. But it was just fear from seeing an armed man that would make you forget.' People felt guerrilla pressure to be happy and spirited at *moraris*. 'If you weren't, you could get beaten', said a *youth*. The appearance of *parents*' symbolic support through singing and repeating slogans masked their anxieties. 'We the women [referring to the group of women she was speaking of before] would be so afraid of the comrades. When we got to the *moraris*, we'd just sit with our eyes down, not looking and too nervous to listen.' To enforce attendance at *moraris*, guerrillas used coercion, chiefly against *parents*. *Youth* often expressed how much they enjoyed *moraris*, after which they would spend the night with the guerrillas. The elite felt guerrillas preferred them not to be present at *moraris* because they could feel less inhibited saying what they liked without worrying about educated people evaluating them.

Even when circumstances were beyond their control, chairmen were responsible for meeting demands for food and other resources. A village war chairman, also the village headman, said: 'Once I and all the *youth* in the village got beaten by comrades. My village was supposed to collect money. I failed to because soldiers were there. I explained to the comrades, but they said: "You must have sold-out. Why are they just in your village?"' Guerrilla coercion against *parents* on the war committees is apparent in a special appointee's account of his job. 'A chairman had been collecting much less than letters called for on several occasions. He'd collect $10 when the letters were asking for $40–$60 . . . Such a chairman would be beaten by comrades for all his people.' In this particular case, 'the chairman knew there was trouble', quickly collected the money, and never went to the 'comrades'. A war chairman related that whenever *youth* came to tell him that the guerrillas wanted to see him, he was 'always afraid why they might want me'. Heeding the call, he would go to them only to be given a letter specifying their demands. 'I'd go to Mutoko, quickly give the letter to one of the few businessmen we dealt with, and then run out of the shop and wander around . . . Only when I gave the food and other things to the comrades and they sat around and talked could I feel relaxed.' A *youth* leader recalled how he would get beaten if he could not collect money from *parents* to buy the guerrillas clothes. 'The letter may request $40 but *parents* could only collect $5 . . . I'd get beaten.' His plight was so widely shared by other *youth* that a black clergyman claimed to be able to distinguish *youth* from government groups masquerading as *youth* because '*mujibas* would be scared of taking back nothing'. Another *youth* leader got punished for not being able to find enough blankets for the guerrillas in the winter months. 'We'd go house to house, but a house may only have one blanket and would not give it up. Then comrades would beat me and say I was not explaining properly to the people.' Guerrilla coercion was used against *parents* to ensure that they contributed resources. By using coercion against *youth* who failed to deliver the resources that the guerrillas requested, the guerrillas invited the *youth* to coerce resource contributions from *parents*.

From the vantage point of *parents* and the elite, there were many cases in which the guerrillas killed innocent people as 'sell-outs' without investigation. Appalled at the superficial investigations of alleged informers, a principal commented: 'Comrades had to find out if you were a genuine supporter. If you were thought to be a reluctant supporter, then slaughter. Ten *parents* before my eyes.' Another said: 'Comrades did not follow principles to try a sell-out. They only wanted to show the *povo* [masses] they had the power to do anything and instil fear so that none would repeat the mistake.' Again, it is necessary to distinguish *youth* from adults in their response to guerrillas killing or punishing 'sell-outs'. *Youth* played an important role in identifying 'sell-outs' for the guerrillas, and were primarily responsible for many of the deaths or punishments of innocent people (see chapter 5). Consequently, the deaths or beatings of innocent people alleged to be 'sell-outs' concerned *parents* and the rural elite rather than *youth*. 'Sell-outs' were usually killed or beaten publicly at *moraris*. It is impossible to know how many 'sell-outs' were killed, but official figures show that the guerrillas killed more African civilians than regime force members. In small communities where people know one another, incidents of guerrilla coercion spread quickly. According to official figures, between 1977 and 1980 the guerrillas allegedly killed 2,751 black civilians; the Security Forces reportedly killed 3,360 black civilians, but this figure excludes those killed in attacks on camps in Mozambique.[133] Official figures, as previously noted, inflate guerrilla deaths by including civilians. If the total deaths recorded are accurate, then it follows that official figures understate civilian deaths. None the less, these figures underline the enormous difficulty the guerrillas had in polarizing society along racial lines when Africans were so involved with the state and the colonial economy.

Inconsistent appeals

Guerrilla appeals to arouse African cultural nationalism and to change morality, and their general instructions to villagers were laced with inconsistencies. Inconsistent guerrilla appeals complicated winning popular support and confused even those who may have wished to be responsive. The effect of inconsistent guerrilla appeals on popular support is not an issue in the literature on the war in Zimbabwe, in part because of the low prominence of peasant voices. Guerrilla warfare is decentralized and one would expect variations in guerrilla appeals from area to area. What occurred in Mutoko though were discrepancies within a guerrilla group and among different groups operating in the same area. Some may attribute these inconsistent appeals to poor guerrilla training. Without dismissing the problems associated with inadequate guerrilla training, I would prefer to emphasize the structural constraints in which the guerrillas operated, and especially the extent of differentiation in rural African society.

Some guerrillas might denounce Christianity as a European religion and forbid attendance at church (see chapter 3). Others were not against Christianity. An African Catholic clergyman claimed: 'Comrades didn't say: "Don't go to church." They were saying: "If you go to church in a group, soldiers will think it's a political meeting and kill you or beat you up. Also, we ourselves are killing so don't go to church where you are taught not to kill. Better not to be hypocritical." They left people free to choose whether to go to services.' A villager who attended United Methodist services regularly before the war remembered, or was told, a different message: 'Comrades said we could go to church after the war. Now we should pray to the spirits to liberate the country.' Still another villager said: 'Comrades said: "Do one thing at a time. Fight the war and then you can go to church."'

Before Muzorewa held constitutional talks with Prime Minister Smith in 1978, the guerrillas expressed different views on him. Some found him acceptable; others regarded his supporters as 'sell-outs'. When Muzorewa's ANC was established in 1971, ZANU and ZAPU leaders had been on its executive. Strains developed between Muzorewa and ZANU members soon after the Pearce Commission left the country in 1972, and escalated when ZANU was pressured by the front line states to accept Muzorewa's leadership of a new umbrella organization, also called the ANC. According to teachers, activists inside the country believed that ZANU and Muzorewa were working together and that Muzorewa supporters sent guerrilla recruits into exile to ZANU for training. The first guerrilla groups had identified themselves simply as freedom fighters but after the split between Muzorewa and ZANU deepened in 1975, some began to identify themselves as ZANU guerrillas and to disassociate themselves from Muzorewa. A *youth* leader recalled what the guerrillas told him on his meeting with them in early 1976. 'We were told to stop collecting money for UANC. In future, all collections should be for them. They said they were ZANU. They said Muzorewa was bribing them [lying to them] that he was fighting for the country. While other nationalists were being detained, he was not being arrested because he was working with the white government. In future, we should only listen to them. We were told to inform people in our villages of this.' But other guerrillas, some of whom had been recruited under Muzorewa's auspices, retained allegiance to him, thus confusing people about the relationship of different parties to each other. The confusion was compounded because some areas had earlier contact with the guerrillas than others, and became aware of the split sooner. Taking their cue from the guerrillas, they began to regard neighbours who still openly supported Muzorewa as 'sell-outs'.

The guerrillas promised Tribal Trust Land cultivators 'freedom in farming' or 'free living' – a life free of government interventions in how much land they could cultivate, where they could farm, where they had to graze their cattle, and how many cattle they were permitted to own. 'Everyone could do whatever he feels like', villagers were told. For Purchase Area landowners and lessees, the imagery of 'free living' and a 'people's government' evoked fears of tyrannical rule by the Tribal Trust Land population. So guerrillas avoided such references to Purchase Area residents, and instead promised them that they would inherit the white farms, and the Tribal Trust Land villagers would move onto their vacated land.

Some guerrillas made wild promises with a millennial tone. A teacher remembered: 'Comrades would tell people how they'd have cars of all the whites who'd leave, TVs, and so on. Other groups would tell them: "It's not true."' The following interchange with the guerrillas, recalled by a villager, underlined how some guerrillas opposed raising false expectations. 'People would ask: "When the war is over, would we go and stay in whites' houses?" Comrades said: "No." People said: "But we also want to live there." Comrades said: "You must farm hard, get jobs, and build your own homes. You can't just go and live in someone else's house."'

The guerrillas' different positions on whether to close schools is perhaps the clearest expression of their lack of a coherent set of appeals. The issue was complex. To close the schools, perceived as arms of the state, had certain advantages.[134] It demonstrated guerrilla control, deprived the government of revenue from school fees, and made available *youth* for full-time logistical work. Guerrilla proponents of closing schools argued that the schooling Africans received was inferior and they were better off without it. However, if schools closed because of the guerrillas' decision, the government would stop paying teachers' salaries that were an important part of 'war taxes'. Also, it would leave many *youth* more exposed to the security and paramilitary forces who suspected they were working for the guerrillas. Opponents of school closings argued that some education, even if inferior to that of whites, was better than none.

A headmaster described how guerrilla instructions on the fate of his school were in conflict. One guerrilla leader stood up at a *morari* and said: 'The schools must stay open. Education is important. The future leaders of our country must be educated. If the headmasters and teachers see soldiers coming, they must dismiss the children quickly so they won't get captured by auxiliaries.' He went to rest and another 'comrade' stood up and shouted: 'Schools must close. Down with schools. This is war. Everything must stop. The whole system must be disrupted.' Another principal described how his school was closed on 29 July 1977 after they all left the 'keep'. In January 1979 some 'comrades' told him to open the school. 'They wanted the children to learn.' Then on 14 March, 1979 'comrades told us to close. Those who were uneducated said: "Close the schools."' Missionaries and teachers often persuaded guerrilla leaders that it was in the best interests of Zimbabwe to keep the existing school system running during the war.[135] Even when they had convinced guerrilla leaders to keep schools open, other guerrillas or *youth* might try to close the school. A headmaster related how the staff at his school had established 'a good rapport with the detachment commander and we'd negotiate with him to keep the school open. Comrades and *youth* wanted the school closed. But the detachment commander wrote us a letter saying the school could stay open. We said that as long as circumstances permitted, we should keep school open . . . So when groups of comrades came and said we should close the school, we'd show them the letter, and they'd say: "Okay, we can discuss it later."'

Sometimes guerrillas gave different messages to the better educated and uneducated. To the uneducated, they postured that schooling was unimportant: lack of education had not hindered them fighting the war; nor would it prevent them from holding jobs after the war. To secondary school students, though, they would stress the importance of schooling. A *youth*, back at secondary school after the war, remembered how 'comrades pointed to a large store owned by a black and said: "If you give this store to an uneducated black, who will run the store?" Comrades would say: "We must have our secrets, otherwise the mass will lose hope and stop supporting us. We have to encourage them."'

Guerrilla appeals to discourage beer drinking were as inconsistent as cultural nationalist appeals, and were undermined by guerrillas openly flouting their own disciplinary code that prohibited drinking. A headmaster noted how 'comrades sometimes prohibited beer-drinks, and sometimes discouraged them . . . Comrades began drinking. If there were none [beer], they could ask for cash to buy it. They were often drunk at the base.' Apostolics' religious code forbids them to drink alcohol, and they find making it repugnant. Their known opposition on religious grounds to political activity and war angered guerrillas, as it had the nationalist parties in the 1960s.[136] To punish them for their anti-war stance, the guerrillas might make them drink beer. According to a war chairman the guerrillas told an Apostolic, 'you say forward with the war at meetings but you go home and say down with the war because God is against war. They forced him to brew beer for them. Two weeks later they came and made him drink with them and gave him drugs. Today he is a drinker!'

Guerrilla instructions to villagers were also often contradictory. One group might tell villagers to move their homes from the road because 'they could easily sell them out to soldiers' who had easy access to them. Another group told them they should not move, 'otherwise soldiers would know they were all in the bush and follow them there . . . Then they got a letter in red ink, signed by G. . . . [a guerrilla leader], telling them this is their last warning, or else they'd come to destroy villages near the road. They never did do this . . .'

In summary, the case of popular support in Zimbabwe's war rests on the effectiveness of guerrillas' normative appeals, particularly their cultural nationalist appeals. Many also assume that government coercion intensified commitment to the guerrilla cause and facilitated mobilization without considering the alternative hypothesis that government coercion complicates mobilization. Arguments for popular support neglect to consider, as peasants did, the costs of their exchange relations with the guerrillas, of compliance coercion, and of inconsistent appeals. These costs must be taken into account in any study of popular support.

Individuals' calculus

It remains to establish the net effect of these forces on rural civilians' responses to the guerrillas. Did guerrilla appeals produce popular support, which I take to mean at a minimum voluntary support from a significant minority? Hirschman's *Exit, Voice and Loyalty* provides useful ways of conceptualizing individuals' strategies in their relations with firms or organizations. Adopting the perspective of the organization, Hirschman seeks to find out what kinds of individual responses will send a signal to a declining organization so that it can improve itself. In a free market, when consumers become unhappy with the quality of a product, they usually either choose an 'exit' or 'loyalty' option. The 'exit' option is impersonal and avoids the unpredictable consequences of a confrontation between the customer and the firm. Alternatively, they may choose to stay in the firm as loyal customers. Rarely, though, do they use 'voice' and articulate to organizations their dissatisfaction directly. The presence of the 'exit' alternative is likely to atrophy the development of the art of 'voice', to the detriment of the firm. Precisely those customers who care most about the quality of the product and who would be the most active, reliable, and creative agents of 'voice' are also the ones who will be the first to take advantage of the easier 'exit' option. Hirschman looks at examples of organizations that encourage people to use 'voice' and that benefit from the opportunity to get immediate information about declining performance rather than wait for the invisible hand of the market to signal their decline.[137] The value of Hirschman's analysis for this study is its focus on individuals' strategies in their interactions with an organization. But Hirschman examines these strategies from the vantage point of what is good for the firm or organization. An organization that has high costs of 'exit' and 'voice' can boast of 'loyal' members, but their loyalty to the organization does not necessarily describe voluntary support.

The concept of strategies of avoidance of direct conflict, sometimes called 'everyday resistance', is also useful in understanding responses to the guerrillas. In repressive states or institutions, it is argued, one should not mistake the absence of formal, organized protest for legitimacy. Protest may be 'informal, often covert, and concerned largely with immediate de facto gains' rather than changing conditions.[138] Proponents of the concept of 'everyday resistance' assume that desertions from employers, non-tax payments, and the like, express genuine consciousness of political realities.[139] Others have criticized the concept for different reasons,[140] but the most compelling critique is that the concept predisposes one to find resistance as the motive behind all behaviour. I try to minimize overstating resistance by using the concept parsimoniously. Strategies of avoidance, like Hirschman's 'exit' option, are a form of protest that avoid direct, personal conflict.

How can one overcome the problem of estimating the extent of popular or reluctant support? Since the 1950s, surveys have been used to quantify political support for regimes, government policies, and leaders.[141] Others have debated the merits of this research technique in largely non-literate societies (as well as literate societies for which they were originally designed). Even if one concludes, as some have, that surveys are appropriate in this setting, research on revolutions differs radically from that on electoral politics, and direct questions about political opinions on sensitive topics are doomed to fail. Some assert it is the intensity of popular opinion among the committed few that is important in a revolution and not the numerical size of popular support.[142] This book adopts that position and uses peasants on war committees as a critical case to investigate popular support for the guerrillas. A priori, one can argue that peasants elected to war committees were most likely to be enthusiastic guerrilla supporters. If these peasants did not meet such expectations, it is unlikely that others would have.

Parents

Parents who stayed in the rural areas chose to seek an accommodation with the guerrillas that involved a combination of 'exit', 'voice', and 'loyalty' strategies. *Parents* claimed that they sought people with special qualities to occupy committee positions. They needed brave members – 'people who were not butterflies' or 'people who did not bend easily' – who would resist informing when coerced by government forces. Messengers should be capable of conveying messages accurately, the treasurer should be of good character, and the secretary should be able to record in writing the payments made by people. However, war-time committee work was perceived as dangerous, and the search for people with ideal qualities was abandoned for anyone who could be pushed into filling the positions. Committee positions often went to those not swift enough to avoid being elected. According to a war-time committee member, 'you'd not look into anything. If the person was a fool, and didn't think quickly enough of an excuse, he'd accept the job.' This was a common theme. Another war committee chairman said: 'It was a difficult job. We wouldn't look into anything. We'd just try to find anyone to take the jobs.' Still another said: 'You didn't look into anything. You'd just choose people. It was a dangerous job. Nobody liked it.'

Given the undesirability of committee work, *parents* sometimes allo-cated committee positions as punishment to people suspected of being 'sell-outs'. A striking number of war leaders had not been present at their election. Not attending election meetings or *moraris* was read as a sign of 'not being interested in the war' or 'not liking the war' by others who themselves were perhaps too afraid to miss a meeting and eager to find an opportunity to push jobs onto absentees. People pointed out that having 'sell-outs' actively engaged in working for the guerrillas also had the advantage of reducing the collective risks to the village of being 'sold-out' to government forces. People rarely provided names and specific cases to support their claims about the practice of using 'sell-outs' on committees. Usually, the information was presented in a general way, with swift denials that anything like it had ever occurred in their villages. This reflected their fears that disclosing such information would stir up village hostilities that were barely under control. Some specific examples of the use of informers and suspects on support committees were given.

In one village people spoke about a man they chose to be their chairman precisely because they knew he was a traitor. They supported their charge by noting that he had once been a government witness in a court case against a fellow villager who had been detained because of his ZAPU affiliations. Moreover, during the war he regularly visited Mutoko centre that was always awash with government forces. It was palpable to them that his purpose was to provide soldiers with information. Why else would anyone risk travelling that distance unless they had been guaranteed a safe passage? His friends were members of the Guard Force, police and soldiers. When others had to flee from the regime forces, he was able to remain in safety at his home. In the 'keep', he could come and go without presenting an identity card. In another village, *parents* mentioned that they had asked the guerrillas if they should give positions to people who had relatives or children in the state forces. The guerrillas had advised them to consider only the individual's loyalty and not trouble themselves with the political allegiances of family members. Later the guerrillas appointed a branch chairman from this village who had been a former policeman and whose children were in the Guard Force and police force. When the guerrillas assigned jobs to 'special appointees', they also sometimes did so either to punish a suspected 'sell-out' or as a test of loyalty.

The rapid turnover of committee personnel also attests to strategies of avoidance. When the first party committee I interviewed spent hours trying to recall who had held particular positions on the war committees, I grew impatient and was certain that I was being manipulated by people who knew, but, for whatever reason, were choosing to withhold the information while pretending to be helpful. But in village after village, I met with the same response. A youthful current branch secretary explained: 'Many people had positions in the war. Jobs changed hands so often, that those who don't have positions today sometimes forget that they ever did.' A man who had the distinction of being a war-time vice-chairman for the duration of the war described the selection of committee members as 'a big game. There could be twenty section [village] chairmen. After one week, one could say one was ill. One can only remember those who stayed in the job for a long time.' Claiming illness to get out of committee work was a common strategy of avoidance. A former committee chairman joked about how difficult it was to find people to do committee work or help the committee. 'Most people when they were asked to go to Mutoko to buy food for the comrades would suddenly feel sick.' Another form of avoidance or non-cooperation was to accept a position but 'not work very hard'. The other villagers might recognize that it was in their interests to find a substitute rather than risk collective punishment by the guerrillas. A vice-chairman described this type of response: 'That man was an organizer for three weeks. Then he got scared. So people told comrades he was ill and couldn't manage the job and another would be given the job.' A group of village heads maintained that in their area 'people just thought to change you after a while. It was an unspoken arrangement. We knew the jobs were difficult.' Often the guerrillas simply intervened and appointed someone themselves. *Parents* might fail to form committees or take too long filling a position because they were too afraid to agree to do a job, or they might not perform their tasks satisfactorily. A former war-time chairman described why he was replaced by guerrillas. 'Comrades just appointed a replacement. They knew people didn't want the job and they couldn't waste time choosing people, They knew A. as he'd been here through the war, so they appointed him at a *morari*.'

The most unambiguous strategy of avoidance was to 'exit'. Many adults fled the rural areas for extended periods. Some joined relatives or husbands in the towns, but townspeople already lived in overcrowded accommodation and people from the rural areas were a heavy burden. A survey of a transitional squatter camp at Harare *Musika* (market) shows that adult women were prominent among refugees. The greatest proportion of adult 'refugees' – those who fled their rural homes because of the war and had nowhere else to go and no one to support them – came from Murewa district (30 per cent), with the next highest percentage from Mutoko (13 per cent).[143] Married men were also leaving the district in large numbers according to the district commissioner who was having difficulty tracking down ratepayers.[144]

These strategies of avoidance and non-cooperation attest to the difficulties of using 'voice' to refuse to participate in committee work. 'You couldn't just say: "I'm tired"', said a *parent*. 'The people could beat you and say: "You are a rebel. You are a sell-out". Comrades could also beat you and say: "So you don't like the war."' On occasions, though, *parents* used 'voice' to complain to the guerrillas. Those who confronted guerrillas were described by fellow civilians in heroic terms for their daring and bravery. They complained about guerrillas and *youth* killing innocent people as 'sell-outs' and other kinds of misconduct, and the onerous guerrilla demands for resources. Husbands complained about guerrilla intervention in their personal lives. They especially resented guerrillas beating them for beating their wives. The intermediaries were sometimes war chairmen, but usually teachers and missionaries. I provide only one illustration of the use of 'voice' because there are many more in the next chapter. The following dialogue with headman Nyakuna reveals how he was given an opportunity by guerrillas to defend himself against allegations of being a traitor.

Q. In these difficult times, was your life ever threatened?

A. Yes.

Q. By whom?

A. The mass who alleged to the comrades that I was doing this or that. I challenged them when I was brought before the comrades and refuted all their allegations against me. A contact had happened here [at the primary school]. It was alleged that I carried the injured comrade to the headmaster at Mutoko Secondary [School] and that we took the injured comrade to the JOC [Joint Operations Command] in a scotchcart. We did not do this. I was brought to where the headteacher was and he was tied with his hands behind his back . . . It was difficult to convince the comrades of my innocence. I did not attend these meetings. We had our hands tied with wire while these meetings were held.

Parents, one must conclude, were at best reluctant supporters of the guerrillas. The costs of 'exit' were high, but many people fled the rural areas; others risked strategies of avoidance of committee work. 'Voice' was also risky but *parents* were sometimes driven to complain to the guerrillas about their behaviour and *youths'* behaviour. *Parents* on war committees adopted strategies that make it difficult to characterize them as fervent and committed nationalists.

To argue that peasants were reluctant supporters of the guerrillas appears to pose problems for explaining why they voted for ZANU-PF in the 1980 elections. As previously noted, ZANU-PF won a majority of the Africans' parliamentary seats, leading observers to understand the electoral results as a validation of the popular support the guerrillas had established during the war. If peasants did not voluntarily support the guerrillas during the war, why would they voluntarily vote for the guerrillas' political party? Electoral commitments are undemanding compared to revolutionary war commitments, so it is not surprising that people who were unwilling to provide voluntary support to the party during a war would be willing to vote for it. Peasant support for ZANU was consistent with their reluctant support for it during the war. Besides an end to the war, what peasants hoped for when they voted for ZANU was that it would compensate them for the sacrifices – the loss of resources, labour time, and lives – forced upon them by ZANU guerrillas. Mutoko peasants, and peasants in Shona areas where ZANU guerrillas had operated, had no such claim against other parties. In Ndebele-speaking areas exposed to ZANU guerrillas, the guerrillas' insensitive efforts to impose Shona cultural nationalism were an early signal to expect nothing from ZANU. Shona-speaking peasants in predominantly Shona areas did not encounter such cultural conflicts with the guerrillas. This interpretation is also consistent with peasants' post-war preoccupation with compensation and disillusionment with the ZANU-PF government because it failed to compensate them (see chapter 6).

Rural elite

Ranger has argued that the rural middle class lacked the ideological commitment of peasant radical nationalists. 'By 1979 the rural middle class did not know . . . who had brought them into their present situation; by contrast with the clarity of radical peasant ideology, they did not know even what to hope for, except for an end to the war.'[145] Ranger reaches this conclusion partly by linking progressive farmers to the Methodist church. Ranger draws on Norman Thomas' study of religion and politics in Manicaland to make the point that the Methodists 'largely abstained from nationalist politics in the early 1960s'.[146] But Thomas' point was that high church attenders in all the older churches 'have no time for politics' while low attenders constitute the pool from which the 'nationalist political groups draw the bulk of their membership and leadership'.[147] Rather than finding the Methodists less likely to produce participants in nationalist parties in the rural areas, Thomas found that they ranked alongside Roman Catholics as the strongest participants since the 1960s: 35.6 per cent of adult Methodists reported membership in a political party and 41.8 per cent of Roman Catholics.[148]

According to my informants, villagers who were ZAPU activists and the rural elite had disdain for the peasants mobilized by ZANU during the war. A villager referred to the contempt ZAPU activists had for the political neophytes mobilized by ZANU. 'Active nationalists did not easily get convinced to support the comrades. They had been in politics and would argue with the people, saying: "You know nothing about politics. My party will be the one to liberate the country."' A headmaster, himself a longstanding nationalist, endorsed this perception of war-time committee members as politically ignorant. He described them as 'novices who came in from nowhere. They were only mobilized in the war and they don't really understand what went on in the war. The UANC-ZANU struggle confused them. They don't know of ZANU-Sithole, which was a party for elites. For them, ZANU began with ZANU-PF.' These remarks turn Ranger's argument about elite's lack of understanding compared with peasants upside down, and support my earlier argument that his case for peasant nationalism is weak. Moreover, peasants frequently made comments such as 'we thought the war would never end' or 'we never thought we'd live', suggesting that they were as eager as the 'rural middle class' to see an end to the war. Studies of the 1979 election explain peasants' vote for Muzorewa as partly a vote to end the war; similarly, studies of the 1980 election recognize that peasants voted for the guerrilla parties partly because they alone could end the war.

The African rural elite such as storekeepers and teachers and even agricultural demonstrators, often chose to return to their home villages, where they felt safer among people they knew well. Some teachers whose schools were close to Mutoko township went to live there because it was well fortified by regime forces and they could commute to work. At other rural schools, they were able to get jobs because the teacher shortage was so great during the war. Leaving their original home and job did not constitute escaping the war. They still contributed to the war and faced its dangers. Others went to live in Harare but this 'exit' option was costly as it meant losing work.

There is no evidence that the elite attempted to avoid contributing to the guerrillas, and many seemed unresentful. This I attribute to their strong support for the nationalist cause. The rural elite did not seek to exploit the war to fulfil other agendas, as *youth* and *parents* did (see chapter 5). They understood that they would reap the benefits from a nationalist victory. More than the *parents*, the elite often complained to the guerrillas about problems in the support organizations, the guerrillas' behaviour, *youths'* misdemeanours, and the closing of the schools. Their education and social status gave them the confidence to debate with the guerrillas. Loyal nationalists, the elite expressed no enthusiasm for the guerrillas.

Youth

While it was easier for *youth* to leave than for *parents* with children and property, there were enormous pressures from guerrillas and other *youth* to stay in the rural areas. 'Who'd be left to fight the war?', the guerrillas would say. Also, 'other *youth* didn't like it that you had gone to town and they'd remained with the bad job'. 'They could report you to the comrades', said a *youth* who had managed to escape to town. There were reports of guerrillas going to town to search for *youth* who had escaped.

A strategy of avoidance was available to young girls. If they married, their tasks as *parents* were generally less demanding. A local stated, matter of factly: 'Guerrillas were sometimes reasonable. Married men and women had other duties to do at their homes and could not spend all day in the bush as the *youth* had to.' The case of a young primary school teacher illustrates how marriage was used as a strategy of avoiding the more demanding work of *youth*.

> I was so afraid during the war that I thought it might help if I married. Even though the comrades respected that teachers had a job to do and often excused us from meetings so that we did not have to teach class after a *morari* that ended at four in the morning, I was always afraid of what might happen to me at those meetings. Unmarried girls had to attend meetings with comrades and spend the next day with them; married mothers could be excused from the meetings. Initially the comrades would not touch a woman. That was their policy. But as time went on, they were sleeping with the girl *youth*. I know that if a comrade approached me, I'd be too frightened to refuse him.

After military contacts, *youth* were often reluctant to fulfil their duties. A *youth* described how 'A base at K. was bombed. Most of the *youth* and comrades at the base died. Then the *youth* here were afraid to go to the G. base. They said they were sick . . . A comrade was injured in a contact at our base. *Youth* feared to go to the base a day or two later when the comrades came again.'

Some of the behaviour of *youth* lends itself to being interpreted as 'everyday resistance' to the guerrillas. It is possible to argue that when *youth* defied guerrilla instructions to cook more quickly, not to kill or report innocent people as traitors, and not to masquerade as guerrillas, they were challenging the guerrillas. Although some of the ways in which *youth* violated their code of conduct may indeed reflect a deliberate act against the guerrillas, I attribute this behaviour to different motives (see chapter 5).

On the whole, however, based on what *youth* themselves said and did, and how *parents* and the elite described them, one must conclude that they provided the enthusiastic guerrilla supporters. There is little evidence of *youth* complaining to the guerrillas or to anyone else whereas *parents* sometimes reported problems with the *youth* to guerrillas and dwelled in interviews on their violent behaviour. One might interpret *youths'* silence as due to their fear of the guerrillas. However, the weight of evidence suggests otherwise. *Youth* were available for recruitment for the nationalist cause: they had no lineage or other loyalties at this stage of their lives. Participation entailed no resource losses for them, although schooling was disrupted for some. They were usually eager participants in identifying 'sell-outs' rather than victims of the search for traitors. Finally, their overzealous execution of their duties in the support organizations and the spirit of camaraderie that seems to have existed between them and the guerrillas all point to *youth* being enthusiastic supporters of the guerrillas, even though often for reasons other than their nationalism (see chapter 5).

The importance of *youth* in the war (as guerrilla supporters and in government armies) comes as something of a surprise. On the one hand, there is a literature that discusses the availability of youth for recruitment in revolutions and counter-revolutions: 2,500 years ago Aristotle wrote of youths' 'exalted notions' making them feel equal to great things and hence their disposition to seek revolutionary change. On the other hand, the literature on twentieth-century guerrilla wars of national liberation has been mostly about peasant participation. The Zimbabwe case points to the need to deal with *youth* as a distinct social category. Some will object that the class differences among *youth* exceed their common interests. Perhaps further research will confirm this, but in societies where age stratification is rigid, *youth* may find more in common with their age cohorts than with class comrades. Who is a youth and how important youth is as a social category are questions that have been discussed for European societies.[149] The questions warrant attention in newly independent states too, especially given that today children under fifteen constitute over 50 per cent of the populations of many of these societies and often fight in their armies.

Conclusion

The concept of popular support is of tremendous importance in theories and studies of guerrilla wars of national liberation. Yet the evidence for it is almost always inferred from secondary sources rather than from what active participants themselves say and do. I have argued that the evidence for peasant popular support for ZANLA guerrillas is flawed: it does not rely on peasant voices, attributes too much mobilizing power to cultural nationalist appeals, too little influence to the lack of positive utilitarian appeals and the adverse effects of negative utilitarian appeals, and insufficient attention to the negative effects of guerrilla coercion and the potential obstacles of government coercion to mobilization and participation. Oral data from active participants about their behaviour in the civilian support organizations challenge the entrenched view of popular peasant support for the guerrillas. At best, peasants were reluctant supporters. Enthusiasm for the guerrillas and the war came from *youth* whose participation in guerrilla wars has been overshadowed in the literature by a preoccupation with peasants. But even *youth* had reasons beyond a commitment to the guerrillas and their nationalist cause for participating in the war. There is a real danger of cultural nationalism serving as a convenient residual category to explain peasant participation in anti-colonial wars of liberation. This is particularly likely in cases where the guerrillas cannot liberate territory and offer utilitarian benefits. A focus on what factors might produce a mutually supportive relationship between guerrillas and civilians diverts attention from civilian relationships during a guerrilla war and how these may produce strong reasons independent of the guerrilla cause for participating in a national liberation war. This is the subject of the next chapter.

5

Struggles in the struggle

This chapter is about struggles inspired by agendas other than African nationalism and African majority rule that were central for the guerrillas and the parties they represented. Sometimes they converged with the guerrilla agenda; othertimes they were in conflict with guerrilla goals. The theme of revolution(s) within a revolution occupies a prominent place in the literature on revolutions. An example is Debray's *Revolution in the Revolution?* that addresses ideological and strategic disputes about how to bring about revolution in Latin America. It is intended to discredit Marxist–Leninist communist parties in Latin America for failing to bring about revolutionary change. Debray rejects the Leninist concept of a vanguard party providing revolutionary leadership as inappropriate for Latin American conditions and popularizes instead the lessons he has drawn from the Cuban revolution. He begins by denying political agitation a role in the first stage of revolutionary guerrilla war and advocating propaganda through armed action. This is tantamount to abrogating the leadership role of the party and is heresy to Marxist–Leninists. He goes on to attack directly the role of communist parties in Latin America and claims that they have unwittingly played a counter-revolutionary role by creating obstacles for the guerrillas. Communist parties do not devote their full energies to military struggle but try to maintain several forms of struggle including legal struggle in the city which he regards as incompatible with armed struggle. Moreover, communist parties often use the guerrillas to try to increase pressure on governments to extract concessions whereas the guerrillas' objective is to seize power.[1]

The literature on Zimbabwe's war of national liberation has given considerable attention to leadership struggles within ZANU and ZAPU, and the extent to which these have been over ideological and strategic differences, ethnic-based competition for dominance in the movement, or petty bourgeois factionalism. Moore's dissertation is the most extended treatment of the internal conflicts that beset ZAPU and ZANU. He examines the guerrillas' challenge to ZAPU's leadership in the March 11 movement (1970–1) and to ZANU's leadership in the *Nhari* rebellion

(1974–5). Moore highlights ideological issues behind these struggles within the parties, whereas John Saul attributed these conflicts to petty bourgeois factional infighting and Masipula Sithole stressed their ethnic dimension. Moore gives most attention to ZIPA leaders, initially consisting of ZANU and ZAPU military commanders, but later of only ZANU commanders. He compares ZIPA favourably with ZANU's exiled political and military leaders who were detained by Zambia after their acting president's assassination and who displaced ZIPA leaders (with the Mozambican government's help) soon after they were released. These men became the rulers in Zimbabwe at independence. Moore rails against official ZANU history that labels ZIPA as 'counter-revolutionary', and analysts who, in his view, have misrepresented it or minimized its significance. Martin and Johnson called ZIPA infantile and ultra-leftist; Andre Astrow dismissed it as limited and superficial; Ibbo Mandaza remarked that it did not go much beyond the African nationalism of the victorious parties in 1980; and Terence Ranger characterized it as militarist and unreflective. Moore's analysis builds on the work of John Saul and Lionel Cliffe, who both identified ZIPA as representing a left-wing challenge to the ultimately victorious ZANU. Unlike the 'old guard' ZANU leaders who came to power in Zimbabwe, ZIPA's military leaders made the guerrilla war a priority. To accomplish a guerrilla victory, they were willing to lay aside temporarily the tendentious issue of who would lead the party because it was consuming energy that should have been devoted to the armed struggle. Opposed to the petty jousting between ZANU and ZAPU for political leadership of an independent Zimbabwe, they sought to maximize military strength by uniting the guerrilla armies of ZAPU and ZANU. Critical of the 'old guards'' lip-service to Marxist–Leninist ideology, they sought to ensure a Marxist–Leninist future for Zimbabwe by establishing an ideological school to train guerrillas. Moore acknowledges, like others, that although ZIPA was crushed, its brief existence influenced positively the ideological development of the victorious 'old guard' but he is less sanguine than Terence Ranger about the extent of transformation. While Ranger argues that on the eve of independence there were no indications that the 'old guard' had not committed itself to a socialist Zimbabwe, Moore perceived the 'old guard' to have been essentially untransformed.[2]

This chapter is about grassroots or micro-level struggles within the Zimbabwean revolution rather than leadership or macro-level struggles. It describes how pre-existing conflicts within peasant communities became entangled in the organization of logistical support for the guerrillas, sometimes complicating peasant mobilization and organization but also providing compelling motives for various groups to participate in the war. Chapter 1 examined several influential works on peasant revolution and argued that they were unlikely to uncover struggles internal to the peasantry even if they were important because their concepts and methodologies predisposed them to emphasize peasant opposition to states, markets, and other classes. This bias towards peasant grievances against external actors and forces such as capitalism and imperialism was attributed to several factors: inferences about peasant motives from non-peasant data; a concept of peasants that places them on a continuum between primitives and farmers and regards them as 'other' because of their different relationships to external actors such as the state, elites, and markets; a bias toward the revolutionary elite's prerequisites and goals for success and hence toward popular support, unity, and collective action; and finally, for some, a characterization of peasants as embued with nationalism that deepens the bias inherent in the peasant concept in favour of peasants acting as a united group against external actors.

Analysts of Zimbabwe's war of national liberation have also attributed the grievances that peasants sought to resolve through participation in the revolutionary war to external actors, and in particular peasant resentments against the functioning of the state and markets. In an article, Cliffe and his co-authors maintain that peasants participated in the war because they wanted to remedy their grievances associated with racially discriminatory legislation.[3] Astrow's *Zimbabwe: A Revolution That Lost Its Way?* argues that peasants sought to replace the white settler state with an African one and transform capitalist social relations that restrict production.[4] In *None But Ourselves* Julie Frederikse understands peasant participation in the war in terms of their grievances against racial and cultural oppression.[5] Ranger's *Peasant Consciousness and Guerrilla War in Zimbabwe* depicts peasants as motivated by a desire to recover their lost lands and introduce a state that would cease to discriminate against black farming and would support it against white agriculture through favourable pricing and marketing policies.[6] In *Guns and Rains* Lan perceives peasant participation in the war to have been motivated by their grievances about discriminatory legislation that limited their freedom and development, and, most importantly, the appropriation of African land by whites.[7] All these analysts agree on the centrality of peasant grievances against a racially discriminatory state. Grievances internal to the peasantry might be expected to surface more in grass roots approaches to the study of revolutions. For this reason, Ranger's *Peasant Consciousness and Guerrilla War in Zimbabwe* and Lan's *Guns and Rain* are exemplary in highlighting how peasant grievances located outside peasant society become so dominant in understanding peasant participation in revolutionary wars. These studies also illustrate how, when potential conflicts internal to the peasantry are considered, they are perceived as obstacles to the revolutionary organization.

Ranger's neglect of internal peasant grievances during the war is surprising because he makes a great deal of the internal socio-economic differentiation in the peasantry and the resulting differentiation in peasant consciousness that is reflected in different peasant religions.[8] In the pre-war history, these differences sometimes become the source of conflicts but the thrust of Ranger's analysis is about how peasants understand their grievances as a class.[9] During the war, these socio-economic differences within the peasantry become the basis of class conflicts between peasants and the rural middle class because Ranger narrows the implicitly defined peasant category that he uses for his study of the pre-war period. Teachers, storekeepers, and other business people, once members of the internally differentiated peasantry, become the 'petty bourgeosie' or the African rural middle class.[10] He also separates out Purchase Area farmers, master farmers, and other 'progressives' from his peasant concept. Even class conflict is not a central theme though. He argues that rural class warfare seemed likely after the internal settlement in 1978, but it was averted because 'the presumed petty bourgeois supporters of Muzorewa in the rural areas' who came under guerrilla attack after 1978 'did not come under the protection of the new regime'.[11] Also, if other members of the bourgeoisie 'were prepared to cooperate with the guerrillas . . . they were regarded as invaluable allies'.[12] Later, when he is discussing the post-independence period, he alludes to class tensions between peasants and Purchase Area farmers, rural businessmen and foreign migrants, only to bypass them as 'a minor theme by comparison with peasant participation in the attack on white farm and ranchland during the war'.[13]

Ranger is also not insensitive to gender, generational, and chiefly status distinctions within the peasantry during the war and the difficulties that they posed for the guerrillas in their quest for popular support. Initially, he says of the male elder peasants' relations with the young guerrillas:

> There were some substantial discontinuities also which made it difficult for there to be intermediate or total collaboration between the peasant elders and the young guerrillas. To begin with the guerrillas *were* young and they were closer to the teenagers of Makoni District than they were to the resident elders. Men in their fifties, who had hitherto dominated Makoni peasant radicalism and who were used to controlling a flock of dependent women – wives, daughters, daughters-in law – now found that the initiative had passed to young men with guns. These young men called upon the unmarried women of Makoni to act as their cooks, informants and messengers and in these latter two roles teenage girls were able to exercise a good deal of power, for the first time in Makoni's history.[14]

Ranger also differentiates elders and *youth* to exculpate guerrillas from much of the killing of civilians and to blame *youth* for it. He refers to 'a good deal of remembered resentment among elders and parents directed against the power exercised by the *mujibas* during the war', and cites an informant who says 'most of the people who are said to have been killed by the guerrillas are the direct victims of the *mujibas*. These sometimes robbed civilians, abused the populace at beer parties, and in most cases misrepresented the comrades' aims and commitments.'[15] Finally, Ranger also recognizes differences between chiefs and headmen *via-à-vis* other peasants. Although at one point he implies conflicts between chiefs and headmen and other peasants when he asserts that 'the administration was totally wrong to suppose the chiefs and headmen did or could command such [peasant] support',[16] these differences were apparently not great because guerrilla attacks on the 'tribal authorities' were unsettling to peasants. Ranger grants chiefly status, gender, and generation importance during the war, not because they affected the way peasants interacted with each other, but because they interfered with the guerrillas attaining their objective of winning peasant support. 'All in all, some means was urgently required to give the guerrillas legitimacy in terms of Makoni's own past and to give the peasants some way of controlling the young men with guns. The spirit mediums provided just such a means.'[17] With the endorsement of the mediums, 'there was no danger that the guerrillas would be repudiated by the peasant elders'. The mediums 'most effectively' laid down 'norms of conduct' for the guerrillas.[18] Hence the potential for conflicts arising between guerrillas and peasants from differences of gender, generation, and chiefly status within the peasantry are eliminated early in the war.

We learn about conflicts concerning gender, generation, and chiefly status that were internal to the peasantry as well as peasant conflicts with other classes primarily through a discussion of the relationship between guerrillas and peasants. These internal conflicts appear as obstructions to the guerrilla organization's quest for unity and popular support. In this sense, Ranger adopts the perspective of the guerrilla organization despite his interest in peasant agency. Peasant consciousness, by definition, refers to the peasants' understanding of their grievances as a class, which relate to how white farmers and the state undermine their commitment to agricultural production.[19] Peasant consciousness is narrowly constructed to incorporate only peasant interactions as a class with the state and white farmers in the sphere of agricultural production. Of particular relevance here, his peasant consciousness concept does not allow for generation, gender, or other factors internal to the peasantry or inter-African class conflicts to become important. The importance he attributes to peasant nationalism in understanding why peasants offered support to the guerrillas only entrenches peasant class action against whites and the state. Cultural nationalism serves as an ideological bond that not only unites peasants but also guerrillas and peasants. Finally, Ranger's evidence largely excludes the diverse voices of peasants (as he defines them for the war period) – *youth* and *parents*, males and females, those with chiefly status and those without it. Ranger's concepts and methods, and concern with guerrilla goals of winning popular support help to orient him away from grievances internal to the peasantry that might constitute important motives for participation in a revolutionary war.

Lan's *Guns and Rain* is the only study of the war to consider the potential significance of status differences between *strangers* (*vatorwa*) – defined in chapter 2 as those who did not belong to the chiefly clan/totem – but his objective is to show how they become unimportant within the peasantry. Lan points out that *strangers* in Dande district outnumber by three to one the Korekore, the conquerors of the land, but he finds

> the real danger of a 'second conquest' is not great because the *strangers* are not all members of one lineage or one clan. They have allegiance to a variety of different *mhondoro* and chiefs. They have no lineage basis for uniting and mounting a campaign against their hosts. Nonetheless the royal lineages assert their dominance over the *strangers* and affines living in their midst by transforming them all into *vazukuru* or descendants of the *mhondoro* in whose spirit province they live.[20]

The literal meaning of *vazukuru* (singular, *muzukuru*) is descendants two or more generations down in one's own patrilineage or descendants of any woman of one's lineage.[21] Lan goes on to describe how *strangers* become the 'kin' of the *mhondoro*.

> It is not enough simply to live in the spirit province to become the *mhondoro*'s *muzukuru*. When a newcomer arrives in a spirit province he must apply to the *mhondoro* for permission to live there and to plough his land. This request must be accompanied by a gift (*mukowho*). If you have not made the gift and received permission you can never be accepted as a *muzukuru* of the *mhondoro*, a legitimate resident in his territory and beneficiary of the fertility he provides. But even the making of this gift is not sufficient. To be a *muzukuru* you must also do the work of the ancestors. You must take part in the rituals of the agricultural cycle and in the rituals of possession. If any household head resident in the province fails to do so, this reduces the likelihood of the ritual achieving the desired affect. By doing these things *strangers* come to regard themselves and to be accepted as *vazukuru* of the *mhondoro*. In this way is the threat that they pose to the authority of the royal lineage dispelled.[22]

Lan proceeds to emphasize how *stranger* lineages lose their significance as forms of identity and common agricultural interests unite lineages.

> These *vazukuru*, these *strangers*-become-kinsmen are defined not in terms of lineage but of territory. The imagery that characterises times [sic], social identity is a question of action not of essence. All the *vazukuru* of the *mhondoro* think of themselves and of others as such because they all live within the same spirit province, they all work the same land and they all take part in the same rituals that maintain its fertility.[23]

So although Lan is aware of a status distinction between *strangers* who cannot inherit chiefly office and royal lineages that can, what he emphasizes is how unity between them is achieved. In this way, well before Lan comes to discuss the war, the importance of chiefly as opposed to *stranger* lineages as a source of differentiation with political content is eliminated.

Bourdillon's review of Lan notes that *strangers* do not have to come from outside the spirit province, as Lan suggests, but may have lived in them as long as, or longer, than the chiefly clan. More importantly, Bourdillon rejects Lan's claim that *strangers* eventually become accepted as descendants of the *mhondoro*: 'I was called *muzukuru* by *mhondoro*, and I am quite sure there was no connotation of descent in the title. Anyone, including a

175

real *stranger*, who pays respect to a *mhondoro* calls the *mhondoro sekuru* (grandfather, mother's brother, etc.), and is called *muzukuru* in turn. He does not thereby become a kinsman.' Bourdillon argues that it is wrong to reduce the relationship between *strangers* and chiefly clans to a simple cognitive opposition revolving around the issue of land ownership because it ignores the importance of power and status. Bourdillon makes his point by charging that Lan's criticism of his writings on the subject reveals Lan's misunderstanding of the issue.[24] Apart from Bourdillon's evidence, Lan himself presents data that may be used to counter his case for the insignificance of status and power in the relationship between *strangers* and royal lineages. He refers to the higher prestige of the Korekore as 'conquerors' and as members of a group with marginally higher economic status and mobility influencing many Tande autochthons to claim to be Korekore. Lan reports that the Tande, thought to be the people who lived in the territory earliest, are regarded derogatorily by some (though not the royal lineage) and are associated with poverty, backwardness, and so on.[25] Also, Lan cites the removal of inequalities between *strangers* and royal lineages stemming from the latter's exclusive rights to the chieftainship as one of the major accomplishments of the committee system established during the war. The implication is that this status differential was more significant than he allowed for before the war.[26] Giving prominence to the status and power aspects of the relationship between *strangers* and chiefly clans, or alien and royal lineages, restores its potential political content.

Lan regards the other two major accomplishments of the structure of the war committees to be the challenge that they posed to inequalities between men and women and between elders and the young.[27] But the centrality Lan gives to the effective use of ancient symbols to give the guerrillas legitimacy among peasants and others leads him to give almost no attention to gender and generational inequalities within the peasantry, or other potential inter-African differences, despite his awareness of them.

> The guerrillas, all the residents of Dande – Korekore, Tande, Chikunda and Dema – the poorest peasants and those who farmed about fifteen hectares, the schoolteachers, the shopkeepers, the mothers, the young women who disappeared from their homes and returned as armed fighters, the widows, the youngest children organised in their *mujiba* platoons, the elders, the headmen, the healers, the mediums – all of these and all of their ancestors, in opposition to the conquering whites, were placed in one category: the children of the soil, rain-makers, landowners, autochthons. In this most recent formulation of an ancient set of symbols all the local populations are grouped together in opposition to those lineages whose home territories are, ultimately, not within Zimbabwe, but in another land, on another continent, in Europe.[28]

Lan's case for guerrilla legitimacy, as discussed in the previous chapter, has several problems: is the reader hearing Lan, the mediums, peasants, or guerrillas? To the extent that Lan's case requires the acceptance of guerrilla legitimacy by the entire local population, the direct and diverse voices of differentiated peasants, schoolteachers, and others is necessary. Also, Lan's peasant concept, although never explicit, orients him to the discriminatory state and agricultural markets and especially the whites' appropriation of land. He sidesteps the possibility that grievances internal to the peasantry, or even grievances against other African classes, may be important. Lastly, Lan's concern with guerrilla legitimacy reflects a bias in favour of the guerrilla organization's goals of establishing unity, popular support, and collective action: he alludes to differences within the peasantry and between peasants and other Africans only to underline how the cultural symbols that the guerrillas used united Africans against whites.

In summary, both Ranger and Lan, who are interested in grassroots politics in the war of national liberation in Zimbabwe, conceive of peasants as preoccupied with external grievances against a racially discriminatory state and market. By making the cooperation between guerrillas and peasants and the coordination of peasant action central to their studies, both unwittingly favour the guerrilla organization's goals of popular support, collective action, and unity at the expense of potential competing goals emanating from grievances internal to the peasantry. Consequently, they are ultimately more interested in how sources of peasant disunity, and more generally African disunity, lose their importance. Moroever, both provide few opportunities for peasants to express themselves and thereby preclude voices that might offer agendas that compete with the guerrilla goals of unity, popular support, and collective action.

Data from peasants, *youth* and the rural elite in Mutoko suggest that the positions of *youth* and peasants in the civilian organizations, and the guerrillas themselves, were useful resources that empowered them in their struggles to bring about political and social change inside peasant communities and to alter peasant relations with the elite. These struggles within peasant communities and between peasants and African elites often complicated the functioning of civilian support organizations and undermined the guerrillas' quest for collective peasant action and popular support. However, internal peasant conflicts and peasant relations with the rural elite help to explain why peasants participated in the war, even when they were reluctant guerrilla supporters and provide additional reasons, besides their nationalist sentiments, for why *youth* participated. This chapter examines *youths'* revolt against rigid age-based hierarchical relations, resentment by the least well-off against better-off peasants and between peasants and the African rural elite, women's attempts to transform their domestic lives, and efforts by *stranger* lineages to break the royal lineages' monopoly of specific village powers. All these challenges had their roots in inequalities that emerged or deepened during the colonial period and have been described in chapter 2. The war-time agendas of the most oppressed in peasant communities had more radical implications for peasant social relations than the guerrillas' platform that focused almost excusively on attaining racial equality. To the extent that the guerrillas introduced appeals directed at peasant grievances against other Africans, the initiative appears to have emanated from peasants. Bent on winning popular support, the guerrillas could not employ these appeals with any consistency. Guerrilla concerns with unity were constantly undercut by their uneven attempts to satisfy diverse groups within the peasantry.

Chapter 4 discussed guerrilla appeals, emphasizing their cultural nationalist ideological content and their use of coercion against whites and certain categories of Africans. But these appeals were obtained from interviews with peasants and the rural elite, and it may be argued that their memories were deficient or selective, leading them to ignore other appeals. A fruitful method of obtaining guerrilla appeals without inviting distortions introduced by intermediaries is to examine the songs that they and civilians sang at *moraris* and that constituted a primary vehicle of political education. Alec Pongweni collected in a volume nineteen songs that were written in exile and performed in secret in Rhodesia (exile songs) and thirty-three that were written and performed publicly in Rhodesia (home artist songs).[29] Will Moore, a doctoral dissertation student, examined both types of songs, together and separately, to identify the appeals used by the guerrillas. Rather than the threefold typology used in chapter 3 – coercive, normative, and utilitarian appeals – he adopts a fivefold classification: appeals to relative deprivation, appeals that identify the state as the source of relative deprivation, appeals to corporate identity, normative appeals to justify taking up arms, and utilitarian appeals about the value of taking up arms. In private correspondence with Moore, he clarified that he had not examined the songs for guerrilla appeals to different groups of Africans and that he had focused exclusively on guerrilla appeals to all Africans. Examining the appeals in exile and home songs separately, he found that appeals to corporate identity were most prominent, constituting 34 per cent of appeals in exile songs and 44 per cent in home songs. Of these corporate identity appeals, the overwhelming majority in both types of songs – 30.5 per cent in exile songs and 39.8 per cent in home songs – was to establish African corporate identity. Normative (23 per cent) and utilitarian (18 per cent) appeals to take up arms were the next most salient type of appeals in exile songs. Appeals to relative deprivation *via-à-vis* whites in exile songs constituted 16.5 per cent of the total, and surprisingly, given the prominence of the state in academic accounts of peasant grievances, appeals that identified the state as the source of relative deprivation were only 8.5 per cent of the total. Except for the lead rank that their corporate identity appeals shared with exile songs, the content analysis of home songs produced different rankings of appeals. Next most important in rank were relative deprivation appeals (37.5 per cent). Not surprisingly, normative and utilitarian appeals to take up arms were less prominent in the home songs than in the exile songs, since the exile songs were performed clandestinely whereas home songs, performed within hearing of the repressive state, had to have less explicit and more cautious messages. Moore subsequently did analyze the songs to see if they contained appeals to transform intra-African relations and found that they had virtually no place in their songs.[30] Content analysis invites quibbling with classification schema and how data are assigned to one category rather than another. But Moore's data point to the overwhelming importance of race in guerrilla appeals. Jessica Sherman's impressionistic study of war songs collected in August 1980 mainly in the townships surrounding Harare supports the findings of Moore's attempt to classify and quantify the type of guerrilla appeals. Like him, she found the songs aimed to inspire unity and solidarity among the various oppressed African groups, hence the prominence of the ancestors and the spirit of nationalism in the war songs.[31]

Generational conflicts

Civilian organizations established by the guerrillas to provide for their logistical needs respected a major generational division in peasant society. *Parents* were organized separately from *youth*. The division of civilian organizations into *parents* and *youth* wings laid the organizational basis for young people to challenge the authority of their elders. They were aided by the personal influence they sometimes developed with the guerrillas. In the long hours that *youth* were obliged to spend eating and sleeping with the guerrillas at their base after *moraris*, they had an opportunity to develop personal relationships with them. Like *youth*, most guerrillas were young, single, and of low status and these actors helped to strengthen the bonds between them. *Parents'* duties required much less interaction with the guerrillas and their generational differences in an age-stratified society were barriers to them developing close ties with *youth*. At the same time, the relationship between *parents* and *youth* changed. *Youth* became less dependent on their families for food and shelter because they ate and slept with the guerrillas. *Youth* used the power they acquired from their duties in the support organizations to challenge *parents'* authority and control over their lives. The opportunity to alter oppressive constraints imposed by elders on their daily life provided an important impetus that helped sustain *youths'* participation in the guerrilla war. At the same time, their zealotry was costly for elders and interfered with the smooth functioning of the civilian organizations.

When collecting food and money from the chairmen, *parents* dwelled on how *youth* often defrauded them. They produced counterfeit letters requesting money and food from the guerrillas, masqueraded as guerrillas demanding food and money from elders and even holding *moraris*, and appropriated money they were supposed to transfer to the guerrillas. *Youth* often confirmed elders' allegations but were largely unconcerned about them. It was elders, deeply disturbed by the *youths'* abuse of their organizational power, who volunteered information about *youths'* behaviour. The following comments by war chairmen describe such abuses by the *youth*.

> You might get a letter asking for $100 with a signature of a comrade known to you. Then the same day, or soon after, another letter might arrive with the signature of the same comrade. You get suspicious and take it to the comrades. They could sometimes kill *youth* who were doing this.

> Four G. [the name of the village] *youth* disguised themselves as comrades. They went to K. [a village name] and other villages, carrying wooden guns that looked as if they were comrades' guns. The war was still young and we'd not had much experience of it. That night they collected $15 from *parents* in K. They even held a *morari* at a *parent's* home in K. and the *parents* cooked for them. It was late in the night. Two days later they were arrested and had to give cattle to the villages from which they had taken money. After two days, they wanted to do it again. M. [a village name] *youth* arrested them. They were carrying wooden guns. One *youth* managed to flee that night. The other three were taken to the village chairman. He took them to their *parents*. Over fifty *youth* from the affected villages went with. Their *parents* were made to each pay three cattle to each of the villages that had been affected . . . About two weeks later, the G. *parents* went to complain privately to comrades. They said: 'This is what our children have done. But we have been overcharged.' 'What overcharged', said the comrades. 'Your children have been using our name to cheat the people.' And they then beat the *youth* at a *morari*. Then comrades told *parents* that *youth* would carry letters but the chairman and secretary would carry money to them. The *youth* would only accompany them.

> *Youth* could forge letters or demand more than the comrades were asking and take the difference. Comrades could beat *youth* in public at *moraris* for this.

A young primary school teacher accused *youth* of cheating teachers.

> *Youth* were sometimes cheating. They'd come with a letter ostensibly from comrades and then they'd keep the money. Some brave teachers would tell comrades that we'd received two letters in one week, each asking for $70. Was this not unreasonable, as we only got paid once a month? Comrades would then say they'd only sent one letter, and the *youth* could be beaten.

My interpreter and a war chairman discussed how a *youth* leader had posed as a guerrilla, demanding items from *parents*. The interpreter, once a neighbour of the *youth's* brother, said:

> He'd been very popular. But towards the end of the war he started coming into Area B and telling people he was a comrade and needed a radio, etc. He'd say comrades want a radio. It would be night, and he was a *stranger* in Area B. So he got away with it a few times. But then he was caught and Area B comrades beat him to death.

In the guise of executing guerrilla instructions, *youth* challenged established social strictures. '*Youth* may want to see a girl *youth*', said a female *youth*. 'They would tell the *parents* that comrades had come and wanted to see the girl. *Parents* would know it was a story and would say no. *Youth* would then beat *parents*.' Providing another example, she continued:

> A *youth* might come and ask for *sadza* [porridge]. There'd be some girls in the house and the *parents* would think the boy *youth* is just trying to take advantage. *Parents* could refuse *sadza*. He could beat them. Some *youth* were cruel.

Perhaps suggestive of different attitudes between male and female *youth*, a male *youth* leader empathized with *youth* and lambasted *parents* for not letting their daughters stay with them in the mountains.

> They feared that their daughters would become pregnant. But we had our rules not to touch women. We would have to beat the *parents* sometimes before they let their daughters live in the mountains.

Youth repeatedly exceeded guerrilla instructions. When the guerrillas instructed *parents* to avoid using roads they had land-mined, *youth* on occasions tried to stop *parents* from using all roads. Also, the guerrillas had requested that neither they nor the *youth* be fed okra, certain vegetables, and certain groundnuts. *Youth* might stretch this order, demanding that *parents* stop growing these foods for themselves too, and dig up their gardens or stand in their fields killing the plants. *Youth* sometimes interpreted guerrilla orders to limit beer drinking as an instruction to outlaw it or beat *parents* who refused to attend *moraris* although their disciplinary code prohibited them from beating people. Even when *youth* merely informed elders of a *morari*, the latter found the imperiousness with which they did so offensive. A war chairman related how 'there was a time for three to four weeks before the ceasefire when *youth* tried to overpower elders by hearing cases among them. The elders reported this to the comrades and they immediately stopped this.' The following statements by *parents* and the rural elite address these abuses of power by *youth*.

> *Parents* would raise the question of movement with comrades. *Youth* could tell *parents* that they weren't allowed to move at all. This made it difficult for *parents* who were supposed to raise money and food for comrades. Yet the *youth* would not allow them to even move a scotchcart.

> Comrades told us not to cook okra for them. It would make their guns slippery. Also the *youth* shouldn't eat it . . . *Youth* could stand in the *parents*' fields killing the okra growing. Comrades never said *parents* couldn't grow okra.

> Youth were sometimes intimidating elders . . . Comrades did not eat okra, certain vegetables and certain groundnuts because they were sacred. *Youth* came and would make *parents* dig these sacred foods out of the garden. *Parents* told comrades: 'We know you don't eat these foods, but we can. Why are *youth* telling us to dig them up?'

> Comrades had told us not to drink too much beer. *Youth* found K., my brother at a beer-drink. There was nothing illegal about drinking. They took him to his house and beat him thoroughly with clubs and thick sticks. One night I was brewing beer. *Youth* came and spoke offensively to me. I told them it was not an offence and they left.

> . . . *youth* came to our houses and commanded us: 'Wake up. Immediately.' We had to remind them that we were elders and not children. We told comrades and comrades warned them.

A *youth* said: 'We'd get annoyed if *parents* wouldn't give us blankets to give to the comrades.' His mother replied: 'You wouldn't just get annoyed. You'd beat us.'

Many *youth* defied guerrilla instructions that prohibited them from killing or beating alleged 'sell-outs'. *Youth* were merely supposed to report and take them to the guerrillas, who would investigate the case. A village head who survived to tell the story of how he had been called an informer and assaulted by *youth* illustrates *youths'* heavy-handed abuse of power.

> *Youth* came once and threatened to kill me. They called me sell-out. It was night and very dark. They knocked on my door and took me to where there was a *kurova guva* [the ceremony a year after a funeral at which the deceased's assets are distributed]. They'd been drinking. I could not see them clearly because it was so dark. I thought they were comrades because they'd made themselves guns like comrades' guns. At the *kurova guva* they beat me hard. The blamed me for being a sell-out because I was always being seen with the soldiers. It was the time the Guard Force engine had been stolen and soldiers were daily taking me to the keep for interrogation. I couldn't explain this to them. They gave me no chance to talk. They just beat. I think this happened in the year the war ended. Someone else reported it to the comrades. I didn't. I thought that they were comrades.

A villager who had been appointed a 'special messenger' by the guerrillas also spoke of how *youth* violated their instructions by killing 'sell-outs'.

> If new people came to the village, you couldn't just take them to a *morari*. *Youth* had to introduce them to comrades. If a new person just arrived, *youth* could say: 'Who are you?' You could just automatically be killed because they'd think you'd been sent by soldiers and would sell-out people.

Speaking before his colleagues, a teacher said:

> Many killings occurred when they [comrades] were drunk. Once they shot ten people in less than two hours. One time they even exchanged fire among themselves . . . *Youth* were even less disciplined than comrades. If you saw two or three *youth* approaching you, you'd really fear them. They could be instructed to take a sell-out to the comrades, but murder you en route. If they came only with a message that you were wanted at the base, or with letters requesting contributions, then you'd feel more settled.

Youth might even inform against their parents. Kersten England hints at conflicts between female *mujibas* and their parents. According to a 1978 report, 'many women have been beaten to death . . . after they had been reported to the guerrillas of practising witchcraft . . . daughters have been indirectly responsible for the deaths of their parents'.[32] *Youths'* challenge to the *parents* was summed up in their assertive claim: 'We are not your sons. We are the sons of Zimbabwe.'

Although critical of the speed with which guerrillas resolved cases involving 'sell-outs', elders depicted them as judicious, reasonable, and less cruel when contrasted with *youth*. When *youths'* violations of their rules of conduct were reported to the guerrillas, they would intervene and punish the offenders. The village head, whose troubles with *youth* were described earlier, related what happened when comrades found out.

> I learned it'd been *youth*, and comrades had beaten them for their behaviour. That same day they beat the *youth*, they [comrades] came to my home and held a *morari*. Only people from G. village were here. That night they just said: 'Old man, can we see you.' Privately they asked me what had happened. They understood my story about the soldiers always calling to interrogate me about the engine. There was another old man whom *youth* had reported to the comrades for selling beer to the Guard Force. But there was nothing wrong with it. Comrades listened privately to his story and understood.

Three weeks later, though, the *youth* had their revenge.

> They said comrades had sent them to beat me. They broke into the house and beat me and my wife so hard that we were ill for three weeks. I never reported this because they said they'd been sent by comrades. They accused me of being a good farmer and using medicines that enabled me to farm better than others.

A black Catholic clergyman also stressed the role of *youth* in unnecessary killings of villagers and how guerrillas sometimes tried to intervene.

> *Mujibas* would use personal hatred to identify sell-outs. Many people who were innocent were killed by *mujibas*. *Mujibas* would condemn sell-outs before the comrades. Comrades might trust their version and kill innocent people. *Mujibas* themselves killed people. Many *mujibas* were killed by comrades for killing innocent people.

Too often, according to a war chairman, the guerrillas' intervention was belated.

> Sometimes people would get beaten as sell-outs when they weren't really. It was just hatred . . . Some days later it'd be discovered that you were innocent. There was nothing that could be done. You'd been beaten. Comrades could apologize to you.

A government agricultural extension officer who worked in the Purchase Area addressed the limits on the control guerrillas had over *youth* even though they did punish *youth* who abused their powers.

> *Mujibas* would kill a person and only afterwards comrades would hear of the incident. What could they do? They did punish *mujibas*. In Mutambwe in 1979, auxiliaries were staying at a farm. When they left the farm to patrol elsewhere . . . the *mujibas* came. They took the farmer to the comrades on the grounds that he was cooperating with the auxiliaries. Comrades said: 'Leave him. He's cooperating [with us].' All the farmers were cooperating with the boys unless they were unlucky enough to have auxiliaries on the farm, which made it difficult. *Mujibas* tied the farmer to a tree and hit him until he was nearly dead.

A headmaster described how he would deliberately try to leave *moraris* before alleged 'sell-outs' were publicly beaten. On the other hand, '*youth* were very interested in this. They'd usually find the traitor and then join in beating the person.'

Why *youth* were so prominent in killing and reporting 'sell-outs', according to a black civil servant in Mugabe's government, had to do with their low status in Shona society.

> The *mujibas* were very poor. They usually came from the fifth class in African society. They had no cattle or animals of any kind. They were essentially implementing vendettas against rich people in the community. Class one are businessmen; class two are employed people – teachers and government officials; class three are people with cattle and a plough; class four are people with cattle but no plough; and class five are people without any animals.

Yet if *youth* were depicted as the villains, they were paradoxically also seen by elders as the real heroes of the war. Like many others critical of the *youths'* cruelty, a teacher still paid tribute to them.

> In fairness to the *youth*, they were very important. They were like a telegraph system. They worked harder than many comrades. While the comrades ate good food and slept at the base, they'd run messages all night, often going hungry. They slept in caves. With their few grenades, they killed many. They were more effective and daring than comrades.

Elders' greater respect for the role of the *youth* during the war may reflect their continuing personal links to village *youth* whereas guerrillas left the villages after the war. Also, the praise of *youth* may have been influenced by the widespread perception after the war that they had been unfairly treated. While ex-guerrillas were integrated into the army or received government money to retrain and enter the civilian sector, *youth* were not compensated for their war-time sacrifices, including the disruption of their schooling (see chapter 6).

Parents and the rural elite were concerned about the reversal in the authority relationship with *youth*. Denying any problem with *youth* in his area, a war chairman offered a commonly held prescription for retaining control.

> A chairman should have control over the *youth*, the children. Some lost control. If the *youth* did something wrong the first time, he should question them. Otherwise they keep doing more and more things wrong.

He goes on to suggest why *parents* often let their authority slip: 'Maybe the reason for the chairman not asking the *youth* in the first place is that they were frightened of them.' Even after the war, the arrival of a former *youth* leader could intimidate a group of elders. Later my interpreter inquired: 'Did you notice how frightened they were of him? They all became quiet and hardly looked at him.' On another occasion, he contrasted the lack of aplomb of *youth* interviewees with their self-assurance during the war and with the elders' fearfulness during the war.

> If you had seen the girl *youth* leader from my village during the war, you would not believe it were the same person today. Today she is useless. But then! You would have been scared of her. She was frightening. People who were very good in the war are useless today. If people came from town, the rural people could make them look silly with the way in which they would interrogate them, because all townspeople were suspected of being UANC supporters. Now the townspeople come with the cars and the rural people feel silly.

A man who had been a member of a *parents'* village committee described how even when *youth* abused their power and exceeded guerrilla instructions, he dared not challenge them.

> One day I and M. were travelling in a truck on the Nyakabau school road. M. had come to get mangoes from me to sell in Harare. *Youth* stopped the truck and said we weren't supposed to use the road because of the possibility of the comrades having laid land-mines. But comrades here had never told us not to use the road. It had been told in other areas. Comrades said the land-mines were expensive and couldn't be wasted. They were for soldiers, and if one of us hit it, we'd have to pay for it. *Youth* took a watch and $10 from us. We wouldn't stop using the truck. It was just hatred . . . When I returned from selling mangoes in Mutoko once, the same *youth* surrounded my house. They took $40 I'd got from selling mangoes. I didn't report either incident. I feared the *youth* too much.

Fear is thinly veiled behind a teacher's remarks about *youth*.

> *Youth* could say: 'We've come to teach you politics!' If they were friendly, you could joke about it. If not, you'd just listen to them.

Intimidated by *youth*, elders sometimes preferred to try to retain some control of *youth* by developing personal ties with the 'comrades' and having them confirm instructions passed on from *youth*. A teacher described how he and his colleagues tried to establish 'a direct relationship with comrades, so when *youth* would come and say: "Close schools, burn books, no religion – there's no God", we'd say: "Let's go to the comrades."' Those adults, notably missionaries or teachers, who tried to establish a relationship with the guerrillas often managed to retain control.[33] Even without such personal ties, elders who were brave enough reported *youth* to the guerrillas and sought their mediation. If a chairman was suspicious of guerrilla demands conveyed by *youth*, he could take them

185

to the guerrillas to authenticate the messages. Other cases of elders intervening between guerrillas and the rural population have already been recorded in this chapter and additional instances are scattered throughout the rest of it.

The war gave *youth* the opportunity to challenge elders' tight control over their daily lives. It kept their enthusiasm for the war high, but also injected considerable random violence into the day-to-day functioning of the civilian organizations. If one accepts that *youth* targeted *parents* because they were protesting against their low status and strict parental control, then one must acknowledge that one of their central grievances was not part of the guerrilla programme. Had ZANU been concerned with changing African social relations, it would have attacked the lineage organization of Shona society that is at the heart of generational relations.

Anticipating the discussion of gender conflicts, it is instructive to contrast the behaviour of *youth* and women – both oppressed groups but divided by education, religion, and other variables. Rather than engage in violent acts themselves, women relied on guerrilla violence to express their anger towards their husbands. Why *youth* – and it was almost uniformly male *youth* – were so violent towards their elders is difficult to answer. Perhaps it was related to the example of settler violence,[34] family violence,[35] or guerrilla violence.[36] Perhaps their use of violence against elders helped to foster bonds – a widely held view of the tactical value of violence.[37] Fanon's idea of the value of therapeutic violence does not apply: he specifically advocated violence against European settlers and regarded inter-African violence as a sublimation of anger and resentment toward the colonial oppressors.[38] Two and a half millennia ago, Aristotle may have been closer to the truth when he noted that youths 'have exalted notions, because they have not yet been humbled by life or learned its necessary limitations; moreover their hopeful disposition makes them think themselves equal to great things – and that means exalted notions . . . All their mistakes are in the direction of doing things excessively and vehemently . . . They love too much, hate too much, and the same with everything else.'[39] To accept that there is some validity to Aristotle's perception of youthful excesses is not to deny that their elders also often hate excessively and are more likely to have control of weapons of war when giving vent to their excesses. But in the context of understanding the behaviour of *youth* towards their elders in villages in Zimbabwe, the notion of youthful excesses may be insightful.

Stratification-related conflicts

The organizational features of support work not only coincided with pre-existing generational tensions but also with socio-economic divisions. *Parents* and *youth* in the Tribal Trust Land were organized according to villages. Their organizations were independent of those in the Purchase

Area where the lower population density and the individual farmers' greater food supplies reduced the need for cooperative *parents*' committees found in the Tribal Trust Land. Also, teachers, missionaries, storekeepers, nurses, and others, who constitute part of the rural elite, were not part of the committee system, but contributed as occupational collectivities at their work place. The organization of civilian support entrenched socio-economic divisions among rural Africans and gave an organizational basis for the expression of existing socio-economic tensions. Africans at the bottom of the socio-economic ladder could also manipulate guerrilla appeals to Africans, usually the better-off, to withdraw from participating in European institutions. In the guise of performing their duty as civilians and reporting 'sell-outs' to the guerrillas, the less well-off could appear as loyal guerrilla supporters when in fact they were using the guerrillas to unleash their resentments against the better-off and better-educated. In the hunt for 'sell-outs', villagers were advantaged over the guerrillas. They lived among their co-villagers and could observe them day and night whereas the guerrillas interacted with villagers mainly at night. Consequently, they came to exercise a considerable power in identifying and reporting 'sell-outs' to the guerrillas. The behaviour of *parents* and *youth* in the guerrilla support organizations in the Tribal Trust Land and how the better-off interpreted this behaviour suggests that socio-economic conflicts were important. An opportunity to vent their resentment against the uneven distribution of wealth among rural Africans sustained the interest of many of the poorest and least educated in the war. The guerrillas, preoccupied with appeals directed at redressing racial inequities, did not address these local concerns about stratification within the peasantry and between peasants and African elites.

Youth and *parents* defied guerrilla instructions to raid only white farms for cattle, and stole from African Purchase farmers especially in those parts of the Tribal Trust Land that lay close to Budjga farms. An elected councillor of the post-war district council in Mutoko Tribal Trust Land related how the guerrilla strategy of raiding cattle on white farms 'went wrong'. 'Individuals began to steal from black farmers and ordinary people and sell the meat.' A Purchase Area farmer described how 'initially, people in the reserves gave us a hard time. They stole our cattle, chopped our trees, and were eating so much meat that they called it meat cabbages.' Better-off farmers were also likely victims of trumped up charges. The African Farmers' Union, a national body of Purchase Area farmers, reported that 'prominent African farmers are being killed simply because they are better off than most of the people'.[40] As already recounted, a village head described how he and his wife were beaten by *youth* who accused him of 'being a good farmer' as well as using medicines – witchcraft was prohibited by state law and the guerrillas – that enabled him 'to farm better than others'.

A black Methodist clergyman claimed that the key targets were 'teachers, ministers, businessmen . . . people would make up stories against them'. In the words of a headmaster: '*Parents* resent us and businessmen. They see us as having worked with the previous regime. *Parents* would ask at *moraris*: "What can we do about teachers getting pay from Muzorewa?"' Teachers resented and scoffed at the memory of *youth* (and guerrillas) telling them that they had 'come to teach them politics', and saw in *youths'* intimidating approach to them a generational and socio-economic challenge.

Villagers often envied those who had jobs in town, seemingly because they perceived migrants to be wealthier. A 'special messenger', given this position to test his loyalty after being reported as a 'sell-out', claimed:

> People who sold me out to the comrades and told them I was cooking for the army in town were just jealous that I had a job in town. When you stay with people here, they feel that you are the same as them, and then they are happy.

Tensions between employed migrants and rural residents surface in the following account of what happened when members of a migrant's family sought refuge with the head of their household who worked in Harare.

> When we returned here, everything had been taken from the home – even the cement in the kitchen. Only six of the twenty-seven cattle were left. And someone was using our land. It was just hatred because my father was the only man that age from K. village working in town. Even today, if we all leave the home, we come back to find sugar and flour all mixed together.

The perception that migrants were often better-off than other villagers is interesting because of debates about the relationship between migration and economic development. Those who have adopted dependency approaches to development have often argued that the colonial policy of migrant labour was intended to undermine peasant agriculture to ensure adequate supplies of cheap labour for Europeans. Proponents of this view saw it as nearly universally destructive of subsistence agriculture.[41] Earlier studies, cast in modernization approaches to development, found some positive linkages between migrant labour and development. Yudelman was concerned that male migration left farming in charge of women whom he alleged were resistant to technological change because they lacked exposure to the modernizing influences of the European wage economy, but he also found that: 'The most progressive producers are frequently those who have been in the wage economy for some time.'[42] Weinrich found migration harmful because it drew away the more educated males who were most likely to be innovative and who seldom invested their money in land because their interests lay outside of agriculture. The less educated migrants earned so little that there was nothing to send home after having maintained themselves.[43] Yet later she shows that ordinary peasant cultivators depended on migrant labour for about one-third of their income and it helped them to live above subsistence. Migrant labour was also profitable afterwards for master farmers in the Tribal Trust Lands and successful Purchase Area farmers – both of whom were more dependent on agriculture for income than were ordinary peasant cultivators – because it familiarized them with a cash economy and weaned them from 'tribal' values.[44] Recent research suggests that migrant labour made market-oriented farming possible for a minority but kept most at subsistence.[45] Whatever the objective reality about the relationship between migrants and farming success, individuals perceived that migrants were a privileged group.

Envy of better-off people operated among resident villagers as well as between them and migrants. The following observations were made by other villagers about why certain individuals were killed as 'sell-outs'.

> Some would go privately to the comrades and complain. For instance, if you were jealous of someone who had a lot of cattle . . .

> People might hate you because you have a lot of property; or maybe because you are cruel.

> It was just hatred. Maybe you have money to drink beer; maybe you have the same girlfriend; maybe you have a lot of property in your house.

Relatives also sometimes 'sold out' wealthier or better-educated family members. A man who had been detained under martial law during the war, an ex-teacher and a district councillor, drew attention to the ways in which relatives would abuse their powers to name informers:

> . . . if relatives were against you, they'd make it difficult for you by reporting you to comrades. Relatives could be against you because you are wealthier than they are. You must not get too far ahead of them or else there'll be jealousy.

The experience of a *youth* base commander illustrates how jealous family members might endanger one's life.

> One girl reported to comrades that I was bad and intimidated *youth* and I was nearly killed. But comrades said: 'We know S. He's worked with us for long. He's a very good man.' They beat the girl publicly in front of the *parents*. The girl was a relative. She'd failed grade seven and was just jealous of me because I was educated and the comrades liked me very much. They gave me grenades and later even a gun.

When a man who had served as branch chairman for several years was labelled a 'sell-out' and killed by the guerrillas, many stories circulated about just what he had done and if he deserved his fate. His widow was not alone in defending him. She blamed his death on jealous relatives. Her story refers to Area B and Area C which require some elaboration. Towards the end of 1978 the guerrillas divided Mutoko and Mudzi districts into Area A, Area B, and Area C. Each was under the control of a detachment commander who had responsibility for thirty-six platoons. Platoon commanders were in charge of sections comprising seventeen comrades each. These divisions were intended to alleviate two problems that had become serious. As guerrilla groups operating in the districts grew rapidly, it was often difficult for guerrillas to tell whether a new guerrilla group was a government Selous Scout group masquerading as guerrillas. By confining particular guerrilla groups to an area of operation and making them responsible to the authority of a specific detachment commander, groups could identify each other by their detachment commanders' names. The reorganization was also intended to reduce the pressures on chairmen who were receiving letters of 'request' from multiple guerrilla groups, some of whom were not even operating in the district. The widow of the branch chairman killed as a 'sell-out' presents her version of why her husband was killed.

> In the keep there was once trouble between my husband and people from K. and M. [villages in Area C]. They accused him of not giving money to the comrades. He showed them a receipt which comrades would give when they received money. This trouble then passed. P. [her husband] told the comrades. They said he should bring those who scolded him to them. But they wouldn't come. Comrades couldn't come to the keep and it was difficult to send the *youth* to the keep. The accused could tell the Guard Force that *youth* had come. These people who scolded did support the comrades but not very much . . . Another time he found an axe in one of his cattle, with a note threatening to kill all his cattle. I think this was by one of those from the other villages who wanted to be overall leader.[46] He reported the incident to the comrades. They didn't know who did it. Those were the days in which he died . . . In 1979 P. [her husband] told B comrades [i.e. comrades from Area B] he just wanted to rest . . . Comrades also wanted him to rest. But others – some relatives – were unhappy and said he was now working for some other party. These relatives just hated him from the beginning. He had more than them and he'd been elected overall chairman. The UANC borrowed his bicycle while he was in the keep and didn't return it. So he went to their office in Mutoko with a *youth* from Area B as a witness to demand his bicycle. They gave him a new bicycle. He even used the bicycle to take food to the comrades in Area B. Relatives knew he was well-liked by Area B comrades so they went and told Area C comrades he had a UANC bike. When two *youths* from Area C came, they fooled him. They said there was trouble between C *youth* and comrades and they wanted him to solve it. So P. [her husband] took with him an elder and two *youth* and accompanied the C *youth*.

These *youth*, she alleged, killed her husband.

The different responses of villagers of different socio-economic backgrounds to school closures also suggests the political importance of internal stratification. Teachers and headmasters saw some clustering of opinion according to socio-economic background on the issue of school closures among *parents* and *youth*. According to a headmaster, 'not all parents wanted the school open. Those whose children weren't at school and were jealous, and ignorant ones, wanted the school closed.' Another noted that 'parents who could not afford to send their children to school or who were having trouble paying school fees would support the idea of closing the schools. Others would want it to stay open.' Some poorer parents, according to a headmaster just cited, 'associated education with the enemy. The only educated people whom they knew were blacks in the government – Guard Force, police, soldiers.'

Like the assault of *youth* on elders, the attacks on better-off people occurred without any formal organization. They were piecemeal, individual acts apparently chiefly by low-status single, unmarried *youths* but also all those at the bottom of the socio-economic hierarchy who used the opportunity presented by the war to vent their anger. The targeting of better-off people may have been motivated by the perception that these groups were collaborators but there does also seem to be an attempt at revenge against the better-off. Moral economists such as James Scott and Eric Wolf, if they may be grouped together as such, might interpret their behaviour as a defensive action to try to restore precapitalist norms whereby the rich were responsible for redistributing some of their wealth to the community so that subsistence for all was guaranteed.[47] Others might, and did, interpret their behaviour as an expression of their envy of those who had advanced. To the extent that they aimed at redistributing wealth among Africans, their goal was more radical than guerrilla goals that were almost exclusively concerned with racial equity. The vengeance that socio-economic differences among peasants provoked suggests, contrary to many Marxist analyses, that intra-class antagonisms may have at least as much power for mutual brutalization as inter-class ones.[48]

Gender conflicts

During the war, women had roles as fighters, educators in the refugee camps, providers of food and shelter to the guerrillas, and *chimbwidos* or female *youths*. ZANU and others have pointed to female participation in the war as evidence of its commitment to changing gender relations.[49] Naomi Nhiwatiwa, a ZANU official, reported to a group in Los Angeles in July 1979 on the results of a ZANU conference on women held in Mozambique some three months earlier. She told her audience that women comprised one-third of ZANU's guerrilla forces, who numbered about 20,000 inside the country by December 1979 and at least 2,000 outside the country – a statistic reiterated by Sally Mugabe, wife of Robert Mugabe, in an address to a conference in Copenhagen.[50] Julia Zvobgo, ZANU's representative for women's affairs in Mozambique, distinguished between women combatants in the army and women in the camps, and put the number of trained female fighters in Zimbabwe at between 1,500 to 2,000.[51] In her study of women in national liberation struggles, Miranda Davies also notes that the numbers of women combatants was small, and that females who left Zimbabwe hoping to join the guerrillas were usually asked to look after children.[52] By conflating women who were full-time fighters with those who did some military training in the

191

camps but were primarily engaged in agricultural work, education, or other tasks, Sally Mugabe and Nhiwatiwa create a misleading picture of the extent to which women participated as fighters in the guerrilla army. In his opening address to the women's conference, Robert Mugabe traced the unfolding ZANU policy of treating women as equals with men on the battlefront. He said women fighters 'have demonstrated beyond all doubt that they are as capable as men and deserve equal treatment, both in regard to training and appointments. It is because of their proven performance that we have agreed to constitute a Women's Detachment with its own commander who should become a member of the High Command. It is also necessary . . . that . . . we should promote more women to the High Command.' He proceeded to examine the role of women in ZANLA.

> Although in the High Command there is only one woman . . . in the General Staff, there are now scores of women officers, while in the Army generally several thousands of women cadres gallantly serve in one role or another. In the various operational departments of ZANLA, our women cadres can be found daily performing set tasks. We find them in the Department of Operations, in the Army Commissariat, in the Logistics and Supplies Department, in the Department of Security and Intelligence as officers and cadres, in the Department of Training as instructors, in the Department of Personnel, Production and Construction, Medical Services, Education and Culture, Welfare and Transport. In the Medical and Educational Department, women nursing cadres and teachers are performing wonderful work.[53]

Female participation during wars in roles from which they are normally excluded is not sufficient evidence of changing attitudes to women. Nor was female participation in wars an entirely new phenomenon for African women in this region, if there is validity to Mutunhu's claim that some of the best combat regiments during the Monomotapa period were composed only of women, mainly young and unmarried.[54]

Nhiwatiwa gave her North American audience examples, besides numbers of women participating in roles normally associated with men, of ZANU's progress in establishing gender equality. She reported that the women's conference in Mozambique had eliminated the concept of dowry, and 'right now in the liberated areas the Zimbabwe African National Union arranges the marrying of people, so people get married in the Party. People are getting married, and they are not getting married with the dowry system.' She went on to say that having women fighters holding more important ranks than men had rapidly improved gender relations. 'So a woman may be holding a more important rank than men, leading her husband. So the husband will have to take orders from his wife. That has helped to educate men very, very quickly to accept orders from women.' What women were seeking was equality regardless of whether they chose to become mothers or work for Zimbabwe's development and growth in other ways. Progress was being made on all these fronts, although she stressed that they were part of a 'working program'.[55] But women at the conference were less sanguine about their gains than Nhiwatiwa or Robert Mugabe and voiced resentment at ongoing gender discrimination: only 5 per cent of cadres sent for special courses by ZANU were women; all ZANU representatives abroad were men; leadership selection was biased in favour of men even though women often did much more work. They also condemned *lobola* and polygamy.[56] According to Julia Zvobgo, ZANLA had difficulty deciding how far to intervene in African customs. It did not go very far: it decided not to introduce family planning in the camps and, contrary to Nhiwatiwa's claims to her North American audience, it warned those young couples whose marriages the party registered that their parents would eventually be informed should they want *lobola* payments and other traditional rites.[57] ZANU concerns about clashing with African custom and tradition imposed a limit on the attainment of its goal of liberating women from their double burden of racism and tradition.

More data are needed about the attitudes of male and female combatants and camp and army personnel if problems encountered in eliminating gender discrimination are to be better understood. While some of the females in camps claimed equal treatment with males, others complained that leading 'comrades' thought they were entitled to the services of women.[58] A female guerrilla's report about the attitudes of her male comrades to birth control also raises questions about the depth of their commitment to changing gender relations. In her words, 'some of the male comrades did not like contraceptives because they thought it was murder, but really it was our duty and we female comrades were ready to defend it'.[59] Weinrich asserted that 'nowhere in southern Africa have women obtained as influential a position as have those in the liberation movements'. Yet she reproduced an extract dealing with obstacles to gender equality in ZANU that was allegedly from a captured report of the Department of Administration to the first session of ZANU's enlarged Central Committee in Maputo, dated August 1977. The extract reproduced was entitled 'Place and Role of Female Comrades in the Revolution' and should be treated with appropriate caution given that there is no way of knowing its authenticity as a ZANU document. It underlines obstacles to gender equality that arise from male sexist attitudes to females, and from females' own unwillingness to participate as equals with males.

> Since the March-April Chimoio meeting at which two of our female comrades were appointed to positions on the Central Committee, the Department of Administration has been pleased to see continual efforts by the Executive Committee to get as many as possible of our women comrades to participate in more challenging and satisfying tasks. But it must be pointed out that the ground is still insignificantly scratched. The party still badly needs to revolutionize its attitude towards female comrades and to urgently supervise the development and practice of a new attitude. There is an overwhelming resistance to invite and challenge female comrades to the more significant tasks of the revolution . . . Male comrades still think it

> humiliating to salute their senior-ranking female comrades. Our female comrades are also to blame. Many are still just 'women' in the old traditional sense. They still think it is anathema for them to take up the challenge of the revolution on an equal footing with male comrades . . . The party badly needs to define with much greater exactness what role the women of Zimbabwe must play along the path of revolution.[60]

Civilians inside Zimbabwe support the report's complaints about sexist male attitudes. Civilians reported that male guerrillas frequently defied their disciplinary code that prohibited sexual intercourse on duty. A teacher said:

> Comrades . . . became sexual. They took other people's wives and slept with them . . . They were tempted by money, young girls and women with husbands in Mozambique. They called these women 'their' women . . . They [youth] would have to go and get women for the comrades, yet they were told not to touch women.

Guerrilla attitudes and behaviour to women could not have made them suitable promoters, as they were, of family unity and new standards of morality that prohibited divorce and adultery and made it mandatory for men to marry women who bore their children. Guerrillas themselves fathered many children during the war. The evidence on guerrilla attitudes and behaviour raises questions about Lan's explanation that male elders reasserted their dominance on committees after the war because of 'the absence of the political will which the guerrillas provided' during the war. Nor is the evidence on guerrillas' gender attitudes consistent with his assertions that the guerrillas 'had wished to institute full-scale democracy that would include women and unmarried men too', and that the female guerrillas 'acquired practical experience of living and fighting alongside men as their moral and intellectual equal'.[61]

An emphasis on young women fighters, female *youth*, and aspirant female fighters in the refugee camps as evidence of progress in removing gender discrimination and on guerrilla attitudes as obstacles to further progress overlooks important individual initiatives of married women to change gender relations. Guerrilla appeals to families to be united and to men to stop beating their wives and drinking excessively originated with married women who saw in the guerrillas potential allies. Their initial success in winning the support of guerrillas gave them a strong motive to continue to provide support for the guerrillas. However, the guerrillas backed off from promoting their agenda when there was a backlash from married men. Demands for changing African social relations were ultimately abandoned by the guerrillas whose central platform was against racial discrimination. The limits to gender equality in the army, its secretariat, and the camps as well as data on guerrilla attitudes and behaviour to women also suggest that male guerrillas themselves had difficulties accepting gender equality in practice.

Wife-beating appears as a prominent grievance in accounts of females who left the country to join the guerrillas.[62] It was also a major complaint of rural women inside the country. According to villagers, guerrillas stumbled on women's grievances against their husbands. 'Comrades could come through a village at night, hear a woman crying and find her husband beating her', said a woman. From all accounts, the guerrillas then punished the husbands by beating them. Men felt threatened and 'husbands would be afraid to do or say anything to wives', said a primary school headmaster. 'They [wives] could even call you a sell-out and have you killed.' With the guerrillas as their new allies, women felt empowered and reported to the guerrillas whenever their husbands beat them. Men were not only afraid, but they also resented young people intervening in their private lives and constraining them from wife-beating. They believed that their behaviour to their wives, however violent, was their unquestioned right. A village head found the women's behaviour and the guerrillas' intervention on their behalf unacceptable.

> . . . women could purposely refuse to listen to husbands. They knew if they got beaten, the comrades would beat their husbands. Then husbands wouldn't easily get angry when their wives refused to listen to them.

A primary school headmaster pilloried women during the war, evincing his resentment towards their alliance with the guerrillas.

> Women were asked: 'How are you living with your husbands?' 'We are being harassed', they answered. 'Would you like us to beat them now?', the comrades would say. 'Yes, yes', the women would say . . . Comrades were pressing for equal rights in the home, especially as the war drew to an end. Comrades promised equality but they never explained whether they meant equal pay – which we are for – or equality in the home – which we oppose. If a letter comes to a woman, does the man still have the right to open it? 'Yes', they say.

For a brief period, wives acquired control over their husbands. Without a trace of remorse, a woman said: 'Comrades would beat the husbands publicly. This pleased wives a lot. It brought an end to beatings of women.' And for a while, when 'men complained that comrades were interfering in their private lives', the comrades said: 'We know what men are doing: they go to beerdrinks, get drunk and go home to beat their wives.'

Over time, though, the pleas of men prevailed. A war chairman reported how men in his area negotiated an arrangement with guerrillas:

> We said to them: 'In your home areas, did you ever settle cases between husband and wife?' The comrades then relented. They told women they'd be beaten if they ever brought complaints about their husbands to them. They would deal only with cases relating to the party.

Married women tried to change their husbands' behaviour towards them, and competed with men for the ear of guerrillas in their campaign. After initially supporting women, the guerrillas were won over by husbands' protests that they stay out of their personal lives. To appreciate why women participated in the war, one must take into account their efforts to take advantage of the war to try to improve their domestic lives. Like *youth*, women protested as individuals rather than in an organized way. Angela Cheater has raised the question of why Zimbabwean women did not develop a class consciousness. She points to their failure to realize the significance of bridewealth as a means of controlling female labour and the inherent conflict of economic interest between men and women. Instead, she says, women believe that marriage ties women's economic interests to their husbands in one family.[63] This study does not have data on women's understanding of marriage but why women did not use the organizations established to provide for the guerrillas collectively to challenge men must be raised especially given that *strangers* sometimes used these organizations to pursue their agendas.

Stranger/royal lineage conflicts

Hereditary rulers still exercised, albeit as government subordinates, their pre-colonial powers to hear court cases and allocate land. Except where the chiefly clan had allocated positions to them, *strangers* were excluded from holding such positions. The war offered them two resources with which to compete against hereditary leaders: the war committees and the guerrillas' suspicion of chiefs and headmen. Guerrillas' primary concern was their physical security. Chiefs, headmen, and village heads, as government paid employees, were possible government collaborators. They had to be carefully observed and if they informed on the guerrillas or their supporters, they usually paid with their lives. Moreover, there was often widespread hostility among villagers to chiefs, headmen and village heads, which *strangers* could exploit in their battle against hereditary rulers. The following exchanges with headmen underline their perception of opposition to them in many parts of the district.

> Q. Do you know any headmen or chiefs killed during the war?
>
> A. Kadiki, Kawere, Mujari, Makochera, Nyamanza, chief Nyamkoho and one of his headmen, Dehwe, Nyamatsahuni (suicide), Acting Chief Chimoyo.
>
> Q. Who killed them?
>
> A. They were murdered. They were said to be sell-outs.
>
> Q. Who said they were sell-outs?
>
> A. Our own people. The mass.
>
> Q. Why did the mass turn against chiefs and headmen?
>
> A. We were under whites and were receiving allowances. They were saying we were being paid by the whites. That is the only reason we were being called sell-outs.

Q. How did you survive?

A. I escaped through the hole of a needle.

Q. Were you ever threatened?

A. Yes. I had a shotgun that I'd bought myself. The people were telling the terrorists that my shotgun was to kill terrorists. I'd bought the shotgun to kill animals. Terrorists listened to what I said and then asked for food. It was the ancestral spirits that saved me.

Headman Nyakuna's answers were similar.

Q. Why were so many chiefs and headmen killed during the war?

A. It was the wish of the mass. The mass thought every chief and headman was supporting the whites. The previous government had held meetings with chiefs and headmen and paid us allowances. We were not all assisting whites. It was merely the thought of the mass.

This was the interchange with another headman.

Q. Why do you think so many headmen and chiefs were killed during the war?

A. They were called sell-outs by the mass, in their meeting.

Q. Why did the mass call them sell-outs?

A. Because we as headmen were approaching the DC [District Commissioner]. At the end of the month, we receive our allowances from the DC.

Q. What was the biggest problem in Mutoko during the war.

A. Only death.

Q. Was your life ever threatened?

A. Yes.

Q. By whom?

A. Would I know?

Q. How did you know your life was threatened?

A. From those who liked me.

A village head said:

> People said we could sell them out based on previous experience. We used to collect tax, give it to the DC's office and get $1 or $2 if we are lucky. But we weren't paying tax once the war started. They hated us because we'd been visiting the DC's office and they thought we could report comrades.

The evidence for *strangers* sometimes using the war as an opportunity to challenge 'traditional' leaders comes from examining the composition of village committees in four wards (Nyakuna in Mutoko chiefdom, Nyamatsahuni and Charewa in Charewa chiefdom, and Nyamanza in Chimoyo chiefdom – see map 3) and interviews with war committee members and those who managed to avoid positions. In both Nyamatsahuni and Nyakuna, war committees were dominated by *strangers*. In these wards, the ruling clan's totem was *shumba*. How did they come to occupy a virtual monopoly of the committee positions? On the one hand, they repeatedly claimed that *shumba* rulers and their relatives eschewed positions and 'pushed' them into committee work, upholding a time-honoured division of labour in which *strangers* did all the undesirable tasks.

> It is true that the war jobs were done by us. We are the *varanda* or *tonga* [slaves] of the *shumba*. Traditionally, the difficult jobs are done by us. The *shumba* only lead when the jobs are easy.

> Yes, the *shumba* were afraid to die during the war. They could just give their sons-in-law and nephews the jobs. You could hardly refuse. The father-in-law could just say: 'Son-in-law, you take the job.' [Intra-clan marriages are unusual, and most of the men in his village were married to *shumba* women.]

> I could not have refused, I am a *nhari* [totem]. If I had refused, the people would have reported me to the comrades as a sell-out. The *shumbas* could refuse and not be reported. It was their right to refuse, because they are *shumba*.

> Don't think it was a position given to me out of respect. They pushed these jobs onto us. They were cowards. Traditionally, in Mutoko people who were not *strangers* were called *varanda*. They were given a little land by the *shumba*. The land would be smaller than the plots given to *shumba* and usually less fertile too. We were never given gardens. They were reserved for the *shumba*. At *dares* [traditional court hearings], we could not participate. But after the *dare*, they might send us to skin a goat for them to eat. We used to do their dirty work. The messengers of the headman were always *varanda*. How had the district commissioner's office made the mistake of registering the Rukau people as one of the families amongst whom the headmanship rotated? Because the messenger was from the Rukau family, and he was always going to the district commissioner's office, so that the people there thought that he was the headman himself! We sweep the ancestral graves of the *shumba*; we collect the wood to make the fires for traditional beerdrinks, the *munga* [bulrush millet] or *rapoko* [finger millet] to make the beer, and we cook it. Then the *shumba* drink the beer and clap hands to the spirits. The following morning, when they have already had lots to drink, they will give us some beer and tell us to disperse. We cannot go into the chief's *dare* where the *shumba* drink. Since Nehoreka [the founding father] and Makati [a chief who once occupied the land] fought and Nehoreka won, this has been going on. Before the war, if they did not like us, they could chase us off their land. But during the war we were building our homes near to their houses and using land we were not supposed to. They were too scared to do anything. Today, they are starting again.

> *Shumba* were happy not to do the jobs in the war because they were dangerous.

> *Shumba* were afraid to die . . . The *shumba* didn't respect war leaders.

But *strangers* were not passive as *shumba* 'pushed' them onto war committees, and by collective action tried to use the war committees to take control of local politics from the *shumba* ruling families. 'Maybe other totems used the war as an opportunity to choose other people as their leaders', said a *stranger* who was on a war committee. '*Shumba* are proud and they claim they are the owners of the land.' Another committee member said: 'The whole village committee was not *shumba*. We deliberately left *shumba* out because they were always so proud. When they'd go to listen to a case at their headman, they'd not tell us.' Another justification for consciously excluding *shumba* ruling families from committees, in accord with a desire to wrest power from them, was that they were collaborators or potential traitors.

> For sure there were no *shumba* on war committees. Most of the kraalheads [village heads], etc. were *shumba* and were being referred to as sell-outs. That's why they weren't chosen. Take this village. The kraalhead is *shumba*. You can't elect his children. They are not kraalheads, but they are his children.

Once *strangers* had control of the committees, they behaved in ways that support the view that they intended to take power from hereditary rulers. Although the exercise of power over civilian affairs was limited by the war, chairmen sometimes tried to redistribute unused land that village heads had appropriated unfairly for their 'unborn children and unmarried sons' to those who had no land or insufficient land. More frequently *strangers* simply took the initiative and began to plough land wherever they liked, realizing that the *shumba* leaders had no effective civilian powers during the war. War committees also tried to assert power by settling disputes. *Shumba* rulers' judicial powers were eroded by martial law and the guerrillas' arbitration in cases ranging from divorce and adultery to alleged informers. Through negotiation with guerrillas, committees carved out a space where they could assert power: the settlement of disputes that arose in the context of the support organizations.

The perspective of *shumba* from non-ruling families adds credence to the perceptions of *strangers*. They acknowledged that hereditary rulers were not interested in committee positions and disregarded committee work. A *shumba* villager explained that Headman Nyakuna had not been involved in committee work 'partly because he was a government servant, so if he took up such a position, he might get into trouble from the government'. Implicitly condoning the hierarchy of power relations, he continued: 'Also, people respected him as a headman and didn't want him to run risks running back and forth to the comrades.' When asked why the *shumba* did not choose a person they respected to be a war leader, he answered that 'the headman had enough to do as headman'. Another *shumba* denigrated committee work and confirmed the *strangers'* view that it was 'pushed' onto them.

> During the war we chose other totems to lead the people. *Shumba* had other positions: kraalheads and chiefs . . . We thought it was just a position for

> organizing things in the war . . . The other totems also did not want *shumba* to have positions because they said that we already had positions. People don't like *shumba* – they say we are proud.

A *shumba* teacher claimed that hereditary leaders were too old for physically demanding work and hinted that it would be improper to expose them to the dangers of support work.

> Kraalheads were not usually elected to committees. They were important people and often old. They couldn't be expected to move around much. Also, it was dangerous work.

The *shumba* ruling families also supported the *strangers'* account of how they came to control the war committees. In both Nyamatsahuni and Nyakuna, ruling families were content to let *strangers* take control of the war committees, perceiving them as temporary organizations that would cease to exist after the war and fully anticipating a restoration of the status quo. This expectation was strengthened by the respect the guerrillas showed the ruling *shumba*, calling on them to offer prayers to the spirits at the beginning and end of *moraris*. Over time, the responses of the ruling families in each ward diverged. In Nyamatsahuni, the ruling families continued to ignore the committees' challenge; in Nyakuna, the ruling families fought back and reasserted control. How can one explain their different responses? Two factors seem pertinent. First, in Nyakuna ward *strangers* were a numerical minority. If the *shumba* acted collectively and rallied around their rulers, they could stymie an assault from *strangers*. By contrast, *strangers* were a majority in Nyamatsahuni ward and even if the *shumba* ruling families had assumed a leadership role the power of numbers was against them. Secondly, Headman Nyakuna had a history of being anti-government and a member of nationalist parties, whereas the former Headman Nyamatsahuni had been a government collaborator. Headman Nyamatsahuni had angered even villagers from the ruling clan shortly before the war by reporting the authentic medium of their ancestral spirit to the government as an impostor. What happened when the guerrillas visited him in 1976 unfolded slowly, in 'dribs and drabs', because members of his family who had been there were too intimidated to report the incident. Apparently, he was accosted by 'a gang of terrorists' who stripped him of his badge of office, symbolizing the removal of his powers, and some cash. 'They told him they would probably visit him at his kraal the next day. Although not clear, it appears they did so and this time took a pair of handcuffs and a muzzle loader.' They instructed him to call a meeting of his village heads and inform them he was no longer 'chief' and that they were no longer rulers in the area. One day later, he committed suicide, of which there was some history in his family.[64] No-one was willing to fill the headmanship after his death, and so the most important political position of the ruling lineage in that ward remained vacant during the war.

The initiative to challenge inherited leadership in local politics came from rural people themselves. Thrust onto the committees, *strangers* then united in an organized assault on ruling lineages. The availability of lineage as a basis for organization made the challenge against the ruling lineage the only organized rural civilian protest during the war. The guerrillas opposed hereditary rulers because of their involvement with government but never challenged the institution of hereditary offices. When they killed incumbent rulers or encouraged committee members to take power from them or share power with them, their intent was to punish individual rulers for collaborating with the government and allow the new committees some status and power. The guerrillas' agenda never included eliminating the lineage-based, hereditary political system and broadening the basis for political competition for local power. They might follow majority opinion on the issue, but opposition to hereditary rule was not part of their platform. Even today, the Mugabe government accepts the institution of chiefship (see chapter 6).

In the other two wards studied, the relationship between *strangers* and royal lineages was markedly different. In Charewa ward it is difficult to detect the same challenge to hereditary rulers. Its unique indigenous power structure probably goes a long way to explain the apparent absence of *strangers* seeking to control the committees or hostility towards ruling families. Both in Charewa chiefdom and Charewa ward, one of six in the chiefdom, chiefly clans/totems did not monopolize positions as they usually do. Hence there was no lineage basis for animosity toward members of the chiefly clans.

The unusual power structure in Charewa may be traced to arrangements made between two of the founding fathers. In the seventeenth century two men, Nehoreka who belonged to the *nzou* (elephant) totem, and Mapatwe who belonged to the *shumba* (lion) totem (subclan: *nyamuziwa-hara*), led *shumba* families from near the town of Tete in what is today Mozambique to the area between the Nyadiri and Mudzi rivers in what is today Zimbabwe. According to oral traditions, Nehoreka and Mapatwe used magic to defeat the powerful chief Makati, the leader of the *soko* (monkey) clan and established control of the lands to the east and west of the Chitora river. Out of gratitude for his help in the conquest, Mapatwe gave Nehoreka control of the land west of the Chitora river (i.e. Charewa chiefdom) while Mapatwe ruled to the east and was considered the founding chief of the entire area (known today as Mutoko chiefdom after the reigning chief at the time of British conquest). Soon competition developed between Nehoreka and Mapatwe. Nehoreka was eager to assure his continued influence in the conquered area. To do so, he had to overcome a serious problem. According to Shona custom, usually the deceased leader of the patrilineage that first settles an area becomes the tribal spirit, and his patrilineal descendants become hereditary leaders. This meant that Mapatwe's spirit would prevail and his descendants would be the future leaders. During his lifetime, however, Nehoreka laid the groundwork to ensure that his spirit would prevail over Mapatwe's for all the Budjga people. He first created the closest possible ties between himself and Mapatwe by marrying his relative. Then he adopted the *shumba* totem of the new owners of the land. Finally, he mixed powerful medicine in Mapatwe's food to ensure that his own spirit and not Mapatwe's would in due time become the Budjga's spirit. The result of these machinations was an unusual split between secular and spiritual authority that persists today. The people look to Nehoreka as their *mhondoro* but to Mapatwe's descendants as the supreme secular rulers. Consequently, Nehoreka's descendants do not rule in the Charewa chiefdom and the reigning chief Mutoko (Mapatwe's descendant) nominates the ruler of Charewa. The Charewa ruler must always be a woman who is not a member of the *shumba* clan and must be approved by Nehoreka. Nehoreka's spirit medium, always a woman who lives with the appointed secular leader of Nehoreka's area, Chieftainess Charewa, also asserts spiritual authority over Mapatwe's descendants and must approve the appointments of Chief Mutoko and his presumptive heirs.[65] Chieftainess Charewa is unusual in at least three ways. She is appointed by a neighbouring chief but approved by Nehoreka's medium; her power derives from her spiritual importance as the guardian of Nehoreka's medium, rather than her secular significance; and her four principal councillors, all village heads, are hereditary positions, and from different lineages, their totems being *shumba, soko, nhari,* and *chirandu.*[66]

The political structure of Charewa ward has further peculiarities. Usually when a ward headman becomes chief, his ward does not appoint a headman for as long as he is the reigning chief. In Charewa ward, the incumbent Chieftainess Charewa is always also the ruler of Charewa ward. The headmen in the other five wards are all descendants of Mapatwe and hence members of the *shumba* clan. Usually, all or some of them would be eligible for the chiefship but the special arrangements governing the Charewa chiefship make them ineligible. Charewa ward would not have a headman were it not for the white administration's insistence that the ward produce a representative other than the chieftainess because until recently successive chieftainesses refused to meet with whites. Because its existence is entirely wrapped up with the demands of the white administration, the Charewa headmanship has low status in the indigenous polity. The headman is appointed by the chieftainess in consultation with her inner council of four men, other elders, all headmen in the Charewa chiefdom, and Nehoreka's spirit medium. According to government records, the headman cannot be of the *shumba* totem, must not belong to the lineage of the chieftainess, and must reside permanently in Dzimbahwe village where she and Nehoreka's spirit medium live.[67] In short, leadership positions in Charewa ward and Charewa chiefdom are not always hereditary and are shared by people of different totems/clans in a way that make this chiefdom and ward distinctive. Unlike most chiefdoms and wards, no single chiefly clan monopolizes political positions. Moreover, the strong spiritual power of Chieftainess Charewa probably lends a sanctity to political arrangements throughout the chiefdom.

Nyamanza, one of four wards in Chimoyo chiefdom, represents the final case study of the relationship between *strangers* and the chiefly clan. Nyamanza presented a striking contrast to Nyakuna and Nyamatsahuni wards. While the latter are close to a major bus route to Harare, near to Mutoko centre and better linked to the capitalist world of the settlers, Nyamanza was strikingly isolated and poor. There were few brick houses, homes seldom had items bought in stores, and the arrival of a bus was an event. According to the historian David Beach, the ruling *soko* clan (subclan: *mbire-murehwa*) claims to have accompanied the Budjga on their journey to the present area from Tete. They lived for a while as subordinates of the original ruler before supplanting him in an episode described in a myth.[68] The Nyamanza headmanship was created by the government in 1951 and is not eligible for the Chimoyo chieftainship. All three other headmanships – Mujari, Manyange, Chimoyo – once were eligible but the Manyange headmanship was disqualified during the pre-colonial period by the *soko* clan when one of its incumbents committed a serious offence.[69]

In Nyamanza ward, hereditary rulers, regardless of lineage assumed the leadership of the committees, with each village head acting as chairman until the ceasefire. People appeared to have accepted their leadership in the war, reflecting what I maintain was a respect for them and their wishes. Why, though, did village heads try to maintain the status quo by aggressively seeking leadership of the committees, when in Nyakuna and Nyamatsahuni they were content to let *strangers* acquire new positions? Perhaps rulers volunteered to lead their people in war too because, as a *youth* leader maintained, they never foresaw how grim the war would be. But this is unsatisfactory as they appear to have made no effort to rid themselves of leadership as the war intensified. Maybe it made a difference that the headman had a history of opposition to the government. But then Headman Nyakuna also opposed the government but had initially avoided committee work. People in Nyamatsahuni raised the possibility that village heads had been made chairmen to prevent them from collaborating with the government and to punish them for past collaboration. However, if everyone in Nyamanza believed that their village heads were collaborators and they were concerned about their collective safety, they would probably have reported them as 'sell-outs' to the guerrillas and had them liquidated – the fate of one of the three chiefs and six of the fifteen headmen in the district. Moreover, leaders in Nyamanza appear to have been respected by their subjects. Perhaps hereditary rulers were responsive to the initial efforts of guerrillas to try to use 'traditional' authority to spur mobilization and collective action.

Towards the ceasefire, all village heads lost their positions as chairmen. I did not obtain the totems of section chairmen, but of the five branch chairmen only one belonged to the ruling clan. How can one account for this sudden change in committee leadership, and did it imply a changing relationship between hereditary rulers and *strangers*? The answer to the first question seems to be related to the death of Headman Nyamanza who, along with his medium, was murdered by guerrillas, probably on the last day of 1978.[70] Headman Nyamanza strikes one as a surprising guerrilla victim, given the government's perception of his guerrilla loyalties. In April 1977 the district commissioner complained about Headman Nyamanza to his superior, the provincial commissioner.[71]

> He's long had the reputation of being anti-government and is suspected of having been implicated in the murder by terrorists of the rival candidate for the Chimoyo chieftainship approved by my predecessor.
>
> His people have been unruly and are known to have participated in the recent extensive cutting of the fence at the P.V. [protected village] on two occasions. Information indicates that he has frequently held discussions with the terrorists in his area. Recently he failed to attend a meeting with Mr. Ford [DEVAG supervisor] as did half of his kraalheads . . .
>
> I have told Nyamanza that his allowances will be suspended until there is a noticeable improvement in his ability to control his people and lead them along the paths of righteousness.

Why would the guerrillas kill him, and, soon thereafter, call on the village heads to relinquish their chairmanship of the committees? The guerrillas presumably received information that the headman had betrayed them. Perhaps he had been tortured by government, or perhaps internal rivalries for the Chimoyo chieftainship hinted in the letter I have just quoted, resulted in him being reported as a 'sell-out'. To protect themselves, the guerrillas requested that village heads step down as chairmen. But aware of local respect for village heads, the guerrillas presented their case in terms of their concern for the safety of village heads and the need to protect them from government harassment. Nyamanza villagers brushed aside all questions about their headman's murder, denying any knowledge about what had happened. It seemed a protective silence, especially when compared with the open gloating about how Headman Nyamatsahuni had committed suicide when intimidated by guerrillas.

Even when *strangers* got control of the war committees there is no evidence that they tried to wrest control from their village heads. Disputes continued to be taken to village heads or the guerrillas. Had *strangers* wished to challenge hereditary authority, they might at least have tried to exploit the headman's alleged betrayal of the guerrillas and their resulting fears about village heads' loyalty. Several informants maintained that *strangers* were outnumbered by the ruling *soko* clan. For this reason, *strangers* might have seen the futility of challenging the status quo. But this did not inhibit *strangers*, who were a minority in Nyakuna. All evidence points to *strangers* accepting the status quo.

Despite information gaps the four case studies underline the diversity in the relationships between *strangers* and incumbent rulers. When these relationships were conflictual, the outcomes of competition for power appear to have depended on the ratio of *strangers* to the chiefly clan. The war offered the first opportunity in the colonial period to subject 'traditional' institutions and individual rulers to majority opinion without the government intervening. Although the guerrillas intervened, they tried to do so with due regard for public opinion. In Nyamatsahuni and Nyakuna *strangers* used the committees to launch an assault against hereditary rulers. In Charewa and Nyamanza, no such lineage competition occurred. The unique indigenous administrative system in Charewa does not exclude *strangers* from positions of political power. Hence there is no basis for *strangers*/ruling clan conflicts. Nyamanza ward provides an example of hereditary rulers leading in the war committees. When replaced towards the end of the war, they still continued to hear disputes relating to party issues. This seems to point to their popular acceptance as leaders. In Nyakuna and Nyamatsahuni, *strangers* opposed the ruling lineages and clans, but only in the latter did *strangers* have a numerical majority. Together with the aggressive action of Headman Nyakuna to assert power, the size of the chiefly clan relative to that of *strangers* may go a long way in explaining the ultimate failure of *strangers* in Nyakuna and their success in Nyamatsahuni.

These findings on the composition of village committees may be usefully contrasted with Patrick Chabal's statement about the committees established during the national liberation wars in the former Portuguese colonies in Africa. Chabal maintains that where political mobilization succeeded, the parties relied on existing local political structures, that is, 'traditional' authorities. 'In most instances, anti-colonial sentiments in the village amounted to a desire for a return to "traditional" socio-political institutions rather than for integration into a modern socialist party organisation. The extent to which the three parties actually managed to change the structure of local political institutions must have been limited.' He goes on: 'Although village committees did form the linchpin of local administration in the liberated areas and although they enjoyed a certain degree of autonomy in their dealings with the party, it is unlikely that they acted as instruments of political change. There is thus little ground to suggest that the experience of political mobilisation, and of war-time collaboration between villagers and party turned village committees into "revolutionary cells".'[72] The absence of 'traditional' leaders on the war committees in at least two of the four wards in Mutoko district makes an interesting comparison with the apparent prominence of 'traditional' leaders on the committees in lusophone Africa. Perhaps more interesting, though, is how Chabal assumes that any change in the structure of local politics would depend on the effectiveness of party mobilization. In this respect, he discounts peasant agency. Also, he identifies two types of political change: the return to 'tradition' sought by peasants and revolutionary socialism. This assumes united peasant action in support of 'tradition' and does not allow for divergent peasant responses to 'tradition'. The Mutoko data underline peasant agency and peasant differentiation that on occasion pitted peasant supporters and opponents of hereditary rule against each other.

Problems of overdetermining political motives

The behaviour and attitudes of peasants and *youth*, interpreted here as a challenge to the immediate socio-political environment, can sustain alternative interpretations. The same behaviour often had multiple and even contradictory motives, most of which were suggested at different times by rural people themselves. Take, for example, the behaviour of *youth* towards elders. Some of their violence towards elders reflected their fear of guerrilla retribution if they did not meet their demands. For example, *youth* sometimes stole cattle from the Purchase Area farms rather than face the guerrillas' anger if they returned empty-handed from the increasingly well-fortified European farms. Instances of their overzealous enforcement of guerrilla instructions may be interpreted as reflecting their desire to please the guerrillas. Two war chairmen made this point.

> *Youth* in many areas caused many deaths by trying to please comrades by collecting sell-outs.

> Comrades really trusted me. I saved many people whom comrades were about to kill for no reason. Once at Masango [a guerrilla base], they were about to kill seven people whom *youth* had said were sell-outs. I think *youth* were reporting cases of sell-outs to comrades when they were not really sell-outs because as the comrades grew in numbers, they thought that if they reported many sell-outs, they'd gain the favour of comrades and be rewarded with a gun.

Not all *youths'* embezzlement of funds can be attributed to an act of resistance against elders' authority. Sometimes they and *parents* exploited opportunities for individual material gain. For example, *parents* – especially treasurers – were often accused of appropriating money intended for the guerrillas. A *youth* leader had this to say about chairman P., whose widow had blamed jealous relatives for his death as a 'sell-out':

> M. and P. were crooks. P. sold blankets from Red Cross intended for widows . . . M. was angry because P. wouldn't give him an equal share. So M. tried to sell P. out to C *youth*. They found he was eating money for the comrades. He'd been sent to Harare with $200 to buy clothes, and they never saw the clothes.

There were also occasional references to *youth* not passing on to the guerrillas clothes, money and items received from other *youth*. Some people were alleged to be 'making a good business' profiting from the sale of cattle raided from white farms.

It is similarly difficult to disentangle motives for material gain from anti-government behaviour or anger against the better-off for not sharing some of their wealth. For example, people stripped vacated government housing for teachers and extension assistants, council offices, and schools. Windows, window frames, roofs, furniture, and library books were removed. Many motives may have coincided to produce this behaviour. An agricultural officer, employed by the government, claims that *youth* denounced him, not because he was a government employee, but because they wanted him to leave his house so that they could get material from it.

> In Christmas 1978 I returned and found a letter from the *mujibas*. It said: 'Down with you, and forward with the war.' They threatened to kill me. They were not against everyone working. They wanted me to get out. They wanted to get material from the houses and sell them for money.

The battle lines were also sometimes more complicated than *youth* against their elders. It would be wrong to create the impression that *youth* never clashed with each other or that *parents* never sided with *youth*. Soon after Mutoko and Mudzi had been divided into Areas A, B, and C, tensions developed between *youth* in a few villages in Area B and those in some villages in Area C. A headman of villages involved in Area B tells of how he and others tried to talk to the guerrillas in their area about the evolving conflict, initially between *youth* and later uniting *youth*, *parents*, and guerrillas from the villages in Area B against those in Area C.

> Maybe it was just hatred that they called us Muzorewa supporters. C *youth* once took B *youth* who were in Area C. They didn't know they weren't allowed in Area C and had gone to see C comrades. C *youth* . . . took them to comrades and said they were Muzorewa supporters. Comrades beat them at Gute [a guerrilla base]. When B *youth* were released, they reported to B comrades who told them to report to them if they ever saw a C *youth* in Area B. The B comrades said: 'These C comrades might be Selous Scouts. Why else are they beating you?' . . . Later B *youth* found C *youth* in B. They didn't know where C *youth* were going, but they captured them. B *youth* took them to comrades based at Mukomeka. I got a letter from C comrades . . . It said: 'We want those children, if we don't get them, there'll be chaos'. I only learned from this letter that *youth* had been captured. So I went to get Mr M. and N. and we followed footprints, looking for *youth* and comrades . . . We told the comrades in very strong terms that we'd have to go to town if this situation continued. Guard Force were killing us and we were having to run from comrades too . . . Next morning the comrades told us to go and give B *youth* a letter for the C comrades. When we arrived back here, I found the villages deserted. I thought Guard Force had been here. I learned C comrades had spent the previous night at my house singing. They'd left early that morning before I got back. They'd left bundles of poles that they'd intended to beat me with. When I heard comrades had spent the night at my house, I went back to collect the C *youth* because they had not come back yet. While I was still there Mr M. received a letter from C *youth* giving the B comrades till 12:00 that morning to return their *youth*. Mr M. replied to the letter and said C *youth* would be back that day, but not by 12:00. Then M.

207

> followed to the guerrilla base at Mukomeka . . . Days later B comrades went to C comrades and beat Chiwororo [a guerrilla leader in C] and he was sent back to Mozambique. Some comrades had even suggested killing him – they disliked him so much. They beat Chiwororo because he had been the one who had slept at my house and beaten B *youth*.

A *parent* related the following story of conflict among *youth* living in different villages and working for different guerrilla groups. Like the previous story, it suggests that some *youth* prodded others to be more supportive of the guerrillas. Based on my knowledge of the layout of the villages, those located close to roads were more susceptible to being labelled 'sell-out' or accused of not supporting the war enough. Their location close to the roads meant that they were more often visited by soldiers than guerrillas, thus creating the impression that they were 'selling-out'.

> G. [name of village] *youth* caused trouble here. They told comrades our *youth* were sell-outs because they were disciplined and didn't support the war much. The comrades told G. *youth* to intimidate them so they'd be more supportive. *Youth* from G. were told to get *youth* from this area to carry schoolbooks to their base. They wanted the schools closed. *Youth* were to fetch the teachers and the headmaster to explain why the school was still open. *Youth* from here were embarrassed to push their teachers to the base at Kadiki and take out the books. Only two *youth* from here helped – my son and a young girl. They were forced by G. *youth*. I was furious. Then I had to send my son to learn at Nyadiri, in bad living conditions.

Neat categories created to interpret motives always simplify the messiness and complexity of reality. These problems are unavoidable in studies that try to understand human behaviour that may only rarely, if ever, be interpreted monocausally. In interpreting behaviour as resistance, there is a risk of overstating or overdetermining the significance of locally based popular struggles. Even if internal peasant grievances and resentment toward the rural African elite have been overdetermined in this study, it does not diminish the case for their importance.

Conclusion

Wolf has commented on the shift since World War II from a concern with the social and cultural concomitants of life in closely knit, face-to-face networks of relationships in peasant communities to an interest in peasant involvements with the market, the state, and wide-ranging systems of ideological communication. According to Wolf, the role of peasants in the Chinese, Cuban, and Vietnamese revolutions accelerated interest in wider peasant relations.[73] Put differently, the interest in peasants in revolutions derives from an interest in revolutionary organizations. Analysts of peasant revolutions tend to disregard internal peasant grievances or to perceive them as obstacles to a revolutionary organization or to acknowledge their mobilizing power but also the need for organizational control. In doing so, they unwittingly accept the revolutionary organization's need for unity, popular support, and collective action. If peasant involvement in successful revolutions hastened academic interest in wider peasant relations, other factors also predispose analysts to focus on peasant relations with external actors. Definitions of peasants emphasize their relations with markets, states, and elites. Hence the peasant concept itself orients analysts away from the study of internal peasant grievances. This outward orientation is deepened in studies that emphasize the role of peasant nationalism. In the absence of peasant voices, it is difficult to challenge the entrenched external orientation in studies of peasant revolutions (see chapter 1).

Oral testimonies of peasants, *youth*, and the rural elite who participated in the war of national liberation in Zimbabwe provide such a challenge. They suggest that internal peasant grievances and peasant resentments against the African rural elite were stronger motives to participate in the war than was the state's racial discrimination. The state, settlers, and capitalist imperialism all shaped local conflicts and created grievances. But peasants experienced resentment against those closest to them rather than the more distant white state. Conflicts within peasant communities and between elites and peasants were not merely impediments to guerrilla goals of collective action and popular support but also powerful spurs to participate in the war. Further, the goals of groups in peasant communities cannot be dismissed as inferior to those of the guerrillas. Indeed, peasants were much more concerned with ending hereditary rule and effecting social change within African communities than were the guerrillas. From the perspective of various local groups, the war was an opportunity to express grievances openly. Formerly powerless, they used their positions in the civilian organizations established to support the guerrillas in their fight for African majority rule, and the guerrillas themselves, as resources to press their own agendas. Guerrilla appeals for national liberation were mediated by the different interests of peasants and their children. Subsistence-oriented villagers and poor, uneducated *youth* rejected socio-economic stratification. Their actions are consistent with a desire for greater egalitarianism within the villages or envy of the better-off. *Strangers* belonging to different totems united in two of the four wards to end hereditary political rule in the villages. Women tried to improve their marital relations and *youth* their social status and lack of autonomy. Women and *youth* protested through individual acts and women also appealed to the guerrillas to intervene on their behalf. Only *strangers* launched an organized assault on royal lineages by uniting in an entirely unprecedented way.

Peasant motives during a revolution raise questions about rational choice theories. Chapter 4 discussed how, even though peasants shared a common interest in removing white state power, the guerrillas had to rely on coercion to induce peasants to participate in an organization set up to support them and make possible their defeat of whites. The argument had a striking similarity to Mancur Olson's 'logic of collective action' according to which rational individuals will not participate in providing a collective good unless they are coerced (in which he would include denied benefits) or offered special incentives. But the similarity has its limits.[74] Rational choice theories assume that an organization serves a common interest. In this case, the civilian organizations were intended to meet guerrilla needs so that they could overthrow white rule. But the emergence of civilian organizations to feed the guerrillas, and the presence of the guerrillas themselves, opened opportunities for groups within peasant communities, such as *strangers* and *youth*, to pursue other interests. Whereas rational choice theory assumes that individuals have fixed interests, this chapter highlights how interests are contingent on political action and opportunities. Rational choice theorists also assume that individuals will only engage in voluntary collective action if the organization gives them special incentives. But the behaviour of *strangers* suggests how individuals may voluntarily engage in group action without any organizational incentives. In chapter 4 peasants appear paralyzed by fear of the guerrillas, who are coercing them to engage in collective action to support them, and thereby overthrow white rule, but in this chapter groups within peasant communities are willing to take risks to pursue their own agendas. This apparent inconsistency may be understood if one assumes that peasants were more willing to take risks for their own agendas, than for the guerrillas' agenda, that only indirectly might benefit them.

The argument that internal peasant grievances were more important than peasant resentments against the state and other external actors may undeniably inflame elites. David Beach, an historian, has found it 'sensitive' to discuss how in the 1890s Shona chiefdoms often collaborated with Europeans rather than join other Africans to oppose white rule. Some Shona regarded the Ndebele as a greater threat to them than the whites; others saw the whites as potential allies against chiefdoms with whom they were competing for power. Beach sees in this behaviour 'a measure of the way the past gripped the minds of people in 1896–7'.[75] The war of national liberation occurred almost a century later when self-determination had become a widely accepted principle by African elites in the few remaining colonies and in the international community. To argue that internal peasant politics in Zimbabwe were more important to peasants than removing the white state is potentially more inflammatory given the enormous racial inequalities that characterized the colonial period. At independence 3 per cent of the white population commanded nearly two-thirds of national income, leaving 97 per cent of Africans with at most the remaining third. The tiny white minority also had exclusive ownership of almost half the land (and two-thirds of the best quality land) and together with foreign interests owned nearly all the capital in industry and mining.[76] But people generally, and not necessarily only peasants, do not always understand their oppression as systemic, and instead hold individuals responsible for their misery. Bettelheim's work on concentration camp victims found that they often perceived individual SS guards rather than Hitlerism to be the source of their oppression (see chapter 4). The data of this study, and perhaps also Beach's analysis of the 1890s, would appear to lend support to Anthony Wallace's suggestion that human beings 'generally reserve their settled fears, suspicions, and hatreds to those closest to them: kinsmen, neighbours, and colleagues'.[77] Fanon attributes internal conflicts among the colonized to the effects of colonial policy. This internalized aggression will be released against the colonial power in armed struggle and will unite the colonized as they come to understand who their real enemy is. Colonial rulers undoubtedly sought to divert conflict against the state and encourage internal divisiveness. But the data of this study suggest that peasants, even during the anti-colonial war, ranked coming to terms with their internal enemies as more pressing and more worthy of risks than eliminating the white state. Fanon's descriptions of how the colonized behaved before armed struggle in Algeria bears a striking resemblance to peasant behaviour during the war in Zimbabwe.[78]

> In the colonial context . . . the natives fight amongst themselves. They tend to use each other as a screen, and each hides from his neighbour the national enemy. When, tired out after a hard sixteen-hour day, the native sinks down to rest on his mat, and a child on the other side of the canvas partition starts crying and prevents him from sleeping, it so happens that it is a little Algerian. When he goes to beg for a little semolina or a drop of oil from the grocer, to whom he already owes some hundreds of francs, and when he sees that he is refused, an immense feeling of hatred and an overpowering desire to kill rises within him: and the grocer is an Algerian. When, after having kept out of his way for weeks he finds himself one day cornered by the caid [underworld slang for bigshot, top man or gang leader] who demands that he should pay 'his taxes', he cannot even enjoy the luxury of hating a European administrator; there before him is the caid who is the object of his hatred – and the caid is an Algerian. The Algerian, exposed to temptations to commit murder every day – famine, eviction from his room because he has not paid the rent, the mother's dried-up breasts, children like skeletons, the building-yard which has closed down; the unemployed that hang about the foremen like crows – that native comes to see his neighbour as a relentless enemy.

The Algerian liberation war allegedly changes everything.

> The whole foodstocks of a family . . . may in a single evening be given to a passing company. The family's only donkey may be lent to transport a wounded fighter; and when a few days later the owner learns of the death of his animal which has been machine-gunned by an airplane, he will not begin threatening and swearing. He will not question the death of his donkey, but he will ask anxiously if the wounded man is safe and sound. Under the colonial regime, anything may be done for a loaf of bread or a miserable sheep . . . To live means to keep on existing.

6

Legacies of the war for peasants

Understanding the revolutionary mobilization process is important in itself but also because of its alleged links with post-revolutionary outcomes. Chapter 1 discussed how extensive peasant mobilization during a revolution is often linked to peasant participation in state and party institutions and potential for socialist transformation after the revolution. Such propositions, whether applied to China, Mozambique, or Guinea-Bissau, attribute the potential for socialism to the role of a party with a socialist ideology that controls liberated areas and enjoys peasants' popular support during the revolutionary process. Linked as these propositions are to the mobilization process, it is unsurprising that they too focus on peasant relations with the state and revolutionary party, neglect internal struggles within the peasantry, and rely on sources other than peasant interviews.

In contrast to studies of China, Mozambique, and Guinea-Bissau, that highlight the role of the revolutionary party's socialist ideology and control of liberated areas, studies of Zimbabwe usually acknowledge that ZANU's socialist ideology was poorly developed and that ZANU guerrillas did not win control of liberated areas. Yet several analysts of Zimbabwe link party mobilization during the war to post-independence outcomes. John Saul and Lionel Cliffe argue that armed struggle raised the political consciousness of guerrillas and peasants and made the latter more aware of their grievances as an exploited class. Moreover, the radicalizing effect of popular guerrilla struggle also promoted the ideological development of some leaders in the armed struggle, even though the most radical of them (i.e. those most closely involved in the guerrilla war) were defeated in a leadership struggle. The legacy of protracted armed struggle contains, therefore, the potential for socialist transformation in the post-independence period, but how far this develops will depend on factors such as the character of the nationalist leadership, the class dialectic between the new political leadership and the popular classes (workers and peasants), and other factors.[1]

Ranger's *Peasant Consciousness and Guerrilla War in Zimbabwe* contains a variant of this thesis. He argues that peasants' political consciousness and their central role in providing the popular base for the guerrillas placed them in an unusually advantageous position *vis-à-vis* other African peasantries in the post-war period and enabled them to impose a radicalizing influence, albeit not socialist, on the nationalist leadership.[2] The new government had to take into account peasant aspirations or encounter conflict and resistance from peasant radical nationalists.[3] By the end of 1982, the government had been quite responsive to peasant goals of ending administrative coercion and had gone some way to returning some of their lands.[4] But Ranger expected that the unusually advantageous position of peasants *via-à-vis* the state would give way to 'quite another balance of power'.[5] None the less, he felt there was a prospect, 'however utopian it may sound, that a fruitful interaction between peasant consciousness and official inputs may be achieved'.[6]

An understanding of the mobilization process that emphasizes reluctant peasant support rather than popular support for the guerrillas, and depends on peasant data rather than other sources, leads to a different interpretation of the grassroots legacies of the war in Zimbabwe. Whereas proponents of the radicalization thesis stress the war's participatory and democratic legacy for local party structures, I emphasize villagers' lingering fear of the party, guerrillas, and the government, and how the village committees and *youth* sometimes emulated guerrilla coercion during the war. And while adherents of the radicalization thesis attribute the demobilization of local party structures to the rise of competitive local government institutions, I, like other critics of the radicalization thesis, highlight the role of the state in demobilizing peasants, as well as the effects of the lack of material incentives on party participation. The radicalization thesis also overstates the role of peasants' political consciousness in clashes with the state after the war by not taking into account the antagonism inherent in peasant–state relations. Finally, proponents of the radicalization thesis neglect internal peasant struggles after the war. These revolved around new issues created by the war, such as who had sacrificed resources for the guerrillas and deserved compensation, and continuing conflict between local party committees on the one hand and chiefs and headmen on the other.

ZANU's democratic legacy: neglect of fear of party, guerrillas, and government

Cliffe and his co-authors (1980) believed that popular mass mobilization had led to the creation of people's committees during the war. They perceived them to be evolving in certain areas of the country into alternative administrative bodies that settled disputes and initiated self-help projects. They associated these grassroots structures with participatory democracy and envisioned them serving as mechanisms for reconstruction and post-war development and as organizational weapons to ward off the assault of neo-colonialism on popular peasant interests.[7]

David Lan's *Guns and Rain* identifies the establishment of village committees as the most important outcome of the struggle besides independence. In mid 1979, the guerrillas handed over their authority to elected committees. Just as the mediums had conferred legitimacy on the guerrillas, so they legitimized the authority of the elected village committees.[8] By doing so, the mediums 'endorsed the system of participatory democracy that the committees put into practice and thus a radically new and fully legitimate political era began'.[9] And the mediums' influence over these new, fully elected committees persisted: party meetings began and ended with ritual clapping to the local *mhondoro* and members of the committees reported to their local spirit medium and sought their advice.[10] Mediums introduced a new task for the committees' political commissars of protecting the area from witches.

> This should come as no surprise. The concept of 'witch' is, today as in the past, the negative of the concept *mhondoro*. Because the *mhondoro* have given their support to the committees, the committees defend the moral code they represent. If anyone breaks the code and is therefore categorised as a witch, it is the duty of the Political Commissar, as it was of the chiefs of the past, to take action against them.[11]

Ranger's *Peasant Consciousness and Guerrilla War in Zimbabwe* describes how peasants developed a network of elected village and district committees in Shona areas after the war. They remained outside the control of the party hierarchy for the first twelve months of independence. Village committees were effective centres of administration, allocating land and settling disputes. Village committees established peasant power at the village level as never before but also represented a conservative revolution in that they were comprised of resident junior elders. These were men and women who had been dominant in peasant nationalism before the war but whose influence had been superseded by young guerrillas and *youth* in the war. Ranger asserts that people were happy with elected village committees that were a vehicle for their radical nationalism.[12]

Some variety in these accounts about village committees probably reflects differences that occurred from district to district and even within districts. For example, in Dande, where Lan did his study, committees were elected several months before the end of the war whereas Makoni, where Ranger did his fieldwork, only acquired elected village committees after the war. What should be stressed, though, is that the radicalization thesis adopts a positive view of village committees as the first opportunity for elections at the village level and democratic participation. There is no question of the importance of introducing elected village committees to replace the hereditary rule of chiefs and headmen. I have already described how village and branch committees were most often elected in Mutoko, even during the war. Afterwards, when ZANU-PF established party headquarters inside the country, it made extending the party structure to the district and provincial level a top priority. Branch committees were to elect district committees; they in turn would elect provincial committees that would link up with the central committee appointed by top-ranking party leaders. This was consistent with the party's policy of democratic centralism. Nor can one question the important active role of village committees in various political and economic development projects and reconstruction in the first two years of independence. The party participated in deciding the shape of local councils and in nominating council candidates. When village courts were introduced in 1981 to replace headmen's courts, the party again nominated court officials for election. Party committees handed out application forms for the new resettlement schemes and helped determine who was eligible. They continued to settle disputes, usually party conflicts but also non-party disputes. And, lastly, they administered the food relief and rehabilitation programmes, both of which were sponsored by the United Nations High Commission for Refugees, international donors, and the government. The rehabilitation programme provided packages of seeds, fertilizer, and agricultural implements to help restore agricultural production so that there would be no need for food relief the following year.

Peasant voices, rarely heard in other accounts, as well as other evidence, provide additional insights into the character of village committees that make them less unambiguously positive developments and link them to peasants' experience of guerrilla coercion. Considerable evidence points to non-democratic aspects of village committees' administration. To settle disputes, village committees often used coercion against other villagers, provoking fear of the party. Party headquarters allowed the village committees to continue settling cases relating to breaches of party rules, but they had no legal authority to punish people. The main reason for party headquarters allowing this was that the government had not yet established local government institutions, in particular elected district councils and elected village courts, that would take over the functions formerly performed by chiefs and headmen. Seemingly influenced by guerrilla courts, some party committees took it on themselves to punish people who did not obey party rules. A man who experienced such party justice took the matter to the Mutoko magistrate's court. His crime was that he did not obtain permission to visit an area. Monitoring visitors to an area was a war-time hangover from guerrilla instructions to villagers to watch people, especially those new to an area, to detect potential 'sell-outs'. His evidence against the party chairman suggests that villagers continued to be alert to potential 'sell-outs' after the war and adopted guerrilla methods against suspects.[13]

On the 26th December 1980 I was with Mazarura coming from . . . and going to his kraal . . . On the way we asked for water at a certain kraal. When we left this kraal we saw a group of people – about fifteen – running towards us. The group consisted of juveniles and adults. They were armed with sticks, stones and knives. Some of them tried to assault us and others intervened and suggested that they take us to the chairman. We were taken to the chairman's kraal and ordered to lie on our backs and we were searched. They were looking for our registration certificates and ZANU(PF) membership cards. There was one person searching our pockets and giving to the other what he found in our pockets.

A short while after our arrival, we saw the accused. He appeared when our money was being taken from us. The accused said: 'We have to question thoroughly this one [Mazarura]. He will tell us the truth. Mazarura was taken and made to lie down on his stomach and assaulted with a thick stick on the buttocks by a certain man present. I do not know him. I was interrogated by a group of people and taken into accused's hut. In the room, some people were sitting on chairs, others on the bench. The accused was there. In the room one person was questioning me, the other recording my particulars – name, kraal, chief and where I live. The man who was questioning me asked what I would prefer between letting him take my money or lose my life. I asked whether I was to pay a fine. He got up and said: 'You all hear what he says. He is mad and must be assaulted.' He slapped me several times in the face. The man who was recording ordered me to put my head under a chair, and rise from the ground with the chair on my head. When I was slapped and ordered to put my head under a chair, accused had left the hut. He is the one who removed the chair from me. Accused did not question me in the hut. Accused said he was going away and left us with his police-boy. Later the policeman took us to his huts after he had received a report that guinea fowls were eating his crops in the lands.

In the evening after we had been given something to eat, a group of boys arrived at the policeboy's huts. One of the boys started to ask us where we had come from and what we wanted in the area. The person who had questioned me about money was in the group. This man then said he was not satisfied with the answers we had given. He then said that I had plenty of money and that I do not know how to shout the slogan. He then told me to shout: 'Pamberi ne ZANU. Pamberi ne Kunswisisa.' [Forward with ZANU. Forward with Understanding.] He then said he had come a long way and was not going to waste his time and that he was giving us five minutes and then we will be dead. I then said that what I had told them was the truth. He then ordered that I be tied up and taken outside. My hands were tied up with sisal fibre. Mazarura who was a local man was tied up first. He was taken outside and assaulted. I remained in the hut being assaulted by another man. The accused then came into the hut and Mazarura was taken back into the hut. The accused said: 'What are you doing at my kraal? I do not want this to happen.' He was saying this to those assaulting us. The boys who were assaulting us went outside and left.

Mazarura's kraalhead then arrived. The accused asked Mazarura whether he had seen his kraalhead and announced his presence together with the fact that he had come with me, his friend. He said he did not know he had to do that. The accused then said to him: 'You will receive twenty-seven switch cuts for that.' Mazarura was then tied up for accused to deliver the cuts . . . The stick used was about a metre long and about one inch in diameter . . . After he had assaulted Mazarura, he said he wanted to assault me. I was tied up by some people in the hut and ordered to lie on my stomach by the accused. He then started to assault me with the same stick . . . He said I was to receive twenty-seven cuts as well. When he was assaulting me, some people were holding me down by sitting on my legs and neck . . .

The magistrate's warning suggests that this was not an isolated case of a party committee holding a 'kangaroo court'.

> I want it to be clearly understood that this court will not be found wanting in its duty to punish those who think they are a law unto themselves and commit crimes under the pretext of furthering the interests of the ruling party. I sincerely hope that the people, particularly those who have been put in positions of authority . . . will take my warning seriously and try to carry out their functions according to the law . . .

Peasants' behaviour toward other parties also raises questions about characterizing party committees as democratic and participatory. Once the Mugabe government took office, it instructed district commissioners to form informal commissions to make recommendations on the framework that the proposed district councils should take. Each commission was to be composed of political leaders from all parties, leading businessmen, chiefs, and other influential locals from the Tribal Trust Lands (renamed Communal Areas) and Purchase Areas (renamed small-scale commercial farming areas). The inclusion of all political leaders on these commissions reflects Mugabe's reconciliation policy towards whites, ZAPU, and other parties. On the evening of 4 March 1980 Mugabe, the Prime Minister-elect, told the nation: 'We will ensure that there is a place for everyone in this country. We want to ensure a sense of security for both the winners and the losers.' There would be no sweeping nationalizations, the pensions and jobs of mainly white civil servants were guaranteed, and white farmers would keep their land. Mugabe said: 'Let us forgive and forget. Let us join hands in a new amity.'[14] But peasants (and evidently also many ranking ZANU-PF officials) rejected reconciliation towards other parties. Mutoko villagers attacked the commission because all parties were represented. They said ZANU-PF had won the war and only it should be on the commission. The chairman, a businessman appointed by the district commissioner, explained that the commission was supposed to be a non-partisan body and that he himself had been nominated as a businessman rather than a politician. People denounced him for not supporting the party during the war. The provincial party chairman, a ZANU-PF member, assumed the chairmanship to try to conciliate villagers. But the commission continued to encounter opposition because it had been appointed by a white district commissioner and it was not a monolithic ZANU-PF commission. It was forced to abandon holding meetings with villagers to discuss the future councils.[15] Only ZANU-PF contested the district council elections. The government official responsible for the election reported that 'whether other parties had been intimidated or not . . . was difficult to see'.[16] In Makoni district, Manicaland, parties other than ZANU-PF failed to respond to the district commissioner's invitation to send a member to serve on the commission to discuss the future district council, and he attributed it to intimidation from ZANU-PF.[17] At Wedza in Mashonaland East Province, the public 'demanded that persons serving on the Commission who were not members of ZANU-PF should be removed'. The district commissioner's report gives a sense of the mood, and the villagers' willingness to use coercion to enforce their wishes.[18]

> At this stage the atmosphere was quite tense as some members of the public suggested the Commission Members be beaten. Trouble was prevented when the local ZANU(PF) Chairman intervened but it is understood Chief Ruzane (one of thirteen commissioners) was manhandled. After the meeting had closed the Commission Members were made to return to the meeting place, where the people were still gathered, and asked to explain their presence at Chisasike. After some discussion they were set free and allowed to leave.

It is tempting to attribute intolerance of other parties to an intense commitment to ZANU-PF. Also, one might wish to discount references to intimidation by party members and other villagers as being from white district commissioners who may well have been hostile to ZANU-PF and unhappy about working with elected party officials rather than chiefs and headmen. But villagers' negative reactions to other parties and their willingness to use coercion against their supporters must be understood in the context of their war experiences. Guerrillas' political education had included denouncing other parties and their members as 'sell-outs' and coercing them to stop supporting traitors. There had also been guerrilla promises that supporters of other parties who survived the war would be punished. A woman said matter-of-factly: 'We were told all sell-outs would be put in keeps; that Muzorewa would be tried by the *parents*; that there'd be tarred roads and electricity. The comrades lied.'

Although the ruling party continued to officially pursue a policy of reconciliation, its attitude to other parties hardened, especially after arms caches were found on ZAPU farms. By early 1982 ranking party officials were openly denouncing other parties as traitors. 'Down with fat stomachs', referring to Nkomo, the leader of ZAPU, renamed the Patriotic Front (PF), and 'Down with Muzorewa', referring to the leader of the United African National Council, became ritual slogans at party meetings. The records of a Mashonaland Central provincial party meeting show the party hierarchy's security concerns, and challenge Lan's view that the directive to weed out witches, the embodiment of evil, came from mediums.[19] 'Members were advised to be vigilant, be resourceful and report all peculiar activities and knowledgeable [knowledge of] saboteurs of Government to the police, central intelligence organization, the local members of parliament and the party level in the bid to preserve our hard won independence and cultivate peace.'

By 1982, with elected district councils responsible for local administration and elected village courts settling disputes, the grassroots party structures – the village and branch committees – and even district committees had become instruments of information for the party hierarchy. They conveyed information to the provincial and central party and received information from above. Fanon's grim depiction of militants being turned into party informers after independence, and of coercion against opposition parties, resonates more with the political reality for opposition parties than does the official reconciliation policy.[20]

> The progressive transformation of the party into an information service is the indication that the government holds itself more and more on the defensive. The incoherent mass of the people is seen as a blind force that must be continually held in check either by mystification or by the fear inspired by the police force. The party acts as a barometer and as an information service. The militant is turned into an informer. He is entrusted with punitive expeditions against the villages. The embryo opposition parties are liquidated by beatings and stonings . . . In these conditions, you may be sure, the party is unchallenged and 99.99% of the votes are cast for the government candidates.

There were many other instances of villagers' fear of the party. Mutoko teachers who questioned villagers for the new census in 1982 marked the houses they had visited with a sticker to prevent double-counting. They reported that villagers often asked them to remove the sticker because they were afraid that it would be read as a symbol of support for another party. In some districts, including parts of Mutoko, people refused food aid, also fearing that it had come from another party and would get them in trouble later. When I asked questions about the new resettlement programme, which did not meet many villagers' expectations, or ZANU-PF, many people simply refused to answer or said 'one cannot say anything bad about the party', by which they implied that it was foolish to ask them what they felt about policies.

Fear of the party, the government, and ex-guerrillas was also evident in the court testimonies of villagers involved in the witchhunt in Mutoko after the war. The witchfinder was a Tanzanian who was a registered member of the Zimbabwe National *Nganga* (traditional doctors) Association. According to the prosecutor, Mr Mataka was invited to come to Mutoko from Arcturus Mine in Goromonzi district in Mashonaland East Province by Chieftainess Charewa in February 1979. He settled in Charewa ward where Chieftainess Charewa used him as a witchfinder. In 1981 he employed two former guerrillas as messengers. Between March and May 1981 he operated in the Katsukunya area of Mutoko Tribal Trust Land. He sent his messengers to invite people to come to Katsukunya township to be examined for evil spirits and treated if necessary. One by one, complainants and others were brought into his hut where he would examine them, with the assistance of his messengers, for a fee of fifty cents. Anyone found to be possessing dangerous magic or to be a witch was charged money, cattle, or both. Those who refused to pay were followed by the two messengers who assaulted or threatened them. Mr Mataka was accused of extorting Z$3,652 and ninety-five head of cattle.[21]

Mr Mataka pleaded not guilty. He claimed that he was merely carrying out a brief, with the support of Chieftainess Charewa, spirit mediums, and party officials, to cleanse the area of evil.

> I came to Charewa in 1979. I was giving treatment to freedom fighters who were mentally disturbed. On being satisfied with my work Chief Charewa gave me place to build my home. Before I started operating, a meeting was convened and attended by over 5,000. Nine spirit mediums attended. They told the people I had to cleanse the area. I asked to see the district officials [of the party] before I started to work. They allowed me to operate. Each person who wanted to see me would see officials and the Chief first. Any person with bad *muti* [medicine] I would refer to the district office. I was not sending James and Stewart [the messengers] to call these people. I am surprised they reported against me when I was helping them. If I knew I was doing wrong, I would not have done it. I admit these people gave me their *muti*. I still have it now.

Excerpts of complainants' testimony before the magistrate's court convey their fear of the party, the ex-guerrillas, and the government.

> In April, 1981 I was called by Chairman Misheck Vhavha to come to Katsukunya. All villagers were told to pay 50 cents each, which was for calling accused Mataka to the villagers. Vhavha told them to get into a hut in which a *nganga* by the name Mataka was. I went into the hut. The accused Mataka was in the hut. He was with his two messengers. The accused took a book. He started to read it in a foreign language. He then said to me: 'You old man, you have a horn (*nyanga*) which you keep in your granary hut.' I said: 'No, I have no horn.' He said: 'I want that horn together with a charm that you have. If you do not bring them, you are going to bring me a beast' . . . He told his messengers to cut me incisions . . . and that I had to pay $10 for that. This was done and I gave him the money. I was frightened. He said he had been sent by the government and Comrade Mugabe had sent him to do all this, so I was frightened. I had to comply with the government order. He told me to go home and bring another $10 for photographs. The following day I brought the horn and the charm and $10. I gave them to the accused. Because I had no *mombe* [cattle], I paid him $82 . . . I was photographed holding the horn and the charm. He said the $82 was a penalty for keeping a horn which I was using for killing innocent people.

The following exchanges between the witchhunter Mr Mataka and some of those he accused of being witches and wizards occurred during cross-examination.

> Mataka: You paid after you were satisfied with my work?

> Witness X: That is not correct. I paid in fear. We had just come out of the war and you were telling us of JOC Assembly Point [where ex-guerrillas were in barracks] and the government. You were saying they were all behind you.

> Witness Y: I agreed to have these incisions when he threatened he had the authority of the leading spirit medium Nehoreka and ZANU (PF) and comrade Mugabe.

Witness C: He said: 'You are a wizard.' He said: 'I want the horns. If you refuse, I will send you to JOC Assembly Point.' He said: 'Do you not know I am a real comrade?'

Mataka: Why did you not report the incident to the police?

Witness C: I was afraid. You called yourself a comrade and threatened me with death.

Mataka: Did you hear me say I was a comrade at the chairman's place?

Witness C: Yes and everybody present was placed in fear.

Witness K: . . . he threatened that he was doing this [taking my cattle from my kraal] with the authority and protection of the government and comrade Mugabe. He said he had been given comrades from JOC Assembly Point to protect him. He produced photographs of people holding guns. He said anyone who does not comply would be taken to JOC Assembly Point and killed by comrades.

Mataka: Why did you not report to Chief Charewa?

Witness Z: The comrades were above the chiefs. Even the chiefs were afraid of being killed.

To focus solely on the participatory aspects of the party and the introduction of elected positions obscures the important influence of fear of the party that many peasants continued to experience even after the departure of the guerrillas from the rural areas. Also, the coercive methods adopted by peasants and their party committees suggest a less sanguine heritage of the war, namely the influence of guerrilla slogans and punishments against traitors, among whom were included not only government supporters but also those who identified with parties other than ZANU. Peasants also continued to be alert to potential security threats and to fear unknown visitors.

Peasant relations with the party-state

Adherents of the radicalization thesis accepts that once local government institutions were in place, the balance of power shifted in favour of the state and away from peasants. Cliffe and Stoneman lament how top-down initiatives by the party-state after independence created new local structures – district councils and party branches – without trying to build on the 'spontaneous people's committees'. After 1985, when the party-state attempted to build on people's committees in establishing village and ward development committees, they had already all but disappeared. People's committees were active till 1980–1. They participated in mobilizing self-help labour for reconstruction and for distributing food, seeds, and implements in United Nations sponsored projects to stave off hunger in the war-torn rural areas. Thereafter, people's committees began to wither, leaving the party hierarchy, even in the four Shona provinces, without a presence at the village level.[22] Cliffe and Stoneman maintain that the strength of the grassroots committees 'lay decisively in the best instances, in the *interaction* of peasants *with* guerrillas. With the withdrawal of the latter, there was a draining away of much of the initiative in charting goals and of the broader raising of consciousness, plus, moreover, of the actual strength to withstand pressures.'[23] Before Lan left the field, he found that power had been removed from the village committees to government institutions (district councils and village courts) established after the war, leading mediums who had allegedly conferred legitimacy on village committees to complain of government neglect.[24] Ranger, despite his optimism about the continuing influence of peasant radical nationalism on government policies, also predicted that the new local government institutions would alter the balance of power between peasants and the state. He stated: 'It is clear, also, that as the new administrative system stabilizes and as the negative peasant achievement of ending agrarian coercion and the positive peasant achievement of exerting pressure for land redistribution come to their natural term, the unusual advantageous position of Zimbabwean peasants *vis-à-vis* the state will give way to quite another balance of power.'[25] These accounts emphasize the negative effect on village committees of newly created local government institutions that constituted a new administrative system exercising the powers briefly enjoyed by the village committees.

In explaining demobilization, critics of the radicalization thesis focus on the state's interests while accepting the notion of peasants' popular support for the guerrillas. Ronald Weitzer acknowledges the importance of popular mobilization of peasants during the war but maintains that post-war outcomes will depend on changes in the state sector too. He shows how the state security sector has continued to expand during the post-independence period, dominating both the legislature and judiciary, as it had from the late 1950s. Despite the party's avowed intent to make itself supreme over government at its congress in 1984, the state security sector dominated ZANU-PF too. The expansion of the state security sector, he argues, reflects the new political leadership's choice to preserve the inherited state security system because of its interests in consolidating power. Even at the Lancaster House constitutional negotiations, debate centred on who would control the security apparatus rather than on changing the structure of the internal security state. The British were not interested in state-building and simply wanted majority rule and a settlement, and each of the other parties was convinced it would win the elections and would need a security state to eliminate pockets of unpopularity. Zimbabwe's post-independence leadership has continued to concern itself with regime security or maintaining itself in power rather than with public order. It has exaggerated threats to its supremacy, leading it to over-react. The regime has the resources to remove the dominance of the security sector in the executive but its political will is lacking.[26] Others, too, have maintained that the regime's priority interest was to maintain itself in power rather than promote development and change.[27] For Astrow and Callinicos, like Weitzer, the nationalist leaders' lack of political will is crucial in influencing post-war outcomes. During the war ZANU had popular support because its leaders relied on socialist rhetoric but from the time of the Lancaster House talks they revealed their petty bourgeois class origins. Their acceptance of the Lancaster House settlement and failure to implement socialist policies after the war reflect their class interests in capitalist development and stability.[28]

Ibbo Mandaza, like other critics of the radicalization thesis, also accepts that the guerrillas mobilized the popular support of peasants during the war but rejects the usefulness of predicting post-independence outcomes from war mobilization. Mandaza, like Weitzer, maintains that such predictions require a thorough understanding of the structure of the state. But he is interested in its class structure whereas Weitzer analysed the balance of power between branches of the state and within the executive. Mandaza highlights the political, military, and ideological weakness of the liberation movements on the eve of the Lancaster House agreement vis-à-vis the white settler colonial state and its imperialist props. The African petty bourgeois leadership's own class interests and need to maintain the state compel it to follow the dictates of international capital. To meet capital's interests, the petty bourgeois leaders must control popular demands by demobilizing those whom it sought to mobilize during the war.

> The point . . . is that international finance capital has, since the Lancaster House Agreement, been the major factor in the character of the internal and external policies of the state in Zimbabwe. The role of the settlers is important only in as far as it tends to coincide with and reinforce the overall interests of international finance capital and those of imperialism. The African petit bourgeoisie remains quite weak and is forced, in the interests of both its class and the need to maintain the state, to make compromises with both the former white settlers and international finance capital; not to mention the fact that there would be a significant and influential section within the African petit bourgeois class that would rather see Zimbabwe's destiny continue in the sphere of the West than move towards socialism.[29]

Where some see leadership choice, Mandaza sees the hand of international finance capital imposing constraints on even those leaders who might wish to fulfil their war-time promises to the masses.[30] Cliffe and Stoneman, while accepting a version of the radicalization thesis, also weight heavily the constraints on the leadership of the Lancaster House agreement and the inherited institutional framework of the colonial settler state.[31]

Hodder-Williams, writing before the elections of 1980, made basic assumptions about the post-war outcomes regardless of which party or coalition came to power. By asserting that the central issue that would determine Zimbabwe's future was who would control the formal apparatus of state power, Hodder-Williams rejected the emphasis on the effects of the war on the peasantry that characterizes variants of the radicalization thesis. He assumes that the key political leaders, irrespective of party, would continue the previous regime's centralizing tendency and top-level government officials would be primarily nationalists with a bourgeois tendency that would disincline them towards radical solutions and predispose them to reformist policies. While less sophisticated than the top echelon of leaders, middle-level political workers and administrators would also be nationalists, most of whom would see the end of colonial rule as a chance to inherit the state and would favour reformist policies. A minority of positions would be filled by those who were radicals seeking profound change, such as those who had been promoted within the exile movements, ex-detainees and articulate guerrilla leaders. While accepting the importance of politicization of guerrillas and peasants during the war, Hodder-Williams cautions that in Zimbabwe radical guerrillas lacked the opportunity to engage intensively with peasants in liberated areas as they did in Mozambique. This difference makes him 'tend to argue against those who foresee a radicalised peasantry and a determinedly progressive cadre of potential leaders'. For him, reformist and radical governments differ in that the latter seek to transform the rural sector, and hence see the peasantry as 'peculiarly relevant' whereas the former 'do not grant a greater relevancy to the peasantry than is required by their need for continuing labour and a successful subsistence sector'. Moroever, reformist governments are often associated with 'a measure of depoliticisation' of 'ordinary people'.[32]

The state's interests and policies unquestionably played a role in demobilizing a mobilized peasantry. Whether intentional or not, its repeated efforts to restructure the party at the local level also hastened demobilization as people wearied of endless and time-consuming elections. There were elections for the new village courts and district councils, for district and branch committees immediately after the war, and then for village and cell committees. In 1982 the central party called for fresh elections as part of an exercise to restructure the party. Men, women and youth were to have separate committees and party organization was to be formalized. Each village committee was to represent 100 members, branch committees 500, and district committees 5,000. Men's committees, referred to as 'the main committees', had representatives from the women's and youth committees.[33] Local party officials found themselves counting party membership cards to make sure that party committees covered the required numbers of people. All over Mutoko district there was little interest in this bureaucratic exercise or the time-consuming task of fresh elections.

In addition to the role of the state, the lack of material incentives to encourage peasants to serve the party must also be taken into account in understanding demobilization at the grassroots level. The lack of utilitarian appeals by the guerrillas was omitted in analyses of the efficacy of party mobilization and contributed to a spurious conclusion of popular peasant support that depended crucially on the success of cultural nationalist appeals or pre-existing peasant nationalism. The importance of utilitarian appeals in affecting peasant decisions about party participation, apparent during the war, continued to influence peasant participation. Once early expectations of pay for party work had proved starry-eyed and village committees had lost their powers, peasant interest in the party flagged.

Neglecting lack of material appeals

Party work, as in the war, was time-consuming and without immediate material rewards. Initially, party positions were seriously contested because villagers saw them as instruments of power and expected to be remunerated. District councillors and village court officials got paid by the government, but party officials did not. Even chiefs and headmen whose former responsibilities for village justice, district administration, and land allocation had been removed, continued to receive salaries. Chiefs and headmen with over 500 followers received allowances of Z$178 per month and Z$46 per month respectively, making them better paid than village court officials and district councillors who had assumed most of their responsibilities. District council chairmen received a monthly allowance of Z$50, deputy chairmen earned Z$40 per month, and district councillors Z$30.[34] The Cabinet Committee on legislation commented in December 1981 that the government was paying over one million dollars per annum to maintain 264 chiefs and 452 headmen for doing little other than act as 'custodians of tribal culture and tradition'.[35] The Mutoko district council made representations to the Minister of Local Government because, according to its chairman, 'councillors are pained by allowances being given to headmen and chiefs'. But it was to no avail. And a man who had been active in nationalist parties before and during the war had this to say. 'The comrades never promised leaders any rewards. I never expected any reward. I was only fighting for liberation. I think today we should be rewarded. If one is not rewarded, one feels tired today. Those who get positions should be given money.'

By 1982, peasants had lost interest in party activities and the vibrancy of the immediate post-war period had given way to dispirited passivity. Party committees seldom held meetings, and when they did, it was difficult to get a quorum. Party meetings were poorly attended, and party elections were often rescheduled because of poor electoral turnout. For example, a district committee election was arranged by members of the provincial party. When few people came to vote, another date was set for the election. Local party officials threatened that provincial party members would report back to Harare that they did not support ZANU-PF. That brought people out to vote in large numbers. A district councillor addressed the large crowd, touching on one of the reasons for lack of interest in the party.

> I'm glad about the gathering today. We have never had such a big gathering before. It shows people are now very cooperative. Some officials don't attend meetings which is very bad. So when electing someone you should look into people who don't get tired easily. Some don't come because when they were elected they thought they could get paid. So today you should elect people who need not be paid but just to work for the benefit of Zimbabwe.

Most peasants and *youth* had not expected rewards for their war efforts but when guerrillas were absorbed into the army and paid salaries, they wondered why they had been unrewarded. From their perspectives, guerrillas were amply rewarded. At independence, the guerrilla armies were integrated with the ex-Security Forces, making for an army of about 80,000. By early 1982 the army had been reduced to some 40,000, partly because the government had offered guerrillas who chose to be demobilized Z$185 per month (US$400) for two years. During this time they were expected to equip themselves for civilian life.[36] Some guerrillas used the pay to set themselves up in the private sector, and some combined their resources to purchase businesses or land. Many properties that ZAPU guerrillas purchased with demobilization pay were confiscated by the ZANU-PF government in its crackdown on ZAPU after some of its properties were found to have arms' caches. The government also helped to employ guerrillas: males as security guards, males and females as local government promotion officers whose jobs entailed working at the grassroots to encourage participation in government projects and to convey information about government development policies, and females as secretaries of local government bodies. The more than 5,000 disabled ex-combatants have been employed or placed in skill acquisition programmes.[37] The government gave priority to ex-combatants along with refugees, people displaced by the war, and the landless in its resettlement programme.[38] Despite government efforts to employ ex-guerrillas, about 25,000 were unemployed in March 1988.[39] In contrast to its efforts to reward guerrillas – many argue that they have been inadequate – the government refused to compensate peasants for their property losses during the war. Only the disabled, widowed, and orphaned were eligible for compensation. Few of them had the death and medical certificates that had to be produced to claim compensation. Between October 1981 and August 1982 only 183 applications had been submitted to the Social Services office in Mutoko.[40]

Repeatedly people expressed disappointment and sometimes anger at not receiving compensation. One young man was bitter:

> People who suffered in the war are angry with the party for not giving them compensation for losses of property and injury after the war. If they go to the party office, they are told they are not so badly off; some people's children were bombed in Mozambique. Also many children have not returned and they don't even know if they are dead or alive. 83 Manica Road [the former party headquarters] doesn't help. The girls there are very rude. When it comes to funerals, the government pays for the burials of people like Chitepo

[a nationalist leader who was assassinated in Zambia in 1976]. These people expect the government to at least pay the costs of funerals of those children killed in the war, or presumed dead. They must kill a cow for each person killed. It's expensive.

A war chairman whose one child had been an important *youth* leader addressed the inequity of rewarding guerrillas but not *youth*.

> If you talk to some of the *youth* today, they might even cry. They worked so hard in the war, but they have got nothing today. The comrades have got positions in the army. No, the *youth* were not promised any positions by the comrades. But when they saw the comrades being rewarded, they were very upset. The *youth* could sometimes walk to Shinga; sometimes they'd deliver messages to *youth* in Area C. The *youth* would also be the ones to run the kitchen in some places. The kitchen would be near where the comrades were. If soldiers came and saw fire from the cooking, they could bomb the *youth* and the comrades would be safe. The job of *youth* was very dangerous – more dangerous than the comrades. My son was a *youth*. He walked as far as Mozambique sometimes.

Today his son works for the government in Harare as a medical laboratory technologist. Others have not been so lucky and even young people completing secondary schooling for which opportunities have expanded enormously – the number of secondary schools grew from 177 in 1979 to 1,484 in 1989 and the number of pupils from 75,000 to 650,000 – cannot find jobs.[41] In 1987 there were about 100,000 secondary school leavers but the unchanged economic structure of the country creates at most 10,000–20,000 jobs per annum. Bernard Chidzero, the Finance Minister, estimated that 30 per cent of the total labour force was unemployed in July 1988.[42] At the end of the war many *youth* were no longer so young and not all whose schooling had been disrupted by the war returned to further their education. They too faced a grim job market. A brief visit to Mutoko in January 1989 found many of the same people still volunteering their unhappiness about not having been compensated for their sacrifices during the war.

Independence did indeed produce benefits for peasants. In September 1980, the government had introduced free medical services for those earning less than Z$150 per month (the minimum wage then was Z$70 per month) and universal free primary education. The government kept the decision taken during the British governor's interim rule to make cattle dipping for Tribal Trust Land inhabitants free and also held off reintroducing council rates for several years. Marketing depots were established in every district, access to credit was improved to reach about 12 per cent of peasant producers, and agricultural pricing policies have benefited peasants.[43] Land once inhabited by white commercial farmers was purchased by the government for resettling villagers. Villagers could elect their district councillors and village court officials. But these benefits were available to villagers whether or not they engaged in unremunerative party

227

work. Peasants came to perceive party participation as unrewarding work. They saw guerrillas get rewarded for their war efforts and knew that chiefs, district council and village court officials were being paid for their labour. In contrast, party participation had no material appeal.

Peasant nationalism versus peasant anti-state attitudes

Ranger has documented instances where peasants challenged the state after the war. They rejected the authority of white district commissioners and African officials of the former regime. By 1981, it should be noted, only twenty-five of fifty-eight white district commissioners remained in the country and African district administrators were appointed to take their place.[44] Peasants also opposed the introduction of district councils that they associated with the former African councils and their taxing authority; they resented the slow and bureaucratic methods of implementing the resettlement projects and the lack of security of tenure for new settlers.[45]

My data from Mutoko district and sketchy illustrations from other districts are strikingly similar to Ranger's Makoni data. When the white former district commissioner appeared in Mutoko with a plan to introduce district councils, peasants demanded that only the Minister of Local Government should explain government policy to them.[46] In another district in Mashonaland East province, 'there were shouts of approval when a person said that the Commission was "as good as the District Commissioner"'.[47] In Chilimanzi district in the Midlands province, a party member told the district commissioner people were suspicious of him as he had worked for two governments. People decided that in future the district commissioner should address them only if accompanied by a ranking party member or an ex-guerrilla who would verify what he told them was government policy. The district commissioner was also told to give party slogans in future when addressing meetings.[48] A district commissioner's report from Selukwe district in the Midlands also described people's dismay, anger, and confusion at the reappearance of the hated former government officials.[49]

> It was made very clear to me that the people will not discuss a District Council until they have been spoken to by MP Mr. X. Mativenga. They do not trust the DC who previously worked for 'Smith and Muzorewa', and they do not believe that such a DC can possibly represent PM Mugabe through Minister Zvobgo.

Mutoko people reacted when they learned that councils were going to be reintroduced. They claimed that they 'had a hard time' with councils in the past.[50] In Selukwe and Beitbridge districts people opposed councils because they associated them with unpopular destocking, soil conservation, and taxes.[51] In Lupane district in Matabeleland North, a ZAPU stronghold, people were so suspicious of the councils policy that members of the commission insisted on senior representatives of the party accompanying them to ensure others that the party supported the policy. People in a district in Mashonaland West said they were more interested in 'fresh land and the handouts of fertilizer, etc. etc.',[52] while residents in Gwanda district in Matabeleland South wanted their children released from assembly points and more grazing land.[53] In the end, electoral participation in council elections was high, and there was competition for most seats. In Mutoko, twenty-seven seats were contested by fifty-three candidates, all nominated by ZANU-PF, and an estimated 75 per cent of the electorate voted.

African agricultural extension staff were received with the same hostility as the white district commissioners and were unable to work in Mutoko between March and August 1980.[54] One who had worked in Mutoko throughout the war recalled:

> People would say: 'We don't see any change. Why is it that we see you whom we used to see during the Smith regime?' We had to explain and branch leaders helped us. They said a new government had taken over. Top officials had to explain to local party leaders.

To attribute all peasant resentment towards officials of the old regime to their nationalism overstates the influence of political education by the guerrillas or pre-existing peasant nationalism (see chapter 4). Peasant relations with states are characteristically overtly or latently antagonistic. Many peasants wanted, as before, to keep the state from imposing demands on them. Cognisant of peasant attitudes to taxes, the new regime introduced its councils policy without requiring that they pay taxes. Peasant preferences for a life without state demands is illustrated by their responses to the new resettlement schemes. Many had understood guerrilla promises of 'free living' to mean that they could select whatever land they wanted, and farm free of any rules or regulations. A war chairman understated his disillusionment.

> Comrades used to lie to us a bit. They told us you could live where you like after the war. They would say: '*Parents*, you can't live like this in the mountains. You must go and live in the valleys on the white farms.' Now they give us twelve acres at Zinanga.

Twelve acres or five to six hectares of arable land for individual cultivation was what the major type of government resettlement scheme offered prospective settlers. It was more land than most people in the Tribal Trust Lands or Communal Lands had. What troubled villagers was that they would have no security of tenure and could be removed from the scheme at the whim of a government official. In 1982 rumours were rife that the government would specify production quotas and insist on all the land being used; failure to conform to these requirements would lead to eviction. Additionally, there is evidence that while people wanted more land they had problems of too little labour and no oxen to plough the little land they did have – 40 per cent of peasant producers in the Communal Areas reportedly had no oxen and had to hire them for ploughing.[55] A *youth* leader referred to the absence of 'free living' when he compared extravagant guerrilla promises with the realities of independence.

> Comrades said at independence people would get piped water, flush toilets, jobs. Everyone could do whatever he feels like. The people in the reserves believed this. I didn't. But it was difficult to tell people then that it was just lies.

Peasant hostility toward ex-regime officials, although consistent with an expression of nationalism, may also be interpreted as peasant conformity with guerrilla teachings during the war. Peasants had learned the dangers of challenging guerrilla commands, and it was safer to insist that ZANU-PF deliver policy statements, especially when, as for councils, policies seemed similar to the previous regime's. Guerrilla appeals against whites had raised peasant consciousness and emboldened them without necessarily converting them to nationalists. Peasants wanted to be free of onerous demands from any state, but if they had to take orders, caution dictated that they hear them from ZANU-PF's top officials so that they would not invite punishments.

Internal peasant struggles

The absence of peasant data, the peasant concept, and the focus on peasant relations with the state have obscured struggles within the peasantry after the war. These revolved around new resentments arising from the war between those who had sacrificed resources for the guerrillas and felt they deserved to be compensated and those who had escaped such demands. Some war-time conflicts also persisted after independence.

The government stipulated that the food aid and rehabilitation programmes should give priority to refugees returning from neighbouring countries and displaced people – those who had been in 'protected villages' or had fled the rural areas to live as squatters in the urban areas. At the end of the war there were an estimated 750,000 people in 'protected villages', 150,000 refugees and 250,000 displaced people. That is, roughly one-seventh of the African population qualified for priority assistance.[56] Those who were employed or had employed spouses were ineligible for aid. Peasants and the elite who had stayed in the rural areas during the war felt they ought to be given priority over refugees and the displaced whom they regarded as fortunate at having avoided burdensome contributions to the guerrillas. Teachers and businessmen, when informed that they were ineligible for food rations because they were employed, complained that the guerrillas had not distinguished between employed and unemployed when demanding contributions. Moreover, they had contributed more than the average peasant. They, too, pointed out that those outside the rural areas now heading the list for aid had skipped 'war rounds'. Those who had been in the rural areas during the war and demanded a share of aid found support from local ZANU-PF committees who spread the word that aid was a reward for those who had contributed to the guerrillas. The Minister of Local Government and Housing reportedly propagated this notion in a policy statement relating to councils.[57] Political committees generally managed to ensure that aid reached those on the government's priority list. Sometimes political pressures to share aid with everyone or to exclude refugees and displaced people led committees to split agricultural packages. This defeated their purpose because each package had been designed to provide adequate nutrition for families. At other times, committees excluded refugees and urban squatters. In some districts, notably Nkai in Matabeleland, this resulted in refugees commandeering supplies.[58]

Mugabe's policy of reconciliation, announced immediately after his party's electoral victory, won approval in the West. The policy was directed chiefly at whites, but also at Africans who had fought on the side of the Rhodesian government or who had supported parties other than ZANU-PF. People who had contributed to guerrilla support were in no mood to be reconciled with those who had fled their rural homes in the war and now wished to return. They had kept careful records of how much each individual had contributed in 'war rounds'. Money was owed to people for cows, chickens, and other animals that had been used to feed the guerrillas. People hoped to pay these debts by charging returning villagers a resettlement fee but the government acted against local party committees that tried to collect retroactive war taxes. Few people were willing to admit that party committees were involved in such activity after the government had informed committees that it ran counter to the policy of reconciliation. A war chairman expressed his indignation at the injustice of prohibiting committees from charging returnees resettlement fees.

> Yes. Don't be fooled. It happened all over the district and the country. Sure, it was worth it for those returning to pay us to be able to live in unity with us. During the war we got beaten, gave comrades first eggs, then chickens, then goats and then cattle. If the Prime Minister had not told us to stop, we'd still be doing this. My younger brother was a secretary during the war but then fled to town in the middle of the war. He never sent any money here, even though he knew we were fighting and paying 20 cents today, giving cattle and goats. At the end of the war when he came back, we held a meeting at the village and decided he should pay $40 before he could begin to build his house [it was burned in the war]. He'd paid $26 and was in town still when the PM announced this must stop. So he never had to pay the $14 balance. The purpose of collecting money was to repay those from whom we'd bought cows and other things for the comrades. This village owed people $85. We had to call people together and explain we wouldn't be able to pay them back because of the government announcement.

The hunt for witches, spearheaded by Mataka and apparently supported by Chieftainess Charewa, Charewa mediums, and ZANU-PF seems to suggest serious internal conflicts among villagers and a search for the enemy within to establish solidarity. Meanwhile Nehoreka's spirit medium called all *youth* and guerrillas to Chieftainess Charewa's village. Local informants said many *youth* had 'gone mad' after the war because they had killed innocent people in the war. The medium, asserting her authority, claimed she could protect them from the avenging spirits of the dead. In a clandestine cleansing ceremony, each person was given some 'medicine' and ordered to obey certain rules that included no beer-drinking at funerals and prohibitions on eating certain kinds of okra. In 1982 a visitor to the district could observe many young people wearing black necklaces. Locals said the beads symbolized that *youth* and guerrillas would be protected from the wrath of avenging ancestors because they had killed in war. In contrast, David Lan interpreted guerrillas in Dande wearing black bead wristlets as reflecting guerrilla legitimacy. 'For some this indicated that they themselves had become mediums of their own lineage ancestors. For the rest it served to identify them with the local source of political authority which had adopted and endorsed them, the *mhondoro*.' Writing in 1928, a colonial official noted that people wore black beads on their wrist or around their waist as a sign of possession by evil spirits (*mashave*) that were making them ill. Instead of possession by such evil spirits being a sign of the individual having done anything wrong, it was taken to be the person's bad luck. Historian David Beach has described how people put on black beads, the 'badge of the Mondoro', before the uprising of June 1896.[59]

For Dande, Lan describes the close relationship between mediums and village committees and suggests the possibility, albeit remote, that mediums might in the future withdraw support from the government and ZANU-PF in favour of chiefs if the government continues to displease them.[60] If Lan is correct about the legitimacy the mediums gave to village committees in Dande and how committed they were to village committees continuing to exercise powers that once belonged to chiefs, Mutoko district presents an interesting contrast. Here the mediums, and especially the powerful medium of Nehoreka, bitterly resented the government's introduction of elected village courts that removed the power to hear court cases from headmen and chiefs – unless they happened to get elected. Mediums were asking rhetorically whether Mugabe thought he or Nehoreka was the chief in that part of the country. There were also scattered instances of mediums vying with elected village courts to settle disputes. In Nyamatsahuni in Charewa ward, even though elected village courts were functioning, a medium settled a case arising from a villager having had sex with someone else's cow. The case was considered too serious for the novices elected to the village courts to preside over.

Competition between parties and chiefs continued in parts of the district and elsewhere in the country. Some parties regarded the chiefs as potential competitors and others tried to appoint chiefs to posts left vacant by deaths during the war or remove those that survived the war. The acting district commissioner for Mutoko reported:[61]

> Under the present situation, they [chiefs and headmen] don't feel free and feel the present situation is worse than during the war. The party is now oppressing them. They say there are now so many 'officials' in the Tribal Trust Lands that people don't know who to go to. In an area, there are various committee chairmen and area chairmen all of whom are holding courts, distributing lands and giving orders. They wonder whether the party or the government is running the country. Grazing land has been ploughed up . . .
>
> I believe this has arisen due to the fact that the chiefs and headmen have been told that they can carry on their traditional roles and the party is preventing them from doing so. They claim the party and the government tell them different things and they no longer know whom to believe.
>
> Chiefs and headmen are angered by politics entering into the election of chiefs and headmen. They say when Rhodes came to the country, he found chiefs here and kept the system going. Now their own government comes to power and is rejecting them. They resent interference of parties in the election of chiefs and headmen.

It is tempting to dismiss this defence of chiefs and attack on party committees as the carping of a white government official, more comfortable with the old leaders than the new ones. However, the Minister of Local Government, also a member of the central committee of the ruling party, issued the following countrywide warning to parties.[62]

> It has come to my notice that in some cases, elements of political parties are seeking the removal of a particular Chief or Chiefs.
>
> Similarly, those same elements are trying, in some instances, either to install Chiefs of their own choosing, or, where a vacancy exists because of the death of the incumbent, to interfere with the normal customary rules of succession in an endeavour to ensure that their own candidate is nominated for the chieftainship.
>
> I wish to make it quite clear that Government will not, under any circumstances, permit elements of political parties to remove Chiefs from office, or to interfere in the normal selection procedures, for purely political reasons.
>
> In terms of the law the President may remove a Chief for just cause. Before making any recommendation to the President, I, as Minister, must be satisfied that just cause exists. Furthermore, if it is alleged that it is the general wish of inhabitants of an area to have their chief removed, I will need to be satisfied, once again on material evidence, that that is the majority wish, for good cause, and that it is not based simply on political considerations.
>
> A Chief may only be removed from office for failing or neglecting without reasonable excuse to carry out any of the duties imposed upon him by law and custom.

Local party committees might have hoped for spirited support from the ostensibly Marxist-Leninist government, but Prime Minister Mugabe (today the President) made it clear that the party had not challenged the institution of chieftainship during the war and the new ZANU-PF government was also not going to.[63] The cultural and traditional rationale for defending the chieftainship was articulated in the House of Assembly by Eddison Zvobgo, a member of the central committee and also the Minister of Local Government.[64]

> I put it to you that it is not reasonable for members to proudly proclaim that as a nation we ought to preserve and conserve our culture and on the other hand to want to abolish certain traditional institutions that go along with it.

On other occasions, the Minister repeated the cultural rationale for retaining the chieftainship. For instance, he said:[65]

> We felt, in the end, that we could not do away with our tradition. If we had done so we would have looked like people who did not know where they came from. We would have lost our tradition and dignity if we threw that away. We therefore agreed that chieftainship was part and parcel of our culture.

Government support for the chieftainship should be contrasted with its deliberate efforts to demobilize local party committees. It should not be surprising that chiefs won the competition for power with village committees. But chiefs faced numerous other competitors after the war, underlining how much local political participation had increased. They competed with elected village court officials to settle disputes and with district councillors who were the local elected administrators and formally had the power that once belonged to chiefs to allocate land. Chiefs and headmen were elected by some wards as council representatives or by villages as village court officials but in the first few years their position was insecure. Government bolstered them in councils, as it had protected them in competition with party committees. Initially, government policy made the inclusion of chiefs as ex-officio district councillors a matter to be decided by the informal commissions. But when the informal commissions chose to exclude chiefs as ex-officio members in seventeen of fifty-three districts,[66] the government insisted that at least one chief and at most three in each district be made ex-officio members. As a concession, ex-officio members did not have to be given a vote on the council.[67] The government reduced the power of chiefs in the reconstituted provincial councils, but still allowed them a limited ex-officio role. The Mashonaland East Provincial Authority, mostly members of the urban and rural elite, discussed removing the three chiefs who were ex-officio members, arguing that they were not prepared to serve with people who had not been elected.[68] In 1988 the government's support of chiefs, and possibly a shift in local sentiment in their favour, heralded a return of their powers to settle disputes.

Direct and open generational struggles seemed to lose their significance quickly once the guerrillas departed from the rural areas and *youth* left to seek work in the towns or returned to schools, often in other districts. Similarly, the public attacks on wife-beaters seemed to subside but gender struggles undoubtedly continue. If new legislation is enforced, and it is a big if, the position of women should improve. The Legal Age of Majority Act of 1982 gave women majority status and full contractual capacity on attaining the age of eighteen. The Labour Relations Act of 1984 makes it an offence for an employer to discriminate against any employee or prospective employee on grounds of gender in job advertisements, recruitment, creation or abolition of jobs, determination of wages and benefits, choice of persons for jobs, training, advancement, transfer, promotion or retrenchment. This Act also enables women to take ninety days maternity leave, with up to 75 per cent of salary. More relevant for rural women, the Matrimonial Causes Act of 1985 recognizes the direct and indirect contribution of women to family wealth and gives women a right to a share of property on divorce.[69] These laws advance the legal status of women but to what extent rural women can use the law to their advantage is unclear. Progress on other fronts looks less promising. ZANU's war promises to remove *lobola* (bridewealth) remain unfulfilled. Although the first new ministry created was the Ministry of Community Development and Women's Affairs in 1981, in 1983 it got just over 1 per cent of the national budget. The Adult Literacy programme aimed especially at women had to close temporarily at the end of 1982 because of lack of funds. And the government seemed determined to follow historical practices of preserving certain spheres for male employment: female combatants were channelled into sewing and typing and those in the army can no longer bear arms but serve as clerical workers and cooks. A few females trained in Denmark as electricians were unable to find employment when they returned to Zimbabwe despite a shortage. Women hold only 10 per cent of the positions on the urban and district councils even though in the rural areas they constitute a majority of adults.[70] Gender struggles are likely to take place in the home and courts, where records should provide interesting data.

Conclusion

The Zimbabwe war, like other revolutions, has produced variants of a thesis that link mobilization to positive post-war outcomes for peasants. They are built on the premise, unsubstantiated by direct peasant voices, that mobilization was popular among peasants. The thrust of the argument is that popular mobilization during the war led to the creation of village party committees that became vehicles for democratic participation for peasants. These committees and peasants' heightened political consciousness from war-time mobilization gave peasants at least the potential to join battle against the state with some success. About two years after the war, though, local state institutions were introduced and they acquired the powers formerly exercised by the village committees, thereby contributing to peasant demobilization. Critics correctly charge that proponents of the so-called radicalization thesis place too much emphasis on social change during revolutions when predicting post-war outcomes. Despite this objection, critics accept the central assumption of the radicalization thesis that characterizes the revolutionary process as resting on the popular support of peasants.

This book's finding that mobilization did not rest on peasant popular support, along with peasant voices and other evidence on their post-war experiences, permits a reinterpretation of the relationship between mobilization and outcomes for peasants. While accepting that elected village committees advanced local participation in politics, this chapter has argued against labelling them as democratic and instead focuses on party coercion. This chapter highlights not only the role of the state in demobilizing peasants but also its failure to offer material incentives for party participation. Peasant hostility to the state is attributed to factors other than peasant nationalism, such as peasant fears of not conforming with party directives and characteristic peasant resentments of states. Finally, the chapter rectifies the external bias in the radicalization thesis by examining the effects of mobilization on internal peasant relations. Some war struggles, rooted in pre-colonial and colonial history, continued but the war itself created new, perhaps short-lived, peasant divisions such as between those who contributed to the guerrillas and those who fled the rural areas. By highlighting these new divisions that were a product of the war, the chapter underlines the way in which political interests are constantly formed by contingent events and challenges rational choice theorists who regard political interests as fixed.

7

Conclusion

I began by posing the following questions. How do revolutionary organizations win popular support, what is the evidence for popular support, and how satisfactory is it? Who in the peasantry is most likely to participate in revolutions? What motivates peasants to participate in revolutions? And what are the outcomes for peasants from participating in revolutionary movements? Influential studies of peasant revolution were selected to examine how they approached these questions, and the first chapter pays particular attention to their methodologies and concepts. I also analyze how the literature on ZANU's guerrilla war answers these questions, and how its concepts and methods influence its findings. Using alternative concepts and methods, I reinterpret ZANU's guerrilla war from the perspectives of peasants in Mutoko district. A basic premise of this book, like others that make mobilization a topic of investigation, is that individual choice has an important influence on political outcomes. In this assumption, it differs from studies that downplay or dismiss the role of human agency in affecting outcomes. Such alternative studies are more likely to highlight how structures inhibit individual choice and action and to focus on the causes and consequences of revolutions rather than their processes. The findings of this book, despite its different initial assumption from structural analyses, illuminate the significance of structures, particularly the structure of the state and of peasant communities.

Organizational appeals, popular support and its evidence

Studies of peasant revolution in Zimbabwe and other countries tend to accept the notion that revolutions rest on popular support, although few, if any, define what that means. Studies of revolutions in other contexts emphasize the efficacy of a revolutionary organization's utilitarian or normative appeals in winning popular support. The effects of guerrilla coercion against those whom the organization seeks to mobilize are usually ignored or considered only to be dismissed as making no dent in its popular support. Analysts of ZANU's war of national liberation emphasize the

237

importance of cultural nationalist appeals in mobilizing peasants, all but ignore utilitarian appeals, and although they often acknowledge the frequency of guerrilla coercion, never allow it to interfere with ZANU guerrillas' success at winning peasant popular support. The evidence for popular support, whether in studies of Zimbabwe's rural-based revolution or in the other contexts that were examined, rests on inferences based on sources other than peasant data. But it is well known that to infer attitudes through such indirect means is even more problematic than inferring attitudes and motives from what people themselves say.

This book draws on peasants and others to reassess the case for peasant popular support in the literature on ZANU's guerrilla war. Existing studies of the war overemphasize the effectiveness of cultural nationalist appeals in winning popular support by underestimating the effects of guerrilla coercion on peasants and the lack of utilitarian appeals. They limit guerrilla coercion to brief spates of inadequate guerrilla training and fail to see it as systematic and linked to the difficulties that confronted guerrillas as they tried to mobilize peasants while the military power of the colonial state was still intact and even increasing. Similarly, they fail to link the guerrillas' inability to offer utilitarian incentives to peasants to the power of the settler colonial state. Rural schools, clinics, and other services – symbols of a racially discriminatory state – came under guerrilla attack. But this guerrilla strategy denied rural people access to those few benefits they had become accustomed to and even helped to pay for. Taking into account the effect of all these appeals, positive and negative, leads to an emphasis on the costs of guerrilla support for peasants rather than the effectiveness of cultural nationalist appeals. Relying on direct peasant voices, I examined how peasants, *youth*, and the rural elite responded to the mixture of guerrilla appeals. The prominence of peasant strategies to avoid active involvement in supporting the guerrillas underlines their lack of enthusiasm and their fear of guerrillas and government forces. In emphasizing how the lack of utilitarian appeals meant that the guerrillas had to coerce individual peasants to participate, even though each of them would have liked to remove the settler state, my conclusions are consistent with the findings of rational choice theorists. They assert that rational individuals will not engage in collective action, even when they all agree on the desirability of a collective good, unless the organization can offer special incentives or force participation.

Peasant motives to participate in revolutions

Revolutionary organizations seek popular support by manipulating peasant grievances. Hence the study of mobilization is inextricably linked to the question of why peasants participate in revolutions. Whether studies stress peasant responsiveness to normative or utilitarian appeals, almost all locate the primary peasant grievances outside peasant communities and focus especially on peasant grievances against the state or other classes. I criticized the literature on peasant revolutions for its external bias. Whether based on peasant participation in Zimbabwe or in other revolutions, studies neglect peasant grievances against others in peasant communities. Why should this so consistently be the case across a large body of influential writings on peasant-based revolutions? I believe that the external bias in understanding why peasants participate in revolutions has its origins in the peasant concept, the reliance on inferred evidence from non-peasant data about peasant motives, scholars' elite bias that leads them to adopt the agenda of revolutionary organizations, and, in some cases, the concept of peasant nationalism.

Definitions of peasants abound, but, for all their differences, they display a remarkable similarity in defining peasants in terms of others. Peasants are commonly defined as being on a continuum between primitives and farmers. Unlike primitives, peasants are subjected to the dictates of the state or the influence of elites. In contrast to farmers who produce to maximize profits, peasants produce chiefly for subsistence. Hence states, elites, and markets are prominent in studies that seek to understand why peasants become active participants in revolutions.

This outward-oriented bias is reinforced by the absence of direct peasant voices to challenge it. All data sources contain their own bias. State archives on peasants reflect government concerns with maintaining order and production and are unlikely to delve into the internal politics of peasant communities. Military records are likely to exaggerate the strength of states with which they are in conflict to justify additional defence budgets. Peasants are unlikely to enter into these records except as pawns to bolster arguments about military performance or military needs. Revolutionary elites' documents are also likely to give short shrift to internal peasant grievances. Elites are interested in taking state power and are likely to emphasize why all or most groups would benefit from removing the incumbent regime. While they may understand the need to manipulate peasant grievances for their own ends, they fear the mobilizing potential in conflicts within the peasantry because they pose a threat to the revolutionary organization's goals of popular support, unity, and collective action. Hence their records are unlikely to illuminate peasant internal grievances. There are also extensive data on how peasants are exploited by the state and other classes. But such data cannot provide information about the subjective perception of exploitation. And to uncover motives, peasants' subjective experience of exploitation rather than their objective exploitation is critical. That the state and oppressive classes are the central cause of peasant misery does not mean that peasants will understand their condition in that way. There is no substitute for the direct voice of peasant data if one is interested in peasant motives for participating in revolutions.

Analysts of revolutions have been predisposed to adopt the perspective of revolutionary organizations, thereby allowing the external bias in

239

studies of revolution to pass unchecked. Scholars give priority to revolutionary organizations' goals of popular support, unity, and collective action. Like elites, they are often aware of the mobilizing potential of conflicts among peasants based on ethnicity and lineages, but they too regard them as dangerous to exploit because they clash with revolutionary organizations' goals of unity and collective action. Finally, those who emphasize peasant nationalism as the main reason for peasant participation in revolutions add to the existing external bias in studies of revolutions. The concept of nationalism, like that of peasants, is outward-oriented and assumes that peasant differences with each other pale in significance to their differences with alien others. Peasants appear as a class motivated against an alien state, whether characterized as capitalist, imperialist, or colonialist.

Zimbabwean peasant voices highlight how internal conflicts within peasant communities motivate revolutionary participation. Coerced to participate in committees that organized logistical help for the guerrillas, groups of peasants and *youth* exploited opportunities to further their diverse agendas to transform peasant society. Their positions in the organizational network established to support the guerrillas, their access to the guerrillas, and their ability to manipulate guerrilla appeals empowered them. *Strangers* sought to challenge the monopoly powers and abusive rule of chiefs and headmen. Women tried to end their husbands' domestic violence; the poorest and most disadvantaged peasants struck out at the better-off; *youth* challenged their elders' authority. To seek a uniform peasant motive, as if peasants behave as a united class, is misleading. Peasants with structurally different positions in their communities had different motives for exploiting their coerced participation to support the guerrillas. The peasant concept, with its external bias, vitiates against examining gender, lineage, generational, and socio-economic differences as they affect internal peasant relations during a revolution. Also, the emphasis on peasant responses to organizational appeals gives too much weight to organizations as agents of change and too little to peasants' agency. The agendas of oppressed groups in peasant communities were more radical than those of guerrillas. While oppressed groups in peasant society rebelled against the exploitative organization of peasant society, the guerrillas aimed at altering race relations. Undoubtedly, the diverse agendas of groups in peasant communities interfered with the efficient organization of guerrilla support. But they also provided the impetus for oppressed groups to respond creatively to their coerced participation for the guerrilla cause.

Who participates in revolutions?

Twentieth-century studies of peasant revolutions have focused too much on socio-economic differences in explaining who in the peasantry participates in peasant revolutions. In doing so, they have missed investigating the contribution of young unmarried boys and girls who have few, if any, rights in peasant societies. Barred by their single status from obtaining their own land and by their age from exercising any power in their communities, youth constitute a potentially important group for recruitment. Examining conflicts within peasant villages in Zimbabwe's guerrilla war draws attention to the especially important role of *youth* – those unmarried boys and girls who were over fifteen years old. There is some evidence that nationalism played a more important role in *youth's* support of guerrillas than it did for peasants, but even *youth* had other and more important motives. The war empowered *youth* in their communities as never before and they sought to challenge their elders' authority. Unmarried boys and girls over fifteen years old also constituted the bulk of the guerrilla armies and were important in paramilitary armies opposing the guerrillas.

The manner in which groups of oppressed peasants and *youth* used the civilian organizations that were established to aid the guerrillas for their own ends presents a challenge to rational choice theorists. They posit that an organization's primary purpose is to meet a fixed common interest, either through coercing members or offering them selective benefits. But the pursuit of interests is contingent on political circumstances and although the civilian organization was coerced into existence to provide for guerrilla needs, groups found it could serve simultaneously their own particular ends which they regarded as more important. Rational choice theorists also assert that individuals will only act cooperatively if they are coerced or provided with utilitarian benefits. But I show groups of peasants, in particular *strangers*, acting voluntarily to meet their collective ends. The description of peasants as paralyzed by guerrilla coercion but sometimes defying guerrilla commands to act in their own interest might appear to be inconsistent rather than rational behaviour. But I attribute this apparent inconsistency to individuals being more willing to take risks to satisfy their own agendas than the guerrilla agenda.

Popular mobilization and revolutionary outcomes

I also examine propositions that link popular mobilization to revolutionary outcomes that benefit peasants. The literature on ZANU's guerrilla war, like some other studies of peasant revolutions, sometimes links popular mobilization during a revolution to more peasant participation in state and party institutions after the revolution. Interpretations of revolutionary outcomes as positive for peasants rest on concepts and methods similar to those that underpin arguments for peasant motives for participating in revolutions. Such interpretations assume that the revolutionary process had popular support; they focus on peasant relations with the state and ignore the consequences of mobilization for internal peasant relations; and they depend on non-peasant sources. Using peasant interviews and other sources, I examined links between mobilization and post-war consequences in Zimbabwe. Peasant participation in state and party bodies had increased and guerrilla coercion had a residual influence on the character of local party institutions. The war also affected internal peasant relations. New divisions rooted in who had supported the war and who had fled guerrilla exactions were important and mediums and witchhunters were engaged in trying to re-establish community solidarity after the war-time killing, much of which had been unnecessary. Other battles within the peasantry continued, although once the guerrillas departed, competing groups lost an important resource to manipulate. The new government, less immediately dependent on peasants, was not as easy to manipulate and did not always side with groups who had benefited from the guerrillas' presence.

Generalizability of Zimbabwe findings

Zimbabwe, like other cases of revolution, has its distinctive features. The guerrillas had to contend with a still powerful settler state. The power of the white minority state is partly reflected in its ability to expand its military and paramilitary forces by drawing chiefly on new African recruits to fight against African guerrilla armies. Had the state been able to draw on troops from its metropolitan power, as was the case in Malaya, Algeria, and Kenya, its power would have been even greater. The strength of the colonial settler state helps to account for the guerrillas' reliance on cultural nationalist appeals and their scant utilitarian appeals. Some might argue that the guerrillas' failure to establish liberated areas and offer utilitarian incentives disqualifies it from being included as a revolution. Lastly, the guerrilla army, unlike its counterparts in China and Vietnam, never evolved into a regular army.

I make no claim for the generalizability of my findings but I have tried to highlight conceptual and methodological similarities between existing studies of ZANU's guerrilla war and other rural-based revolutions. Most studies of revolution accept that revolutionary organizations had popular support and downplay the effects of guerrilla coercion against peasants. These studies also explain peasant motives for participation by their resentment of states, markets and other classes, and see peasants as beneficiaries of mobilization after the new regime comes to power. Methodologically, they rely on non-peasant sources for data on peasant attitudes and behaviour. For these reasons, I conclude that findings of the Mutoko district study of Zimbabwe's war of national liberation have relevance for the concepts and methods used to study peasant revolutions. Abandoning the assumption that the collective behaviour of peasants is more important to peasants in revolutions than internal peasant struggles and using direct peasant data might lead to reinterpretations of other revolutions, as they have helped to contribute to reinterpretations of ZANU's guerrilla war in Zimbabwe. Relying on fieldwork, wherever possible, to ascertain peasant experiences of mobilization could revolutionize theories of revolutionary process.

Appendix

Field Research

Because of the importance of subjective factors in field research, discussed in chapter 1, the appendix provides additional information that may or may not have bearing on my findings. My field experiences also help to convey something of the atmosphere at the time in Zimbabwe.

Choosing peasant participation in the war as a subject of study

When I went to Zimbabwe at the end of 1981, I intended to examine how international sanctions had affected the domestic political system. By doing so, I hoped to fill a lacuna in the literature that focused on the economic impact of sanctions. But all my presuppositions about why it should have been a propitious time for such a study were contradicted by the realities in Zimbabwe. The atmosphere in Zimbabwe in 1981 was charged with an excitement about the possibilities of development, and I found myself drawn to the rural areas where many held that the hopes for a future Zimbabwe free of the chains of neo-colonialism lay. The armed struggle had left these areas physically ravaged, but scholarly accounts converged on how the war in ZANU's areas of operation had resulted in a remarkable political mobilization that had helped the guerrillas to create 'semi-liberated' or 'liberated zones'.[1] The well-organized party structures that had been established seemed to promise that at independence there would be a nationalist party with a grassroots presence. It would be responsive to rural needs, and would help to reverse the massive rural–urban inequalities that plague so many recently independent countries. The well-organized peasantry could also be a popular force against a state that did not meet its interests.

Accepting the premises of ZANU's successful rural mobilization, organized rural party structures, and 'liberated' or 'semi-liberated' areas, I decided to find out what continuities existed between the political activists who had controlled the party committees during the war and those who occupied positions of local power afterwards. This led me to examine grassroots party organization, the recently established local governments or district councils, and the newly constituted village courts. I was also interested to learn how 'traditional' rulers were responding to changes that were designed to undercut the privileged monopoly of local power they had secured during the colonial period. Lastly, I wanted to find out how much weight local powerholders had in interactions with state agencies in rural rehabilitation and development projects. When my premise of well-organized party structures began to crumble in the face of counter-evidence, I continued to pursue these questions but also expanded my interests backward in time to include the mobilization process itself.

Meeting people and early interviews in the district

I worked on government records at the Ministry of Local Government and Housing from which I hoped to get an understanding of what had happened to African local government in the rural areas during the war and the post-war period of reconstruction. At the same time, I began to make short trips to Mutoko district, equipped with letters granting me government and ZANU permission to do this research. I began with the white farming community where I correctly surmised that my reception would be easiest. On these trips, I stayed with a white family on their farm. The woman was very active in agricultural and administrative bodies – she was the chair-lady of Mutoko Rural Council, the European commercial farmers' local government body – and helped me to meet other white farmers, and white and African government officials. White farmers were very willing to talk and from them I learned about

243

their war experiences, a little about their history of the white farming community, and their anxieties about the future.[2]

Still on white terrain, I decided to interview farm-workers if I could find a translator. An African librarian whom I had met while reading old newspapers had expressed interest in my work, and was especially intrigued by my experiences in the European farming area. Interviewing farm-workers had little intrinsic interest to him, but he was delighted that it would give him the experience – unusual for Africans in Zimbabwe – of formally playing anthropologist with European subjects. He conducted the interviews by himself, and recorded and transcribed them. The outcome was disappointing but instructive. Using an interpreter was enough of a disadvantage; to lose even more control by being removed from framing the questions and having the ability to intervene with further questions was obviously undesirable.

Through my host on my short trips to Mutoko, I met a former district commissioner's court interpreter. He spoke fluent English and I did not feel that his links with the previous regime would jeopardize interviews with 'traditional' leaders or Purchase Area farmers. The former were often portrayed in the literature as government stooges, while the latter were depicted as kulaks. Neither image suggested that he would be found politically unacceptable. Again, this hunch was vindicated and he worked quite well with these two groups.

My host also introduced me to an African agricultural officer working for CONEX, the Department of Agricultural Conservation and Extension, which then operated in the white farming areas and the Purchase Areas. He and his family were extremely helpful, introducing me to agricultural advisors who had worked in the area and providing me briefly with accommodation. During this period, I was also spending time at the district headquarters, speaking to local government officials and using whatever records I could find on local government, dynastic disputes, and the district commissioner's court. I was also interviewing, in English, African teachers, European missionaries, African ministers of religion, and storekeepers throughout the district.

Urban interludes

Before starting to work in the four selected wards, I chose to track down refugees from Mutoko in Harare and Chitungwiza – a huge sprawling area that has municipal status. The idea came to me from old newspapers that noted that many of the refugees in the city were from Mutoko and Murewa. It seemed worth pursuing, chiefly to provide me with more background. The local housing authorities generously provided me with several staff members, with knowledge of the indigenous languages and the area, to help with interviews. The authorities also made available remarkably detailed housing records that document the inhabitants of each government housing unit, which district they came from, and when they arrived. However, the records turned out to be less useful than I had expected, and interviews with refugees were filled with tensions I had not foreseen. In the early 1900s when the mines were unable to recruit enough Zimbabweans because they paid such low wages and conditions were so atrocious, they recruited foreign Africans. In 1910 a recruiting agency was established at Mutoko. For Africans from the north (Malawi, Mozambique, and Zambia), Mutoko was also the first place where they could obtain a government registration certificate without which they could not seek work in the country. To encourage this flow of foreign migrant labour, a free government lorry service was introduced in the 1930s. One of its routes, operative until 1961, brought Africans from Nyasaland and Mozambique to Mutoko.[3] Consequently, many Africans who had come from these countries had registration certificates that listed them as having come from Mutoko. It took many interviews before it became apparent that those listed in the housing office records as coming from Mutoko may only have passed through the district decades ago. When we did find people who had come from Mutoko during the war, they had their own reasons for not wanting to talk. The government was trying to persuade people who had left their rural homes in the war to return to them.

Many were living in squatter communities and there was a housing shortage in the urban areas. Those who had acquired housing and who showed up on the housing lists feared that information about the war might be used to evict them. Learning about the war through refugees proved unproductive, and after a street incident in which we were challenged by party members, it seemed better to simply leave.

I made one further effort to speak to people living in the urban areas about their war experience in the rural areas. I had been given interesting data in the Harare housing office about the composition of the squatter populations in Harare during and since the war. A housing official volunteered to introduce me to four or five young men who had worked closely with the guerrillas in the north-east during the war, and now lived in Harare hostels for single males. I leapt at the opportunity, although the Friday night appointment after pay day at a hostel struck me as less than ideal. I went accompanied by the African librarian who had earlier helped me with interviewing farm-workers and who again agreed to translate if necessary. The evening's events may convey something of the tensions at the time, the perception among party members of their powerlessness, and why I felt vulnerable.

We were led into a large room on the top floor of a hostel, into which scarcely another person could have fit. As soon as we entered, everybody stood up and greeted us with songs. I knew then there had been a serious misunderstanding, and suggested we raise the issue immediately. The librarian thought otherwise, and I deferred. We were seated with party officials behind a table at the front of the room. A party official introduced me as an honoured guest of the government from America, who wanted to learn something about their heroic struggles during the war. The speaker appealed to the crowd to cooperate. The floor was mine, and I had to think quickly of innocuous questions that were war-related – an impossible task. Party officials were trying to persuade their reluctant audience to be more talkative. In the midst of this incredible spectacle, I noticed a woman scuttling from the audience to the party officials at the table, and she began to take notes on the exchanges at the meeting. By this time, my companion too sensed a need to end the show. Someone in the audience then asked if she could ask me a question. 'Why was I interested in their war? Where had I been when they were suffering?' Another person wanted to know who had given me permission to address the party. I tried to explain through my friend what had happened. Pandemonium broke out. When some order was restored, my friend was asked for his ZANU-PF party card, his home and work address, and before an aroused crowd, he had to recount his political history. The atmosphere was very tense, and party officials requested that everybody leave, except the party committee. People wanted to stay, and some fighting broke out. Eventually, the hall was cleared and we were confronted by angry party officials – almost all young men in their twenties, except for an older man in his forties. Again and again, we tried in vain to explain what had happened. My crime, they told me, was to call a party meeting without first getting permission from the appropriate level in the party hierarchy. I was asked to call the Minister of Local Government and Housing to come immediately. If they were to try to get him to come, they said, it would take forever. It seemed as if the stalemate would never end, but police had been called into the hostel, because someone had been stabbed in the outbreak after the meeting had been dismissed, and had found their way into the hall. What followed further underlined the powerlessness of the party structure in the hostels. We were all taken to the police station where the officials were berated for holding a meeting without first obtaining party permission. Afterwards I learned that most of those young people had fled the war for the relative safety of Harare, where they found themselves unemployed and living in grim squatter camps. At independence they had been moved into these hostels formerly for employed single African males.

Finding a place to stay in Mutoko

After these urban experiences, I returned to work in the four wards in the Tribal Trust Land that I had selected for study. From this point on, I stayed for about twelve months continuously in Mutoko. For a few weeks, I enjoyed the hospitality of an African agricultural officer and his wife, a primary schoolteacher. I had met the agricultural officer through the white chairwoman of the commercial farmers' local government body. He and his wife lived in a government house in the district centre. He was to transfer at the end of the month to a post in Matabeleland and the plan was that I would stay on with his wife who would complete the school semester and join him a month later. One stormy evening I was having a telephone conversation when I was thrown down the hallway by a flash of lightning. Over the next few days I experienced increasing difficulty with my peripheral vision and went into Harare to see a doctor. I returned about a week later to Mutoko to find that the agricultural officer had left for Matabeleland and his wife had moved in with neighbours. She believed that her husband's colleague, senior to him in age but junior in rank, had intended to direct the lightning against him and she feared to stay in the house. So I needed to find a place to stay immediately.

My preference was to stay within the African community. But the district administrator, a graduate from a West African university who dressed and behaved like the office-bound urban bureaucrat he aspired to be, told me accommodation was at a premium and he could not help to arrange anything for me. I tentatively explored staying at rural schools, but it was obvious that I would be a potential burden on the hosts, for whom I would attract unwanted attention.[4] Moreover, living facilities were basic and I was reluctant to spend a good part of every day, as local people do, collecting water and wood. So I stayed with the local garage owner, the last remaining white living in the district centre. He lived in what used to be called the 'European suburb', which since independence has been Africanized, and spent weekends with his family in Harare. He was extremely generous and helpful and it is an understatement to say that I could not have done my research without his support. Gas was in short supply and rationed but I enjoyed privileged treatment and only rarely had to go without. Car problems plagued me throughout my stay – one was stolen, another lasted only a few weeks on the rough roads, and its replacement was in need of almost daily attention. Every fresh difficulty was quickly attended to, and spare parts were ordered or brought in from Harare when necessary. When I was without a car for an extended period he let me use one of his vehicles. Just how much help it was to have a car was most appreciated when my interpreter and I had to use local buses and wait along with villagers for the unpredictable hour they would arrive, hitch rides, and walk incredible distances in intense heat, hoping one would return home before it grew dark.

Finding an interpreter

At a party in Harare, a young man introduced himself and expressed an interest in helping me. He knew of the work I was doing in Mutoko through an American working for Zimbabwe Publishing House. He seemed an ideal assistant. He spoke good English so we could communicate. He was enrolled in a teachers' training programme at Nyadiri, the heart of an American Methodist mission complex in Murewa district, and could commute to Mutoko on the bus service linking the two districts. An added advantage was that he had grown up in Mutoko and knew the area. His first project was to try to find out who the party officials were in one of the four wards. After only two days he was 'arrested' by suspicious village party officials – a power they still exercised in the 'spirit of the war' even though the government had removed the party's war-time policing functions. The ZANU-PF district party chairman had been called to the scene, ordered his release, and explained to villagers that he was working for me and I had government and party permission. Villagers had been alarmed, I was told, when the young man came to find out who ZANU-PF party officials were because he was known to support Muzorewa's party. Even after ZANU-PF had won the independence elections, the district party chairman said that the young man had 'stubbornly' refused to switch his allegiance. In a celebrated case in his home area, his mother, who had supported the guerrillas by knitting them berets, was identified as a 'sell-out' by youths from another ward. Without adequate interrogation, the guerrillas had killed her, only to be told later that they had been misinformed. The district party chairman suggested I inform him before I went into an area, and he would explain to people what I was doing to avoid potential misunderstandings. He also offered to provide a translator, an offer I preferred not to accept given his prominent position in the party and local government. Ultimately, I worked with the young man to whom I was introduced by an American Methodist missionary in the district.

A researcher's sense of vulnerability

In the colonial era, the relationship between fieldworker and subject was based on an unequal power relationship, perhaps best symbolized by the protection of the imperial government enjoyed by the researcher and the likelihood of punishment for subjects who refused to cooperate.[5] Even today, villagers' fears suggest their perception of a continuing unequal power relationship with a researcher. But for the researcher, there are no longer guarantees of physical safety but more likely, as in my case, warnings and proposals about how to avoid dangerous situations. As I sat through meetings where I was the centre of controversy – at least before the purpose of the gathering became murky and entangled in other issues as it invariably did – it was difficult to comprehend how people could be so oblivious of my own powerlessness.

A sense of vulnerability was not mitigated by the government's silence on events pertinent to one's physical safety. Whole battalions of ex-guerrillas were rumoured to have escaped from Murewa barracks after fighting had broken out among soldiers. These barracks lie off the main road between Harare, the capital, and Mutoko. Talk in Mutoko centre revealed anxiety about the possibility of armed men wandering about the district. The army was also said to be searching the district for the escaped soldiers. But one could get no information from the press in the days following the apparent conflict. One night the unmistakable sound of gunshots could be heard in Mutoko centre. Preferring to know what was happening, I called the local exchange – as one had to – to connect me to Mutoko police station. The police denied having heard anything. The following morning, when the centre was abuzz with speculation about what might have happened, the police station still disavowed that anything had occurred. The government's preference for hushing up security problems rather than informing the public made one feel less secure. As so often happens in such situations, one was more likely to hear about important events from the British Broadcasting Corporation or local rumours than from national media.

As one would expect after a war, there had been cases of banditry. Also, tensions in the national army between the guerrillas who had fought in Nkomo's army and those who had fought in Mugabe's army had resulted in many of the former escaping with arms. Political dissidents had been reported largely in Matabeleland and the Midlands provinces, where, among other activities, they had vowed to disrupt the government census planned for 1982. On one occasion, my interpreter and I set out for an area where the colonial government had prohibited people from settling because of malaria, but where many people had begun to settle during the war and continued to do so after the war. The area was more remote than any other place we had yet visited. We had just left familiar terrain, when armed men in uniform flagged us down. I was reluctant to stop, but heeded my interpreter's advice. They wanted a ride to a nearby school. Again, my instinct was to refuse but my interpreter reminded me, as informants often had, that 'you don't say no to armed men'. As we drove along a dirt road, we saw small groups of armed men walking through wooded areas and villages. When we got to the school, my interpreter asked our passengers what was going on and was it safe to carry on to our planned destination. We could get no explanation of why they were out in such large numbers, but were told that we could carry on if we liked. One man volunteered to accompany us, and two others wanted to be taken further. We continued, both apprehensive about who we were carrying and what we were heading for. As things turned out, the day went quite smoothly and we were able to get rid of our armed escort before interviewing people. We returned to the district centre and learned that the army was looking for the killers of two teachers who had been murdered while conducting the government census in the general vicinity in which we had travelled. This was a most unusual day and it would be misleading to convey the impression that a military presence was the norm during fieldwork. The point, though, is that one could not rely on the national media or the local police and army to advise you about the security situation. To talk about security problems was evidently regarded as making matters worse. So one moved around often in ignorance and dependent on what one picked up from local talk.

Notes

Introduction

1 Legum, Colin (ed.), *African Contemporary Record*, 1979–1980; Moorcraft and McLaughlin, *Chimurenga!*, p. 249, for the 1981 estimate of guerrilla returnees; *Africa South of the Sahara 1988–9*, p. 1, 162 for 1989 estimate of guerrilla returnees.
2 *Africa Confidential*, 19 August 1987.

1 Peasant revolutions: theories and methods

1 Skocpol, *States and Social Revolutions;* Himmelstein and Kimmel, 'Review Essay', provide a succinct summary. Skocpol examines the 'conjuncture' of two structural crises: a political crisis that occurs when weak states are faced with military or economic competition from stronger states and a crisis in peasant–landlord relations. Whether or not the state can enact relevant reforms successfully will depend on two other structural relationships: the role played by the landed upper class in national government and the amenability of agrarian class relations to raising productivity. If international tensions are moderate, if the landed upper class is weak *vis-à-vis* the government, and if agricultural relations are suitable for high productivity, the state can introduce reforms and overcome its crisis. If any or all of these structural conditions do not prevail, the state will be unable to solve its crisis. A combination of state crisis and upper class insurrection immobilizes the state and opens the way for peasant uprisings. The potential for peasant revolt in turn is determined by another set of structural factors – the degree of peasant autonomy and solidarity and the local strength of the upper class. Peasant uprisings are likely when the peasant community is strong and peasants have some economic and political autonomy and when landlords lack direct economic and political control at the local level.
2 Manicas, 'Review Essay'.
3 Skocpol, *States and Social Revolutions*, p. 18.
4 Ibid.; Popkin, *The Rational Peasant;* Johnson, *Peasant Nationalism and Communist Power*; Wolf, *Peasant Wars of the Twentieth Century*; Scott, *The Moral Economy of the Peasant*; Moore, Barrington, *Social Origins of Dictatorship and Democracy*; Migdal, *Peasants, Politics and Revolution*.
5 E.g. Gurr, *Why Men Rebel*.
6 Skocpol, *States and Social Revolutions*.
7 Tilly, *From Mobilization to Revolution*.
8 Skocpol, Reuschemeyer, and Evans, *Bringing the State Back In*.
9 Skocpol, *States and Social Revolutions*, p. 16.
10 Moore, *Social Origins of Dictatorship and Democracy*, p. 480.
11 Ibid., p. 473; see Rothman, 'Barrington Moore and the Dialectics of Revolution' for

other ways in which Moore departs from objective exploitation as a cause of peasant revolt.

12 Moore, *Social Origins of Dictatorship and Democracy*, pp. 222–3.

13 Wolf, *Peasant Wars of the Twentieth Century*. Party mobilization of peasant support is not a central concern in Wolf's introduction or conclusion, but in his case discussions that constitute the bulk of the book he does give this factor explicit attention. Wolf discusses at length the phases of the Communist Party's strategy to win peasant support, including its introduction of radical land reform, progressive land taxes, and new organizations that gave poorer and landless peasants some political leverage (pp. 146–50). In his conclusion, he alludes to the organizational fusion between 'rootless' intellectuals and their constituency or rural supporters among the peasants (p. 289). Organizations succeed when they appeal to peasants' sense of landlord violations of existing arrangements. So, despite an emphasis on the objective conditions that make peasants potential revolutionaries, Wolf also permits the notion of peasant popular support and organizational behaviour to matter in his analysis.

14 Popkin, *The Rational Peasant*, p. 253.

15 Ibid., p. xi.

16 Migdal, *Peasants, Politics and Revolution*, p. 241.

17 Johnson, *Peasant Nationalism and Communist Power*, p. x.

18 Ibid., p. 93.

19 Mao, *On Guerrilla Warfare*, p. 82.

20 Schram, *The Political Thought of Mao Tse-Tung*, p. 314.

21 Ibid., pp. 343–4.

22 Bienen, *Violence and Social Change*, pp. 44–5.

23 Guevara, *Guerrilla Warfare*; Debray, *Revolution in the Revolution?*

24 Paret and Shy, *Guerrillas in the 1960s*, pp. 33–4.

25 De Nardo, *Power in Numbers*, p. 4.

26 Ibid., pp. 217–18.

27 Paret, *French Revolutionary Warfare from Indochina to Algeria*, p. 66.

28 Dunn, *Modern Revolutions*, pp. 132–3.

29 Paret and Shy, *Guerrillas in the 1960s*, pp. 76–7. Bienen, *Violence and Social Change*, p. 59 dismissed their proposal to investigate guerrilla terror, asserting that it may not be the most interesting or important phenomenon of insurrections.

30 Crenshaw, *Revolutionary Terrorism*, p. 48.

31 Ibid., p. 48.

32 Ibid., p. 48.

33 Leites and Wolf, *Rebellion and Authority*, chapter 6.

34 Ibid., p. 126.

35 Ibid., p. 129.

36 Ibid., p. 101.

37 Wolf, *Peasant Wars of the Twentieth Century*, p. xv.

38 Ibid., pp. 294–5.

39 Ibid., p. xi.

40 Scott, 'Review Article. Peasant Revolution: A Dismal Science'.

41 Ibid.; Scott, *The Moral Economy of the Peasant*.

42 Scott, 'Revolution in the Revolution: Peasants and Commissars'.

43 Popkin, *The Rational Peasant*, pp. 223–9.

44 Wolf, *Peasant Wars of the Twentieth Century*, pp. 290–3.

45 Redfield, *The Little Community*, pp. 17–22.

46 Silverman, 'The Peasant Concept in Anthropology', p. 56. These themes are already apparent in Redfield's *Tepoztlan*, a study of a rural community in Mexico that sought to find out about the process of cultural change by which a 'folk culture' (the term he usually

uses for peasants in this study) becomes 'modern' or 'civilized' or 'urban'. Redfield portrays Tepoztlan as 'no longer a primitive tribal society nor yet an urbanized community, it must nevertheless be defined, as it tends to define itself, with reference to the world-wide city culture within which it is now included.' (Redfield, *Tepoztlan*, p. 51).

47 Wolf, *Peasant Wars of the Twentieth Century*, p. xiv.
48 Silverman, 'The Peasant Concept in Anthropology', p. 64.
49 Hill, *Development Economics on Trial*, p. 14.
50 Skocpol, *States and Social Revolutions*, e.g. p. 291.
51 Solomon, *Mao's Revolution and the Chinese Political Culture*, p. 239; also pp. 6 and 196–7.
52 Ibid., pp. 216–17.
53 Ibid., pp. 234–7.
54 Massell, *The Surrogate Proletariat*, especially pp. xxii–xxiii, 249, 285–303, and 394–7.
55 Chabal, 'People's War, State Formation and Revolution in Africa', p. 111.
56 Scott, 'Revolution in the Revolution: Peasants and Commissars', p. 97
57 Scott, 'Review Article. Peasant Revolution: A Dismal Science', p. 288 and 'Revolution in the Revolution: Peasants and Commissars', pp. 127–8.
58 Kahn, 'Peasant Ideologies in the Third World', p. 71.
59 Hodgkin, *Nationalism in Colonial Africa*.
60 Smith, *State and Nation in the Third World*, discusses Nairn and Kautsky.
61 Plamenatz, 'Two Types of Nationalism', pp. 23–4.
62 Hodgkin, *Nationalism in Colonial Africa*, p. 115.
63 Kamenka, 'Political Nationalism – the Evolution of an Idea', p. 12.
64 Kamenka (ed.), *Nationalism*.
65 Skocpol, 'Review Article: What Makes Peasants Revolutionary?', p. 363.
66 Skocpol, *States and Social Revolutions*, p. 279.
67 Ibid., p. 287.
68 Mazrui, 'Political Engineering in Africa', p. 289.
69 Chabal, 'People's War, State Formation and Revolution in Africa?'
70 Southern Rhodesia Parliamentary Debates, vol. 84, July 1973, Columns 1,141, 1,149; Maxey, *The Fight For Zimbabwe*, pp. 128–9, notes that a decision was also taken in February 1973 to divide Umtali, Murewa, and Sipolilo, where the war was also intense. Days earlier, the regime had also tried to tighten its control over the movement of Africans by making it mandatory that Africans in Tribal Trust Lands in these districts carry identity documents in addition to the registration documents they already carried.
71 District assistants, vols. 4 and 5, Telex, 2 July 1976; Secretary of Internal Affairs to provincial commissioner, 24 March 1977.
72 Stiff, *Selous Scouts Top Secret War*, p. 196; Cilliers, *Counter-Insurgency in Rhodesia*, p. 127.
73 Caute, *Under the Skin*, p. 421.
74 Maxey, *The Fight for Zimbabwe*, pp. 141–4 for discussion of biases in official and ZANLA statistics on casualties and other data.
75 1979 Army Report. Villages varied in population.
76 Todorov, *The Conquest of America*, p. 232.
77 Ibid., p. 246.
78 Gregory, 'Zimbabwe 1980: Politicisation Through Armed Struggle and Electoral Mobilisation', p. 74; Cliffe, Mpofu, and Munslow, 'Nationalist Politics in Zimbabwe: The 1980 Elections and Beyond', pp. 54-8.
79 Garbett, 'The Rhodesian Chief's Dilemma: Government Officer or Tribal Leader?', p. 126, argues differently. He maintains that the Ndebele system of government had been more completely overhauled after 1896 than that of the Shona and that this helped to account for Ndebele chiefs being more pro-government than Shona chiefs.

80 Ranger, 'Traditional Authorities and the Rise of Modern Politics in Southern Rhodesia', p. 173; Ranger, *The African Voice in Southern Rhodesia*, pp. 26–9.
81 Shamuyarira, 'A Revolutionary Situation in Southern Africa', p. 166; *Africa Report*, January 1969, p. 26.
82 Caute, *Under the Skin*, p. 423.
83 Seidman, 'Women in Zimbabwe: Postindependence Struggles'.
84 *Africa Contemporary Record*, 1979–1980, B. 987.
85 Wasserman, 'The Economic Transition to Zimbabwe', p. 43.
86 Maxey, 'The Armed Struggle in Zimbabwe and The Gaps in Our Knowledge', p. 14.
87 *Africa Report*, January 1969, p. 26; Shay and Vermaak, *The Silent War*; Wilkinson, 'From Rhodesia to Zimbabwe', pp. 247, 268. See Kapuscinski, *Another Day of Life*, on the FNLA paying pressganged Bakongo per battle.
88 Rake, 'Black Guerrillas in Rhodesia', pp. 24–5.
89 Weiss, *The Women of Zimbabwe*, pp. 28–9.
90 Ibid., pp. 83–4.
91 Ibid., p. 86.
92 Ibid., p. 88.
93 Seidman, 'Women in Zimbabwe: Postindependence Struggles', pp. 425–6.
94 Mufuka, 'Rhodesia's Internal Settlement'.
95 E.g., comment of Sister Janice McLaughlin who worked in the camps, cited in Weiss, *The Women of Zimbabwe*, p. 93.

2 Inequalities and peasant grievances

1 E.g. Yudelman, *Africans on the Land* uses interchangeably peasants, producers and the 'traditional' agricultural sector to refer to African producers in the Tribal Trust Lands and Purchase Areas. 'Modern' producers (Europeans) are market-oriented while 'traditional' producers (Africans) distrust the market and exchange relations and give primacy to social kin obligations (pp. 10–23). He recognizes that not all African producers share the same traditional attitudes and that some are more like 'modern' producers. Weinrich, *African Farmers in Rhodesia* includes in her peasant category Africans in the Tribal Trust Lands, in the Purchase Areas and on irrigation schemes in Tribal Trust Lands. She refers to Tribal Trust Land producers as peasant cultivators, Purchase Area producers as peasant farmers, and those on irrigation schemes as plotholders. She emphasizes the differences among them but what they appear to share is that they earn most of their income from the land, and they do not sell all their produce.
2 Weinrich, *African Farmers in Rhodesia*, pp. 65, 114 includes teachers and civil servants in a survey of peasant households even though they earn more income from non-agriculture than agriculture, which, from her own definition, would mean they should not be classed as peasants. Manungo, 'Peasants and Guerrillas: An Oral History'; Ranger, *Peasant Consciousness and Guerrilla War in Zimbabwe* employs two different peasant concepts, one broadly inclusive and the other narrower (see chapter 4).
3 Mason, *The Birth of a Dilemma*.
4 For details on the Charter and the 1923 constitution, see Gann, *A History of Southern Rhodesia*; for an overview of constitutional history, see Wills, *An Introduction to the History of Central Africa: Zambia, Malawi and Zimbabwe*.
5 Phimister and Van Onselen, *Studies in the History of African Mine Labour in Colonial Zimbabwe*; Phimister and Van Onselen, 'The Political Economy of Tribal Animosity: A Case study of the 1929 Bulawayo Location Faction Fight'; Good, 'Settler Colonialism in Rhodesia', p. 597; Emmanuel, 'White-Settler Colonialism and the Myth of Investment Imperialism'.
6 The discussion up to here relies on Gray, *The Two Nations*; Palmer, *Land and Racial*

Domination in Rhodesia; Mason, *The Birth of a Dilemma*; Yudelman, *Africans on the Land*. Legislation in the colonial era refers to whites as 'Europeans', and this usage has been followed here.

7 Weinrich, *Chiefs, Commissioners and Councils*, p. 4, fn.4; Weinrich, *Black and White Elites in Rural Rhodesia*, pp. 17–19.

8 Yudelman, *Africans on the Land*, p. 81.

9 Rifkind, *The Politics of Land in Rhodesia*. Purchase Areas that were converted to communal tenure were called Special Native Reserves until 1961 when they, and the Reserves, were renamed Tribal Trust Lands.

10 Riddell, *The Land Question*, p. 11.

11 Palmer, *Land and Racial Domination in Rhodesia*.

12 Mudzi and Ngarwe had been set aside for European cattle ranches at one point but the scheme was abandoned because of low rainfall and lack of surface water (Murphree, *Christianity and the Shona*, pp. 19–20).

13 Ibid., p. 20.

14 See Commercial Farmers' Union. *Resettlement of Farms in Mutoko and Mt. Darwin*. Cyclo No. 11783. In the 1970s, European farmers tried to attribute their poor performance to the poor quality of their land and claimed that all their land fell in natural region 4 (Agricultural Development Authority Report, 1972).

15 Department of Physical Planning, 1981.

16 This refers to population in Mutoko Intensive Conservation Area (an agricultural unit), the borders of which differ slightly from the Mutoko European Area (an administrative unit).

17 Floyd, 'Changing Patterns of African Land Use in Southern Rhodesia', pp. 220–2.

18 Agro-Economic Survey of the Mazoe Area, pp. 109–10.

19 The need for government assistance arose because most European farmers, who had obtained cheap land as returning veterans or as immigrants after World War II, had pursued tobacco farming. At the time the international tobacco market was buoyant, and by 1958, there were over 100 European farms specializing in tobacco. But the climate and soil are unsuited for intensive tobacco production, and when the boom tobacco-market conditions changed and international sanctions were introduced in 1965–6, the farms were too small for mixed farming or specialized livestock production to which the soil and climate were better suited. After sanctions were imposed in 1965, Mutoko farmers experienced a much more serious agricultural decline – measured by the drop in hectares allocated to tobacco production, number of farms, and in permanent African male labour – than elsewhere in the country. Farm amalgamations did occur, but too often the farms were not even adjacent to one another – a pattern encouraged by the forced sales that led to speculative buying. The government then offered assistance by selling off Unassigned Land at cheap prices to European farmers in Mutoko and Mayo. Annual Report of Native Commissioner, Mtoko, 1941, 1952–3, 1954–5, 1958. Archives S 1563 and 100355 18.17.3F; Agro-Economic Survey of the Mazoe Area, pp. 75, 86–9; Agricultural Development Authority, 1978; Robinson Commission, Third Report of Working Party D, District Survey, Mtoko.

20 Clarke, *Domestic Workers in Rhodesia*, pp. 26, 55–6.

21 Gray, *The Two Nations*, pp. 99–106.

22 Shamuyarira, *Crisis in Rhodesia*, p. 111; Astrow, *Zimbabwe: A Revolution That Lost Its Way?*, pp. 23, 31, 49.

23 Weinrich, *Black and White Elites in Rural Rhodesia*, p. 24. The table also reveals how in the years of economic downturn (1958–61, 1965–7), African wage workers were vulnerable while European workers enjoyed job protection.

24 Gray, *The Two Nations*, pp. 61–6; Yudelman, *Africans on the Land*, pp. 115–17, 159–61.

25 Rifkind, *The Politics of Land in Rhodesia*; Duggan, 'The Native Land Husbandry Act of

1951 and the Rural African Middle Class of Southern Rhodesia'; Gray, *The Two Nations*, pp. 70–1; Floyd, 'Changing Patterns of African Land Use in Southern Rhodesia'; Yudelman, *Africans on the Land*, pp. 53 and 117.

26 Pilditch Report, 1965; African Production and Marketing Development Fund. Third Report of Select Committee on African Production and Marketing Development Fund Estimates.

27 Agro-Economic Survey of the Mazoe Area, 1976, p. 110.

28 International Labour Office, *Labour Conditions and Discrimination in Southern Rhodesia (Zimbabwe)*, p. 45; United Nations, *Zimbabwe. Towards A New Order. An Economic and Social Survey*, pp. 57–8; Weinrich, *African Farmers in Rhodesia*, pp. 27, 32–3; Yudelman, *Africans on the Land*, pp. 157–8.

29 Yudelman, *Africans on the Land*, pp. 179–80.

30 Ibid., pp. 22–3, 89.

31 The preceding section draws on Nziramasanga, 'Major Trends in the Rhodesian Economy, 1955–77'; United Nations, *Zimbabwe. Towards a New Order*, pp. 57–8; Tickner, *The Food Problem*, pp. 25–32; Gray, *The Two Nations*; Yudelman, *Africans on the Land*, pp. 178–91.

32 Yudelman, *Africans on the Land*, pp. 165–7; Weinrich, *African Farmers in Rhodesia*, p. 149.

33 Gray, *The Two Nations*, pp. 307–9; Clarke, 'Economic and Political Aspects of the Rhodesian Franchise'; Meredith, *The Past is Another Country*, pp. 28–9, 62–3; Gann, *A History of Southern Rhodesia*; Wills, *An Introduction to the History of Central Africa*.

34 Holleman, *Chief, Council and Commissioner: Some Problems of Government in Rhodesia*; Weinrich, *Chiefs, Commissioners and Councils*; Passmore, 'A History of Policy on African Involvement in Local Administration and Development in the Tribal Areas of Rhodesia'.

35 Passmore, 'History of Policy on African Involvement', pp. 246–7; Passmore, *The National Policy of Community Development in Rhodesia*, p. 59.

36 Letter from regional commissioners, Mashonaland East, to all District Commissioners, Mashonaland East, 26 September, 1977.

37 Weinrich, *Chiefs and Councils in Rhodesia*, pp. 166–9, discusses reasons for opposition to councils and the community development policy. Chiefs feared competition from elected councillors. Missions regarded handing over schools to revenue-poor councils with forebodings of a loss of Christian influence in African education, a drop in academic standards and a reduction in the expansion of schools. Teachers anticipated interference from illiterate chiefs in the running of the schools. Peasants had all the influence they wanted over education through parents' school committees and feared councils would eliminate these. They regarded community development and councils as another excuse for taxing them.

38 Weinrich, *Black and White Elites in Rural Rhodesia*, p. 28.

39 Passmore, 'History of Policy on African Involvement', pp. 286, 292–3; Passmore, *The National Policy of Community Development in Rhodesia*, p. 141; Bratton, *Beyond Community Development: The Political Economy of Rural Administration in Zimbabwe*, p. 23.

40 Provincial Authorities: A Background Paper. 1980/1. Division of District Administration, p. 1.

41 People in Mutoko Tribal Trust Land had experimented in the 1960s with community boards. Although government-inspired, these bodies were non-statutory and voluntary. They received no government money, and relied on local contributions of labour and money for community projects. Women were especially active, helping to mould bricks for building schools and clinics, and constructing roads, dams, and bridges. Despite active government discouragement against community boards working together, all the

community boards in Mutoko district cooperated to raise R$8,000 to build an agricultural show hall and a women's club training room in Mutoko Tribal Trust Land close to Mutoko centre. Passmore, 'History of Policy on African Involvement', p. 374; Mr Sharples, Regional Training Officer, interview 22/1/82; Annual Report of District Commissioner, Mtoko, 1969. Archives.

42 Mtoko district files on councils and administration c/a/117/1; c/a/117/2, c/a/117/3, c/a/117/11, c/a/140/1, c/a/129/12.

43 Mtoko district files on councils and administration c/a/2/1; Mtoko district files on councils and administration, notes by Dave Ford, 1971.

44 Mtoko district files on councils and administration c/a/2/1; Mtoko district files on councils and administration, notes by Dave Ford, 1971.

45 An amendment to the Land Apportionment Act in 1941 authorized local authorities to establish African townships in African (rural) areas. This provision reflected official recognition of the emergence of 'detribalized' Africans: those who having worked in European areas would not want to return to live under chiefs. Africans were not allowed to buy property in the rural townships. Yudelman, *Africans on the Land*, pp. 70, 73.

46 Gray, *The Two Nations*, pp. 128–44; Riddell, *Education for Employment*, p. 10.

47 Martin and Johnson, *The Struggle for Zimbabwe. The Chimurenga War*, pp. 57–8.

48 International Labour Office, *Labour Conditions and Discrimination in Southern Rhodesia (Zimbabwe)*, pp. 59–62.

49 Weinrich, *Black and White Elites in Rural Rhodesia*, pp. 29–30.

50 Gilmurray, *The Struggle for Health*, pp. 33–9.

51 For example, Annual Report of Native Commissioner, Mtoko, 1936, archives S 1563; Annual Reports of Native Commissioner, Mtoko, 1956–7, archives 100355 18.17.3F.

52 The Jesuits had tried unsuccessfully to open a mission at Mutoko in the 1890s. See Keppel-Jones, *Rhodes and Rhodesia: The White Conquest of Zimbabwe. 1884–1902*, p. 417.

53 Murphree, *Christianity and the Shona*, pp. 62, 80; Annual Reports of Native Commissioner, 1955–7, Mtoko, archives 100355 18.17.3F.

54 Murphree, *Christianity and the Shona*, pp. 65, 81. Africans contributed labour by helping to build schools and clinics. More so than Catholic members, Methodists were required to give cash to help pay teachers' salaries. The government prohibited these payments when it tried to limit the influence of religion on education (Ibid., p. 87).

55 Clans often take the name of some animal, and usually their members are not allowed to eat the flesh of the animal or some part of it. To do so, it is believed, would court misfortune. This suggests that clan and sub-clan names have religious and symbolic connotations but this should not be over-emphasized because occasionally names have been changed simply to conceal the identity of a group or to adjust its relations with other groups.

56 This clan structure arises because of the way villages grow. When a village is founded, its nucleus is made up of the founder's patrilineal descendants. Some *strangers* come to the village when the men marry because Shona marriage is exogamous and virilocal: Shona are not supposed to marry people within their clan, and wives ought to reside in their husbands' villages. Shona women retain their fathers' clan name after marriage. Relatives from the wife's family may go to live with her thus increasing the *stranger* community. A few men married to daughters in the patrilineal clan may come to live in their wives' villages, perhaps because their families cannot afford to pay the brideprice to entitle them to bring their wives to their villages. Some men may also prefer to live with their wives' families because they have bad relations with their own kin. Another reason for men living in their wives' villages or away from their own villages is that they may prefer to live with friends. In subsequent generations, the children of these sons-in-law or totally unrelated men will form the nuclei of further patrilineal families and hence

stranger lineages proliferate. Bourdillon, *The Shona Peoples. An Ethnography of the Contemporary Shona, with Special Reference to their Religion*, pp. 76–8.

57 Holleman, 'Some "Shona" Tribes of Southern Rhodesia', p. 372.

58 The following example illustrates how some houses come to be excluded from the chiefship. Suppose the first chief (A1) has three wives (A2, A3, A4). Each wife has three children: A2 has children B1, B2, B3; A3 has children B4, B5, B6; A4 has children B7, B8, B9. The children of B generation belong to the C generation. When the chief dies, ideally the chiefship should be inherited by the house of each wife in order of seniority. So the second chief should be B1, the third B4, the fourth B7. On the death of B7, there may be younger brothers in his house (B8 and B9) still alive while all of that generation in the other houses are dead. If the junior wife of the first chief was very much younger than the senior wife, it is possible that all of generation C will have died in the senior house before the last of generation B in the junior house. The senior house is then likely to be excluded from the chiefship since members of generation D in the senior house should not rule over their 'father' of the senior generation C in the junior houses. Certain branches of the chiefly family may also be excluded because of an alleged offence by an ancestor. Bourdillon, *The Shona Peoples*, pp. 124–6.

59 Weinrich, *Chiefs and Councils in Rhodesia*; Gann, *A History of Southern Rhodesia*.

60 Ministry of Internal Affairs. Delineation Report, Mtoko District, November 1965, Delineation Officer B.P. Kaschula, p. 6.

61 Chimoyo chiefdom file, Mutoko.

62 Garbett, 'Religious Aspects of Political Succession Among the Valley Korekore (N. Shona)'; Weinrich, *Chiefs and Councils in Rhodesia*, p. 13.

63 This section on chiefs' religious and ritual powers draws on Bourdillon, *The Shona Peoples*, pp. 136–8. See also Bourdillon, 'Suggestions of Bureaucracy in Korekore Religion: Putting the Ethnography Straight'.

64 Weinrich, *Chiefs and Councils in Rhodesia*, pp. 10–11; Gann, *A History of Southern Rhodesia*, pp. 81–4, 104, 148–9.

65 Cuerden, 'Human Development Opportunities in Community Development: The Gutu Exploratory Case Study', p. 18.

66 Passmore, 'History of Policy on African Involvement', p. 308.

67 Southern Rhodesia Parliamentary Debates, 84, 3 August 1978, column 1,451.

68 J.M. Leach, Provincial Authority Adviser, Mashonaland East Provincial Authority, Seke, June 1978.

69 Provincial Authorities Act, 1972; R.G.N. 939/72 amended by R.G.N. 245/76 and Statutory Instrument 593/79 make provision for the election of provincial councils. All chiefs who were senators were ex officio members, and every district was represented by a chief who was not a member of the senate. The provincial assembly of chiefs elected one member per district from among the African council chairmen in the Tribal Trust Lands and one from among the Purchase Area council chairmen.

70 Bratton, *Beyond Community Development*, pp. 27–9; Meredith, *The Past is Another Country*.

71 Weinrich, *Chiefs and Councils in Rhodesia*, pp. 13, 16–18.

72 Ibid.; Bratton, *Beyond Community Development*, pp. 27–9; Meredith, *The Past is Another Country*, pp. 225–6.

73 Gray, *The Two Nations*, pp. 155, 164; Weinrich, *Chiefs and Councils in Rhodesia*, pp. 21–2; Murphree, *Christianity and the Shona*; May, *Zimbabwean Women in Colonial and Customary Law*, pp. 53–4.

74 Floyd, 'Changing Patterns of African Land Use in Southern Rhodesia', pp. 118–19.

75 Chavunduka, 'Social Change in a Shona Ward', p. 2.

76 Weinrich, *African Farmers in Rhodesia*, pp. 68–9.

77 Nyamfukudza, *The Non-Believer's Journey*, p. 84.

78 Bourdillon, *The Shona Peoples*, Ch.4.
79 Day, 'The Insignificance of Tribe in the African Politics of Zimbabwe Rhodesia'; Weinrich, *African Farmers in Rhodesia*; Weinrich, *Black and White Elites in Rural Rhodesia*; Garbett, 'Prestige, Status, and Power in a Modern Valley Korekore Chiefdom, Rhodesia'.
80 Thomas, 'Christianity, Politics, and the Manyika: A Study of the Influence of Religious Attitudes and Loyalties on Political Values and Activities of Africans in Rhodesia'.
81 Survey cited in Bourdillon, *The Shona Peoples*, p. 140.
82 Beach, *The Shona and Zimbabwe 900–1850*, p. viii.
83 Cobbing, 'The Absent Priesthood: Another Look at the Rhodesian Risings of 1896–7'; Beach, '"Chimurenga": The Shona Rising of 1896–7'; Tsomondo, 'Shona Reaction & Resistance to the European Colonization of Zimbabwe, 1890–1898'; Hodder-Williams, 'Marandellas and the Shona Rebellion'. For a contrary argument about the coordinated action of the rebellion, see Ranger, *Revolt in Southern Rhodesia, 1896–7. A Study in African Resistance*.
84 Garbett, 'The Rhodesian Chief's Dilemma: Government Officer or Tribal Leader?'
85 May, *Zimbabwean Women in Colonial and Customary Law*, pp. 51–2.
86 Beach, '"Chimurenga"'; Schmidt, 'Hunters, Farmers and Gold-Washers: A Re-evaluation of Women's Role in Precolonial and Colonial Zimbabwe', pp. 2–11.
87 Bourdillon, *The Shona Peoples*, pp. 81–2.
88 Annual Report of Native Commissioner, Mtoko, 1937–59. Archives S 1563 and 100355 18.17.3F; Robinson Commission, Third Report of Working Party D, 1962.
89 Tribal Trust Land data from Ministry of Internal Affairs, Intensive Rural Development Area, IRDA Report No. 3; Purchase Area data from Agro-Economic Survey of the Mazoe Area, pp. 75, 86–9, 104–7.
90 Department of Conservation and Extension. Seventh Annual Report of African Purchase Lands Recording Scheme, 1975/6.
91 Weinrich, *African Farmers in Rhodesia*, pp. 162–3.
92 Ibid., pp. 173–5, 306.
93 Ibid., pp. 173–5, 202.
94 Cheater, *Idioms of Accumulation*, pp. 173–9; Pollak, 'Black Farmers and White Politics in Rhodesia', pp. 269–76.
95 At least initially most Purchase Area farmers who acquired capital to buy or lease farms were members of the British South Africa Police, evangelists and teachers from missions, and a few boss-boys from European farms and mines. Most were old too. Between 1953 and the early 1960s, government rules required that applicants for freehold farms have a master farmers' certificate which indicated that they had attained a reasonable standard in farming techniques. Ranger, *The African Voice in Southern Rhodesia, 1898–1930*, p. 230; Weinrich, *African Farmers in Rhodesia*, p. 23.
96 Gray, *The Two Nations*; Ranger, *The African Voice in Southern Rhodesia*, pp. 16, 19, 191–2.
97 International Labour Office, *Labour Conditions and Discrimination in Southern Rhodesia (Zimbabwe)*; Bratton, 'The Public Service and Public Policy in Zimbabwe: Opportunities and Constraints', p. 31; United Nations, *Zimbabwe. Towards a New Order*, p. 241.
98 Ranger, *The African Voice in Southern Rhodesia*; Gray, *The Two Nations*.
99 Davidson, Isaacman and Pelissier, 'Politics and Nationalism in Central and Southern Africa, 1919–1935'; Gray, *The Two Nations*, pp. 325-6.
100 Van Velsen, 'Trends in African Nationalism in Southern Rhodesia', p. 156.
101 Fanon, *A Dying Colonialism*, p. 132.
102 Shamuyarira, *Crisis in Rhodesia*.
103 Weinrich, *Black and White Elites in Rhodesia*, pp. 224–5, 227.
104 Ibid., p. 225.

105 Ibid., pp. 225–6.
106 Ibid., pp. 194–208, 226.
107 Yudelman, *Africans on the Land*, pp. 140–1.
108 Ibid., p. 142.
109 Weinrich, *African Farmers in Rhodesia*, p. 23; Yudelman, *Africans on the Land*, p. 142. Floyd, 'Changing Patterns of African Land Use in Southern Rhodesia', pp. 115, fn. 4, 224, 246–7 and Duggan, 'The Native Land Husbandry Act of 1951', pp. 234–5 estimate that 25 per cent of Tribal Trust Land cultivators followed or attempted to follow the standards set by government agricultural advisors in the 1950s and 1960s.
110 Tickner, *The Food Problem*, pp. 19–22, thinks the figure for market-oriented Tribal Trust Land farmers is an underestimate because it ignores those cultivators who engage in trading with their neighbours or illegal trading outside their areas. The estimates of Weinrich, *Women and Racial Discrimination in Rhodesia*, p. 51, are on the low end of the spectrum: she believes that only 3 per cent of Tribal Trust Land cultivators were market-oriented.
111 Weinrich, *Black and White Elites in Rural Rhodesia*, p. 192, adopts the contradictory view that cash crop farmers in the Tribal Trust Lands were accepted and admired locally.
112 Weinrich, *African Farmers in Rhodesia*, p. 203.
113 Ibid., pp. 131, 135–7.
114 Ibid., p. 310.
115 Ibid., pp. 57–8, 115, 303.
116 Tickner, *The Food Problem*, p. 18, citing a Whitsun Foundation study, 1978.
117 Riddell, *The Land Question*, p. 10.
118 Weinrich, *Black and White Elites in Rural Rhodesia*.
119 Cliffe and Stoneman, *Zimbabwe. Politics, Economics and Society*, pp. 69–70.
120 Bourdillon, *The Shona Peoples*, pp. 134–5, also fn. 22, p. 134.
121 Ministry of Home Affairs, Circular No. 148, File Number: Chk/14, 25 April 1980; Provincial Authorities (Allowances) Regulations, 1979, gazetted 29 November 1979; Provincial Authorities (Allowances) (Amendment) Regulations 1980. No.1, gazetted 28 March 1980.
122 The discussion of these laws draws on May, *Zimbabwean Women in Colonial and Customary Law*, unless otherwise indicated.
123 Except for the Purchase Areas, polygyny declined everywhere for several reasons. As children spent more time in school and educational fees had to be paid, they were seen as an economic burden rather than as workers in family fields who produced wealth. In the Tribal Trust Lands, the need for many wives and children to work the shrinking fields also discouraged polygyny. The rising cost of bridewealth made polygyny less viable. Finally, church teaching against polygyny had an effect, as did the churches' refusal to admit polygynously married Africans as church members. Weinrich, *Women and Racial Discrimination in Rhodesia*, p. 29; Jeater, 'Women and Bridewealth in the Restructuring of Shona Society 1890–1930'; England, 'A Political Economy of Black Female Labour in Zimbabwe, 1900–1980'; Schmidt, 'Hunters, Farmers and Gold-Washers'; Schmidt, 'Women are the Backbone of Agriculture'.
124 Bourdillon, *The Shona Peoples*, p. 70, fn. 61; May, *Zimbabwean Women in Colonial and Customary Law*.
125 In traditional law, a married woman may own certain property which is inherited by her children or her father's family. A woman may accumulate property consisting of livestock from her daughter's husband as part of marriage payments or from his family during her daughter's pregnancy. A woman may also acquire property from income she earns in her own field or from special skills.
126 Bourdillon, *The Shona Peoples*, p. 43.
127 For the status of women in other African countries, see Strobel, 'Review Essay: African

Women'; Robertson and Berger (eds.), *Women and Class in Africa*; Van Allen, 'African Women, "Modernization" and National Liberation'.

128 Bratton, *Beyond Community Development*.

129 Fry, *Spirits of Protest*, pp. 12–17.

130 May, *Zimbabwean Women in Colonial and Customary Law*, pp. 33–4.

131 Weinrich, *Women and Racial Discrimination in Rhodesia*; Weinrich, *African Farmers in Rhodesia*, p. 104, fn. 2; Schmidt, 'Hunters, Farmers and Gold-Washers'; Schmidt, 'Women are the Backbone of Agriculture'; Jeater, 'Women and Bridewealth'; England, 'Political Economy of Black Female Labour in Zimbabwe'; Chavunduka, 'Polygyny among Urban Shona and Ndebele Christians. A Case Study'.

132 May, *Zimbabwean Women in Colonial and Customary Law*, pp. 67–8.

133 Cheater, *Idioms of Accumulation*.

134 Weinrich, *Women and Racial Discrimination in Rhodesia*, p. 29.

135 Cheater, 'Women and Their Participation in Commercial Agricultural Production: The Case of Medium-Scale Freehold in Zimbabwe'; Cheater, *Idioms of Accumulation*.

136 May, *Zimbabwean Women in Colonial and Customary Law*; see also Fry, *Spirits of Protest*, on likelihood of women being accused of witchcraft.

137 Bourdillon, *The Shona Peoples*, pp. 44–5.

138 Jeater, 'Women and Bridewealth'; Schmidt, 'Hunters, Farmers and Gold-Washers'; Schmidt, 'Women are the Backbone of Agriculture'.

139 E.g. Yudelman, *Africans on the Land*, p. 132.

140 E.g. Gray, *The Two Nations*, for child labour in towns; Weinrich, *African Farmers in Rhodesia* – case studies in chapter 6 show males younger than fifteen becoming migrants.

141 Weinrich, *Women and Racial Discrimination in Rhodesia*.

142 Weinrich, *African Farmers in Rhodesia*, p. 168.

143 Ibid., pp. 60–3.

144 Ibid., pp. 164–70.

145 Murphree, *Christianity and the Shona*, pp. 94–109, 143; Jules-Rosette, 'Women as Ceremonial Leaders in an African Church'; Kileff and Kileff, 'The Masowe Vapostori of Seki'; Ranger, 'Religion and Rural Protest in Makoni District, Zimbabwe, 1900–1980'; Ranger, 'The Early History of Independency in Southern Rhodesia'.

146 E.g. Shamuyarira, *Crisis in Rhodesia*, for youth in nationalist movement; Ranger, *The African Voice in Southern Rhodesia*, pp. 157, 159, although not focusing on youth, discusses how protonationalist organizations such as the Industrial and Commercial Workers' Union appealed to 'native youth'.

3 Strategies, goals and appeals: continuity and change

1 Measures of state capacity, see Adelman, *Revolution, Armies and War*; Skocpol, Reuschemeyer and Evans (eds.), *Bringing the State Back In*, pp. 16–17. Skocpol identifies sovereign integrity and stable administrative-military control of a given territory as preconditions for any state to be able to implement policies. State effectiveness also requires loyal and skilled officials and plentiful financial resources.

2 Gray, *The Two Nations*; Wills, *An Introduction to the History of Central Africa*; Ranger, *The African Voice in Southern Rhodesia, 1898–1930*.

3 Nyangoni and Nyandoro (eds.), *Zimbabwe Independence Movements*, pp. 3–20; Van Velsen, 'Trends in African Nationalism in Southern Rhodesia'.

4 Nyangoni and Nyandoro, *Zimbabwe Independence Movements*, see N.D.P. constitutional proposals, pp. 34–43.

5 Ibid., p. 32.

6 Van Velsen, 'Trends in African Nationalism in Southern Rhodesia', pp. 142, 148–52;

Wilkinson, 'From Rhodesia to Zimbabwe', pp. 223–5, 322–40; Shamuyarira, *Crisis in Rhodesia*, pp. 43–4, 49, 59, 66, 70.

7 Moore, David, 'The Contradictory Construction of Hegemony in Zimbabwe: Politics, Ideology and Class in the Formation of a New African State', p. 90. He cites Eshmael Mlambo, *Rhodesia: The Struggle for A Birthright*.

8 Day, 'Southern Rhodesian African Nationalists and the 1961 Constitution'; Nyangoni and Nyandoro, *Zimbabwe Independence Movements*, pp. 21–45.

9 Nyangoni and Nyandoro, *Zimbabwe Independence Movements*, pp. 52–6.

10 Shamuyarira, *Crisis in Rhodesia*, pp. 63, 69, 72, 175, 202; Wilkinson, 'From Rhodesia to Zimbabwe', pp. 226–7, notes that nationalist leader Chikerema claimed that the decision to use violence was made in 1960. Astrow, *Zimbabwe: A Revolution That Lost Its Way?*, pp. 31, 46, 49, argues that sabotage was decried by nationalist leaders of the NDP and of ZAPU who preferred constitutional politics and always lagged behind the masses in their militancy (see also Palmer, *Land and Racial Domination in Rhodesia*, p. 244). In early 1964, Astrow argues, the leaders continued to dissociate themselves from sabotage but probably by then did not discourage its members if they helped to create a breakdown in law and order and forced Britain to act (pp. 38–9). Whether sabotage was a tactic adopted partly because of lack of active mass support is an interesting question to which Shamuyarira and Mugabe provide different answers. Shamuyarira, *Crisis in Rhodesia*, p. 74, claims that ZAPU could have mobilized mass support but found it tactically advantageous to employ a small number of saboteurs. Speaking before ZANU women in Mozambique in 1979, Mugabe said: 'It was because of the men's reluctance to participate in strikes and demonstrations that we decided, when we formed ZAPU, to avoid the method of strikes, boycotts and demonstrations. Then we also had concluded that it was better to strike at the settler's property through acts of sabotage and cause the enemy economic loss than to expose our supporters to torture and suffering through mass strikes and demonstrations that invited brutal police action.' (Women's Liberation in the Zimbabwean Revolution. Materials from the ZANU women's seminar, p. 13.)

11 Nyangoni and Nyandoro, *Zimbabwe Independence Movements*, pp. 64–71.

12 Ibid., pp. 75–85.

13 Ibid., p. 84.

14 First, the new constitution would give white Rhodesians independence based on the 1969 constitution that was openly white supremacist. Secondly, the improvements that the British government claimed were against this constitution rather than the 1961 constitution that had been the context of the five principles. Finally, the improvements were small, prospective rather than immediate in effect, and dependent on the good faith of the white community. The franchise formula would delay even parity in the legislature until well into the next century.

15 Nyangoni and Nyandoro, *Zimbabwe Independence Movements*, pp. 231–42, 248. On the ANC refusing to support its members who were arrested, see Moore, 'The Contradictory Construction of Hegemony in Zimbabwe', p. 101.

16 FROLIZI came into existence in 1971 when some Shona broke away from ZAPU and ZANU to form it. Instead of being a unity movement as it claimed, it represented a third force that competed with ZANU and ZAPU for control of the nationalist movement. FROLIZI, soon under the leadership of the former Acting President of ZAPU, contrasted its revolutionary socialism with the alleged reformist politics of the older nationalists in the two exiled movements. Peasants and workers, FROLIZI asserted, were ready for revolution but the bickering nationalist leaders were squandering opportunities to organize them for armed struggle. FROLIZI promoted the virtues of a collective military leadership as opposed to party leadership to guide the armed struggle, but its contribution to the armed struggle never amounted to more than sending a few armed groups to commit sabotage in Rhodesia. FROLIZI was responsible for at least

one military exercise inside Rhodesia in 1973 that alarmed the Security Forces. Nyangoni and Nyandoro, *Zimbabwe Independence Movements*, pp. 171–84, 224–30; Kirk, 'Politics and Violence in Rhodesia'.

17 Nyangoni and Nyandoro, *Zimbabwe Independence Movements*, pp. 277–85.
18 Wills, *An Introduction to the History of Central Africa*.
19 Wilkinson, 'From Rhodesia to Zimbabwe', p. 232; Moorcraft and McLaughlin, *Chimurenga! The War in Rhodesia 1965–1980*, p. 16; Maxey, *The Fight for Zimbabwe*, pp. 54–5.
20 Wills, *An Introduction to the History of Central Africa*, pp. 378–9, maintains that ZAPU and the South African African National Congress declared their objective to be the overthrow of the white governments in Rhodesia and South Africa. Wills, like others, questions whether the armed struggle was inspired by the nationalist parties themselves or by external actors such as the Organization of African Unity.
21 De Braganca and Wallerstein (eds.), *The African Liberation Reader*.
22 Moorcraft and McLaughlin, *Chimurenga!*, pp. 80–1; Seegers, 'Revolution in Africa: The Case of Zimbabwe', p. 231; Wilkinson, 'From Rhodesia to Zimbabwe', pp. 222–30, 236–9; M'gabe, 'The Beginnings of Guerrilla War', p. 46; Maxey, *The Fight for Zimbabwe*, pp. 11, 41, 64, 81.
23 Moorcraft and McLaughlin, *Chimurenga!*, p. 21.
24 Wilkinson, 'From Rhodesia to Zimbabwe', p. 235; M'Gabe, 'The Beginnings of Guerrilla War', p. 73, cites a Rhodesian propaganda package that conceded that 'the men encountered in the valley were well trained and well armed, employing everything from small arms to machine guns, rifles and bazookas'.
25 Wilkinson, 'From Rhodesia to Zimbabwe', pp. 241, 244–5.
26 Shay and Vermaak, *The Silent War*, p. 79; Maxey, *The Fight for Zimbabwe*, pp. 9, 89, 116.
27 Moore, 'The Contradictory Construction of Hegemony in Zimbabwe', pp. 107–8.
28 Some regard conflicts between Shona and Ndebele leaders in ZAPU as the chief reason for the upheaval that erupted in ZAPU in February–March 1970. Others put more emphasis on ideological differences between the disputing parties, with those challenging James Chikerema's leadership desiring a socialist ideology and a swift change from conventional warfare to Maoist guerrilla tactics.
29 Moorcraft and McLaughlin, *Chimurenga!*, pp. 76, 83.
30 ZANU Political Programme. No. 2. Lusaka. 1972.
31 Moorcraft and McLaughlin, *Chimurenga!*, pp. 30, 73, 84.
32 Thompson, *Challenge to Imperialism*; Astrow, *Zimbabwe: A Revolution That Lost Its Way?*; Martin and Johnson, *The Struggle for Zimbabwe*; Meredith, *The Past is Another Country*; Smiley, 'Zimbabwe, Southern Africa and the Rise of Robert Mugabe'; Moore, 'What's Left of Liberation in Zimbabwe? Socialism, Democracy and the Legacy of a Guerrilla War'; Day, 'The Insignificance of Tribe in the African Politics of Zimbabwe Rhodesia'.
33 Sithole, *Zimbabwe. Struggles Within the Struggle* expresses the view that ethnic conflicts split ZANU and led to Chitepo's assassination. However, *Serving Secretly*, the memoirs of Ken Flower, director of Rhodesian intelligence, admits that Rhodesian intelligence agents killed Chitepo. Martin and Johnson's study also holds the Rhodesian regime responsible for Chitepo's assassination.
34 Alperin, 'The Distribution of Power and the (June 1979) Zimbabwe Rhodesia Constitution'; Mufuka, 'Rhodesia's Internal Settlement: A Tragedy'; Zvobgo, 'Rhodesia's Internal Settlement 1977–1979. A Record'.
35 Delap, 'The April 1979 Elections in Zimbabwe–Rhodesia'; Cilliers, *Counter-Insurgency in Rhodesia*, p. 239; Moorcraft and McLaughlin, *Chimurenga!*, p. 210, mention that in some places the guerrillas encouraged voting.

36 Moorcraft and McLaughlin, *Chimurenga!*, pp. 73, 229; Cilliers, *Counter-Insurgency in Rhodesia*, p. 50; Meredith, *The Past is Another Country*, pp. 235–6; Legum (ed.), *African Contemporary Record*, 1979–80, B.982.

37 Wilkinson, 'The Impact of the War', p. 116; Mufuka, 'Rhodesia's Internal Settlement: A Tragedy', p. 446. Moorcraft and McLaughlin, *Chimurenga!*, p. 76, date ZANU's request for recruits to stay inside Rhodesia from 1979.

38 See Wilkinson, 'The Impact of the War', for other indicators of intensifying war; see also Caute, *Under the Skin. The Death of White Rhodesia*, p. 369.

39 Legum (ed.), *Africa Contemporary Record*, 1979–80.

40 Lan, *Guns and Rain. Guerrillas and Spirit Mediums in Zimbabwe*, p. 133.

41 Ibid., p. 167.

42 Ranger, *Peasant Consciousness and Guerrilla War in Zimbabwe*, p. 179.

43 Ibid., p. 181.

44 Ibid., p. 212.

45 Ranger, 'Bandits and Guerrillas: The Case of Zimbabwe', pp. 387–8.

46 Caute, *Under the Skin*, pp. 245, 314.

47 Ibid., pp. 18, 253, 350, 406–7.

48 Gann and Henriksen, *The Struggle for Zimbabwe*, pp. 88–9, 94–5.

49 Callinicos, *Southern Africa After Zimbabwe*, p. 35.

50 Linden, *The Catholic Church and the Struggle in Zimbabwe*, p. 272.

51 Ibid., pp. 272–3.

52 Cliffe, Mpofu and Munslow, 'Nationalist Politics in Zimbabwe: The 1980 Elections and Beyond', p. 50.

53 Ibid., p. 50.

54 Ibid., p. 50.

55 Ibid., pp. 63–4.

56 Mandaza, 'The State and Politics in the Post-White Settler Colonial Situation' and 'Introduction: The Political Economy of Transition 1980–1986'.

57 Callinicos, *Southern Africa After Zimbabwe*; Astrow, *Zimbabwe: A Revolution That Lost Its Way?*, pp. 135, 140–1, 148, 173.

58 Cliffe and Stoneman, *Zimbabwe. Politics, Economics and Society*, pp. 38–9. They suggest that in this short period even though the integration of Marxism was only partial in nationalist ideology, Marxist ideology affected guerrillas who went into Zimbabwe and they in turn influenced peasant consciousness. It is only a suggestion, and they produce no evidence, but it does seem far-fetched.

59 Mandaza, 'The State and Politics in the Post-White Settler Colonial Situation', p. 29.

60 Frederikse, *None But Ourselves*, quotes a few guerrillas who claim the importance of socialist appeals, but other guerrillas she cites refute this. Ranger, *Peasant Consciousness and Guerrilla War in Zimbabwe*; Lan, *Guns and Rain*, both found socialist appeals to have been unimportant.

61 Shamuyarira, *Crisis in Rhodesia*, p. 62.

62 Ibid., p. 62.

63 Thomas, 'Christianity, Politics and the Manyika', p. 174.

64 Shamuyarira, *Crisis in Rhodesia*, p. 68.

65 Ibid., pp. 42–3.

66 Mtoko District files on councils and administration. Statement to police, March 27, 1963.

67 Mtoko District files on councils and administration. Detective Sergeant, Criminal Investigation Department, Marandellas.

68 Shamuyarira, *Crisis in Rhodesia*, p. 203.

69 On the use of songs to analyse culture, see Scott, *The Moral Economy of the Peasant*, 'Revolution in the Revolution', and *Weapons of the Weak: Everyday Forms of Peasant Resistance*. For liberation songs, see Pongweni, *Songs that Won the Liberation War*. For a

content analysis of the appeals in Pongweni, see Moore, 'Rebel Music: Appeals to Rebellion in Zimbabwe'.

70 Bullock, *The Mashona*, p. 13, fn. 1, describes how the head of a murdered aspirant chief would be sent back to his people in the beak of this bird.

71 Lan, *Guns and Rain*, pp. 157–9. He gives a fascinating account of the symbolic meaning of the prohibitions, pp. 159–66.

72 See also Linden, *The Catholic Church and the Struggle in Zimbabwe*, p. 272.

73 Cliffe, Mpofu and Munslow, 'Nationalist Politics in Zimbabwe', p. 64.

74 Nyangoni and Nyandoro, *Zimbabwe Independence Movements*. Muzorewa appeals to men to stop excessive drinking in the 1970s.

75 Pennell, 'Women and Resistance to Colonialism in Morocco: The Rif 1916–1926', pp. 112–13, describes similar appeals in the early resistance in colonial Morocco, where rooting out interpersonal violence was seen by the guerrillas as especially important.

76 Bayles, 'A Concept of Coercion'.

77 Lyons, 'Welcome Threats and Coercive Offers'; Pennock, 'Coercion – An Overview'.

78 Shay and Vermaak, *The Silent War*, pp. 10–12, 14–16; Wilkinson, 'From Rhodesia to Zimbabwe', pp. 226–8; Thomas, 'Christianity, Politics, and the Manyika', pp. 112–14; Fry, *Spirits of Protest*, p. 111. Nyamfukudza's novel, *The Non-Believer's Journey* describes urban political violence and intimidation in this period, p. 17.

79 Van Velsen, 'Trends in African Nationalism in Southern Rhodesia', pp. 152–3, 157.

80 Statement taken by assistant magistrate Simmonds from Headman Charewa at Mtoko hospital, 19 October 1961. Headman Charewa seemed oblivious to how his own actions had challenged the indigenous hierarchy, angering both the elders and the nationalists. The Charewa headmanship was created by the government because Chieftainess Charewa who had jurisdiction over Charewa ward refused to attend government meetings or have any contact with Europeans. Consequently, his status was low in the eyes of the Charewa people. When in May 1961 he was elected to the newly created Council of Chiefs – a government body to give chiefs a national platform – the government raised his status to that of Deputy Chief to overcome the status inconsistency of a headman being on a body of chiefs. Leaders in the Charewa administration and nationalists opposed his acceptance of a position on the Council of Chiefs. Six months later his hut was burned.

81 Murphree, *Christianity and the Shona*, p. 155, fn. 1.

82 Ibid., pp. 153–5.

83 Detective sergeant, Criminal Investigation Department, Marandellas district.

84 Acting District Commissioner, Mtoko to Provincial Commissionei, 12 August 1964.

85 Acting District Commissioner, Mtoko to Provincial Commissioner, 12 August 1964.

86 Murphree, *Christianity and the Shona*, p. 155, see also p. 156 for youths' intimidation of church members in Charewa ward, and the reversal in the relationship between nationalists and church members here only six months later.

87 Moore, David, 'The Contradictory Construction of Hegemony in Zimbabwe', p. 90.

88 For general description of ZANU's lack of a mass base, see Van Velsen, 'Trends in African Nationalism in Southern Rhodesia', pp. 155–6. For Mutoko, I rely on interviews, mostly with teachers.

89 Hancock, *White Liberals, Moderates and Radicals in Rhodesia 1953–1980*, pp. 153–5.

90 Letter from Mtoko District Commissioner, Mr Markram to Provincial Commissioner, Mashonaland East, 6 March 1980 on Headman Kabasa. Ref.: per 5/hm/mtk; for suicide, see ch. 5.

91 Letter from Mtoko District Commissioner, Mr Markram to Secretary of Internal Affairs, 28 November 1978.

92 Unsigned and undated note in district file. Ref.: Per/5/hm/mtk.

93 Letter from Mtoko District Commissioner, Mr J.F. Saunders to the Provincial

Commissioner, Mashonaland East, 10 September 1976. Ref.: PER 5/hm/mtk; for death of Headman Nyamanza of Chimoyo chiefdom, see chapter 5.

94 Letter from Mtoko District Commissioner, Mr Saunders to Provincial Commissioner, Mashonaland East, 12 August 1976. Ref.: Per 5/hm/mtk.

95 Letter from Mtoko District Commissioner, Mr Markram to Provincial Commissioner, Mashonaland East, 11 June 1980. Ref.: per 5/hm/mtk.

96 Letter from Mr M.E. Hayes, research officer, to District Commissioner, Mtoko, 26 August 1977. Ref.: per 5/hm/mtk.

97 Letter from Mtoko District Commissioner, Mr Markram to Provincial Commissioner, Mashonaland East, 3 January 1978; letter from Mtoko Acting District Commissioner, Mr D.G. Rosenhahn to Provincial Commissioner, Mashonaland East, 31 October 1978; letter from Mtoko District Commissioner, Mr Markram to Provincial Commissioner, Mashonaland East, 21 March 1980. Ref.: per 5/hm/mtk.

98 Interviews.

99 Handwritten sheet, 25 August 1977. Ref.: per 5/hm/mtk; letter from Mr M.E. Hayes (research office, Ministry of Internal Affairs) to District Commissioner, Mtoko, 26 June 1978. Ref.: per 5/hm/mtk; letter from Mr L.G. Leach, Provincial Commissioner of Mashonaland East to Secretary for Internal Affairs, 7 December 1978. Ref.: per 5/hm/mtk.

100 Circular Minute No.33, Ministry for Internal Affairs, 'Councils in the War Situation', 19 July 1977. Ref.: c/60.

101 Letter from District Commissioner, Mtoko to Provincial Commissioner, Mashonaland East, 7 March 1977. Ref.: c/22.

102 Minutes of Mutoko district team meeting, 4 January 1980. Archives C36.8.7F 192754.

103 African Production and Marketing Development Fund. Second Report of the Select Committee on African Production and Marketing Development Fund Estimates, pp. 30, 38–9.

104 Interview with head of African Development Fund, 1982.

105 DEVAG extension supervisor, interview 21 December 1981; former DEVAG extension supervisor, interview 30 December 1981. On July 1 1978 responsibility for agriculture in the Tribal Trust Lands was transferred from the Ministry for Internal Affairs to the Department of Agricultural Development (DEVAG) in the Ministry of Lands, Natural Resources, and Rural Development. Circular Minute No. 3, Ministry for Internal Affairs, 6 June 1978. Ref.: DMN/1/30.

106 Caute, *Under the Skin*, describes vividly the effect of the war on white farmers.

107 Mtoko Intensive Conservation Area data, Department of Statistics, unpublished.

108 Ranger, *Peasant Consciousness and Guerrilla War in Zimbabwe*, pp. 206–7.

109 Cliffe and Stoneman, *Zimbabwe. Politics, Economics and Society*, p. 48.

110 Cilliers, *Counter-Insurgency in Rhodesia*, p. 89.

111 Shamuyarira, *Crisis in Rhodesia*, p. 49.

112 Skocpol, 'Review Article: What Makes Peasants Revolutionary?', p. 366.

113 The Unlawful Organizations Act provided for the outlawing of organizations and the Preventive Detention Act for the detention of individuals. The former was used to ban the SRANC and the latter to detain 300 of its leaders, after 500 had been arrested mainly in the rural areas. The Native Affairs Amendment Act made it a crime for any African to make statements or act in any way 'likely to undermine the authority' of, or bring into 'disrepute' government officials, chiefs, or headmen. It also prohibited meetings of twelve or more Africans unless they had the approval of the native commissioner, imposing a serious organizational constraint on a movement less than two years old.

114 After violence in urban townships in 1960, parliament passed the Law and Order Maintenance Act and the Emergency Powers Act. The Law and Order Maintenance Act provided, *inter alia*, for banning publications, prohibiting meetings, arrest without a warrant, and restriction to a designated area without a trial. It created a new category of

crimes: subversive statements, intimidation, the use of violence, sabotage and terrorism, causing disaffection in the police, publishing 'false news', and boycotts. The Emergency Powers Act enabled the state to declare an emergency for three months whereas the existing legislation had restricted an emergency to one month. Also, the Minister of Justice was empowered to make regulations considered 'necessary or expedient' for public order, peace, safety, and the maintenance of 'essential services'.

115 Weitzer, 'The Internal Security State', pp. 42–7.

116 Ibid., pp. 47–8, 52–3, 59–60.

117 A 1970 amendment made the death penalty for petrol-bombing residential properties discretionary.

118 Palley, 'Law and the Unequal Society'; Wilkinson, 'From Rhodesia to Zimbabwe', p. 234; Windrich, 'Rhodesian Censorship: The Role of the Media in the Making of a One-Party State'; Windrich, 'Controlling the Media: Rhodesia Style', pp. 89–90.

119 Wilkinson, 'The Impact of the War', pp. 110, 241–2; Weitzer, 'The Internal Security State', pp. 30, 68.

120 Moore, David, 'The Contradictory Construction of Hegemony in Zimbabwe', p. 97.

121 Under the Emergency Powers Act 1967 the executive's power (especially the police and Minister of Law and Order) to legislate during an emergency through issuing regulations further eroded the powers of the legislature. The Law and Order (Maintenance) Act 1967 was tightened. Sabotage and terrorism were broadly defined, every person charged with a criminal offence was assumed guilty until proven innocent, and the judiciary was required to impose a death sentence on those who could not prove their innocence. The Act was again amended in 1970. It became a criminal offence to knowingly harbour or assist guerrillas, or having harboured and assisted them, to refuse to disclose this to the police within a reasonable time. At the same time, the mandatory death sentence for security offences under the Emergency Powers Act was removed, signifying the regime's confidence that the courts would impose sufficiently severe sentences. See Palley, 'Law and the Unequal Society', Part I, pp. 39–43.

122 Minter, *King Solomon's Mines Revisited*, p. 276; see also Gann, 'Prospects for White Resistance', p. 12, which notes Mugabe's estimate of 1,400 foreign mercenaries and Hodges, 'Counterinsurgency and the Fate of Rural Blacks', p. 16, which estimates 1,200 white mercenaries. Fall, *Street Without Joy*, pp. 279–80, defends the French army's use of foreigners in Indo-China, and then goes on to remark: 'the principle of using foreign nationals in one's armed forces . . . is almost as old as warfare itself; on the contrary, the principle of the single-nationality armed force is quite new and more often than not observed in the breach'.

123 Legum (ed.), *African Contemporary Record*, 1977–8.

124 Ibid.; Gann, 'Prospects for White Resistance', p. 11.

125 Nelson *et al.*, *Area Handbook for Southern Rhodesia*, pp. 330–2; International Defence and Aid Fund for Southern Africa, *Zimbabwe. The Facts About Rhodesia*, pp. 53–4.

126 Stiff, *Selous Scouts Top Secret War*, p. 124; estimate for Selous Scouts is from Cilliers, *Counter-Insurgency in Rhodesia*; Stiff's estimate is 1,000, pp. 97–8.

127 Nelson *et al.*, *Area Handbook for Southern Rhodesia*, pp. 330–2.

128 Ibid., pp. 332–3; Nelson (ed.), *Zimbabwe. A Country Study*, pp. 254–5.

129 Cilliers, *Counter-Insurgency in Rhodesia*; Astrow, *Zimbabwe: A Revolution That Lost Its Way?*, fn. 44, p. 185; Frederikse, *None but Ourselves*; Windrich, 'Controlling the Media'; Circular Minute No. 42, Ministry of Internal Affairs, 'National Service Act: Employers' Return of Africans Liable for National Service, 1978'. Ref.: c/22; Weitzer, 'The Internal Security State'.

130 Rhodesia National Farmers' Union, Bulletin No. 12, August 24 1978; Mr D. Hasluck, Deputy President of Commercial Farmers' Union, interview, 14 August 1981; Mrs Guild,

Chairlady of Mutoko South Rural Council, interviews August 5–7 1981; white farmer, interview, 23 August 1981.
131 Weitzer, 'The Internal Security State', p. 73; Nelson *et al.*, *Area Handbook for Southern Rhodesia*, p. 335.
132 Fall, *Street Without Joy*, pp. 171–2.
133 Moorcraft and McLaughlin, *Chimurenga!*, p. 222.
134 Caute, *Under the Skin*, p. 369.
135 Astrow, *Zimbabwe: A Revolution That Lost Its Way?*, p. 116.
136 Weitzer, 'The Internal Security State'.
137 Martin and Johnson, *The Struggle of Zimbabwe*, p. 45; Thompson, *Challenge to Imperialism*, pp. 154–5; Cohen, 'The War in Rhodesia: A Dissenter's View', pp. 491–2. South Africa supplied pilots who participated in raids into Mozambique, police between 1967 and 1975, and during the Lancaster House negotiations there were two battalions in Rhodesia under South African command, and South African troops in the army.
138 Weitzer, 'The Internal Security State', p. 73.
139 Adas, *Prophets of Rebellion*, p. 174.
140 For example, Wilkinson, 'From Rhodesia to Zimbabwe'.
141 On Mao's guerrilla strategy, see Schram, *The Political Thought of Mao Tse-Tung*; Mao Tse-Tung, *On Guerrilla Warfare*; Moorcraft and McLaughlin, *Chimurenga!*, p. 151. The closest ZANU came to considering conventional war was in late 1979, when ZANLA decided to abandon dispersion tactics inside Mozambique because of repeated Security Force attacks on its camps. To this end, it built a vast new base, New Chimoio. During the Lancaster House negotiations, the Security Forces attacked New Chimoio and killed 3,000 guerrillas without losing any men themselves.
142 Skocpol, 'Review Article: What Makes Peasants Revolutionary?', p. 366; Wolf, *Peasant Wars of the Twentieth Century*; Zagoria, 'Introduction. Peasants and Revolution'; Hofheinz, 'The Ecology of Chinese Communist Success: Rural Influence Patterns, 1923–45'; Dunn, *Modern Revolutions*, pp. 89–90, 152; Worsley, 'The Superpowers and the Tribes', p. 298.

4 Guerrilla – civilian relations: the issue of popular support.

1 District Commissioner Frank Taylor, Mtoko to Provincial Commissioner, 22 March 1972.
2 Lan, *Guns and Rain*, asserts that peasants did not understand the term *magandanga* to be abusive. This differs from the description in Bullock, *The Mashona* who describes a *magandanga* as an animal spirit that enables a man to turn himself into a species of a werewolf. It robs the person it kills, leaving the corpse uneaten.
3 Moorcraft and McLaughlin, *Chimurenga!*, p. 126.
4 Field data; Nyamfukudza, *The Non-Believer's Journey*, chapter 7 has a good description of a *morari*.
5 Cliffe, Mpofu, and Munslow, 'Nationalist Politics in Zimbabwe: The 1980 Elections and Beyond'; Gregory, 'Zimbabwe 1980: Politicisation Through Armed Struggle and Electoral Mobilisation'; Rich, 'Legacies of the Past? The Results of the 1980 Election in Midlands Province, Zimbabwe'.
6 Cliffe, Mpofu and Munslow, 'Nationalist Politics in Zimbabwe', pp. 48–9.
7 Ibid., p. 49.
8 Ibid., p. 49.
9 Ibid., p. 53.
10 Ibid., p. 50.
11 Ibid., p. 45.
12 Ibid., p. 57.

13 Ibid., p. 63.
14 Cliffe, 'Towards an Evaluation of the Zimbabwean Nationalist Movement'.
15 Astrow, *Zimbabwe: A Revolution That Lost Its Way?*, e.g. pp. 37–9, 45–7.
16 Ibid., p. 57.
17 Ibid., pp. 47, 135.
18 Ibid., p. 135.
19 Ibid., p. 135.
20 Ibid., p. 144.
21 Ibid., p. 141.
22 Wilkinson, 'From Rhodesia to Zimbabwe', pp. 226–7.
23 Van Velsen, 'Trends in African Nationalism in Southern Rhodesia'.
24 Astrow, *Zimbabwe: A Revolution That Lost Its Way?*, p. 137.
25 Frederikse, *None But Ourselves*, pp. v–vi.
26 Ibid., pp. 66–7, 72.
27 Ibid., pp. 131, 185–6.
28 Ibid., p. 90.
29 Ibid., p. vi.
30 Ibid., pp. 61–2, 217.
31 Ibid., p. 353, fn.11.
32 Ibid., pp. 301–2, 308.
33 Ranger, *Peasant Consciousness and Guerrilla War in Zimbabwe*, p. 12.
34 Ibid., p. 90, see also p. 137.
35 Ibid., p. 137.
36 Ibid., p. 14.
37 Ibid., pp. 24–5.
38 Ibid., p. 177.
39 Ibid., p. 189.
40 Ibid., p. 206, see also pp. 207–8.
41 Ibid., pp. 177, 179–80.
42 See tables in Kriger, 'The Zimbabwean War of Liberation: Struggles Within the Struggle'.
43 Ranger, *Peasant Consciousness and Guerrilla War in Zimbabwe*, p. 154.
44 Ibid., pp. 13–14, 189, 215–16.
45 Ibid., p. 190.
46 Ibid., p. 194.
47 Ibid., p. 212.
48 Ibid., pp. 190–3; see also Ranger and Hobsbawm (eds.), *The Invention of Tradition*.
49 Ranger, *Peasant Consciousness and Guerrilla War in Zimbabwe*, p. 215.
50 Thomas, 'Christianity, Politics, and the Manyika', pp. 175, 245–6; Murphree, *Christianity and the Shona*, pp. 153–8.
51 Ranger, *Peasant Consciousness and Guerrilla War in Zimbabwe*, p. 179.
52 See Kriger, 'The Zimbabwean War of Liberation', on typicality of Makoni as a case-study.
53 Ranger, *Peasant Consciousness and Guerrilla War in Zimbabwe*, p. xi.
54 Thomas, 'Christianity, Politics, and the Manyika', pp. 308–9.
55 Ibid., p. 185.
56 Ibid., pp. 174–96.
57 Moore, *Injustice. The Social Bases of Obedience and Revolt*, pp. 100–1, on interpreting unformed attitudes.
58 Ranger, *Peasant Consciousness and Guerrilla War in Zimbabwe*, p. 169.
59 E.g. Palley, 'Law and the Unequal Society', pp. 163–4.
60 Ranger, 'Bandits and Guerrillas: The Case of Zimbabwe', p. 381.

61 Ibid., p. 386.
62 Ibid., p. 386.
63 Ibid., p. 389.
64 Ibid., p. 385.
65 Lan, *Guns and Rain*, pp. 140–1.
66 Ibid., pp. 147–8.
67 Ibid., p. 149.
68 Ibid., p. 170.
69 Ibid., p. 207.
70 Ibid., p. 209.
71 Bourdillon, 'Guns and Rain: Taking Structural Analysis Too Far?'.
72 Lan, *Guns and Rain*, p. 125.
73 Ibid., pp. 147–8.
74 Ibid., p. 165.
75 Ibid., p. 170.
76 Ibid., pp. 171–2.
77 Ibid., p. 168.
78 Ibid., p. 168.
79 Ibid., p. 130.
80 Ibid., p. 132.
81 Ibid., p. 166.
82 Ibid., pp. 168, 200. Fry, *Spirits of Protest*, pp. 120–2, also describes the hunt for 'sell-outs' in Marandellas district in the 1960s after the banning of the nationalist parties and how the search for government informers among Africans was accompanied in the religious sphere by a new preoccupation with the public accusation of witches and sorcerers. Mediums who could detect witchcraft and sorcerers and help to remove the source of evil gained in popularity. Fry's main point is that religion became the outlet for politics when open political activity was suppressed by the government.
83 Bourdillon, 'Guns and Rain: Taking Structural Analysis Too Far?', pp. 270–1.
84 Ibid., p. 273.
85 Lan, *Guns and Rain*, p. 131.
86 Ibid., pp. 132–3.
87 Ibid., p. 132.
88 Ibid., p. 128.
89 Ibid., pp. 163, 167. Lan makes the following analogy between chiefs and guerrillas: 'The authority of chiefs had been based on allocation of land, the organisation of the ritual cycles of exchange and the administration of law. The guerrillas could not allocate individual plots to their followers but they did promise that land would be given them and these promises were underwritten with their lives. The old cycles of labour for the chiefs in return for access to land and security in famine which had been broken up by taxation, wage labour and the salaries paid to chiefs were replaced with new cycles. Food, labour and shelter were supplied to the guerrillas in return for guarantees of access to land, of an end to taxation and of restored political and economic autonomy.'
90 Ibid., p. 133.
91 Ibid., p. 133.
92 Caute, *Under the Skin*, p. 16.
93 Ranger, 'Review Article: The Historiography of Southern Rhodesia', p. 67.
94 Linden, *The Catholic Church and the Struggle in Zimbabwe*, p. 265; Maxey, 'The Armed Struggle in Zimbabwe and the Gaps in Our Knowledge', p. 11.
95 Frederikse, *None But Ourselves*, pp. 122–30, 183, 301–2; Cilliers, *Counter-Insurgency in Rhodesia*, pp. 49, 57; Weinrich, 'Strategic Resettlement in Rhodesia', p. 229; Shamuya-rira, 'A Revolutionary Situation in Southern Africa'. For similar arguments in the former

Portuguese colonies, see Jundanian, 'Resettlement Programs'; Bender, 'The Limits of Counterinsurgency. An African Case'.

96 Fanon, *Wretched of the Earth*, pp. 71–2.
97 Sarkesian (ed.), *Revolutionary Guerrilla Warfare*, pp. 507–32.
98 De Nardo, *The Power in Numbers*, pp. 232–4.
99 Ibid., p. 235.
100 E.g. Popkin, *The Rational Peasant*.
101 Amalrik, *Will the Soviet Union Survive Until 1984?*, pp. 21–2.
102 *Weekly Mail*, May 15–May 21, 1987, p. 7.
103 Bettelheim, *Surviving, and Other Essays*, pp. 48–83.
104 Mason, *The Birth of a Dilemma*, p. 193.
105 Moore, *Injustice: The Social Bases of Obedience and Revolt*, pp. 77–80.
106 Bettelheim, *Surviving, and Other Essays*, pp. 48–83.
107 Moore, *Injustice. The Social Bases of Obedience and Revolt*, pp. 113–16.
108 Da Cunha, *Rebellion in the Backlands*.
109 Olson, *The Logic of Collective Action. Public Goods and the Theory of Groups*, p. 2.
110 Circular No 308. 'Per Capita (Tuition) Grants to Private Schools', Ministry of Home Affairs, 1 November 1979. Ref.: CDV/10/17; Farmers' Licensing and Levy (Rate of Levy), (Cattle) (Suspension) Notice 1979; *Rhodesia Herald*, 25 May 1979; Circular No. 11 (Addendum H), Ministry of Home Affairs, 7 January 1980. Ref.: AGR/12/3.
111 *Rhodesia Herald*, 'African Councils Hit by Terrorism', 24 May 1977.
112 Letter from the district commissioner, Mrewa district to the provincial commissioner, Mashonaland East, 'Council Rates: Collection', 11 January 1977. Ref.: c/15; SBV 2/ UZUMB/77.
113 Brand, 'From Compound to Keep: On the Nature of Settler Control in Southern Rhodesia', p. 5.
114 Circular No. 300, Ministry of Internal Affairs, 'Martial Law', 27 December 1978. Ref.: x/364.
115 Letter from Mr Wyatt, Ministry of Home Affairs to the provincial commissioner, Matabeleland North, 7 December 1979. Ref.: c/22, Volume 6; see also letter from Mr Wyatt, Ministry of Home Affairs to Special Forces Headquarters, 29 November 1979. Ref.: CDV/12/14, Volume 2.
116 See Lan, *Guns and Rain*, pp. 162-3, on medium prohibitions on what guerrillas may eat.
117 Tickner, *The Food Problem*, p. 18.
118 Cilliers, *Counter-Insurgency in Rhodesia*, pp. 32, 158–9. Food control had first been introduced in the north-east on white farms. Farmers had to give food rations to their farm labourers to prevent them from having a surplus for the guerrillas. ZANLA guerrillas had turned to farm labourers for food because there was drought in the Tribal Trust Lands and the 'protected villages' made it more difficult for them to get food from villagers.
119 Circular No. 11 (Addendum 6), Ministry of Home Affairs, 'Dipping', 21 September 1979. Ref.: c/16; AGR/12/3; African Production and Marketing Development Fund. Second Report of the Select Committee on African Production and Marketing Development Fund Estimates, p. 36.
120 DEVAG agricultural extension assistants, interviews.
121 Gann and Henriksen, *The Struggle for Zimbabwe*, pp. 88–9; Keppel-Jones, *Rhodes and Rhodesia*, pp. 487–8, describes the easy access rebels had to food in 1896–7.
122 Gann, 'Rhodesia and the Prophets', p. 136; Ibid.; Shamuyarira, 'A Revolutionary Situation in Southern Africa', p. 160, describe how the lack of jungle, great swamps, or alpine massifs meant that the guerrillas were exposed to observation from the air. Johnson, 'Third Generation', compares Mao's guerrillas with the Vietminh and Vietcong. He argues that because the Chinese had no external bases, they were entirely

dependent on the civilian population for supplies whereas the Vietminh and Vietcong had external bases and therefore had to rely less on the population for support and used terror more. Access to external bases and support might reduce the extent of guerrilla dependence on local supplies, but guerrillas still need food daily and must either grow it locally or obtain it from locals. The Zimbabwean movements' external bases and supplies still left guerrillas dependent on local food supplies.

123 Davidson, *The People's Cause. A History of Guerrillas in Africa;* Clutterbuck, *Guerrillas and Terrorists.*

124 Notes by the Council Advisory Office, Mashonaland East Provincial Authority, on visit to councils in Mutoko district, 11–13 July 1979; Reports by the education adviser, Mashonaland East Regional Authority (renamed the Mashonaland East Provincial Authority) on visits to councils in Mutoko district, 16–19 February 1976, 28 July 1976. District files.

125 Reverend Nyanungu; Father Gibbs; interviews, 29 December 1981.

126 *Rhodesia Herald*, 13 March 1980; see Caute, *Under the Skin*, p. 253, for numbers of teachers and students affected by 1978.

127 African Farmers' Union Report, 13 February 1979. Ref.: Files of the Catholic Commission of Peace and Justice.

128 Ranger, *Peasant Consciousness and Guerrilla War in Zimbabwe*, highlights the dilemma of the African elite employed by the government but also required to contribute to the guerrillas.

129 Moore, 'The Contradictory Construction of Hegemony in Zimbabwe', p. 241.

130 Ibid., p. 238.

131 See Ranger, *Peasant Consciousness*; Lan, *Guns and Rain.*

132 Liebenow, 'The Military Factor in African Politics: A twenty-Five Year Perspective', pp. 135–6, discusses how colonial armies assigned Africans to posts outside their home areas; Ulam, *Stalin: The Man and his Era,* pp. 326–7, describes how Stalin used shock troops from the urban areas to collectivize agriculture. In the Zimbabwe literature on the war, Moorcraft and McLaughlin, *Chimurenga!,* pp. 127–8, and Weinrich, 'Strategic Resettlement in Rhodesia', pp. 211 and 219 claim that many guerrillas were sent to their home areas. This did happen on occasion, see interview with female fighter in Davies (compiler), *Third World-Second Sex*, Ch. 9.

133 Caute, *Under the Skin*, p. 386; see also Gann and Henriksen, *The Struggle for Zimbabwe*, p. 91; Moorcraft and McLaughlin, *Chimurenga!*, p. 222.

134 Linden, *The Catholic Church and the Struggle in Zimbabwe*, pp. 271–3.

135 Ibid., p. 271; Ranger, 'Holy Men and Rural Communities in Zimbabwe, 1970–1980'.

136 Murphree, *Christianity and the Shona.*

137 Hirschman, *Exit, Voice and Loyalty.*

138 Scott, *Weapons of the Weak.*

139 On 'everyday resistance' in labour conflict in colonial regimes, see Van Onselen, 'Worker Consciousness in Black Miners' and 'Black Workers in Central African Industry'; Phimister and Van Onselen, *Studies in the History of African Mine Labour in Colonial Zimbabwe*; Isaacman and Isaacman, 'Resistance and Collaboration in Southern and Central Africa, c. 1850–1920'. On 'everyday resistance' by slaves, see Lovejoy, 'Fugitive Slaves: Resistance to Slavery in the Sokoto Caliphate'; Bauer and Bauer, 'Day to Day Resistance to Slavery'. On peasant strategies of avoidance, see Adas, 'From Avoidance to Confrontation'; Scott, *Weapons of the Weak*. Hobsbawm, *Primitive Rebels* regards unorganized, individual acts of resistance as representing a lower level of political consciousness than formal, organized protest. Fanon, *Wretched of the Earth*, never uses the term 'everyday resistance' but regards the colonized's laziness in the workplace as 'the conscious sabotage of the colonial machine'. Like Hobsbawm, Fanon associates this type of resistance with a less mature political consciousness. For Fanon, colonial

situations demand armed struggle and hence only it can be regarded as reflecting mature political consciousness.

140 Frederickson and Lasch, 'Resistance to Slavery', argue that resistance requires conscious, organized action that reflects an understanding of the institutional structure as a whole. Individual acts, often violent, cannot be called resistance because they exhibit a misunderstanding of the nature of power. Orthodox Marxist critiques dismiss the endeavour to elicit the opinions of individuals or even an entire class about motives because what a class imagines to be its aim differs from what it is compelled to do because of the dynamic of class relations. See Cohen, 'Resistance and Hidden Forms of Consciousness Among African Workers'.

141 Easton, 'A Re-Assessment of The Concept of Popular Support'.

142 Edwards, *The Natural History of Revolution*.

143 Seager, 'Housing the Poor in an Urban Environment'.

144 Letter from district commissioner, Mtoko to M.D. bookstore, 1978. District files.

145 Ranger, *Peasant Consciousness and Guerrilla War in Zimbabwe*, p. 275.

146 Ibid., pp. 256, 263.

147 Thomas, 'Christianity, Politics, and the Manyika', p. 328.

148 Ibid., pp. 218, 220.

149 Gillis, *Youth and History*; Raedts, 'The Children's Crusade of 1212'.

5 Struggle in the struggle

1 Debray, *Revolution in the Revolution?*; Ramm, *The Marxism of Regis Debray*.

2 Moore, 'The Contradictory Construction of Hegemony in Zimbabwe'. See also Cliffe, 'Towards an Evaluation of the Zimbabwean Nationalist Movement'; Ranger, 'The Changing of the Old Guard: Robert Mugabe and the Revival of ZANU'; Saul, 'Transforming the Struggle in Zimbabwe'; Sithole, *Zimbabwe. Struggles Within the Struggle*; Martin and Johnson, *The Struggle for Zimbabwe*; Mandaza, 'The State and Politics in the Post-White Settler Colonial Situation' and 'Introduction: The Political Economy of Transition'; Astrow, *Zimbabwe: A Revolution That Lost Its Way?* See also Sylvester, 'Simultaneous Revolutions: The Zimbabwean Case'; Wasserman, 'The Economic Transition to Zimbabwe', p. 44, who accepts ZANU leaders' commitment to socialist transformation; Moorcraft and McLaughlin, *Chimurenga!*, pp. 77, 82, who argue that ZANU and ZAPU used guerrilla warfare to influence their bargaining position, to gain time to build up armies for use after independence, and to heal rifts within their parties.

3 Cliffe, Mpofu and Munslow, 'Nationalist Politics in Zimbabwe'.

4 Astrow, *Zimbabwe: A Revolution That Lost Its Way?*, p. 144.

5 Frederikse, *None But Ourselves*.

6 Ranger, *Peasant Consciousness and Guerrilla War in Zimbabwe*, p. 177.

7 Lan, *Guns and Rain*, pp. 147–8.

8 Ranger, *Peasant Consciousness and Guerrilla War in Zimbabwe*, e.g. pp. 43–4, 88, 90, 185–6, 256.

9 Ibid., pp. 48, 84.

10 Ibid., pp. 254, 275.

11 Ibid., p. 269; see also pp. 264–5.

12 Ibid., p. 272.

13 Ibid., p. 287; see also pp. 284–6.

14 Ibid., pp. 206–7.

15 Ibid., p. 292.

16 Ibid., p. 253.

17 Ibid., p. 208.

18 Ibid., pp. 211–12.

19 Ibid., pp. 15, 42, 48, 84.
20 Lan, *Guns and Rain*, p. 114.
21 Bourdillon, 'Guns and Rain: Taking Structural Analysis too Far?', p. 266.
22 Lan, *Guns and Rain*, p. 115.
23 Ibid., p. 115.
24 Bourdillon, 'Guns and Rain: Taking Structural Analysis too Far?', p. 206.
25 Lan, *Guns and Rain*, p. 14.
26 Ibid., p. 212.
27 Ibid., p. 212.
28 Ibid., p. 172.
29 Pongweni, *Songs that Won the Liberation War*.
30 Moore, 'Rebel Music'.
31 Sherman, 'Songs of the Chimurenga'.
32 England, 'A Political Economy of Black Female Labour', p. 136, fn. 85.
33 Ranger, 'Holy Men and Rural Communities in Zimbabwe, 1970–80'; Linden, *The Catholic Church and the Struggle in Zimbabwe*.
34 Sithole, 'The General Elections, 1979–1985'.
35 See discussion of gender conflicts.
36 See chapter 5.
37 See references to such literatures in Arendt, *On Violence*; Crenshaw, *Revolutionary Terrorism*.
38 Fanon, *Wretched of the Earth*.
39 Quoted in 'Why Youth Revolt', *New York Times*, 24 May 1989, opposite editorial page.
40 African Farmers' Union Report, 13 February 1979, Catholic Commission for Peace and Justice files, Harare, Zimbabwe.
41 For Zimbabwe, see Palmer, *Land and Racial Domination in Rhodesia*.
42 Yudelman, *Africans on the Land*, p. 99.
43 Weinrich, *African Farmers in Rhodesia*, ch. 4.
44 Ibid., pp. 305–7.
45 Phimister, 'Commodity Relations and Class Formation in the Zimbabwean Countryside, 1898–1920'.
46 This was the only case of alleged competition among individuals to be war chair.
47 Scott, *The Moral Economy of the Peasant*; Wolf, *Peasant Wars of the Twentieth Century*.
48 Mazrui, *Soldiers and Kinsmen in Uganda*, pp. 95–6, makes this point in the context of a study of why rural Ugandan men beat suspected thieves, sometimes to death, more readily than such civic violence occurs in the United States, and are also more likely to win community approval.
49 Lapchick and Urdang, *Oppression and Resistance*; Weiss, *The Women of Zimbabwe*; Davies (compiler), *Third World-Second Sex*; Weinrich, *Women and Racial Discrimination in Rhodesia*; England, 'A Political Economy of Black Female Labour'; Women's Liberation in the Zimbabwean Revolution. Materials from the ZANU Women's Seminar.
50 Speech by Naomi Nhiwatiwa, p. 24, in Women's Liberation in the Zimbabwean Revolution. Materials from the ZANU Women's Seminar; Sally Mugabe's estimate appears in Lapchick and Urdang, *Oppression and Resistance*, p. 101.
51 Weiss, *The Women of Zimbabwe*, p. 106.
52 Davies (compiler), *Third World-Second Sex*.
53 Mugabe's speech in Women's Liberation in the Zimbabwean Revolution. Materials from the ZANU Women's Seminar, p. 15.
54 Mutunhu, 'Nehanda of Zimbabwe (Rhodesia): The Story of A Woman Liberation Leader and Fighter', p. 59.
55 Nhiwatiwa's speech in Women's Liberation in the Zimbabwean Revolution. Materials from the ZANU Women's Seminar, p. 32.

56 *Southern Africa*, July/August, 1979, p. 9.
57 Weiss. *The Women of Zimbabwe*, p. 95.
58 Ibid., pp. 94–5.
59 Davies (compiler), *Third World-Second Sex*, p. 105.
60 Weinrich, *Women and Racial Discrimination in Rhodesia*, pp. 136–7.
61 Lan, *Guns and Rain*, pp. 212–13.
62 Davies (compiler), *Third World-Second Sex*, p. 80; Weiss, *The Women of Zimbabwe*, pp. 11, 50, 119, 136, 140; Weinrich, *Women and Racial Discrimination in Rhodesia*, p. 114; see also Marechera, *The House of Hunger*, p. 50.
63 Cheater, *Idioms of Accumulation*, pp. 55–6; Cheater, 'Women and Their Participation in Commercial Agricultural Production: The Case of Medium-Scale Freehold in Zimbabwe', pp. 370–1.
64 Letter from district commissioner, Mr J.F. Saunders to provincial commissioner, Mashonaland East, 16 September 1976. Ref.: per 5/hm/mtk.
65 Holleman, *African Interlude*, pp. 234–6; Holleman, 'Accommodating the Spirit Amongst Some Northeastern Shona Tribes'; Berlyn, 'The Keeper of the Spirit of Nehoreka'; Morkel, 'The Mondoro or Ancestral Spirit of the Wabuja, Mtoko'; Simmonds, 'Charewa, Voice of the Rain God', pp. 60–3. For a somewhat different but less detailed account than Holleman, *African Interlude*, see Beach, *The Shona and Zimbabwe 900–1850*, p. 165.
66 Interviews with the four councillors, September, 1982.
67 Letter from Mr R. Boell, district commissioner, Mtoko district to the Secretary for Internal Affairs, 7 May 1974. Ref.: per 5/1/74; Kaschula, B.P., Delineation Officer, Delineation Report, November 1965, p. 6.
68 Beach, *The Shona and Zimbabwe 900–1850*, p. 175.
69 Chief Chimoyo, Ref.: per 5.
70 Letter from Mr J. Markram, district commissioner, Mtoko district to provincial commissioner, Mashonaland East, 11 January 1977. Ref.: per 5/hm/mtk.
71 Letter from Mr B.H. Lucas, district commissioner, Mtoko district to provincial commissioner, Mashonaland East, 4 April 1977. Ref.: per 5/hm/mtk.
72 Chabal, *Amilcar Cabral*, p. 119; Barry Munslow's study of the revolution in Mozambique raises some question about the empirical accuracy, at least for Mozambique, of Chabal's description of committees being composed of 'traditional' authorities. Munslow's characterization of the role of chiefs in the initial mobilization by FRELIMO party substantiates Chabal's discussion. Munslow notes that however much the authority of chiefs had been weakened by colonial power, chiefs still held the allegiance of the people. To win the support of chiefs was to ensure the support of the people. At least in the beginning, chiefs became chairmen of committees once the colonial power left an area (Munslow, *Mozambique: The Revolution and its Origins*, pp. 90–1). But later, chiefs were replaced as FRELIMO's socialist ideology became influential (Munslow, Ibid., pp. 145–6). Munslow's study of the revolutionary period depends heavily on FRELIMO sources so that it reads more as an analysis of FRELIMO's ideology and strategies than their effectiveness in mobilizing peasants.
73 Wolf, 'Peasants and Political Mobilization: Introduction'.
74 Olson, *The Logic of Collective Action*.
75 Moore, 'The Contradictory Construction of Hegemony in Zimbabwe', p. 75, citing D.N. Beach, *Zimbabwe Before 1900* (Gweru, Zimbabwe, Mambo Press, 1984').
76 Cliffe and Stoneman, *Zimbabwe. Politics, Economics and Society*, p. 42.
77 Wallace, 'Psychological Preparations for War', p. 177.
78 Fanon, *Wretched of the Earth*, pp. 307–8.

6 Legacies of the war for peasants

1 Cliffe, 'Towards an Evaluation of the Zimbabwean Nationalist Movement'; Saul, 'Transforming the Struggle in Zimbabwe'; Saul, 'Zimbabwe: The Next Round'; see Cliffe and Stoneman, *Zimbabwe. Politics, Economics and Society*, pp. 3–4.
2 Ranger, *Peasant Consciousness and Guerrilla War in Zimbabwe*, p. 290.
3 Ibid., p. 295.
4 Ibid., pp. 299, 303–9.
5 Ibid., p. 319.
6 Ibid., p. 325.
7 Cliffe, Mpofu and Munslow, 'Nationalist Politics in Zimbabwe: The 1980 Elections and Beyond', e.g. p. 66. Their article cites primarily ranking party officials, the rural elite (teachers, businessmen), and high-ranking guerrillas; while they interview peasants their voices are barely audible.
8 Lan, *Guns and Rain*, pp. 209, 211–12.
9 Ibid., pp. 226–7.
10 Ibid., p. 210.
11 Ibid., p. 210.
12 Ranger, *Peasant Consciousness and Guerrilla War in Zimbabwe*, pp. 291–2, 296.
13 The state versus the party chairman, sentenced on January 27 1981, Mutoko magistrate's court. Court files.
14 Mandaza, 'The State and Politics in the Post-White Settler Colonial Situation', p. 42.
15 Letter from acting district commissioner, Mutoko to provincial commissioner, Mashonaland East, 27 June 1980. File: SBV2/GEN/80; Minutes of commission meetings, 11 June and 27 June 1980.
16 Report from principal planning officer on local government elections, undated, district files.
17 Letter from Acting Provincial Commissioner, Manicaland to Secretary for District Administration, 'Formation of District Councils: Chipinga and Makoni Districts', 20 June 1980. File Ref.: SBV/2/1.
18 Letter from district commissioner, Wedza to provincial commissioner, Mashonaland East, 26 June 1980.
19 Zimbabwe African National Union (Patriotic Front), Mashonaland Central Province, Inter-district Meeting, 30 January 1982.
20 Fanon, *Wretched of the Earth*, p. 182.
21 Mataka's evidence at Mutoko magistrate's court. The case of Mataka, 10 May 1982.
22 Cliffe and Stoneman, *Zimbabwe. Politics, Economics and Society*, pp. 103, 111.
23 Ibid., p. 111.
24 Lan, *Guns and Rain*, pp. 220–1.
25 Ranger, *Peasant Consciousness and Guerrilla War in Zimbabwe*, p. 319.
26 Weitzer, 'In Search of Regime Security: Zimbabwe Since Independence'; Weitzer, 'The Internal Security State'. Cliffe and Stoneman, *Zimbabwe. Politics, Economics and Society*, misrepresent Weitzer's argument.
27 Kaarsholm, 'Quiet After the Storm'; Bratton, 'Development in Zimbabwe: Strategy and Tactics'.
28 Callinicos, *Southern Africa After Zimbabwe*; Astrow, *Zimbabwe: A Revolution That Lost Its Way?*
29 Mandaza, 'The State and Politics in the Post-White Settler Colonial Situation', pp. 62–3.
30 Ibid. and Mandaza, 'Introduction' to *The Political Economy of Transition*.
31 Cliffe and Stoneman, *Zimbabwe. Politics, Economics and Society*.
32 Hodder-Williams, 'Political Scenarios and their Economic Implications', p. 60.

33 Zimbabwe African National Union (Patriotic Front), Mashonaland Central Province, Inter-District meeting, 30 January 1982.

34 Ministry of Local Government and Housing, 'Memorandum on Chiefs and Headmen', prepared for the Minister by J.D. White, 17 March 1982. File Ref.: CHK/14.

35 Ibid.

36 Cliffe and Stoneman, *Zimbabwe. Politics, Economics and Society*, p. 189; Weiss, *The Women of Zimbabwe*, p. 97.

37 Report on the National Disability Survey of Zimbabwe. Produced by the Ministry of Labour and Social Services, in association with UNICEF. Government Printer, Harare, 1981, p. 26.

38 E.g. Else and Ziswa, 'The Impact of Non-Governmental Organizations (NGOs) on Collective Cooperatives in Zimbabwe'.

39 Weitzer, 'Zimbabwe: Fortifying One-Party Rule'.

40 Clerks at Social Service office, Mutoko.

41 Anthony Lewis, *New York Times*, 'Knowledge is Power', opposite editorial, 12 January 1989. These figures may slightly overstate the gains since independence because during the war years the numbers of schools, pupils, and teachers were lowered by school closures.

42 Cliffe and Stoneman, *Zimbabwe. Politics, Economics and Society*, pp. 68, 126–7, 172.

43 Ibid., pp. 133–4.

44 Interview with Mr Bowen-Davies, Acting Director of the District Development Fund, 28 December 1981. The Fund, responsible for rural reconstruction, absorbed the remaining district commissioners when the government appointed African district administrators to replace them.

45 Ranger, *Peasant Consciousness and Guerrilla War in Zimbabwe*, e.g. pp. 293, 295–6, 303–5, 310–11.

46 Letter from district commissioner, Mutoko to provincial commissioner, Mashonaland East, 27 June 1980. File Ref.: SBV.2/GEN/80.

47 Letter from district commissioner, Wedza to provincial commissioner, Mashonaland East, 26 June 1980. File Ref.: SBV/2/GEN/80.

48 Letter from district commissioner, Chilimanzi to provincial commissioner, Midlands, 13 May 1980. File Ref.: c/22 Vol. VI.

49 Letter from district commissioner, Selukwe to provincial commissioner, Midlands, 30 September 1980. File Ref.: SBV.2/80.

50 Letter from acting district commissioner, Mutoko district to provincial commissioner, Mashonaland East, 27 June 1980. File Ref.: SBV.2/GEN/80. Minutes of commission meetings, 11 June 1980 and 27 June 1980.

51 Letters from district commissioner, Selukwe to provincial commissioner, Midlands, 30 September 1980. File Ref.: SBV.2/80; district commission file on Beitbridge district, Matabeleland South Province.

52 Report by district commissioner, Urungwe district, Mashonaland West, on its district commission.

53 Report by district commissioner, Gwanda district, Matabeleland South, on its district commisssion.

54 Interviews with agricultural staff.

55 Cliffe and Stoneman, *Zimbabwe. Politics, Economics and Society*, pp. 133–4.

56 Estimates obtained from Director of Social Services, Department of Social Services, 27 October 1981.

57 Mr Nyirenda, United Nations High Commission for Refugees, interview, 21 October 1981; Mr Ntunde, Highfields Social Services office, interview; Mr Billing, DEVAG, interview, 3 February 1982. DEVAG was responsible for overall administration of the rehabilitation programmes.

58 Mr Billing, DEVAG, interview, 3 February 1982; Department of Social Services, interview, 28 April 1982; official involved in food progamme, interview 10 September 1981; Department of Agricultural Development. Relief of Distress and Rehabilitation Through Agriculture, 1980–1. DEVAG Programme, Progress Report to 30 April 1981.

59 Bullock, *The Mashona*, pp. 144–8; Beach, 'Chimurenga: The Shona Rising of 1896–97', p. 395; Lan, *Guns and Rain*, p. 166.

60 Lan, *Guns and Rain*, p. 221.

61 Letter from acting district commissioner, M. Sumner, Mutoko district to provincial commissioner, Mashonaland East, 3 December 1980. File Ref.: PER 5/GEN.

62 Circular Minute No.1/1981. 'Statement by Minister on Chieftainships', Division of District Administration, 9 January 1981. Press statement issued on 5 January 1981. File Ref.: CHK/6.

63 *The Herald*, 'Mugabe Tells Chiefs to Get Involved in New Plans', 3 Oct 1980; *Sunday Mail*, 'Support PM at Historic Indaba', 27 July 1980; Mugabe addressed chiefs from Matabeleland and the Midlands on 26 July 1980, and chiefs from Mashonaland, Manicaland, and Midlands at Seke on 2 Oct 1980. Each time he reassured them that they had a role to play.

64 *The Herald*, 5 September 1980, 'Chiefs Still Have Role – Zvobgo'.

65 *The Herald*, 18 January 1982 'Zvobgo Places Chiwashira in Traditional Role'. See also *The Herald*, 15 Feb 1982 'Chiefs' Land Powers Will Go – Zvobgo'.

66 Reports of commissions, Ministry of Local Government and Housing.

67 Division of District Administration, Memorandum: 'Inclusion of Chiefs in District Councils', August 1980. File Ref.: C/22. The Attorney-General's opinion was that it was illegal to have ex officio members who did not have a vote. Letter from R.Y. Phillips for Attorney-General, to Secretary for District Administration, 'District Councils Act (ch. 231): Voting at Council Meeting', 18 November 1980.

68 Minutes of 3rd meeting of Mashonaland East Provincial Authority, 4 June 1981.

69 Made and Whande, 'Women in Southern Africa: A Note on the Zimbabwean "Success Story"', p. 27.

70 Seidman, 'Women in Zimbabwe: Postindependence Struggles': Made and Whande, 'Women in Southern Africa', p. 27.

Appendix

Field research

1 Bratton, *Beyond Community Development*; Cliffe, Mpofu and Munslow, 'Nationalist Politics in Zimbabwe: The 1980 Elections and Beyond'; Gregory, 'Zimbabwe 1980: Politicisation Through Armed Struggle and Electoral Mobilisation'; Saul, 'Zimbabwe: The Next Round'. It is a general theme in the literature on people's war. See ch. 6.

2 Caute, *Under the Skin*, evokes extremely vividly the European farm communities and their war experiences.

3 Annual Report, Mtoko, 1934; Gelfand, 'Migration of African Labourers in Rhodesia and Nyasaland (1890–1914)', p. 296; Clarke, *Contract Workers and Underdevelopment in Rhodesia*, p. 93.

4 Murphree, *Christianity and the Shona*, p. 156, has an interesting account of the impact his research assistants had on the relationship of a mission school and the nationalists in Charewa.

5 Rosaldo, 'From the Door of his Tent: The field worker and the Inquisitor', p. 92.

Bibliography

Abraham, D.P. 'The Roles of "Chaminuka" and the Mhondoro-Cults in Shona Political History' in Eric Stokes and Richard Brown (eds.), *The Zambesian Past. Studies in Central African History* (Manchester University Press, 1966), 28–46

Adams, Paul L. 'The Social Psychiatry of Frantz Fanon', *American Journal of Psychiatry* 127, 6 (December 1970), 809–814

Adas, Michael. *Prophets of Rebellion: Millenerian Protest Movements against the European Colonial Order* (Chapel Hill, North Carolina, University of North Carolina, 1979)
  'From Avoidance to Confrontation. Peasant Protest in Precolonial and Colonial Southeast Asia', *Comparative Studies in Society and History* 23, 2 (1981), 217–47

Adelman, Jonathan. *Revolution, Armies, and War. A Political History* (Colorado, Lynne Rienner Publishers, Inc., 1985)

Africa Research Group. 'Southern Africa: A Smuggled Account from a Guerrilla Fighter', *Ramparts* 8, 4 (October 1969), 8–12

Alavi, Hamza. 'Peasants and Revolution', *The Socialist Register* (1965), 241–77

Almond, Gabriel A. and Sydney Verba (eds.), *The Civic Culture Revisited: An Analytic Study* (Boston, Massachusetts, Little, Brown, 1980)

Alperin, J. Robert. 'The Distribution of Power and the (June 1979) Zimbabwe Rhodesia Constitution', *Journal of Southern African Studies* 5, 1 (January 1980), 41–54

Amalrik, Andrei. *Will the Soviet Union Survive Until 1984?* (New York, Harper & Row, 1970)

Arendt, Hannah. *On Violence* (New York, Harcourt Brace & World, 1970)

Arrighi, G. 'Labour Supplies in Historical Perspective: A Study of the Proletarianization of the African Peasantry in Rhodesia', *Journal of Development Studies* 6 (1970), 197–234

Ashton, Hugh. 'From Spears to Ploughshares: Changes in the Political Structures of the Amandebele' in William A. Shack and Percy Cohen (eds.), *Politics in Leadership. A Comparative Perspective* (Oxford, Clarendon Press, 1979)

Astrow, Andre. *Zimbabwe: A Revolution That Lost Its Way?* (London, Zed Press, 1983)

Barber, James. 'Zimbabwe's Southern African Setting', *Journal of Commonwealth and Comparative Politics* 18, 1 (March 1980), 69–84

Bauer, R. and A. Bauer. 'Day to Day Resistance to Slavery', *Journal of Negro History* 27 (1942), 388–419

Bayles, Michael D. 'A Concept of Coercion' in J. Roland Pennock and John W. Chapman, *Coercion*, Vol. 14 of *Nomos* (Chicago, Aldine, 1972), 16–29

Baylies, Carolyn. 'Imperialism and Settler Capital: Friends or Foes?', *Review of African Political Economy* 18 (1980), 116–26

Beach, D.N. 'The Initial Impact of Christianity on the Shona. The Protestants and The Southern Shona' in Anthony J. Dachs (ed.), *Christianity South of the Zambezi* (Gwelo, Rhodesia, Mambo Press, 1973), Vol. 1, 25–40.

Bibliography

'"Chimurenga": The Shona Rising of 1896–97', *Journal of African History* 20, 3 (1979), 395–420

The Shona and Zimbabwe 900–1850. An Outline of Shona History (New York, Africana Publishing Company, 1980)

Zimbabwe Before 1900 (Gweru, Zimbabwe, Mambo Press, 1984)

Bender, Gerald J. 'The Limits of Counterinsurgency. An African Case', *Comparative Politics* 4 (April 1972), 331–60

Berlyn, Phillipa. 'The Keeper of the Spirit of Nehoreka', *NADA* 10, 4 (1972)

Berman, Bruce J. 'Bureaucracy and Incumbent Violence: Colonial Administration and the Origins of the "Mau Mau" Emergency in Kenya', *British Journal of Political Science* 6 (1976), 143–75

Bettelheim, Bruno. *Surviving, and Other Essays* (New York, Knopf, 1979)

Bienen, Henry. *Violence and Social Change. A Review of Current Literature* (The University of Chicago Press, 1968)

Biermann, Werner and Reinhart Kossler. 'The Settler Mode of Production: The Rhodesian Case', *Review of African Political Economy* 18 (1980), 106–16

Bilha, H.H.K. *Trade and Politics in a Shona Kingdom* (London, Longman, 1982)

Birmingham, David and Phyllis Martin (eds.), *History of Central Africa*, Vol. 2 (London, Longman, 1983)

Birmingham, David and Terence Ranger. 'Settlers and Liberators in the South' in Birmingham and Martin (eds.), *History of Central Africa*, Vol. 2, 336–82

Blok, Anton. 'The Peasant and The Brigand: Social Banditry Reconsidered', *Comparative Studies in Society and History* 14 (1972), 494–503

Bourdillon, M.F.C. 'Is "Customary Law" Customary?', *NADA* 11, 2 (1975)

The Shona Peoples. An Ethnography of the Contemporary Shona, with Special Reference to their Religion (Gwelo, Rhodesia, Mambo Press, 1976)

'Religion and Ethics in Korekore Society', *Journal of Religion in Africa* 10 (1979), 81–94

'Suggestions of Bureaucracy in Korekore Religion: Putting the Ethnography Straight', *Zambezia* 9, 2 (1981), 119–36

'Freedom and Constraint among Shona Spirit Mediums' in J. Davis (ed.) *Religious Organization and Religious Experience* (London, Academic Press, 1982), 181–94

'Guns and Rain: Taking Structural Analysis Too Far?', review article, *Africa* 57, 2 (1987), 263–74

Brand, Coenrad M. 'Race and Politics in Rhodesian Trade Unions', *African Perspectives* 1 (1976), 55–80

'From Compound to Keep: On the Nature of Settler Control in Southern Rhodesia', paper read to 9th World Congress on Sociology, Uppsala, Sweden, August 1978

Bratton, Michael. *Beyond Community Development: The Political Economy of Rural Administration in Zimbabwe.* From Rhodesia to Zimbabwe. Mambo Occasional Paper No. 6. (Catholic Institute for International Relations, 1978)

'Settler State, Guerrilla War, and Rural Underdevelopment in Rhodesia', *Rural Africana* 4–5 (Spring–Fall 1979), 115–29

'The Public Service and Public Policy in Zimbabwe: Opportunities and Constraints' in *Symposium on Zimbabwe's Economic Prospects* (Seven Springs Centre, Mt. Kisco, New York, February, 1980)

'Development in Zimbabwe: Strategy and Tactics', *Journal of Modern African Studies* 19, 3 (1981), 447–75

Bullock, Charles. *The Mashona* (Cape Town, Juta and Co., 1928)

Burchett, Wilfred. *Southern Africa Stands Up. The Revolutions in Angola, Mozambique, Zimbabwe, Namibia and South Africa* (New York, Urizen Books, 1978)

Burton, Anthony. *Revolutionary Violence. The Theories* (New York, Crane, Russak & Co. Inc., 1978)

278

Callinicos, Alec. *Southern Africa After Zimbabwe* (London, Pluto Press, 1981)

Carr, Edward Hallett. *Studies in Revolution* (London, MacMillan & Co. Ltd, 1950)

Caute, David. *Under the Skin. The Death of White Rhodesia* (London, Allen Lane, 1983)

Chabal, Patrick. *Amilcar Cabral: Revolutionary Leadership and People's War* (Cambridge University Press, 1983)

'People's War, State Formation and Revolution in Africa: A Comparative Analysis of Mozambique, Guinea-Bissau, and Angola' in Nelson Kasfir (ed.), *State and Class in Africa* (London, Cass and Co., 1984), 104–25

Chaliand, Gerard. *Revolution in the Third World. Myths and Prospects* (New York, The Viking Press, 1977)

Chanaiwa, D. 'African Initiatives and Resistance in Southern Africa' in A. Boahen (ed.), *Africa Under Colonial Domination 1880–1935*, vol. 2. UNESCO. *General History of Africa.* (London, Heinemann, 1985), 194–220

Chater, Patricia. *Caught in the Crossfire* (Harare, Zimbabwe Publishing House, 1985)

Chavunduka, G.L. 'Social Change in a Shona Ward', Department of Sociology. Occasional Paper No. 4. University of Rhodesia, 1970.

'Polygyny among Urban Shona and Ndebele Christians. A Case Study', *NADA. The Rhodesian Ministry of Internal Affairs Annual* (1979), 10–20

Cheater, Angela P. 'Women and Their Participation in Commercial Agricultural Production: The Case of Medium-Scale Freehold in Zimbabwe', *Development and Change* (Sage) 12 (1981), 349–77

'Effects of the Liberation War in One Commercial Farming Area in Zimbabwe', Department of Sociology, University of Zimbabwe, unpublished paper, 1981/2

Idioms of Accumulation. Rural Development and Class Formation among Freeholders in Zimbabwe (Gweru, Zimbabwe, Mambo Press, 1984)

Chidzero, B. and K. Moyana. 'The Structure of the Zimbabwean Economy and Future Manpower Implications', *Rural Africana* 4–5 (Spring–Fall, 1979), 1–15

Cilliers, J.K. *Counter-Insurgency in Rhodesia* (London, Croom Helm, 1985)

Clarence-Smith, W.G. 'For Braudel: A Note on the Ecoles Des Annales and The Historiography of Africa', *History of Africa* 4 (1977), 275–81

Clark, Margaret. 'The Cultural Patterns of Risk-Seeking Behaviour' in Mary LeCron Foster and Robert A. Rubinstein (eds.), *Peace and War: Cross-Cultural Perspectives* (New Brunswick, New Jersey, Transaction Books, 1986)

Clarke, Duncan G. 'Economic and Political Aspects of the Rhodesian Franchise', *Journal of Commonwealth Political Science* 11 (1973), 67–78

Contract Workers and Underdevelopment in Rhodesia. Mambo Occasional Papers, Socioeconomic Series No. 3 (Gwelo, Rhodesia, Mambo Press, 1974)

Domestic Workers in Rhodesia. The Economics of Masters and Servants. Mambo Occasional Papers, Socioeconomic Series No.1 (Gwelo, Rhodesia, Mambo Press, 1974)

Cliffe, Lionel. 'Towards An Evaluation of the Zimbabwean Nationalist Movement', Political Studies Association of the United Kingdom, Annual Conference, University of Exeter, 31 March–2 April 1980

Cliffe, Lionel, Joshua Mpofu, and Barry Munslow. 'Nationalist Politics in Zimbabwe: The 1980 Elections and Beyond', *Review of African Political Economy* 18 (May–August 1980), 44–67

Cliffe, Lionel and Colin Stoneman. *Zimbabwe. Politics, Economics and Society* (New York, Pinter Publisher, 1989)

Clifford, James and George Marcus (eds.), *Writing Culture: The Poetics and Politics of Ethnography* (University of California Press, 1986)

Clutterbuck, Richard. *Guerrillas and Terrorists* (Ohio University Press, 1980)

Conflict and Violence in Singapore and Malaysia, 1945–1983 (Boulder, Colorado, West-view Press, 1985)

Bibliography

Cobbing, Julian. 'The Absent Priesthood: Another Look At The Rhodesian Risings Of 1896–1897', *Journal of African History* 18, 1 (1977), 61–84

Cohen, Barry. 'The War in Rhodesia: A Dissenter's View', *African Affairs* 76 (October 1977), 483–94

Cohen, Robin. 'Resistance and Hidden Forms of Consciousness among African Workers' in Hazel Johnson, Henry Bernstein, Raul Hernan Ampuero and Ben Crow (eds.), *Third World Lives of Struggle* (London, Heinemann Educational Books in association with The Open University, 1982)

Cokorinos, Lee. 'The Political Economy of State and Party Formation in Zimbabwe' in Michael Schatzberg (ed.), *The Political Economy of Zimbabwe* (New York, Praeger, 1984), 8–54

Connolly, William E. 'On "Interests" in Politics', *Politics and Society* 2 (1972), 459–77

Cooper, Frederick. 'Peasants, Capitalists and Historians: A Review Article', *Journal of Southern African Studies* 7, 2 (1981), 284–314

Coser, Lewis A. 'The Sources of Revolt', *New York Times Book Review* (21 October 1979)

Crenshaw, Martha. *Revolutionary Terrorism: The FLN in Algeria, 1954–1962* (Stanford, California, Hoover Institution Press, 1978)

(ed.), *Terrorism, Legitimacy and Power: The Consequences of Political Violence* (Middletown, Connecticut, Wesleyan University Press, 1983)

Crenson, Matthew A. 'The Private Stake in Public Goods: Overcoming the Illogic of Collective Action', *Policy Sciences* (1987)

Cuerden, Michael. 'Human Development Opportunities in Community Development: The Gutu Exploratory Case Study', unpublished Bachelor of Education thesis, University of Rhodesia, 1977

Cumings, Bruce. 'Interest and Ideology in the Study of Agrarian Politics', *Politics and Society* 10, 4 (1981), 467–95

Da Cunha, Euclides. *Rebellion in the Backlands*, translated and with an introduction by Samuel Putnam (University of Chicago Press, 1944)

Davidson, A.B., A. Isaacman, and R. Pelissier. 'Politics and Nationalism in Central and Southern Africa, 1919–1935' in A. Boahen (ed.), *Africa Under Colonial Domination 1880–1935*, vol. 2. Unesco. *General History of Africa* (London, Heinemann, 1985), 673–711

Davidson, Basil. *The Liberation of Guine. Aspects of an African Revolution* (Harmondsworth, England, Penguin, 1969)

'African Peasants and Revolution', *Journal of Peasant Studies* 13 (April 1974), 269–90

The People's Cause. A History of Guerillas in Africa (London, Longman, 1981)

Davies, Miranda, compiler. *Third World-Second Sex. Women's Struggles and National Liberation. Third World Women Speak Out* (London, Zed Press, 1983), Ch. 6 and Ch. 9

Day, John. 'Southern Rhodesian African Nationalists and the 1961 Constitution', *Journal of Modern African Studies* 7, 2 (1969), 221–47

'The Creation of Political Myths: African Nationalism in Southern Rhodesia', *Journal of Southern African Studies* 11, 1 (October 1975), 52–65

'The Insignificance of Tribe in the African Politics of Zimbabwe Rhodesia', *Journal of Commonwealth and Comparative Politics* 18, 1 (March 1980), 85–109

De Braganca, Aquino and Immanuel Wallerstein (eds.), *The African Liberation Reader* (London, Zed Press, 1982)

Debray, Regis. *Revolution in the Revolution? Armed Struggle and Political Struggle in Latin America* (New York, Grove Press, Inc., 1967)

Deiner, John, D. 'Geurrilla [*sic*] Border Sanctuaries and Counterinsurgent Warfare', *The Army Quarterly* 109, 2 (April 1979), 162–79

Delap, Mick. 'The April 1979 Elections in Zimbabwe-Rhodesia', *African Affairs* 78, 313 (October 1979), 431–8

De Nardo, James. *Power in Numbers. The Political Strategy of Protest and Rebellion* (Princeton University Press, 1985)

Denitch, Bogdan. 'Violence and Social Change in the Yugoslav Revolution. Lessons for the Third World?' *Comparative Politics* (April 1976), 465–78

Denoon, Donald and Adam Kuper. 'Nationalist Historians in Search of A Nation. The New Historiography in Dar es Salaam', *African Affairs* 69 (1970), 329–49

Duggan, William, R. 'The Native Land Husbandry Act of 1951 and the Rural African Middle Class of Southern Rhodesia', *African Affairs* 79, 315 (April 1980), 227–39

Duncanson, Dennis. '"Symbiotic Insurgency" in Vietnam Ten Years After', *International Affairs* 54, 4 (October 1978), 589–601

Dunn, John. *Modern Revolutions: An Introduction to the Analysis of a Political Phenomenon* (Cambridge University Press, 1972)

Easton, David. 'A Re-Assessment of the Concept of Popular Support', *British Journal of Political Science* 5 (1975), 435–57

Edwards, Lyford P. *The Natural History of Revolution* (University of Chicago Press, 1970)

Ekpo, Smart A. 'Book Review', *Journal of Modern African Studies* 21, 2 (1983), 349–52

Else, John and Valentine T. Ziswa. 'The Impact of Non-Governmental Organizations (NGOs) on Collective Cooperatives in Zimbabwe', unpublished paper, African Studies Association, Denver, Colorado, November 1987.

Emmanuel, Arghiri. 'White-Settler Colonialism and the Myth of Investment Imperialism', *New Left Review* 73 (May–June 1972)

England, Kersten. 'A Political Economy of Black Female Labour in Zimbabwe, 1900–1980', unpublished B.A. thesis, School of History, University of Manchester, 1982

Fall, Bernard. *Street Without Joy* (Pennsylvania, The Stackpole Company, 1964)

Fanon, Frantz. *A Dying Colonialism*, translated from French by Haakon Chevalier (New York, Grove Press, Inc., 1959)

Black Skins. White Masks (New York, Grove Press, 1967)

Wretched of the Earth (New York, Grove Press, 1982)

Flower, Ken. *Serving Secretly: An Intelligence Chief on Record: Rhodesia into Zimbabwe, 1964 to 1981* (London, J. Murray, 1987)

Floyd, Barry Neil. 'Changing Patterns of African Land Use in Southern Rhodesia', unpublished Ph.D., Syracuse University, 1959

Frederikse, Julie. *None But Ourselves. Masses vs. Media in the Making of Zimbabwe* (Harmondsworth, England, Penguin, 1984)

Frederickson, George M. and Christopher Lasch. 'Resistance to Slavery', *Civil War History* 13 (1967)

Friedland, William with Amy Barton, Bruce Dancis, Michael Torkind and Michael Spiro. *Revolutionary Theory* (Totowa, New Jersey, Allanheld, Osmun and Co. Publishers, Inc., 1982)

Fry, Peter. *Spirits of Protest. Spirit-mediums and the Articulation of Consensus Among the Zezuru of Southern Rhodesia* (Cambridge University Press, 1976)

Gann, L.H. *A History of Southern Rhodesia. Early Days to 1934* (New York, Humanities Press, 1965)

'Rhodesia and the Prophets', *African Affairs* 71 (April 1972), 125–43

'Prospects for White Resistance', *Africa Report* (September–October 1977), 9–20

Gann, Lewis H. and Thomas H. Henriksen. *The Struggle for Zimbabwe. Battle in the Bush.* (New York, Praeger, 1981)

Garbett, G. Kingsley. 'Religious Aspects of Political Succession Among the Valley Korekore (N. Shona)' in Eric Stokes and Richard Brown (eds.), *The Zambesian Past. Studies in Central African History* (Manchester University Press, 1966), 137–70

'The Rhodesian Chief's Dilemma: Government Officer or Tribal Leader?', *Race and Class* 8, 2 (1966), 113–28

Bibliography

'Prestige, Status, and Power In A Modern Valley Korekore Chiefdom, Rhodesia', *Africa* 37 (1967), 307–26

'Disparate Regional Cults and a Unitary Ritual Field in Zimbabwe' in R.P. Werbner (ed.), *Regional Cults* (New York, Academic Press, 1977), 55–92

'From Conquerors to Autocthons: Structural Transformation in Korekore Regional Cults', Conference in Culture and Consciousness in Southern Africa, Manchester University, September 1986

Garlake, P.S. 'The Mashona Rebellion East of Salisbury', *Rhodesiana* 14 (1966), 1–11

Gates, John, M. 'Toward a History of Revolution', *Comparative Studies in Society and History* 28 (July 1986), 535–44

Geiger, Susan. 'Women in Nationalist Struggle: TANU Activists in Dar es Salaam', *International Journal of African Historical Studies* 20, 1 (1987), 1–26

Gelfand, Michael. 'Migration of African Labourers in Rhodesia and Nyasaland (1890–1914)', *The Central African Journal of Medicine* 7, 8 (August 1961), 293–300

Gillin, Donald. 'Review Article: Peasant Nationalism in the History of Chinese Communism', *Journal of Asian Studies* 23 (February 1964), 269–89

Gillis, John, R. *Youth and History. Tradition and Change in European Age Relations. 1770–Present* (New York, Academic Press, 1974)

Gilmurray, John. *The Struggle for Health* (London, Catholic Institute of International Relations, 1979)

Goldschmidt, Walter. 'Personal Motivation and Institutionalized Conflict' in Mary LeCron Foster and Robert A. Rubinstein (eds.), *Peace and War: Cross-Cultural Perspectives* (New Brunswick, New Jersey, Transaction Books, 1986), 3–14

Goldstone, Jack. 'The Comparative and Historical Study of Revolutions', *Annual Review of Sociology* 8 (1982), 187–207

Good, Kenneth. 'Settler Colonialism in Rhodesia', *African Affairs* 73, 290 (1974), 10–36

'Settler Colonialism: Economic Development and Class Formation', *Journal of Modern African Studies* 14, 4 (1976), 597–620

Gordon, David F. 'Development Strategy in Zimbabwe: Assessments and Prospects' in Michael Schatzberg (ed.), *The Political Economy of Zimbabwe* (New York, Praeger, 1979), 119–43

Gray, Richard. *The Two Nations. Aspects of the Development of Race Relations in the Rhodesias and Nyasaland* (London, Oxford University Press, 1960)

Gregory, Martyn. 'Zimbabwe 1980: Politicisation Through Armed Struggle and Electoral Mobilisation', *Journal of Commonwealth and Comparative Politics* (March 1981)

Guelke, A.B. 'Book Review', *Africa* 59 (1982), 127–8

Guevara, Che. *Guerrilla Warfare*, translated from Spanish by J. Morray (New York, Vintage Press, 1969)

Gurr, Ted Robert. *Why Men Rebel* (Princeton University Press, 1970)

Hampson, Joe and Edwell Kaseke. 'Zimbabwe' in John Dixon (ed.), *Social Welfare in Africa* (London, Croom Helm, 1987), 279–306

Hancock, Ian. *White Liberals, Moderates and Radicals in Rhodesia, 1953–1980* (London, Croom Helm, 1984)

Harris, Peter. 'Industrial Workers in Rhodesia, 1946–1972: Working-class Elites or Lumpenproletariat?', *Journal of Southern African Studies* 1, 2 (1975), 139–61

Harsanyi, John C. 'Rational-Choice Models of Political Behaviour vs Functionalist and Conformist Theories', *World Politics* 21 (July 1969), 513–38

Hastings, Adrian. 'Some Reflections Upon the War in Mozambique', *African Affairs* 73 (1974), 263–76

Hill, Polly. *Development Economics on Trial. The Anthropological Case for a Prosecution* (Cambridge University Press, 1986)

Himmelstein, Jerome L. and Michael S. Kimmel. 'Review Essay: States and Revolutions:

The Implications and Limits of Skocpol's Structural Model', *American Journal of Sociology* 86, 5 (1981), 1,145–54

Hinton, William. *Fanshen. A Document of Revolution in a Chinese Village* (New York, Monthly Review Press, 1966)

Hirschman, Albert O. *Exit, Voice and Loyalty. Responses to Decline in Firms, Organizations, and States* (Cambridge, Massachusetts, Harvard University Press, 1970)

Hobsbawm, Eric. *Primitive Rebels. Studies in Archaic Forms in the 19th and 20th Centuries* (New York, W.W. Norton, 1965)

'Social Bandits: Reply', *Comparative Studies in History and Society* 14 (1972), 503–5

Hodder-Williams, R. 'Marandellas and the Mashona Rebellion', *Rhodesiana* 16 (1967), 27–54

'Political Scenarios and their Economic Implications', *Journal of Commonwealth and Comparative Politics* 18, 1 (March 1980), 55–68

Hodges, Tony. 'Counterinsurgency and the Fate of Rural Blacks', *Africa Report* (September–October 1977), 15–20

Hodgkin, Thomas. *Nationalism in Colonial Africa* (New York University Press, 1957)

Hofheinz, Roy, Jr. 'The Ecology of Chinese Communist Success: Rural Influence Patterns, 1923–45' in Doak Barnett (ed.), *Chinese Communist Politics in Action* (Seattle, University of Washington Press, 1969)

Holleman, J.F. *Accommodating the Spirit Amongst Some Northeastern Shona Tribes*, The Rhodes-Livingstone Papers, No. 22 (Cape Town, published for the Rhodes-Livingstone Institute by Oxford University Press, 1953)

African Interlude (Cape Town, Nasionale Boekhandel Beperk, 1958)

'Some "Shona" Tribes of Southern Rhodesia' in Elizabeth Colson and Max Gluckman (eds.), *Seven Tribes of British Central Africa* (Manchester University Press, 1961)

Chief, Council and Commissioner: Some Problems of Government in Rhodesia (Assen, Netherlands, Afrika-Studiecentrum, 1969)

Huntington, Samuel. *Political Order in Changing Societies* (Cambridge, Massachusetts, Harvard University Press, 1968)

Huyghe, Bernard. 'Toward A Structural Model of Violence: Male Initiation Rituals and Tribal Warfare' in Mary Le Cron Foster and Robert A. Rubinstein (eds.), *Peace and War: Cross-Cultural Perspectives* (New Brunswick, New Jersey, Transaction Books, 1986)

International Defence and Aid Fund for Southern Africa, *Zimbabwe. The Facts About Rhodesia* (London, November 1977)

International Labour Office. *Labour Conditions and Discrimination in Southern Rhodesia (Zimbabwe)* (Geneva, International Labour Office, 1978)

Isaacman, Allen. 'Social Banditry in Zimbabwe (Rhodesia) and Mozambique, 1894–1907: An Expression of Early Peasant Protest', *Journal of Southern African Studies* 4, 1 (1977), 1–30

Isaacman, Allen and Barbara Isaacman, 'Resistance and Collaboration in Southern and Central Africa, c. 1850–1920', *The International Journal of African Historical Studies* 10, 1 (1977), 31–62

Mozambique. From Colonialism to Revolution. 1900–1982 (Boulder, Colorado, Westview Press, 1983)

James, Daniel (ed.), *The Complete Bolivian Diaries of Che Guevara and other Captured Documents* (New York, Stein & Day, 1968)

Jeater, Diana. 'Women and Bridewealth in the Restructuring of Shona Society 1890–1930', African History Seminar, School of Oriental and African Studies, University of London, 13 March 1985

Johnson, Chalmers, A. 'Civilian Loyalties and Guerrilla Conflict', *World Politics* 14, 4 (1962), 646–61

'The Third Generation of Guerrilla Warfare', *Asian Survey* 8, 6 (June 1968), 435–47

Peasant Nationalism and Communist Power: The Emergence of Revolutionary China, 1937–1945 (Stanford, California, Stanford University Press, 1962)

Bibliography

Johnson, Phyllis and David Martin (eds.), *Destructive Engagement. Southern Africa At War* (Harare, Zimbabwe Publishing House, 1986)

Journal of Asian Studies 42, 4 (1983),753–868

Jules-Rosette, Benetta. 'Women as Ceremonial Leaders in an African Church: The Apostles of John Maranke' in Benetta Jules-Rosette (ed.), *The New Religions of Africa* (Norwood, New Jersey, Ablex Publishing Corporation, 1979), 127–44

Jundanian, Brendan, F. 'Resettlement Programs', *Comparative Politics* 6 (July 1974), 519–39

Kaarsholm, Preben. 'Quiet after the Storm. Continuity and Change in the Cultural and Political Development of Zimbabwe', African Studies Association, Chicago, 28–31 October 1988

Kahn, Joel, S. 'Peasant Ideologies in the Third World', *Annual Review of Anthropology* 14 (1985), 49–75

Kamenka, Eugene. 'Political Nationalism – the Evolution of an Idea' in Eugene Kamenka (ed.), *Nationalism. The Nature and Evolution of an Idea* (New York, St Martin's Press, 1976), 2–21

Kapuscinski, Ryszard. *Another Day of Life*, translated from Polish by William R. Brand and Mroczkowska-Brand (San Diego, California, Harcourt Brace Jovanovich, 1987)

Kelly, George Armstrong. 'Conceptual Sources of the Terror', *Eighteenth Century Studies* 14 (Fall 1980), 18–36

Victims, Authority and Terror: The Parallel Deaths of d'Orleans, Custine, Bailly, and Malesherbes (Chapel Hill, North Carolina, The University of North Carolina Press, 1982)

Keppel-Jones, A. *Rhodes and Rhodesia: The White Conquest of Zimbabwe, 1884–1902* (Kingston, Ontario, McGill-Queens University Press, 1983)

Kileff, Clive and Margaret Kileff. 'The Masowe Vapostori of Seki' in Benetta Jules-Rosette (ed.), *The New Religions of Africa* (Norwood, New Jersey, Ablex Publishing Corporation, 1979), 151–67

Kirk, Tony. 'Politics and Violence in Rhodesia', *African Affairs* 74, 294 (January 1975), 3–38

Kotowski, Christoph M. 'Revolution' in G. Sartori (ed.), *Social Science Concepts: A Systematic Analysis* (Beverly Hills, California, Sage, 1984), 403–51

Kriger, Norma. 'Rural Conflicts and the Struggle for Independence: The Case of Zimbabwe', unpublished Ph. D. thesis, Department of Political Science, Massachusetts Institute of Technology, 1985

'The Zimbabwean War of Liberation: Struggles Within the Struggle', *Journal of Southern African Studies* 14, 2 (January 1988), 304–22

Kuper, Hilda. *The Shona and Ndebele of Southern Rhodesia: The Shona* (London, International African Institute, 1955)

Lan, David. *Guns and Rain. Guerrillas and Spirit Mediums in Zimbabwe* (Berkeley, California, University of California Press, 1985)

Laqueur, Walter. *Guerrilla: A Historical and Critical Study* (Boston, Little, Brown, 1976)

(ed.), *The Terrorism Reader* (Philadelphia, Pennsylvania, Temple University Press, 1978)

Lapchick, Richard E. and Stephanie Urdang. *Oppression and Resistance. The Struggle of Women in Southern Africa* (Westport, Connecticut, Greenwood Press, 1982)

Legum, Colin (ed.), *Africa Contemporary Record: Annual Survey and Documents, 1977–80* (London, Rex Collings, 1977–80)

Leites, Nathan and Charles Wolf, Jr. *Rebellion and Authority. An Analytic Essay on Insurgent Conflicts* (Chicago, Markham Publishing Company, 1970)

Libby, Ronald. 'Developmental Strategies and Political Divisions within the Zimbabwean State' in Michael Schatzberg (ed.), *The Political Economy of Zimbabwe* (New York, Praeger, 1984), 144–63

Bibliography

Liebenow, Gus. 'The Military Factor in African Politics: A Twenty-Five Year Perspective' in G. Carter and P.O'Meara (eds.), *African Independence. The First Twenty-Five Years* (Bloomington, Indiana University Press, 1985), 126–59

Linden, Ian. *The Catholic Church and the Struggle in Zimbabwe* (London, Longman, 1979)

Llosa, Mario Vargas. 'Inquest in The Andes', *New York Times Magazine* (31 July 1983)

Lodge, Tom (ed.), *Resistance and Ideology in Settler Societies*. Scuthern African Studies, Vol. 4 (Ravan Press, Johannesburg, 1986)

Lomnitz, Larissa. 'The Uses of Fear: Porro Gangs in Mexico' in Mary LeCron Foster and Robert A. Rubinstein (eds.), *Peace and War: Cross-Cultural Perspectives* (New Brunswick, New Jersey, Transaction Books, 1986), 15–24

Louie, Richard. 'The Incidence of The Terror: A Critique of a Statistical Interpretation', *French Historical Studies* 3 (Spring 1964), 379–89

Lovejoy, Paul. 'Fugitive Slaves: Resistance to Slavery in the Sokoto Caliphate' in Gary Okihiro (ed.), *In Resistance: Studies in African, Caribbean and Afro-American History* (Amherst, Massachusetts, University of Massachusetts Press, 1986), 71–95

Lyons, Daniel. 'Welcome Threats and Coercive Offers', *Philosophy* 50 (1975), 425–36

Made, Patricia A. and Nyorovai Whande. 'Women in Southern Africa: A Note on the Zimbabwean "Success Story"', *Issue: A Journal of Opinion* 17, 2 (1989), 26–8

Makgetla, Neva Seidman. 'Transnational Corporations in Southern Rhodesia', *Journal of Southern African Studies* 5, 1 (January 1980), 57–87

Malaba, Luke. 'Supply, Control and Organization of African Labour in Rhodesia', *Review of African Political Economy* 18 (1980), 7–28

Mandaza, Ibbo. 'The State and Politics in the Post-White Settler Colonial Situation' in Mandaza (ed.), *Zimbabwe. The Political Economy of Transition*

'Introduction: The Political Economy of Transition' in Mandaza (ed.), *Zimbabwe. The Political Economy of Transition*

(ed.), *Zimbabwe. The Political Economy of Transition, 1980–1986* (Dakar, Senegal, 1986)

Manicas, Peter. 'Review Essay', *History and Theory* 20 (May 1981), 204–18

Manungo, Ken D. 'Peasants and Guerrillas: An Oral History', Conference on Culture and Consciousness in Southern Africa, Manchester University, 23–26 September 1986

Mao Tse Tung. *On Guerrilla Warfare*, translated by Samuel Griffiths (New York, Praeger, 1961)

Marechera, Dambudzo. *House of Hunger: Short Stories* (London, Heinemann, reprint, 1984)

Martin, David and Phyllis Johnson. *The Struggle for Zimbabwe. The Chimurenga War* (Harare, Zimbabwe Publishing House, 1981)

Mason, Philip. *The Birth of a Dilemma. The Conquest and Settlement of Rhodesia* (London, Oxford University Press, 1958)

Massell, Gregory J. *The Surrogate Proletariat. Moslem Women and Revolutionary Strategies in Soviet Central Asia, 1919–1929* (Princeton University Press, 1974)

Maughan-Brown, David. 'Myths on the March: The Kenyan and Zimbabwean Liberation Struggles in Colonial Fiction', *Journal of Southern African Studies* 9, 1 (October 1982), 93–117

Maxey, Kees. *The Fight for Zimbabwe. The Armed Conflict in Southern Rhodesia since UDI* (London, Rex Collings, 1975)

'The Armed Struggle in Zimbabwe and The Gaps in Our Knowledge', paper presented at Conference on Zimbabwe, Department of Politics, University of Leeds, 21–22 June 1980

May, Joan. *Zimbabwean Women in Colonial and Customary Law* (Gweru, Zimbabwe, Mambo Press, 1983)

Mazrui, Ali. *Soldiers and Kinsmen in Uganda. The Making of a Military Ethnocracy* (Beverly Hills, California, Sage Publications, 1975)

Bibliography

'Political Engineering in Africa', *International Social Science Journal* 2 (1983), 279–94

Meisner, Maurice. *Marxism, Maoism and Utopianism: Eight Essays*. (Madison, The University of Wisconsin Press, 1982)

Memmi, Albert. *The Colonizer and the Colonized* (Boston, Beacon Press, 1967)

Meredith, Martin. *The Past is Another Country. Rhodesia 1890–1979* (London, Andre Deutsch Ltd, 1979)

M'Gabe, Davis. 'The Beginnings of Guerrilla War', *Monthly Review* (March 1969), 39–47

Migdal, Joel. *Peasants, Politics and Revolution. Pressures Toward Political and Social Change in the Third World* (Princeton University Press, 1974)

Milosz, Czeslaw. *The Captive Mind (New York,* Vintage Press, 1981)

Minter, William. *King Solomon's Mines Revisited: Western Interests and the Burdened History of Southern Africa* (New York, Basic Books, 1986)

Mittelman, James H. 'Revolutionary Nationalism in Zimbabwe', *Monthly Review* 34, 8 (1983), 51–6

Mlambo, Eshmael. *Rhodesia. The Struggle for a Birthright* (London, C. Hurst. 1972)

Moise, Edwin E. 'Review Essay: The Moral Economy Dispute', *Bulletin of Concerned Asian Scholars* 14 (1982), 72–7

Moorcraft, Paul, L. and Peter McLaughlin. *Chimurenga! The War in Rhodesia 1965–1980. A Military History* (Johannesburg, Sygma/Collins, 1982)

Moore, Barrington, Jr. *Terror and Progress. USSR. Some Sources of Change and Stability in the Soviet Dictatorship* (Cambridge, Massachusetts, Harvard University Press, 1954)

Social Origins of Dictatorship and Democracy. Lord and Peasant in the Making of the Modern World (Boston, Beacon Press, 1966)

Injustice. The Social Bases of Obedience and Revolt (White Plains, New York, M.E. Sharpe, 1978)

Moore, David. 'What's Left of Liberation in Zimbabwe? Socialism, Democracy and the Legacy of a Guerrilla War', paper presented to the Conference of the Review of African Political Economy and the Centre of African Studies, Liverpool University, 26–28 September 1986

'The Contradictory Construction of Hegemony in Zimbabwe: Politics, Ideology and Class in the Formation of a New African State', unpublished Ph.D., York University, Canada, 1989

Moore, Will. 'Rebel Music: Appeals to Rebellion in Zimbabwe', Centre for Comparative Politics, Department of Political Science, University of Colorado, Boulder, unpublished, 17 July 1989

Moreno, Jose, A. 'Che Guevara on Guerrilla Warfare: Doctrine, Practice and Evaluation', *Comparative Studies in Society and History* 12, 2 (April 1970) 114–33

Morkel, E.R. 'The Mondoro or Ancestral Spirit of the Wabuja, Mtoko', *NADA* 8 (1930)

Mosley, Paul. 'Agricultural Development and Government Policy in Settler Economies: The Case of Kenya and Southern Rhodesia, 1900–60', *Economic History Review* 35, 3 (August 1982), 390–408

Mtetwa, Richard, M.G., 'The "Political" and Economic History of the Duma People of South-Eastern Rhodesia from the early Eighteenth Century to 1945', unpublished Ph.D., University of Rhodesia, 1976

Mufuka, K. Nyamayaro. 'Rhodesia's Internal Settlement: A Tragedy', *African Affairs* 78, 313 (October 1979), 439–50

Munslow, Barry. *Mozambique: The Revolution and its Origins* (London, Longman, 1983)

Murphree, Marshall W. *Christianity and The Shona,* London School of Economics. Monograph on Social Anthropology No. 36, University of London (New York, Athlone Press, 1969)

'Essay Review: The Study of Religion in Central Africa', *Zambezia* 11, 1 (1981), 67–75

Mutambirwa, Jane. 'Traditional Shona Concepts on Family Life and How Systems Planned on the Basis of These Concepts Effectively Contained The Population Growth of Shona Communities', *Zimbabwe Journal of Economics* 1, 2 (1979), 96–103

Mutambirwa, James A. Chamunorwa. *The Rise of Settler Power in Southern Rhodesia (Zimbabwe), 1898–1923* (Toronto, Fairleigh Dickinson University Press, Associated University Presses, 1980)

Mutunhu, Tendai. 'Nehanda of Zimbabwe (Rhodesia): The Story of A Woman Liberation Leader and Fighter', *Ufahamu* 7, 1 (1976) 59–70

Mzamane, Mbulelo V. 'The People's Mood: The Voice of a Guerrilla Poet', *Review of African Political Economy* 18 (1981), 29–43

'New Writing From Zimbabwe: Dambudzo Marechera's *The House of Hunger*', *African Literature Today* 13 (1983), 201–25

Nehwati, Francis. 'The Social And Communal Background To "Zhii". The African Riots in Bulawayo, Southern Rhodesia in 1960', *African Affairs* 69 (July 1970), 250–66

Neier, Aryeh. 'The Contra Contradiction', *New York Review of Books* (9 April 1987), 5–6

Nelson, Harold D. (ed.), *Zimbabwe: A Country Study* (Washington, District of Columbia, Foreign Area Studies, The American University, 1983)

Nelson, Harold, D. *et al.*, *Area Handbook for Southern Rhodesia* (Washington, District of Columbia, Foreign Area Studies, The American University, 1975)

Newitt, M.D.D. *Portuguese Settlement on the Zambesi: Exploration, Land Tenure, and Colonial Rule in East Africa* (New York, Africana Publishing Co., 1973)

North, James. *Freedom Rising* (New York, A Plume Book, New American Library, 1986)

Nyamfukudza, S. *The Non-Believer's Journey* (London, Heinemann, 1980)

Nyangoni, Christopher and Gideon Nyandoro (eds.), *Zimbabwe Independence Movements* (London, Rex Collings, 1979)

Nziramasanga, M.T. 'Major Trends in the Rhodesian Economy, 1955–77' in *A Symposium on Zimbabwe's Economic Prospects* (Seven Springs Center, Mount Kisco, New York, February 1980)

Olson, Mancur. *The Logic of Collective Action. Public Goods and the Theory of Groups* (Cambridge, Massachusetts, Harvard University Press, 1965)

Paige, Jeffery. *Agrarian Revolution: Social Movements and Export Agriculture in the Underdeveloped World* (New York, Free Press, 1975)

Palley, Claire. 'Law and the Unequal Society: Discriminatory Legislation in Rhodesia under the Rhodesia Front from 1963 to 1969', Part 1, *Race* 12, 1 (1970), 15–47; Part 2, *Race* 12, 2 (1970), 139–67

Palmer, Robin. *Land and Racial Domination in Rhodesia* (Berkeley, California, University of California Press, 1977)

'From Zimbabwe to Azania? A Review Article', *African Affairs* 82, 329 (October 1983) 574–78

Paret, Peter. *French Revolutionary Warfare From Indochina to Algeria. The Analysis of a Political and Military Doctrine,* Princeton Studies in World Politics, No. 6 (New York, Praeger, 1964)

Paret, Peter and John W. Shy. *Guerrillas in the 1960's*, Princeton Studies in World Politics, No. 1 (New York, Praeger, 1965)

Parry, Albert. *Terrorism. From Robespierre to Arafat* (New York, Vanguard Press, 1976)

Passmore, Gloria C. *The National Policy of Community Development in Rhodesia*, Department of Political Science, Source Book Series No. 5 (University of Rhodesia, 1972)

'A History of Policy on African Involvement in Local Administration and Development in the Tribal Areas of Rhodesia', Vols. 1 and 2, unpublished Ph.D. thesis, University of Rhodesia, February 1978

Peltez, Michael, G. 'Moral and Political Economies in Rural Southeast Asia. A Review Article', *Comparative Studies in Society and History* 25 (1983), 731–9

287

Bibliography

Pennell, C.R. 'Women and Resistance to Colonialism in Morocco: The Rif 1916–1926', *Journal of African History* 28, 1 (1987), 107–18

Pennock, J. Roland and John W. Chapman. *Coercion*, vol. 14 of *Nomos* (Chicago, Aldine, 1972)

Pennock, J. Roland. 'Coercion – An Overview' in Pennock and Chapman, *Coercion*

Perinbaum, B. Marie. 'Violence, Morality and History in the Colonial Syndrome: Frantz Fanon's Perspectives', *Journal of Southern African Studies* 3, 1 (January 1978)

    Holy Violence. The Revolutionary Thought of Frantz Fanon. An Intellectual Biography (Washington, D.C., Three Continents Press, 1982)

Perry, Elizabeth. *Rebels and Revolutionaries in North China 1845–1945* (Stanford University Press, 1980)

    'Collective Violence in China, 1880–1980', *Theory and Society* 13, 3 (May 1984), 427–54

Phimister, Ian R. 'Peasant Production and Underdevelopment in Southern Rhodesia, 1890–1914', *African Affairs* 13 (1974), 217–28

    'Rhodes, Rhodesia and the Rand', *Journal of Southern African Studies* 1 (1974), 74–90

    'African Worker Consciousness: Origins and Aspects to 1953' in Phimister and Van Onselen, *Studies in The History of African Mine Labour*

    'Review Article: Zimbabwean Economic and Social Historiography since 1979', *African Affairs* 78 (April 1979), 253–68

    'Commodity Relations and Class Formation in the Zimbabwean Countryside, 1898–1920', *Journal of Peasant Studies* (July 1986), 240–57

    'The Combined and Contradictory Inheritance of the Struggle against Colonialism' in Colin Stoneman (ed.), *Zimbabwe's Prospects. Issues of Race, Class, State and Capital in Southern Africa* (London, MacMillan Publishers, 1988), 8–15

Phimister, Ian R. and Charles Van Onselen. *Studies in the History of African Mine Labour in Colonial Zimbabwe* (Gwelo, Rhodesia, Mambo Press, 1978)

    'The Political Economy of Tribal Animosity: A Case Study of the 1929 Bulawayo Location Faction Fight', *Journal of Southern African Studies* 6, 1 (1979), 1–43

Plamenatz, John. 'Two Types of Nationalism – the Evolution of an Idea' in Eugene Kamenka (ed.), *Nationalism. The Nature and Evolution of an Idea* (New York, St Martin's Press, 1976), 22–37

Pollak, Oliver B. 'Black Farmers and White Politics in Rhodesia', *African Affairs* 74 (1975), 263–77

Pongweni, Alec J.C. *Songs that Won the Liberation War* (Harare, Zimbabwe, College Press, 1982)

Popkin, Samuel L. *The Rational Peasant. The Political Economy of Rural Society in Vietnam* (Berkeley, University of California Press, 1979)

Powell, John Duncan. 'The Adequacy of Social Science Models for the Study of Peasant Movements', *Comparative Politics* (April 1976)

Presley, Cora Ann. 'Kikuyu Women in the "Mau Mau" Rebellion' in Gary Okihiro (ed.), *In Resistance* (Amherst, Massachusetts, University of Massachusetts Press, 1986), 53–70

Prins, Gwyn. 'The End of the Beginning of African History', *Social History* 4, 3 (October 1979)

Pye, Lucian. *Guerrilla Communism in Malaya: Its Social and Political Meaning* (Princeton University Press, 1956)

Race, Jeffrey. *War Comes to Long An* (Berkeley, University of California, 1972)

Raedts, Peter. 'The Children's Crusade of 1212', *Journal of Medieval History* 3 (1977), 279–323

Rake, Alan, 'Black Guerrillas in Rhodesia', *Africa Report* (December 1968), 23–5

Ramm, Hartmut. *The Marxism of Regis Debray. Between Lenin and Guevara* (Lawrence, The Regents Press of Kansas, 1978)

Ranger, Terence O. 'The Early History of Independency in Southern Rhodesia' in *Religion in*

Africa, Proceedings of a seminar held in the Centre of African Studies, University of Edinburgh, 10–12 April 1964, University of Edinburgh, Centre of African Studies, 52–74

'Traditional Authorities and the Rise of Modern Politics in Southern Rhodesia, 1898–1930' in Eric Stokes and Richard Brown (eds.), *The Zambesian Past. Studies in Central African History* (Manchester University Press, 1966), 171–93

Revolt in Southern Rhodesia. 1896–7. A Study in African Resistance (Evanston, Northwestern University Press, 1967)

'Connexions Between "Primary Resistance" Movements and Modern Mass Nationalism in East and Central Africa. Part 1', *Journal of African History* 9, 3 (1968), 437–53

'Connexions Between "Primary Resistance" Movements and Modern Mass Nationalism in East and Central Africa: 11', *Journal of African History* 9, 4 (1968), 631–41

'African Reactions to the Imposition of Colonial Rule in East and Central Africa' in 'Colonialism in Africa 1870–1960' in L.H. Gann and Peter Duignan (eds.), *The History and Politics of Colonialism 1870–1914* (Cambridge University Press, 1969), 293–324

'The "New Historiography" in Dar es Salaam: An Answer', *African Affairs* 70, 278 (1970), 50–61

The African Voice in Southern Rhodesia, 1898–1930 (London, Heinemann Educational, 1970)

'Review Article: The Historiography of Southern Rhodesia', *Transafrican Journal of History* 1, 2 (1971), 63–76

'The People in African Resistance: A Review', *Journal of Southern African Studies* 4, 1 (1977), 125–146

'Growing from the Roots: Reflections on Peasant Research in Central and Southern Africa', *Journal of Southern African Studies* 5, 1 (1978), 99–133

'The Changing of the Old Guard: Robert Mugabe and the Revival of ZANU', *Journal of Southern African Studies* 7, 1 (October 1980), 71–90

'The Death of Chaminuka: Spirit Mediums, Nationalism and the Guerrilla War in Zimbabwe', *African Affairs* (July 1982), 349–69

'Literature and Political Economy: Arthur Shearly Cripps and the Makoni Labour Crisis of 1911', *Journal of Southern African Studies* 9, 1 (October 1982), 33–53

'Tradition and Travesty: Chiefs and the Administration in Makoni District', *Africa* 52, 3 (1982), 20–41

'Religion and Rural Protest in Makoni District, Zimbabwe, 1900–1980', in Janos Bak and Gerhard Benecke (eds.), *Religion and Rural Revolt* (Manchester University Press, 1984)

Peasant Consciousness and Guerrilla War in Zimbabwe. A Comparative Study (Berkeley, University of California Press, 1985)

'Resistance in Africa: From Nationalist Revolt to Agrarian Protest' in Gary Okihiro (ed.), *In Resistance* (Amherst, Massachusetts, University of Massachusetts Press, 1986), 32–52

'Bandits and Guerrillas: The Case of Zimbabwe' in Donald Crummey (ed.), *Banditry, Rebellion and Social Protest in Africa* (London, James Currey, 1986)

'Taking Hold of the Land: Holy Places and Pilgrimages in Twentieth Century Zimbabwe', unpublished paper, Conference on Culture and Consciousness in Southern Africa, Manchester University, September 1986

'Holy Men and Rural Communities in Zimbabwe, 1970–1980' in *The Church and War*, papers read at the 21st summer meeting and the 22nd winter meeting of the Ecclesiastical History Society. Ecclesiastical Studies in Church History, vol. 20, edited by W.J. Sheils (published for the Ecclesiastical History Society by Basil Blackwell, 1983), 443–61

Ranger, Terence O. and Eric Hobsbawm (eds.), *The Invention of Tradition* (Cambridge University Press, 1983)

Redfield, Robert. *Tepoztlan. A Mexican Village* (University of Chicago Press, 1973)

The Little Community, and Peasant Society and Culture (University of Chicago Press, 1969)

Reed, Nelson. *The Caste War of Yucatan* (Stanford University Press, 1964)

Bibliography

Reid Daly, Ron. *Selous Scouts: Top Secret War* (Alberton, South Africa, Galago Publishing, 1982)

Rejai, Mostafa (ed.), *Mao Tse-Tung. On Revolution and War* (Garden City, New York, Doubleday and Co., 1969)

Rennie, J.K. 'White Farmers, Black Tenants and Landlord Legislation: Southern Rhodesia 1890–1930', *Journal of Southern African Studies* 5 (1978) 86–98

Rich, Tony. 'Legacies of the Past? The Results of the 1980 Election in Midlands Province, Zimbabwe', *Africa* 52 (1982), 42–54

Riddell, Roger. *The Land Question. From Rhodesia to Zimbabwe*, No. 2 (London, Catholic Institute for International Relations, 1978)

'Prospects for Land Reform in Zimbabwe', *Rural Africana* 4–5 (Spring/Fall 1979), 17–31

Education for Employment. From Rhodesia to Zimbabwe, No. 9 (London, Catholic Institute for International Relations, 1980)

'Zimbabwe. The Economy Four Years After Independence', *African Affairs* 83, 333 (October 1984), 463–76

Rifkind, Malcolm L. 'The Politics of Land in Rhodesia. A Study of Land and Politics in Southern Rhodesia, with Special Reference to the Period 1930–1969', unpublished M.Sc. thesis, University of Edinburgh, April 1969

Robertson, Claire and Iris Berger (eds.), *Women and Class in Africa* (New York, Africana Publishing Co., 1986)

Roeder, Philip G. 'Legitimacy and Peasant Revolution: An Alternative to Moral Economy', *Peasant Studies* 11, 3 (Spring 1984), 149–68

Rogowski, Ronald. 'Rationalist Theories of Politics: A Midterm Report', *World Politics* 30 (January 1978), 296–323

Rosaldo, Renato. 'From the Door of his Tent: The Fieldworker and the Inquisitor' in James Clifford and George Marcus (eds.), *Writing Culture: The Poetics and Politics of Ethnography* (Berkeley, University of California Press, 1986), 77–97

Roth, Jack. *The Cult of Violence. Sorel and the Sorelians* (Berkeley, University of California, 1980)

Rothman, Stanley. 'Barrington Moore and The Dialectics of Revolution: An Essay Review', *American Political Science Review* 64 (1970)

Rudebeck, Lars. *Guinea-Bissau: A Study of Political Mobilization* (Uppsala, Scandinavian Institute for African Studies, 1974)

Samkange, Stanlake. *On Trial For My Country* (London, Heinemann, 1967)

Sanders, David. 'The State & Popular Organisation', *The Journal of Social Change and Development* 8 (Harare, Zimbabwe, 1984), 6–8

Sarkesian, Sam (ed.), *Revolutionary Guerrilla Warfare* (Chicago, Precedent Publishing Company, 1975)

Saul, John. 'African Peasants and Revolution', *Review of African Political Economy* (1974), 41–68

'Transforming the Struggle in Zimbabwe' in John Saul, *State and Revolution in East Africa* (New York, Monthly Review Press, 1979), 107–22

'Zimbabwe: The Next Round', *Monthly Review* (September 1980), 1–42

Scheer, Robert (ed.), *The Diary of Che Guevara: Bolivia, November 7, 1966– October 7, 1967* (New York, Bantam Books, 1968)

Schmidt, Elizabeth. 'Hunters, Farmers and Gold-Washers: A Re-evaluation of Women's Roles in Precolonial and Colonial Zimbabwe', paper presented to Annual Meeting of African Studies Association, Denver, Colorado, 21 November 1987

'Women are the Backbone of Agriculture: A Historical Assessment of Women's Role in Peasant Production in Zimbabwe, 1890–1939', paper presented to Annual Meeting of American Anthropological Association, Chicago, Illinois, 18 November 1987

Schram, Stuart R. *The Political Thought of Mao Tse-Tung* (New York, Praeger, revised edn, 1969)

Scott, James C. 'Exploitation in Rural Class Relations. A Victim's Perspective', *Comparative Politics* 7 (July 1975), 489–532

The Moral Economy of the Peasant. Rebellion and Subsistence in Southeast Asia (New Haven, Yale University Press, 1976)

'Review Article. Peasant Revolution: A Dismal Science', *Comparative Politics* 9 (1977), 231–48

'Revolution in The Revolution: Peasants and Commissars', *Theory and Society* 7, 1 (1979), 97–134

Weapons of The Weak: Everyday Forms of Peasant Resistance (New Haven, Yale University Press, 1985)

Scott, Joan Wallach. 'Women in History, "The Modern Period"', *Past and Present* 101 (November 1983), 141–57

Seager, Diana. 'Housing the Poor in an Urban Environment. The Example of Salisbury', Research Report No. 1. War Refugees in Harare Musika. Department of Sociology, University of Rhodesia, August 1979

Seegers, Annette. 'Revolution in Africa: The Case of Zimbabwe (1965–1980)', unpublished Ph.D. thesis, Loyola University, Chicago, 1984

Seidman, Gay, W. 'Women in Zimbabwe: Postindependence Struggles', *Feminist Studies* 10, 3 (Fall 1984), 419–40

Shamuyarira, Nathan M. *Crisis in Rhodesia* (London, Andre Deutsch Ltd, 1965)

'A Revolutionary Situation in Southern Africa', *African Review* (Accra, Ghana, New Africa Publications), 4, 2 (1974), 159–79

Shay, Reg and Chris Vermaak. *The Silent War* (Rhodesia, Galaxie Press, 1971)

Sherman, Jessica. 'Songs of the Chimurenga', *Africa Perspective* (Johannesburg Students African Studies Association, Witwatersrand University) 16 (1980), 80–8

Silverman, Sydel. 'The Peasant Concept in Anthropology', *Journal of Peasant Studies* 7, 1 (October 1979), 49–69

Simmonds, R.G.S. 'Charewa, Voice of the Rain God', *NADA* 9, 1 (1964)

Sithole, Masipula. *Zimbabwe. Struggles Within the Struggle* (Salisbury, Rhodesia, Rujeko Publishers, 1979)

'The General Elections, 1979–1985' in Mandaza (ed.), *Zimbabwe. The Political Economy of Transition.*

'Ethnicity and Factionalism in Zimbabwe Nationalist Politics 1957–1979', *Ethnic and Racial Studies* 3, 1 (January 1980)

Skocpol, Theda. 'A Critical Review of Barrington Moore's Social Origins of Dictatorship and Democracy', *Politics and Society* 4 (Fall 1973), 1–34

States and Social Revolutions. A Comparative Analysis of France, Russia and China (Cambridge, Massachusetts, Harvard University Press, 1979)

'Review Article: What Makes Peasants Revolutionary?' *Comparative Politics* 14 (1982), 351–75

Skocpol, Theda, Dietrich Reuschemeyer and Peter Evans (eds.), *Bringing The State Back In* (Cambridge University Press, 1985)

Smiley, Xan. 'Zimbabwe, Southern Africa and the Rise of Robert Mugabe', *Foreign Affairs* (N.Y.), 58 (Summer 1980), 1,060–83

Smith, Anthony D. *State and Nation in the Third World: The Western State and African Nationalism* (Brighton, Sussex, Wheatsheaf Books, 1983)

Solomon, Richard. *Mao's Revolution and the Chinese Political Culture* (Berkeley, University of California Press, 1971)

Southern Africa, 'ZANU Women Meet', special report by Barbara Barnes (July/August 1979), 8, 9 and 30

Southern Africa, 'Zimbabwe's Women: Throwing off the Past', interview with Jane Ngwenya (November–December 1979)

Bibliography

Stoneman, Colin. *Skilled Labour and Future Needs. From Rhodesia to Zimbabwe*, No. 4 (London, Catholic Institute for International Relations, 1978)

Stoneman, Colin and Lionel Cliffe. *Zimbabwe. Politics, Economics and Society* (New York, Pinter Publishers, 1989)

Strobel, Margaret. 'Review Essay: African Women', *Signs: Journal of Women in Culture and Society* 8, 1 (1982), 109–31

Sylvester, Christine. 'Simultaneous Revolutions: The Zimbabwean Case', *Journal of Southern African Studies* 16, 3 (September 1990), 452–75

Thaxton, Ralph. 'On Peasant Revolution and National Resistance: Towards a Theory of Peasant Mobilization and Revolutionary War with Special Reference to Modern China', *World Politics* 30, 1 (October 1977), 24–57

Thaxton, Ralph. *China Turned Rightside Up* (Stanford University Press, 1982)

Thomas, Norman Ernest. 'Christianity, Politics, and the Manyika: A Study of the Influence of Religious Attitudes and Loyalties on Political Values and Activities of Africans in Rhodesia', unpublished Ph.D. thesis, Boston University Graduate School, 1968

Thompson, Carol. *Challenge to Imperialism. The Frontline States in the Liberation of Zimbabwe* (Boulder, Colorado, Westview Press, 1985)

Thompson, Robert. *Defeating Communist Insurgency: The Lessons of Malaya and Vietnam* (New York, Praeger, 1966)

Tickner, Vincent. *The Food Problem. From Rhodesia to Zimbabwe*, No. 8 (London, Catholic Institute for International Relations, 1979)

Tilly, Charles. *From Mobilization to Revolution* (New York, Random House, 1978)

'Revolutions and Collective Violence' in Fred Greenstein and Nelson Polsby (eds.), *Handbook of Political Science*, vol. 3 (Reading, Massachusetts, Addison-Wesley Publishing Co., 1975)

Todorov, Tzvetan. *The Conquest of America. The Question of the Other*, translated from the French by Richard Howard (New York, Harper and Row, 1984)

Trullinger, James Walker, Jr. *Village at War. An Account of Revolution in Vietnam* (New York, Longman, 1980)

Tsomondo, Madziwanyika. 'Shona Reaction and Resistance to the European Colonization of Zimbabwe, 1890–1898. A Case Against Colonial and Revisionist Historiography', *Journal of Southern African Affairs* (1977), 11–32

Ulam, Adam. *Stalin: The Man and His Era* (New York, Viking, 1973)

United Nations. *Zimbabwe. Towards A New Order. An Economic and Social Survey* (United Nations, 1980)

Van Allen, Judith. 'African Women, "Modernization" and National Liberation' in Lynne B. Iglitzin and Ruth Ross (eds.), *Women in the World: A Comparative Study* (Clio Books, Santa Barbara, California, 1976), 25–54

Van Onselen, Charles. 'The Role of Collaborators in the Rhodesian Mining Industry 1900–1935', *African Affairs* 72, 289 (October 1973), 401–18

'Worker Consciousness in Black Miners: Southern Rhodesia, 1900–1920', *Journal of African History* 14, 2 (1973), 237–55

'Black Workers in Central African Industry: A Critical Essay on the Historiography and Sociology of Rhodesia', *Journal of Southern African Studies* 1, 2 (1975), 228–46

'The Regiment of the Hills: South Africa's Lumpenproletarian Army 1890–1920', *Past and Present* 80 (1978), 91–121

'The 1912 Wankie Colliery Strike' in Phimister and Van Onselen, *Studies in the History of African Mine Labour*

Vansina, Jan. 'Once Upon a Time: Oral Traditions as History in Africa', *Daedalus* 2 (Spring 1971), 442–68

'The Power of Systematic Doubt in Historical Enquiry', *History in Africa* 1 (1974), 109–27

'For Oral Tradition (But Not Against Braudel)', *History in Africa* 5 (1978), 351–6

Van Velsen, J. 'Trends in African Nationalism in Southern Rhodesia', *Kroniek van Afrika* 4, 2 (June 1964), 139–57

Von Giap. *People's War, People's Army* (New York, Praeger, 1962)

Wallace, Anthony F.C. 'Psychological Preparations for War' in Morton Fried, Marvin Harris, Robert Murphy (eds.), *War: The Anthropology of Armed Conflict and Aggression* (New York, The Natural History Press, 1968), 173–82

Walter, Eugene Victor. *Terror and Resistance: A Study of Political Violence, with Case Studies of some Primitive African Communities* (New York, Oxford University Press, 1969)

Walton, John. *Reluctant Rebels. Comparative Studies of Revolution and Underdevelopment* (New York, Columbia University Press, 1984)

Wamweya, Joram. *Freedom Fighter* (Nairobi, East African Publishing House, 1971)

Wardlaw, Grant. *Political Terrorism* (Cambridge University Press, 1982)

Wasserman, Gary. 'The Economic Transition to Zimbabwe', *Africa Report* (November–December 1978), 39–45

Weinrich, A.K.H. *Chiefs and Councils in Rhodesia: Transition from Patriarchal to Bureaucratic Power* (Columbia, South Carolina, University of South Carolina Press, 1971)

Black and White Elites in Rural Rhodesia (Manchester University Press, 1973)

African Farmers in Rhodesia. Old and New Peasant Communities in Karangaland (London, published for the International African Institute by the Oxford University Press, 1975).

'Factors Influencing Economic Development in Rural Areas', *The Rhodesia Journal of Economics* 9, 1 (March 1975), 7–13

'Strategic Resettlement in Rhodesia', *Journal of Southern African Studies* 3, 3 (April 1977), 207–29

Women and Racial Discrimination in Rhodesia (Paris, Unesco, 1979)

Weiss, Ruth. *The Women of Zimbabwe* (London, Kesho Publications, 1986)

Weitzer, Ronald. 'In Search of Regime Security: Zimbabwe Since Independence', *Journal of Modern African Studies* 22, 4 (1984), 529–57

'The Internal Security State: Political Change and Repression in Northern Ireland and Zimbabwe', unpublished Ph.D. thesis, Berkeley, University of California, 1985

'Zimbabwe: Fortifying One-Party Rule', chapter 6 in *Transforming Settler States. Communal Conflict and Internal Security in Northern Ireland and Zimbabwe* (Berkeley, University of California Press, 1990)

White, Landeg. 'Review Article: The Revolutions Ten Years On', *Journal of Southern African Studies* 11, 2 (April 1985), 320–32

Wilkinson, Anthony. 'From Rhodesia to Zimbabwe' in Basil Davidson, Joe Slovo, Anthony Wilkinson, *Southern Africa. The New Politics of Revolution* (Harmondsworth, Penguin, 1976)

'The Impact of the War', *Journal of Commonwealth and Comparative Politics* 18, 1 (March 1980), 110–23

Wills, A.J. *An Introduction to the History of Central Africa: Zambia, Malawi and Zimbabwe* (Oxford, Oxford University Press, 1985)

Windrich, Elaine. 'Rhodesian Censorship: The Role of the Media in the Making of a One-Party State', *African Affairs* 78, 313 (October 1979), 523–34

'Controlling the Media: Rhodesia Style', *Journal of Southern African Studies* 5, 1 (January 1980), 90–100

Wipper, Audrey. *Rural Rebels. A Study of Two Protest Movements in Kenya* (New York, Oxford University Press, 1977)

Woldin, Sheldon S. 'The Politics of the Study of Revolutions', *Comparative Politics* (April 1973), 343–58

Wolf, Eric R. *Peasant Wars of the Twentieth Century* (New York, Harper and Row, 1969)

'Peasants and Political Mobilization: Introduction', *Comparative Study of History and Society* 17, 4 (October 1975), 385–8

Bibliography

'Review Essay: Why Cultivators Rebel', *American Journal of Sociology* 83 (1977), 742–50

Womack, John, Jr. *Zapata and The Mexican Revolution* (New York, Alfred A. Knopf, 1969)

Worsley, Peter. *The Trumpet Shall Sound. A Study of 'Cargo' Cults in Melanesia* (New York, Schocken Books, 1968)

'The Superpowers and the Tribes' in Mary Lecron Foster and Robert A. Rubinstein (eds.), *Peace and War: Cross-Cultural Perspectives* (New Brunswick, New Jersey, Transaction Books, 1986)

Yudelman, Montagu. *Africans on the Land* (Cambridge, Massachusetts, Harvard University Press, 1964)

Zachrisson, Per. *An African Area in Change. Belingwe 1849–1946. A Study of Colonialism, Missionary Activity and African Response in Southern Rhodesia*, Bulletin of Department of History, Gothenburg, No. 17 (University of Gothenburg, 1978)

Zagoria, Donald. 'Introduction. Peasants and Revolution', *Comparative Politics* (April 1976), 321–6

Zolberg, Aristide. *Creating Political Order: The Party States of West Africa* (Chicago, Rand-McNally, 1966)

Zvobgo, Chengetai. 'Rhodesia's Internal Settlement 1977–1979. A Record', *Journal of Southern African Studies* 5, 1 (January 1980), 25–38

Party documents

Women's Liberation in the Zimbabwean Revolution. Materials from the ZANU Women's Seminar. Maputo, Mozambique, May 1979 (Published by John Brown Book Club, Prairie Fire Organizing Committee)

ZANU (PF). Zimbabwe African National Union. Speeches and Documents of the First ZANU(PF) Women's League Conference. Zimbabwe, Harare, National Sports Centre, 15–17 March 1984

ZANU Political Programme. 1 August 1972

Zimbabwe African National Union (Patriotic Front), Mashonaland Central Province, Inter-district Meeting, 30 January 1982

Reply of ZANU detainees in Zambia Prisons to the Report of the Chitepo Commission, 1975

Government documents

African Production and Marketing Development Fund. Third Report of Select Committee on African Production and Marketing Development Fund Estimates. Presented to House of Assembly on 25 January 1969, S.C. 3, 1969

African Production and Marketing Development Fund. Second Report of the Select Committee on African Production and Marketing Development Fund Estimates. Presented to the House of Assembly on 6 February 1979, S.C. 1, 1979

African Production and Marketing Development Fund. Annual Reports

Agricultural Development Authority. File Ref.: ARDA DEV/9

Agro-Economic Survey of the Mazoe Area. Report by the Agricultural Development Authority, March 1976 (Government Printer)

Annual Report of Native Commissioner, Mtoko, 1934–59. Archives S1563 and 100355 18.17.3F

Annual Report of District Commissioner, Mtoko, 1965–9, Archives

Central Statistical Office. Unpublished data on Mtoko Intensive Conservation Area and Budjga Purchase Area

Department of Agricultural Development. Relief of Distress and Rehabilitation through Agriculture, 1980–81. DEVAG Programme, Progress Report to 30 April 1981, 20 May

294

1981. Prepared by R.H.G. Howden, Chief Agronomist, DEVAG in collaboration with DEVAG staff at Head office and in the field.

Department of Conservation and Extension. Seventh Annual Report of African Purchase Lands Recording Scheme 1975/76. Compiled by the Farm Management Section of the Department of Conservation and Extension, Salisbury, September 1977.

Department of Physical Planning, 29 June 1981. File Ref.: L20/13

Ministry of Internal Affairs. National Service Research Unit. Resource Survey No.1 Mrewa–Mtoko–Mudzi 1979

Ministry of Internal Affairs. Intensive Rural Development Area, IRDA Report No. 3, Mashonaland East. Compiled by Agricultural Section, Ministry of Internal Affairs, Mashonaland East Province, July 1977

Ministry of Internal Affairs. Delineation Report, Mtoko District, November 1965. Delineation Officer: B.P. Kaschula

Ministry of Internal Affairs. Book I. Index. Tribe, Language, and Relationship of Chiefs and Headmen

Ministry of Internal Affairs, renamed Ministry of Home Affairs. Circulars and Circular Minutes

Ministry of Lands. Report of the Secretary for Lands, incorporating the Report of the Chief Inspector of Lands

Ministry of Local Government and Housing. Division of District Administration. Circulars and Circular Minutes

Ministry of Local Government and Housing. Division of District Administration. Files on councils, community development, chiefs. File Ref.: SBV.2/GEN/80, C/22, SBV/2/1, C/15, C/2, C/11, CHK/14m, PER 5, PER 5/HM/MTK, PER 5/HM/Nyamatsahuni, PER 5/Charewa/4/61, HIS/3/2, C/60, SBV 2/UZUMB/77, CDV/12/14

Ministry of Local Government and Housing. Division of District Administration. Annual African Council Balance Sheets

Mtoko South Rural Council Minutes

Mtoko/Mrewa Farmers' Association Minutes

Mtoko district files on councils and administration. Used at district office before they were transferred to National Archives. C/A/117/1, C/A/117/2, C/A/117/3, C/A/117/11, C/A/140/1, C/A/129/12, C/A/2/1

National Archives. ZBJ 1/1/1, CDV/11/5/70, AGR 7/139, PER 4/48 B.13.4R 158272, C36.8.7F 192754

Pilditch Report, 1965. Erosion Survey of A Portion of Mtoko

Provincial Authority Annual Reports

Robinson Commission, Third Report of Working Party D. District Survey, Mtoko, 11 April 1962. File Ref.: W/P D/3/6

Southern Rhodesia Parliamentary Debates

Non-government papers

African Farmers' Union files

Catholic Commission for Peace and Justice files

Commercial Farmers' Union. Resettlement of farms in Mutoko and Mt. Darwin. Cyclo No. 11783

Rhodesia Herald, renamed *The Herald* (newspaper)

Rhodesia National Farmers' Union. Bulletins.

Southern Rhodesian Elections, February 1980. The Report of the Commonwealth Observers' Group. Commonwealth Secretariat, London, April 1980

Sunday Mail (newspaper)

Index

Index

Other books in the series

LaVergne, TN USA
30 December 2009
168472LV00006B/1/P